MARIA W. STEWART
and the
ROOTS *of* BLACK POLITICAL THOUGHT

MARIA W. STEWART
—————— *and the* ——————
ROOTS *of* BLACK
POLITICAL THOUGHT

Kristin Waters

University Press of Mississippi / Jackson

Margaret Walker Alexander Series in African American Studies

The University Press of Mississippi is the scholarly publishing agency of the Mississippi Institutions of Higher Learning: Alcorn State University, Delta State University, Jackson State University, Mississippi State University, Mississippi University for Women, Mississippi Valley State University, University of Mississippi, and University of Southern Mississippi.

www.upress.state.ms.us

The University Press of Mississippi is a member of the Association of University Presses.

First printing 2022

∞

Library of Congress Cataloging-in-Publication Data

Names: Waters, Kristin, author.
Title: Maria W. Stewart and the roots of black political thought / Kristin Waters.
Other titles: Margaret Walker Alexander series in African American studies.

Description: Jackson: University Press of Mississippi, 2021. | Series: Margaret Walker Alexander series in African American studies | Includes bibliographical references and index.
Identifiers: LCCN 2021029519 (print) | LCCN 2021029520 (ebook) | ISBN 978-1-4968-3674-8 (hardback) | ISBN 978-1-4968-3675-5 (paperback) | ISBN 978-1-4968-3676-2 (epub) | ISBN 978-1-4968-3677-9 (epub) | ISBN 978-1-4968-3678-6 (pdf) | ISBN 978-1-4968-3673-1 (pdf)
Subjects: LCSH: Stewart, Maria W., 1803-1879. | Walker, David, 1785-1830. | African American women political activists. | African American women—History—19th century. | African Americans—History—To 1863. | African Americans—Religion. | Antislavery movements—United States. | African Americans—Politics and government—19th century. | African American women abolitionists.
Classification: LCC E185.97.S84 W38 2021 (print) | LCC E185.97.S84 (ebook) | DDC 323.092 [B]—dc23
LC record available at https://lccn.loc.gov/2021029519
LC ebook record available at https://lccn.loc.gov/2021029520

British Library Cataloging-in-Publication Data available

CONTENTS

First Independent Baptist Church, Belknap St., Boston, also referred to as the African Baptist Church and the African Meeting House. [Isaac Smith] Homans, *Sketches of Boston, Past and Present*. 1851.

"THE AFRICAN MEETING HOUSE"

Regie Gibson[1]

Do not be fooled by paint and window frame.
Nor by landing and step . . . the stream of electric light . . .
by door way . . . by concrete and tempered glass.
This building is more than building. It is body. It is bone.
It is a breathing, living ancestor—a soul that knows and feels.
It asks us to open ourselves to all it has witnessed.
It asks us to listen—to see what it has seen.

See the emaciated, newly self-emancipated
shambling through its aisles . . . small bundles beneath
their quivering arms. See the bloodshot fear in their eyes
as they look over their shoulders for paddyrollers:
slave patrollers who would send them back into chain.
See their branded backs latticed from bullwhip . . .
their manacle-mangled feet torn by travel and travail. Now . . .
see the woman walk toward them . . .
her hand . . . a kindness of food and water.
She opens her mouth: *Here . . . and HEAR:*
this Meeting House is now YOUR harbor and home.

This building that is more than building
wants us to hear the children of the Abiel Smith School
learning their letters—deciphering the code
of written language that had been kept from their grasp.
Imagine their eyes widening as their minds
slowly unweed and begin blooming into blossom.

Feel Mariah Stewart's feminist fire. Her words: burning and blistering
invocations demanding the full and untethered inclusion of women
into the decision making body of this Republic.

Hear David Walker appealing for a vigorous black confrontation
of slavery, and insisting that whites christianize their *actions*
rather than merely their *rhetoric*!

Hear William Lloyd Garrison's abolitionist canter calling for an end
to ALL chains whether they be put on man or woman . . .
On body—or mind!

And, see Fredrick Douglass! Bear witness to his untamable graying head
lathered in lamplight. His determined face tight with nostril-flare
as he indicts this country for not becoming its creed.

Yes, this building is more than building!
More than brick and board.
More than wainscot and two by four.
More than hammer pound and rounded pew.

This building that is more than building is of flesh and blood!

It is an opened mouth singing of freedom!

Is black hands clapping out the rhythm
of this country's collective heartbeat.
Is Thursday evening prayer meetings and Sunday morning saint-shouts
from congregations punctuating the preacher's message
that we so much need to hear now:
Unity of purpose! Respect for each other! Resistance to injustice.

No . . . do not be fooled . . . these pews are still peopled by spirits!
And every rafter and wall is weighted with voices waiting to break into us

and lend us the strength to clench our separate selves into a fist raised against
the fences erected between Justice and For ALL

Yes, this building is more than building!

It is an ancestor filled with ancestors . . . calling us to see!
Calling us to witness!
Calling us to act.

Listen!

MARIA W. STEWART
and the

ROOTS *of* BLACK POLITICAL THOUGHT

MARIA W. STEWART

Her Life and Thought

I feel almost unable to address you; almost incompetent to perform the task.
—Maria W. Stewart, *Religion and the Pure Principles of Morality* (1831) [1]

In 1831 Maria W. Stewart, née Miller (1803–1879), a nearly destitute twenty-nine-year-old widow appeared at the Boston office of William Lloyd Garrison and Isaac Knapp, publishers of *The Liberator*, a periodical destined to become the most influential antislavery newspaper in the United States. Garrison later recalled his thoughts when the young woman whom he might have presumed to be barely literate, placed:

> . . . into my hands, for criticism and friendly advice, a manuscript embodying your devotional thoughts and aspirations, and also various essays pertaining to the conditions of that class with which you were complexionally identified—a class "peeled, meted out, and trodden underfoot." You will recollect if not the surprise, at least the satisfaction I expressed on examining what you had written—far more remarkable in those early days than it would be now, when there are so many more educated persons of color who are able to write with ability. I not only gave you words of encouragement, but in my printing office put your manuscript into type, an edition of which was struck off in tract form, subject to your order. I was impressed by your intelligence and excellence of character. [2]

In doing so, Stewart became, in the words of her biographer Marilyn Richardson, "America's first black woman political writer." Between 1830 and 1833 Stewart wrote a series of meditations and essays delivering several of them publicly on topics ranging from women's potential for success in business, religion, and politics, to the effects of servitude on class advancement and searing critiques of racial and gender inequalities. So passionate was she about spreading her ideas to the public that more than forty years later, in 1879, she fought for a small pension and, shrugging off the temptation to use it for a measure of comfort in her waning years, she compiled and republished her earlier, by then forgotten writings for public consumption. More than one hundred years passed before Richardson, in 1987, meticulously collected and published Stewart's major works along with a beautiful biographical essay in a book that captured the attention of a dedicated group of readers. Still, today, thirty years after Richardson's labors, Maria W. Stewart's writings have not received their full regard. Her work, so profound and so forgotten, stands today as one of the most significant and least well-known foundational voices in African American and Black feminist thought.

Exploring the life and thought of Maria W. Stewart, I consider first her earliest years, then her move from Hartford to Boston, and examine closely the most intellectually productive time in the life of a woman whose journey took her from indentured servitude to recognition as a writer, speaker, thinker, and political philosopher. I leave it to another researcher to unearth the details of the almost fifty years of her life after her Boston days. The early chapters of this book examine the circumstances of Maria W. Stewart's childhood based on the fragments of information available. I was fortunate enough to find a birth record at the Connecticut State Library for Maria Miller that I believe is hers, listing the names of her parents, Caesar and Lib.[3] Beyond the birth location and parents' names, little else about her parentage is definitively traceable; however, what we do know leads to a rich account of a wealthy and well-chronicled community in Greenwich, Connecticut, that affords a view into life in the 1790s, a time when her parents were likely enslaved there.

Partway through this research, a windfall came in the form of a recently discovered essay written by Stewart in 1860 that appears to recount the events of her early childhood. "The First Stage of Life" offers personal insights found in few other of her writings, an essay largely overlooked until now, a rare reflection about a very young girl at the beginning of the nineteenth century, a gift.[4]

The religious and civil histories of early Hartford, Connecticut, are meticulously recorded, as ecclesiastical and town histories were common in the day. Consulting these sources makes it possible to place Maria Miller, a young girl indentured to a clergyman at a time when municipalities were governed by Congregational churches. Historians at the time paid close attention to the lives of ministers, so an account of Miller's decade of servitude may be constructed within the setting of the home, the city, and their relationship to regional and national events—the War of 1812 and the Hartford Convention.

Countering the dearth of direct information about Maria Miller, another surprising source yielded details about her husband-to-be. When Miller was not yet in her teens, James W. Stewart, was a merchant mariner and then a seaman in the US Navy during the War of 1812. We know that he was assigned to a renowned naval vessel commanded by a revered officer, David Porter, who kept a daily diary of their exploits chasing British whalers in the South Pacific. After the war, Stewart served off the Barbary Coast of North Africa as important international treaties were negotiated. James Stewart was a major intellectual influence on Maria Stewart, regaling her with stories of his firsthand experiences of myriad cultural, ethnic, gendered, and racially inflected distributions of power, information generally kept from the masses in the United States in order to perpetuate the myth that white Euro-American supremacy was an immutable, natural, global truth, a "truth" that James Stewart was in a position to shatter.

Reconstructing the intellectual influences that enriched Maria Stewart's thought, we find David Walker, who became her friend and mentor during her Boston years. Prior to that friendship, Walker had witnessed slavery firsthand in the darkest of its dwellings—Charleston, South Carolina—during the planned uprising attributed to a man freed from his enslavement known as Telemaque, or Denmark Vesey. Reprisals for the planned insurrection encompassed hangings, torture on the rack, and deportations, as cruelly executed as can be imagined. Walker, new to the city, witnessed them up close before he scrambled west and then north to safer ground with the memory burning in his chest and the determination to stir his brothers and sisters to action. Walker's *Appeal to the Coloured Citizens of the World* (1829) is perhaps the best-known nineteenth-century abolitionist tract, written during his brief time as an activist in the compact community he shared with Maria W. Stewart.[5]

Before her move to Boston, her indenture behind her, Maria Miller was able to gain a rudimentary education at a newly formed Sabbath School in Hartford, finally in closer company with people of her race, while she formulated a plan to escape the city. With no records of her exodus, I consider that she may have been assisted by another great influence in her life's journey, the Reverend Thomas Paul, first minister of the African Baptist Church, consecrated in Boston in 1806. The Paul brothers, all activists in the cause of Black freedom, had nearly cornered the market on religious ministry in the region with Reverend Nathaniel Paul in Albany, New York, and Reverend Benjamin Paul at the Abyssinian Baptist Church in New York City. In traveling this triangle, growing the Black Baptist religious response to subjugation, Thomas Paul would have traveled through Hartford, quite possibly stopping there to meet with co-religionists in a community preparing to build its own autonomous church. Paul and his family were among the first connections Miller made in her sojourn to Boston.

Whom did Maria Miller meet upon her arrival? One objective of this book is to reclaim the lives and thought of Black women as they co-created community as well as social and political theory, contributing original analysis of the gendered dimensions life, action, and thought. It is no easy task to sort through the prevailing epistemic conditions that dictated that men, not women, did important things and had important ideas.[6] For example, the first autonomous Black church in the Northeast was ". . . officially constituted on 8 August 1805 with twenty-four members, fifteen of whom were women. It is not yet clear whether all available sources have been consulted, but to date only the names of the male members . . . have been identified."[7]

"Fifteen of whom were women"—not one of them named. To rectify the damaging omission, I have reconstructed who those women may have been, carefully tracing the names, families, and occupations of the women of the North Slope, among them, Catherine Waterhouse and Susan Paul, Catherine L. Barbadoes, Eliza Butler Walker, Lavinia Ames Hilton, Louisa Cooper Nell, and Elizabeth Lovejoy Lewis, piecing together their lives and contributions as friends, neighbors, co-congregants, co-theorists and sometimes critics of Stewart, whose writing is replete with gender analyses. As sociologist Patricia Hill Collins makes clear, women's ideas are constructed in dialogue with community. Fortunately, many writers, including Christopher Cameron, Brittney Cooper, Valerie C. Cooper, Thomas Dublin, James Oliver and Lois E. Horton, Joycelyn Moody, Nell Irvin Painter, Carla L. Peterson, Vivian May, Dorothy Porter, Marilyn Richardson, Kathryn Kish Sklar, Dorothy Sterling, Stefan Wheelock, Julie Winch, Jean Fagin Yellin, and the contributors to the co-edited volume, *Black Women's Intellectual Traditions: Speaking Their Minds*, to name a few, in recent years have explored ideas emanating from these early days, including as they pertain to gender.[8]

African American community life held some surprises for the researcher. Throughout this work I have drawn on community festivals and public days of celebration to explore individual, social, and political lives, including almost forgotten festivals and Training Days, particularly the election of Black "governors," public feast days for Black New Englanders culminating with the selection of an esteemed person to serve as a leader and liaison with the white community. There can be little doubt that Maria Miller witnessed one or more of these festivals. In Boston, Bunker Hill Day offered an opportunity to honor and remember the many African and African American men who served in the Revolutionary War, a celebration Maria Miller (as she was then) would not have wished to miss. An exploration of this event occasions a reconsideration of the work of the great Black historian William Cooper Nell (1816–1874) and popular writer Catharine Sedgwick (1789–1867). Nell's writings are a valuable source of information and ideas from one whose family was prominent in the community. Sedgwick, who wrote an account of climbing Bunker Hill in 1825, a year prior to Miller's ascent, has a signal connection to abolition in Massachusetts. Her father, an attorney, prevailed in the legal case of Elizabeth Freeman as she petitioned against her enslavement, setting the stage for the Quock (Kwaku) Walker legal battles that virtually ended slavery in the Commonwealth in 1783. As the summer's celebrations proceeded, the Fourth of July holiday, mostly scorned by the local Black population, was followed by a feast day of greater significance. African Day, celebrating the legal demise of the slave trade as well as the revolution in Haiti, served as a particular source of pride. Shortly thereafter, through a more personal and solemn ceremony, Maria Miller's prospects—her emotional, intellectual, and financial conditions—were enhanced when she married James W. Stewart in Reverend Thomas Paul's esteemed African Baptist Church.[9]

The remaining portions of Maria W. Stewart's life in Boston are significantly easier to trace. Records improve, Black organizing coalesced influenced by the Prince Hall Masons, the creation of the Massachusetts General Colored Association (MGCA), the inauguration of *Freedom's Journal*, a Black-owned and operated abolitionist newspaper, and the publication of David Walker's *Appeal*, as well as the *Liberator* abolitionist newspaper. The written works of Maria W. Stewart—her meditations and essays—and the grueling battle for the estate of her husband allow us to trace and study explicitly her thought before she departed for New York City late in 1833. Stewart's life and thought in Boston, her intellectual production emanating from the cauldron of political ideas there, make it a foundational element of early African American thought in North America.

THE ROOTS OF BLACK POLITICAL THEORY

Black Revolutionary Liberalism[10]

In North America, Enlightenment ideas drifting over from Europe were in the air. Thomas Jefferson, John Adams, James Madison, Alexander Hamilton, Mercy Otis Warren, and John Jay fine-tuned for their own purposes the revolutionary political theories of philosophers such as John Locke, David Hume, Jean-Jacques Rousseau, Adam Smith, Mary Wollstonecraft, and others.[11] Elites and commoners alike absorbed concepts of liberal democracy—natural rights and freedoms—reading the pamphlets, broadsides, and newspapers, listening to speeches, sermons, and everyday conversation. Immersed in the rhetoric of freedom from tyranny and rights to property, free expression and religion, Africans in America were not mere passive receptors. Their understandings created a firm grasp on the hypocrisy of embracing both the noble ideals of liberty and the practice of chattel slavery. Recognition of the wrongs of slavery found expression in the bodies, hearts, minds, and souls of the enslaved long before stolen Africans were in a position to write treatises about it.

Systematic, *written* intellectual productions were rare for Blacks in America and Europe prior to the eighteenth century. When opportunities to publish increased, different voices could be heard. Anton Wilhelm Amo, Benjamin Banneker, Ottobah Cugoano, Olaudah Equiano, Prince Hall, Briton Hammond, Lemuel Haynes, John Marrant, Lucy Terry Prince, Prince Saunders, Belinda Sutton, and Phillis Wheatley all contributed to the growing body of liberation literature including poetry, autobiographical narratives, sermons, petitions, and court cases that gathered steam in the early Republic. As a political philosopher, Maria W. Stewart represents the culmination of a first wave of abolitionist ideas from about 1750 to 1835 that merged in a theory of Black revolutionary or radical liberalism, a theory that shared revolutionary rhetoric across race as a sort of *lingua franca*, but diverged in profound ways in analysis and application. In the late 1700s, African Americans such as Prince Hall, Peter Bestes, and Belinda Sutton wrote petitions to the courts arguing for their civil rights and freedoms. From the pulpit, ministers such as Lemuel Haynes and John Marrant melded ideas of reformed religion and liberation theology. Artistic and literary works from poets such as Phillis Wheatley generated political ideas. In a swelling intellectual continuum, a few generations later, Stewart lectured, and her friend David Walker wrote his *Appeal*, calls to arms.

Maria W. Stewart distilled her political thought into a series of six essays and speeches written over three years. Black revolutionary liberalism, as a political theory created by African Americans, captures and goes far beyond the spirit that justified the colonists' violent resistance to their English oppressors. This is key. Most African Americans understood that an end to slavery and race oppression would require determined, even armed resistance. In contrast, willful ignorance, a concept introduced by the political philosopher Charles W. Mills, fueled by extreme economic advantage and a metaphysics of racial hierarchies meant that a consistent, universal application of natural rights theory would not be countenanced by the practitioners of white supremacy. Black Americans adopted revolutionary liberal theory as a powerful tool to push back against their subjugation—and they did—through armed revolts stretching from the earliest days of enslavement, everyday resistance, and political theorizing.[12]

Stewart's Principles of Morality

Throughout her writings, Stewart develops a moral theory composed of three basic principles. The first, often repeated in her texts, is a *principle of everyday righteousness*. She exhorts her audiences to live *righteous* lives as individuals, families, and community members. Practicing virtue is both a good in itself and the preparatory step for all future actions, political and religious. The idea of everyday virtue leads to her second principle, the *struggle for political freedom and equality*, or universal political rights. For Stewart, the struggle is real and imminent and is based upon her adoption of a political theory of liberal or republican ideals, made consistent by African American writers, thinkers, and ordinary people. Her writing heralds the inevitable push for meaningful equality. She asserts: "This is the land of freedom. The press is at liberty. Every man has a right to express his opinion. Many think, because your skins are tinged with a sable hue, that you are an inferior race of beings; but God does not consider you as such."[13] Likewise, David Walker declares: "Put every thing before us to death, in order to gain our freedom which God has given us."[14]

Stewart's third principle emerges from her deep commitment to an evangelical vision of the future, *a principle of justice on the Judgment Day*. The ultimate goal of virtuous behavior and political enlightenment is to bring about justice now and for eternity. The struggle for political freedom and equality emerges from a fusion of religion and politics. The powerful principles of morality, not just for venial matters but for more profound ones, have far-reaching implications for the "coloured citizens of the world."

Insurrectionist Ethics

Currently, at a time when many ethical theories have shied away from the idea of forceful responses to wrongs, voices have emerged insisting, as did those colonial Americans, that certain circumstances not only permit but in fact *require* the direct action of struggle and resistance. Inspired by the writing of David Walker, Leonard Harris argues that radical action or advocacy thereof is a moral imperative or duty exercised to acknowledge full personhood and the flourishing of all humanity.[15] We may not stand by as we witness the mass suffering of others. Following Harris, scholars have taken up the mantle, contending that the best expression of insurrectionist ethics is to be found in the writings of Maria W. Stewart, since she is explicit about not only the racial but the gendered expressions of oppression, offering a roadmap for creating a society that nurtures the full flourishing of humanity.[16]

In her first published essay, "Religion and the Pure Principles of Morality, the Sure Foundation on Which We Must Build," Stewart levels a series of questions:

"Shall it any longer be said of the daughters of Africa, they have no ambition, they have no force?" Why, if white people tremble at the idea of being "servants forever, to Great Britain . . . then why have not Afric's sons the right to feel the same? Are not their wives, their sons, and their daughters as dear to them as those of the white man's?"[17] One reason the promulgators of insurrectionist ethics have championed the work of Maria Stewart is because they see that "human flourishing" must mean *all* humans and they recognize that women and girls have largely been excluded from the formula—but not by Stewart. The consistency with which she weaves the concept of gender into each of her writings provides a model of intersectional thought.[18]

Knowledge and Power—Epistemologies of and from Oppression

In what may seem a commonplace to our ears, Maria W. Stewart once wrote that "knowledge is power," a persistent theme for her and one that reveals the connections between epistemology and political theory. Stewart keenly perceives the ways that knowledge and ignorance are used as weapons to perpetuate race and gender oppression. Epistemologies—theories of knowledge--are central to and provide handbooks for social control as well as for liberatory resistance. Oppressive ideologies such as ones about racial inferiority are created and enforced through scholarship, law, religion, and popular culture. The ideologies of whiteness employ strict regimens designed to keep oppressed groups un-educated, in poor health, and economically disempowered, creating barriers to effectively countering the false narratives of white exceptionalism. The enforced obliteration of knowledge-creation and accomplishments by oppressed people, *epistemicide*, is designed to perpetuate ignorance on all sides about real lives, ideas, and excellences.[19] The institutionally driven obliteration of knowledge (one crucial example is knowledge of the existence and philosophical thought of Maria W. Stewart and her contemporaries) generates an urgent need for reclamation projects such as this one.[20] Further, the steadfast maintenance by oppressors of a strictly enforced, self-imposed, willful ignorance about Black lives, sorrows, and achievements builds an almost impenetrable wall preventing any recognition of the realities of the whole of humanity. Those with power and privilege vigorously deny to themselves and others the truths of oppression. Any challenge to this stance is met with an inversion of reality, what is some-times known as white fragility or "white tears"—a victim narrative in which the agent of harm takes up the position of the person or group harmed, to deflect, to gain sympathy, to engage in self-pity, and to thwart the narratives of those who are actually harmed. Escaping ignorance could be liberating for everyone.

Double and Triple Consciousness, Labor, and Intersectionality

Among other philosophical concepts explored in this work, I investigate the idea derived from W. E. B. Du Bois of a double consciousness that characterizes the subjective interpretative frame of Black people in a white dominant culture replete with anti-Black racism. It may take the form of internalized oppression that melds an external gaze of disapprobation to a negative self-assessment. It may signify confusion about the conundrum of being both Black and American. In this work I suggest that, in the hands of feminist and antiracist philosophers, the negative psychological repercussions of externally imposed racism may be converted into a steely, enlightening (that is, knowledge-producing) posture. Patricia Hill Collins employs a large body of case studies to demonstrate that her subjects—Black women—formulate Black feminist theory in discourse with each other and may be in a position to take epistemic advantage to assess the intricacies of the white gaze and the mechanisms of white dominance by using "oppositional knowledge . . . collective wisdom to generate a more specialized knowledge, namely, Black feminist thought as critical social theory."[21]

From the standpoint of inside knowledge of white society (the "outsider within"), particularly available to domestic workers such as Maria W. Stewart in her youth, direct observation of white culture combines with organically generated Black feminist theory in ways that stimulate analysis, evaluation, critique, and even subversion of oppressive conditions. The double knowledge of both self and other creates subjective positions that are useful for analyzing white behavior, especially when powerful others suffer from the one-ness of epistemic ignorance. Demonstrating her skill at this type of analysis, Stewart entreats her

> . . . fairer sisters, whose hands are never soiled whose nerves and muscles are never strained, go learn by experience! Had we had the opportunity to improve our moral and mental faculties, what would have hindered our intellects from being as bright, and our manners from being as dignified as yours?[22]

Her "fairer sisters" have polish and manners, but they lack knowledge from experience, *they are ignorant* about social, racial, and class relations, and about life itself, knowledge that Stewart and "outsiders within" possess. Adopting an attitude that promotes critical inquiry (easy to do in the face of white arrogance), the two-ness of double consciousness, of self and other, may become advantageous. Indeed, as Marilyn Richardson observes regarding Stewart, the two-ness may become a three-ness, a triple-consciousness, an intersectional view that stems both from the race/class/gender oppression experienced by the observer, but also from the vantage point of insights seized from the triply oppressive standpoint. Maria W. Stewart has this, a subjectivity akin to what Mariana Ortega designates as a "multiplicitous consciousness or imaging that helps to create survival practices as well as . . . resistance."[23] Decades of servitude and a formidable intelligence combine to produce a brilliant intersectional theory of race/class/and gender oppression. Stewart's focus on the twin threats of excessive labor and educational deprivation unveils a longstanding playbook for subjugation.[24]

A life cannot be told in isolation. A confluence of historical location, political thought and action permeating the communities, and the influences of those around her are part of the narrative in which ideas and places as well as people serve as central characters. I hope that this narrative, one of many that may be told about Maria W. Stewart, may create not just discourse and approval but also disagreement, critique, and other narratives from readers, ones that may be brought to the public arena. Maria W. Stewart deserves it.

Methodology

When I began research for this study, I assumed from the vacancies in my own knowledge that little was known about the theoretical headwork and on-the-ground resistance across the first wave of abolition extending from slavery's beginnings to the 1830s.[25] I could not have been more wrong. A wealth of research, much of it excellent, addresses this period of time, as attested throughout this book and in the bibliography. At the same time, some writers have pointedly ignored the marginalized voices that create a more inclusive and truer narrative. Compounding the obstacles, many sources are riddled with errors that are repeated from source to source.[26] I have worked hard to be as accurate as possible and apologize in advance for any errors, inviting readers to help with the process of correcting the record.

This type of truly interdisciplinary work is challenging and not always loved within the academy, where skirmishes are fought over disciplinary boundaries and perceived encroachments.[27] Philosophy, my field, sometimes teaches that ideas may or must be studied in abstraction from social and political contexts. Historians sometimes view philosophical work as insufficiently grounded in fact, yet they may demure when called upon to identify their interpretive processes. Combining these two endeavors, as I do, may create friction. That said, I have the utmost respect for researchers who do both well.

I have mined every primary source that I could find in a variety of locations: the American Antiquarian Society, the Boston Athenaeum, the Boston Public Library, the Connecticut State Library, the Howard University Archives, the

Massachusetts State Archives, the Museum of African American History/Boston, the National Archives, as well as various local Massachusetts and Connecticut historical societies, especially those in Hartford and Greenwich, and many internet archives. No source has been more valuable than Marilyn Richardson's *Maria W. Stewart: The First Black Woman Political Theorist* (1987). At a time when archival materials were scattered hither and yon, Richardson scoured the landscape and, remarkably, found so much of the historical information presented here that it is not a stretch to say that this book could not have been written without her foundational work. Add to that the fortunate occurrence that when it was possible to do so, Horace Seldon and Michael Terranova furiously scouted out archival materials.[28] They took notes and made copies of primary source documents that contributed to the later work of Kathryn Grover and Janine da Silva who compiled the wonderfully informative *Historic Research Study* of the Boston African American National Historical Site, as the campus that includes the African Meeting House is properly known, as well as to many other studies of this time and place.[29] I strongly encourage anyone who has the means and opportunity to visit this remarkable, sacred place.

The work of philosophers, historians and others, far too numerous to name here, is carefully recorded in the bibliography. The many nineteenth-century secular and ecclesiastical histories, such as those by William Cooper Nell, have been invaluable. More recently, excellent work on Black Boston has been accomplished by James Oliver Horton and Lois E. Horton. For David Walker, no source has been more meticulous, informative, and reliable than the work of Peter P. Hinks. The comprehensive account found in Manisha Sinha's monumental *The Slave's Cause* has served as an invaluable sourcebook.[30]

My philosophical methodology is the culmination of decades of acquiring and then shedding a traditional education in the field. The Afro-American and women's studies movements that came out of the 1960s transformed the face of the academy in ways that, despite fierce resistance, changed forever what counts as knowledge. Scholarship and teaching that excluded marginal voices itself became marginalized to a degree (much to the dismay of its practitioners) and subject to critique.[31] The new fields of study flourished and then faced vigorous backlash. The lives and ideas of so many women and people of color had been buried that reclamation work burgeoned in a heady frenzy of knowledge-production. The desire to contribute to refashioning the canon has infused all my published work over time. My acknowledgments section details the long list of philosophical influences, but it is worth mentioning a few names here. The work of Patricia Hill Collins has been foundational and profoundly influential, helping to create the modern field of Black feminist thought. Originating the concept of "shifting the geography of reason," the founders of the Caribbean Philosophical Association, B. Anthony Bogues, Patrick Goodin, Lewis Ricardo

MEDITATIONS

FROM THE PEN OF

MRS. MARIA W. STEWART,

(WIDOW OF THE LATE JAMES W. STEWART,)

NOW MATRON OF THE FREEDMAN'S HOSPITAL,

AND

Presented in 1832 to the First African Baptist Church and Society of Boston, Mass.

FIRST PUBLISHED BY W. LLOYD GARRISON & KNAP.

Now most respectfully Dedicated to the Church Militant of Washington, D. C.

Meditations from the Pen of Mrs. Maria W. Stewart (widow of the late James W. Stewart). Now matron of the Freedman's Hospital. First Published by W. Lloyd Garrison and Isaac Knapp, republished in 1879. Photo courtesy of Nancy K. Waters.

Gordon, Clevis Headley, Paget Henry, Nelson Maldonado-Torres, Charles W. Mills, and Supriya Nair created a home for a particular, radical approach to the philosophies of the African diaspora, a project later guided by Neil Roberts, Douglas Ficek, Jane Anna Gordon, Rosario Torres-Guevara, and Michael Monahan. Charles Mills' searing assessment of the historically dominant varieties of liberalism and ultimate endorsement of a radical version of liberalism goes to the heart of this philosophical study.

NOTE TO READERS

Some readers may be more interested in the biographical details of Maria W. Stewart's life than in her ideas. I encourage them to skip freely over the denser portions of this work. For example, the first several chapters consist of reconstructed and speculative biography based on historical knowledge or autobiographical narrative. Those who are more keenly interested in her philosophy may wish to read the text catering to their interests. Chapters sixteen through eighteen are densely theoretical, while chapters nineteen and twenty are full of biographical detail based on archival material from the Probate Court and Stewart's diary-like *Meditations*. The final chapters rely heavily on her speeches and essays. I would, however, suggest that for Stewart's philosophical thinking, the context of her life is instructive.

This book is based on facts about Stewart's life and relevant histories. To fill in the historical gaps, I have imagined and speculated about parts or her life and intellectual development. In each case, the speculative portions should be clear from the contexts. In the hope of not perpetuating misconceptions about Maria W. Stewart, her life and thought, I encourage readers and researchers to be similarly cautious when citing from this work, to distinguish between conjectural and historically based claims.

Whenever possible, I draw directly from historical sources, particularly but by no means exclusively from African Americans. Acceptable usage changes over time. For example, the term "Negro" was common for centuries but is not now considered to be an acceptable designation. In almost every instance I retain the original usage and leave it to the reader to understand the deep and often troubling history of this and other terms and expressions.

The delicate issue of what to call the subject of this work has led me to create certain conventions. Born Maria Miller, when she married, she adopted her husband's middle initial as well as his last name: Maria W. Stewart. In the sections that deal with her young life, prior to her marriage, I typically use "Maria Miller" except in those cases where the reference is to the public political philosopher, Maria W. Stewart. I believe that this set of conventions will be easy for the reader to navigate. For the record, in the nineteenth-century, the name "Maria" was generally pronounced "Mariah."

SPEAKING AND WRITING AS RESISTANCE

Why, in the twenty-first century, do so few people know about an early nineteenth-century thinker, Maria W. Stewart, about the roots of Black political theory, about the thousands and more brilliant women and people of color whose accomplishments have not been showcased in scholarly or popular venues? Why is this so when the airwaves, bookstores, theaters, public monuments, internet, and imaginations are so full of stories about the Euro-American heroes of the day? Why were so many people upset when Michelle Obama told the truth about "waking up every morning in a house built by slaves"?[32] The epistemic obliteration, the burying of knowledge, the *epistemicide* is ongoing and in some places, it is almost absolute. Succeeding in her struggle against these practices, Maria W. Stewart is a hero and a warrior. After a life of terrible struggle, including shocking deprivations during the Civil War, she heard about the possibility of a pension for widows of War of 1812 veterans. With tremendous effort and some expense, she marshalled the resources of half a dozen people, some eminent ones such as the Reverend Alexander Crummell, William Lloyd Garrison, and friends such as Louise Hatton, to gather together documents required for filing her claim and to write testimonials as to her character. Once having secured her pension, she might have used the funds to make her final years a little more comfortable. Instead, in the true spirit of fighting against the obliteration of knowledge, she published *Meditations from the Pen of Maria W. Stewart* (1879), her legacy to us.

Chapter One

"MANY FLOWERS AMONG US"[1]

—Maria W. Stewart, *Lecture Delivered at the Franklin Hall* (1832)

These women are the salt
of my sea, the sweat that collects
on the rims of my scars.

I do not need to know their names, their places
of birth, their dates of death,
to know I am their daughter.
—Ruthann Robson *Genealogy*[2]

Five years old, a motherless child. Fatherless too. Her mother, at least, would have been free. Perhaps her father as well, but none of that mattered now. What mattered was that she was to be sent away to work as a servant in someone's home, to clean, wait on family members, sweep, clear out the char and ash from the fireplaces, smooth the rough bed linens, scrub and sweep the entryway. The approach from the street was particularly important since it spoke to those who passed by as well as to those who entered. It spoke of social standing, the ability to provide, ease of living, and also of God's grace and favor. It signaled a fine enough wealth for a pastor—not so much as would be unseemly or so little as to convey shabbiness. It spoke of the good man with his gentleman's library that served as his study for writing sermons and meeting privately with wayward parishioners or businessmen seeking council on civic matters. On the other side of the passageway was the sitting room, domain of the mistress of the house, to welcome visitors—ladies and men. In the rear, a spacious kitchen revealed a large hearth, bread oven, pantry, and door leading to the outbuildings, the pens for chickens and pigs, the kitchen garden—all to be Maria's domain under strict supervision. She was very much a child, unfamiliar with the rigors of domestic labor, so she must have been torn between the inviting bounty of the household and the unsettling newness of servitude. Bound to them for a lifetime—ten years—longer than a young child can imagine.

Years later, reflecting on the ill wind that carried her into hard labor, her memory sought the words of the English poet Thomas Grey: "[T]here are many flowers among us that are ... born to bloom unseen. And waste their fragrance on the desert air."[3] But Maria Miller Stewart's bloom was not wasted. The flower budded, blossomed, spread its fragrance, and bloomed again, broadcasting seeds that in the distant future would grow year after year. True, she was not cosseted in the way that a brilliant child of a different race, gender, and class might have been, but despite harsh conditions and the lack of nurture, from sheer brilliance and force of will, she spread her wisdom. In time it would be seen by others: absorbed, honored, and celebrated. And if, in her old age, she wondered if the intricate flowers of her writing would be recognized, a lifetime of determination, resourcefulness, and strength have brought us the writings of Maria W. Stewart, née Miller—her prescient work the vanguard of Black women's intellectual traditions and, indeed, of Black political thought.[4]

Perhaps her parents died from the epidemic of smallpox so severe that in 1808 Connecticut passed a law to enforce public health through quarantines. Regardless of the cause, die they did. It was common for indigent children to be bound out to someone who would minimally care for their needs in return for their labor. She would have sustenance and shelter, if not the warmth of her own family's care. And Miller seemed bright enough and quick to learn. How can we know what it was like, *what it meant,* to be Maria Miller who grew up to become Maria W. Stewart, an originator of written and published Black women's political theory? In her early years, she was an indentured servant, a Black child in a mostly white community, a member of a household in which the patriarch vigorously devoted himself to saving souls, growing up alongside white children whom she had to serve. And why is her life important, if it is? For that matter, how can we know the biographical, social, and intellectual history of any African Americans in Boston or elsewhere in the early Republic in the absence of detailed and respectful records? If this account is a patchwork—a crazy quilt—it still may serve to embroider the small but beautiful cloth stitched together by previous writers, including Stewart herself and by the hints and documents left to us.[5]

In an 1831 essay of moral and political importance, Stewart recalls,

> I was born in Hartford, Connecticut, in 1803; was left an orphan at five years of age; was bound out in a clergyman's family; had the seeds of piety and virtue early sown in my mind, but was deprived of the advantages of education, though my soul thirsted for knowledge. Left them at fifteen years of age; attended Sabbath schools until I was twenty; in 1826

was married to James W. Stewart; was left a widow in 1829; was, I hope
and trust, brought to the knowledge of truth as it is in Jesus, in 1830; in
1831 made a public profession of my faith in Christ.[6]

This tantalizing morsel serves as an invitation to gather more information
about her birth, her parents, and her young life. Researching someone with
such obscure beginnings presents obstacles, but the challenges are not insur-
mountable. Robert Roberts, an African American who published a guide for
household staff in 1827, describes typical domestic duties like those expected
of Maria Miller: "When you first come down, make as little noise as you possibly can . . . take up your ashes, clean your grates, or fire irons, and tidy up the
hearth."[7] As she labored in the clergyman's home, Maria Miller's mind might
have drifted back to her earliest memories. Most of the people around her, like
herself, were nominally free; still, some in Hartford clung to the old system of
bondsmen and women. Walking to market, did she cast her eyes around and
wonder who her parents were, their origins, and where they had lived? Were
her parents' lives like those of other African Americans she encountered in
Hartford, some friendly, some distant, and some freer than others? Her own
status seemed like a limbo, not like those who moved about more freely or
like others who were clearly less free even than she—bound for life—for she
had been told that when she turned fifteen, she would no longer be bound to
service. Who among them knew or remembered her parents? She felt herself
to be brighter than most, a thought that came to her early as she encountered
a range of people from different races and social standings.

Twenty-six years later, as a published and practicing political theorist,
Stewart asked a group assembled at a meeting of the nascent New England
Anti-Slavery Society:

What literary acquirement can be made, or useful knowledge derived,
from either maps, books, or charts, by those who continually drudge
from Monday morning until Sunday noon? . . . Had it been our lot to
have been nursed in the lap of affluence and ease, and to have basked
beneath the smiles and sunshine of fortune, should we not have naturally supposed that we were never made to toil?[8]

Who were Maria Miller's parents, and how had she come to be orphaned
and indentured? Not "nurtured in the lap of affluence," she has little clear and
distinct genealogy. Still, clues are there for us to trace.

Chapter Two

"CALL ME LIB"

MILLER (MILLIAR), *Maria, d. Caesar & Lib (negro), b. 4 September 1803.*
Greenwich Vital Records 1640–1848, Connecticut Town Birth Records, pre-1870,
Barbour Collection.[1]

THREE SIBS

Maria Miller, daughter of Caesar and Lib (negro), born on September 4, 1803, in Greenwich, Connecticut. The birth of only one Maria Miller is recorded in the state of Connecticut in 1803, or for that matter, for decades before and after, and while later in the century one finds records of Irish immigrants by that name, only one entry, only one person of color, stands out, not in Hartford as Maria W. Stewart recorded in her biographical recollection, but in Greenwich. In keeping with other coastal towns, Greenwich boasted proportionately more people of color than inland communities, a result of proximity with the slave trade ports of Middletown, New London, Bristol, and Providence, relative wealth, and closeness to the sea. In 1831, when Maria W. Stewart wrote, "I was born in Hartford, Connecticut, in 1803; was left an orphan at five years of age," her memory of her birthplace may have been clouded by the circumstances of her young life.[2] Certainly, she was indentured, "bound out to a clergyman" in Hartford at age five in 1808 and lived in Hartford for eighteen years. Why should she not assume that she was born there? Connecticut was known as "the land of steady habits," and in keeping with this designation, the scribes for the established Congregational churches were meticulous about their record keeping. It would be surprising for these record keepers to miss the birth of a child in Hartford, even a descendant of Africans. Other pieces of information about her youth suggest that her caretakers moved from place to place when she was a small child, reinforcing the possibility of a different birthplace—all pieces of the mosaic of her story.

The document records that a daughter, Maria Miller, was born in Greenwich to Lib and Caesar. The slim, scrawled entries on the parchment pages of the church records reveal more than their compact declarations might suggest. No "Lib" appears in the Connecticut records either before or after the 1803 birth of Maria Miller, but there is a rich history of similarly named and placed enslaved women. The accounts of three women named "Sib"—all more or less the same age and in the same location as Lib—help to tell the story of bondswomen in Greenwich. The prosperous, slave-holding community experienced an impulse towards manumission in the 1790s that scattered many of its Black residents. Subtle pressures, bad conscience, religious practice, the recent memory and living evidence of Black veterans' war efforts fighting for independence from Great Britain, and even the principles that underwrote that war converged in a spasm of emancipations—at least 33 in the small Town of Greenwich alone in a span of ten years. Among these are three women, all named "Sib," all of whom were emancipated during the 1790s, each of them with a different story.

Speculatively—just let your imagination roam—consider the connection between Maria Miller's mother, Lib, and these three "Sibs." Consider that when African American men were emancipated, they often marked the occasion by renaming themselves, adopting new monikers, rebaptizing themselves in ways befitting of their new condition: Freeman, Freedman, Beaman (Be a man). Perhaps . . . what if . . . an emancipated Sib, at parturition, imagining liberty for her child, when asked her name for the church accounts, instead of offering the name that had draped her with the mantle of slavery, stated for the record, "Call me Lib."

SIB THE FIRST—"JARED MEAD'S WENCH"

The Mead family wielded power in Greenwich. A commonplace wisdom holds that powerful men insist upon having their way, so crossing the Mead men may not have been a recommended course of action for one of such vastly diminished position as Sib. The first time master Jared Mead came to the enslaved woman, Sib, she was very young, and he was approaching middle age. By that time, Mead had already fathered four daughters with his wife, Lydia, née Smith: Zetta, Lydia, Alma, and Hannah, so intercourse with Sib may have proved a change of pace for him, and no doubt it changed her life, too. She was inexperienced and likely terrified. From this union, Prue, master Jared and enslaved Sib's daughter, was born: Prue, daughter of Jared Mead's "wench," Sib, was born the 16th day of August AD 1790.[3] The master took seriously his duty to "be fruitful and multiply," and by multiplying with his slaves, he could also divide, sending their children away whenever he wished and wherever he

Second Congregational Society Meetinghouse in Greenwich, CT, ca. 1830. Painting by Mary E. Mason (1801–1833). The Greenwich landmark would have been familiar to Maria Miller's parents. Courtesy of the Greenwich Historical Society.

pleased. But it pleased him to keep this child, Prue. The newly minted state of Connecticut was sparsely populated. White children were needed to worship God and rule the polity, while dark children were needed to labor on the land. So, Jared Mead addressed this duty. And while Sib was less able to perform her labor at the farm when she was with child, her diminished abilities were a consequence of Jared's taking *what was his* whenever he wished, and if his wife, Lydia, complained, we have no record of it. Just as her husband took his patriarchal obligations seriously, so Lydia appears to have been earnest about her duties to her husband and to Republican motherhood.[4] Since Lydia, like Sib, spent many years parturient, she may have been grateful to have his attentions focused elsewhere.

Jared Mead's talent was for begetting girl children, four of them so far. Then, as now, sons were favored. Sons could carry on the family name, business, and church pew. Male children born of Christian marriage would be less expensive than similarly situated girls, requiring no dowry. Under the prevailing laws of coverture, men could generate income in ways beyond the reach of respectable girls and women. As a consequence, it must have been a relief and a cause for rejoicing when Jared and Lydia's son, Jared, was born on September 28, 1791.

Then Lucy was born on July 18, 1792, to Sib and Jared—a perfect match for her half-brother Jared—too perfect it seems for at age seventeen, in 1818, Jared followed his father's footsteps away from the marriage bed and impregnated his own half-sister, Lucy, producing a daughter named Prudence after her aunt Prue. In a pitiful irony confounding race and status of enslavement, the Greenwich Vital Records proclaim this incest quite boldly, identifying Lucy as *"formerly negro.*⁵ One assumes they mean "formerly enslaved" since "formerly negro" possesses a metaphysical status of dubious standing. And while Lucy may have been formerly enslaved, she seems not to have been free enough to choose freely her intimate partners. But this moves the story too far into the future, away from the 1790s—so important for Maria Miller's biography.

Following the births of Prue and Lucy to Sib and Jared, and the births of Jared and Alvin to Lydia and Jared, Julie Ann was born to Jared and Sib in 1798, when Lydia was past her childbearing years and, it seems, shortly before Sib was to be freed. What were Jared Mead's thoughts as he signed the papers emancipating Sib in 1799? Did he ponder that she was the mother of his children, Lucy, Prue, and Julie Ann? No records exist to show that these young girls were freed as well. Custom and law prohibited manumitting those who might burden the state. Did he feel sorrow or virtue for this action? And what of Sib? How can we imagine her emotions at the loosening of the bonds that tied her to this man? Was she freed only to remain as a laborer on his estate—a double-edged sword, nursing her one-year-old child and caring for her other small children? Did she choose to stay near her children and her abusive master? Did she flee or remain in place?⁶

The racially entwined Mead genealogy is a common one, an embroidered cloth of differently tinted threads, ripped apart and soaked in the blood of women assaulted by masters who wore their piety proudly. In the absence of details about the external circumstances and interior lives of these individuals, it may not go too far to offer Jared Mead as an example of those who were both sexually rapacious and morally bereft, North and South, while modeling in the community a persona of propriety. Evidence of such couplings is common in the South and a part of the condescension that northerners sometimes heap upon their southern countrymen, but North and South, the bare, bold facts of the records reveal that the agonizing reality of these human relations was not confined to a single family, state, or geographical region.

THE EMANCIPATION OF SIB THE SECOND BY AMOS MEAD

Another Sib was the deeded property of Jared Mead's brother, Amos. The early heroic exploits of the Mead family are well known and documented in *Ye Historie of Ye Town of Greenwich County of Fairfield and State of Connecticut* by Spencer P. Mead, L.L.B. An ancestor, Dr. Amos Mead, was a veteran of the

French and Indian as well as the Revolutionary War, and his descendants possessed material relics from his life.

> One of the descendants of Surgeon Amos Mead . . . has in his posses-
> sion an old flintlock-pistol and powder horn, which were carried by him
> through the campaign of 1759, and upon the powder horn are almost
> perfectly delineated, the relative positions and forts of the hostile armies
> of Ticonderoga.[7]

Less illustriously, Sib's "owner," Dr. Mead's descendant and namesake, Amos
Mead, was appointed to a committee to repair the Cos Cob landing. This Amos
Mead, who held Sib as deeded property, in front of the justices of the peace
John MacKay and Benjamin Mead certified:

> a negro woman belonging to and a Slave of Amos Mead of Greenwich.
> Do find that the said negro woman is about thirty five years old is in
> a common state of health and desireous to be made free we thereupon
> do adjudge her to be a proper person to be emancipated. Dated at
> Greenwich the 17th day of May 1798.[8]

The well-researched Mead family genealogies contain rich details, most of
them not relevant to this study. Amos Mead lived a long life, dying in 1850. Of
course, much less is known about Sib, who ceases to be of interest to the state
once she makes the legal passage from property to person. The emancipation
record reveals something of the ideologies that organized the practice. Notice
in the manumission text the transformation of chattel—property—to something more human. By written declaration, Sib becomes a "proper person"—
legal documents conferring this status upon her, the text further expressing
concerns about her health, not issuing from compassion for Sib, but from a
desire not to have the burden of basic care shifted from the slaveholder to
the town. As philosopher Charles W. Mills notes, in keeping with the Roman
precedent, "European humanism usually meant that only Europeans were
human . . ."[9] When it suited the state to create humans from property, they
did so by legal fiat.

A THIRD SIB—AND A CAESAR

Much of this research was undertaken by Jeffrey B. Mead in *Chains Unbound:
Slave Emancipations in the Town of Greenwich*, descendant of Jared and
the myriad other Meads who to this day populate and leave their mark on

Greenwich, one of the wealthiest communities in the nation. Another powerful Greenwich slaveholding family was eventually to produce two United States presidents: George H. W. and George W. Bush. Yet another prominent family was the Husteds (Heusted) who, like the Bushes and Meads, boasted a full complement of African chattel. When Moses Husted Jr. died in 1795, "he bequeathed his slaves to Lucy, his widow." Within a year, Lucy Husted had also passed away. The inventory of her estate lists "two Negro men & two Negro girls and one Negro child."[10] Among the men were Jeffry and Cesar. The women include a Sib, an unnamed woman (the term "girl" is used for adult women to distinguish them from "children"), and an unnamed child. Since Lucy Husted had no direct heirs, a complicated and perplexing circumstance arose. Among the enslaved persons to be distributed when the estate was settled was Cesar. Mrs. Husted's will complied with the current trend of emancipation in the case of at least four of her inherited human souls and flesh. Joshua Purdy, an executor of her will, filed the following, noting their "desire to emancipate and make free the negro girl called Sib . . . a healthy person and between the age of twenty five and forty five years" (23rd September 1799). This certificate of emancipation establishes that a Black woman called "Sib" was domiciled on an estate that also housed a man named Cesar, who was not emancipated. The documents show a remarkable and highly atypical degree of choice accorded to Cesar, as laid out in Lucy Husted's will:

> I Give and bequeath to Major Brown son of my sd sister Sophiah Brown, Dec'd or to Sophiah Marshall *my negro man Cesar to have his Choice to live with wich he pleases and the person with whom he chooses to live is given & bequeathed twenty Pounds New York money* to be Paid by my executors (viz.) sd Major Brown or Sophiah with wich said *Cesar chooses to live* on condition of receiving twenty Pounds as above said. (Emphasis mine.)

According to this document, Cesar may choose his master. The deference accorded to the bondsman suggests a degree of connection between Lucy Husted and Cesar who was allowed to exercise his agency and express preferences that are then conveyed in the legal document:

> And if said Cesar shall not choose to live with either said Major or said Sophiah then I Give and bequeath said Cesar a Slave for life to any other of my sisters children or brother's Children *with Whoom he is willing to go and live* is to have the twenty Pounds above mentioned and it is my Will that no Person who shall take said Cesar as above mentioned shall sell said Cesar to any person.[11] (Emphasis mine.)

As family historian Jeffrey Mead notes, "The slave Cesar went to live with Lucy Husted's nephew, Major Brown in the Nehemiah Brown House located next to the First Church of Round Hill." Further, a certificate is issued: "I . . . Cesar a negroman do acknowledge before evidence that I make choice of Major Brown for my master to serve him for life agreeable to the will of my late mistress Lucy Heusted late of Greenwich . . ."[12]

The document is signed "Cesar X Negroman." Mead speculates that Cesar may have been too old or infirm to be emancipated if he required a source of support; still, the agency granted to him is unusual. Or perhaps Cesar felt it was somehow to his advantage to remain tied to the Husted family. He may have been of sound mind and body but nonetheless thought that his bonded condition would be preferable to the alternative. Cesar chose to live with Major Brown, and yet within the year, by 1800, no enslaved persons are recorded as living there. Either Cesar had died, he was missed by the census, or somehow, he had moved on. Among the curious features of this story is that the Cesar and Sib connected to the Husteds certainly would have known each other, having lived on the same estate. If Cesar was not old or infirm, if he did not die, they may have had a relationship that in 1803 produced Maria Miller.

Three cases, three Sibs, all of them emancipated in the late 1790s, one of them connected to a Caesar. A motive for a name change and a practice of liberation names. What is clear is that a woman named Lib emerges in 1803, in Greenwich, has intimate relations with a man named Caesar, and they give birth to a child whom they name Maria Miller. When Lib found herself with Caesar by 1803 there is a strong likelihood that one or both were formerly enslaved and had achieved a measure of freedom leading to the birth of their child, Maria. At that moment, Lib, whoever she may have been, experienced the liberation of *choosing* her intimate partner, a man of her own race, and it must have felt emancipating.

Chapter Three

"STOLEN FROM AFRICA"[1]

*Modernity appears when Europe organizes the initial world-system and
places itself at the center of world.*
—Enrique Dussel, *The Invention of the Americas* [2]

MANY CAESARS

Aside from the entry in the Barbour collection at the Connecticut State Library
recording Maria Miller's birth, most of what we know about her parents is a
matter of conjecture. In chapter two I explored what might be pieced together
about Miller's mother, Lib, or similarly situated women in Greenwich, Connecticut. Constructing an account of who her father was presents even more
challenges. We know that he was given the name of "Caesar" and that statistics
about the waves of Atlantic crossings make it possible or even likely that he
was a native of West Africa. In lieu of specific information about her father,
this chapter touches on the origins of the European slave trade and draws on
decolonial analyses addressing the rise of Euro-global dominance, arguing that
the enslavement process was predicated on obliterating the knowledge and
agency of people such as Caesar. Everything written in these pages contributes
to an enterprise of bringing to light knowledge generated by people of African
descent, once buried, now painstakingly reclaimed. Defying this erasure is a
way of combatting what Charles Mills has called the epistemology of ignorance
that veils the realities of race and power.[3]

In her essay "African Rights and Liberty, Maria Stewart wrote:

*Then they stole our fathers from their peaceful and quiet dwellings, and
brought them hither, and made bond-men and bond-women of them and
their little ones; they have obliged our brethren to labor, kept them in utter ignorance, nourished them in vice, and raised them in degradation."*[4]

And yet the "Founding Fathers," itself a troubling designation, self-consciously modeled their new society on classical ideals.[5] Invoking symbols of ancient republics, the enslavers replaced the given names of those stolen from Africa with names derived from classical Greece, Rome, and pagan mythology: Caesar/Cesar, Achilles, Ajax, Phoebe, Daphne, Dido, Nero, Cassius, Jupiter, Venus, Achilles, Ajax, Apollo, Bacchus, Cupid, Daphne, Hector, Hercules, Juno, Neptune, Phoebe, Myrtilla, Philander, Philis, Sabina, and Strephon.[6] More than a thousand years and a drastic change of status mediated the space between the ancient Caesars and the modern ones, connected by the slave-masters' wish to endow with nobility, or to mock those whom they condemned to servitude. It was a façade, a veil of honor shrouding a reality of debasement, countered only by the dignity of knowing one's own value as a human being. As Gertrude Gonzales de Allen observes, "in this process, where branding, naming, labor training, language acquisition, Christianization, racialization, and so forth occur, the human entity is fully transformed into a slave, and object of utility."[7] A duality emerges. The enslaved person embodies and gives consciousness to his or her own subjectivity. For the enslaver, that person becomes an object. Simultaneously, the enslavers strip themselves of their own humanity.

The Caesar who partnered with Lib and fathered Maria Miller died sometime after her birth in 1803 and before she was orphaned in 1808. An anomaly, the Caesar associated with the Husteds commanded sufficient affective connections while enslaved to reject manumission, exercising an extraordinary degree of agency to determine who would be his master, as the Husted estate papers show. It is possible that this Caesar, "Negroman," was the father of Maria Miller, but his absence from the 1800 census puts his status in question. And if not this man, there remains an abundance of enslaved Africans named Caesar who may have been her parent. George Washington claimed ownership in a man whom he called Caesar.[8] In Connecticut alone, the records reveal a number of Caesars: one who died in Farmington in 1808 at age seventy-five, possibly too old to have been Maria's father. There was a Caesar Freeman, a Revolutionary War patriot who was recognized in the rolls, also too old. There were Caesar Smith, Caesar Marsh, and Caesar Wells. Charles W. Mills notes that "there are rituals of naming which serve to seize the terrain of these "New" Worlds . . ." including the terrain of human bodies.[9] The effort to obliterate personal, social, and intellectual knowledge of the past begins with the hardship of the passage, the separation of families and countrymen from each other, the destruction of language, and most personally, the erasure of the name. God gave Adam the power of naming in *Genesis*, an almost mystical force and a speech act that simultaneously confers ontological status.[10] The slavers appropriated that power to themselves. The enslaved carried with them hidden knowledge and power and privately reappropriated the rituals of naming.

Compared with Massachusetts, where the first slave ship, *Desire*, was welcomed into Boston harbor in 1638, Connecticut was slightly later to the trade. The first Africans are recorded as arriving in Hartford in the mid-1600s. Katherine Harris observes that "captivity dominated the African experience" for those identified as Hausa, Igbo, Yoruba, Fante, Ewe, Wolof, Mende, Mandinka, ethnic groups from West Africa whose status on arrival and thereafter may have been as chattel, indentured, or free.[11] Indigenous people had been enslaved in Connecticut after the Pequot War in the 1630s, and in the mid-1700s more than twice as many as Africans were enslaved.[12] This proportion reversed quickly as the availability of Black labor surged through the Triangle Trade. In 1780 almost 6,000 blacks, free and bonded, lived in Connecticut, about 2.3% of the total population. By 1800 fewer than a thousand were still enslaved, possibly among them Maria Miller's father, Caesar, who, like many of his generation, may have been new to the Americas.[13]

FROM WEST AFRICA TO NEW ENGLAND—SHIFTING THE GEOGRAPHY

In an early experiment, the Portuguese engaged in modern chattel slavery modestly in the 1440s stealing twelve human beings from what is now Mauritania and bringing them home to Lisbon. Even with the challenges of clothing, housing, feeding, and training those who were captured, this new form of free labor seemed economically promising. Bolstered by its productivity and new justificatory ideologies, the enterprise accelerated rapidly towards plantation slavery on Madeira and other African coastal islands. In his *Appeal*, David Walker describes the process:

> It is well known to the Christian world, that Bartholomew Las Casas, that very very notoriously avaricious Catholic priest or preacher, and adventurer with Columbus in his second voyage, proposed to his countrymen, the Spaniards in Hispaniola to import the Africans from the Portuguese settlement in Africa, to dig up gold and silver, and work their plantations for them, to effect which, he made a voyage thence to Spain, and opened the subject to his master, Ferdinand then in declining health, who listened to the plan: but who died soon after, and left it in the hand of his successor, Charles V.[14]

Technologies of navigation and the design of sea-faring vessels adapted; the first slave-trading companies established a system that proved lucrative for the slavers and horrific for the captives. Karl Marx delineates the overall economic changes in *The Communist Manifesto*:

The discovery of America, the rounding of the Cape, . . . opened up fresh ground for the rising European bourgeoisie. The East-Indian and Chinese markets, the colonization of America, trade with the colonies, the increase in the means of exchange and in commodities generally, gave to commerce, to navigation, to industry, an impulse never before known, and thereby, to the revolutionary element in the tottering feudal society, a rapid development.[15]

Concomitantly, the slave trade expanded with a vengeance.[16]

For the previous seven hundred years, the Iberian Peninsula encompassing modern day Portugal and Spain, and much of North Africa had been under the control of a thriving Muslim civilization that at times tolerated, protected, and even welcomed Christians and Jews. By 1492 the martial march of Christianity had driven Muslims and Jews from Iberia to the southern and eastern Mediterranean, an expulsion issuing from the Decree of Alhambra, not accidentally coinciding with the agreement that sent Christopher Columbus (Colombo/ Colón) to seek a westward passage to India. In comparison with the great civilizations of the East—India and China—and of the Americas—Inca, Maya, and Aztec—and of Africa—the kingdoms of Aksum, Mali, and Songhai—much of Northern Europe was a backwater plagued by war, pestilence, and a general lack of higher cultural development. Centering global cultural achievement in the East, contemporary decolonial theorists have characterized pre-modern Europe as a "small Asian peninsula," an insignificant protrusion on a mammoth landmass stretching from the Pacific to the Atlantic. On this account, medieval Northern Europe was an afterthought, the detritus of previous civilizations.[17]

Noting the connection between the "purity-of-blood" ideology that fueled the expulsion of Jews and Muslims from Al Andalus and the triumph of Catholicism on the Iberian Peninsula, Enrique Dussel notes,

In the same year, 1492 . . . [that] Granada, . . . fell to the last European Crusade, Columbus, on August 3, set sail. He had only one purpose in mind: to arrive at India by traveling westward . . . The first explorer to complete this journey would acquire nautical knowledge, amass gold, win honor, and expand the Christian faith—purposes that could coexist without contradiction in that Weltanschauung. Although Columbus was one of the last merchants of the occidental Mediterranean, he was at the same time the first modern man.[18]

Along with Dussel, a variety of theorists, including Linda Alcoff, Gloria Anzaldúa, Lewis R. Gordon, Ramón Grosfogel, Alison Jaggar, Serene Khader, Maria Lugones, Lisa Lowe, Nelson Maldonado-Torres, Margaret McLaren,

Chandra Mohanty, Uma Naroyan, Kwame Nimako Mariana Ortega, and Gay-atri Spivak, are among the many who have argued that moving into the modern era Euro/Western geographies began to shape a logic of land and knowledge that ignored Asia, Africa, the Caribbean, Mexico, and Central and South America, announcing Europe as the center of culture globally, in an example of what Grosfogel calls "epistemicide"—destroying knowledge of transnational realities in order to assert and maintain power.[19] They created an imaginary that wiped the original inhabitants of the Americas from the map, socially, politically, and culturally, crafting a *terra nullius* ready for European exploitation.[20] American Indigenous cultures and African ones were obliterated as sites of knowledge and to some degree in their material reality. At the peak of their powers, Maria W. Stewart, David Walker, and other black intellectuals understood the inverted narrative of development and the fall in fortune it brought for women and those not of European descent. In her "Farewell Address," Stewart longed for the days when people of color and women were respected for their intellectual leadership:

> In the 15th century the general spirit of this period is worthy of observation. We might then have seen women preaching and mixing themselves in controversies. Women occupying chairs in Philosophy and Justice, women writing in Greek, and studying in Hebrew. Nuns were poetesses, and women of quality divines.[21]

Walker reminds his readers:

> When we take a retrospective view of the arts and sciences—the wise legislators—the Pyramids, and other magnificent buildings—the turning of the channel of the river Nile, by the sons of Africa or of Ham, among whom learning originated, and was carried thence into Greece, where it was improved upon and refined.[22]

Shifting conceptualizations of cultural production, geography, and conquest, by the midseventeenth century all the primary sites of power in Europe were in on the colonial game, each scrambling to outdo the other. The birth of capitalism, concurrent with and absolutely dependent upon colonization, was premised upon the trade in humans for slave labor. The liberal ideology threatening to overthrow the economically moribund feudal system was premised on a system of *racial patriarchy*, a critical concept developed by Audre Lorde, Barbara Omolade, the Combahee River Collective, Pauline E. Schlosser, and Charles Mills, among others, that identifies a powerful synthesis of race and gender oppression that underlies the colonial project.[23] Class hierarchies of the past, problematic in their own ways, were being cast away. The status of advantaged women and people of color fell precipitously. Princes became slaves.[24] Goddesses were demoted or erased. Prior to the modern period, in medieval Europe, the privileges of aristocratic women and "exotic" princes were recognized and honored in Europe; premodernity rested primarily upon class and not race or gender-based systems, even though male gender privilege often prevailed. The economic and social leveling accomplished in Europe by the development of classical liberalism with its rights and liberties of man raised the prospects of the masses while advancing the whiteness and maleness of a broader swathe of property owners over the varied claims to titled privilege. There, at the creation of the Royal Africa Company, stood John Locke, author of the liberal classic *Two Treatises of Government*, claiming his shares in human trafficking.[25]

RESURRECTING KNOWLEDGE

Broaden the scope of vision. The events in Greenwich and Hartford, the sites of Maria Miller's birth and indenture, in New England generally, indeed in the Americas, North and South, occurred in a known world governed by the ideologies of modernism and colonialism, what has been called the "geography of reason."[26] It is easy to telescope into a New England dominated by the minute and nuanced relations of Anglo-European settlers to each other, as many histories do, relegating the original inhabitants and those who were kidnapped and captive to the sidelines of social, historical, and philosophical analysis. Those on the margins may be seemingly without significant historical roots or ties, or, it is often said, all those ties regrettably have been lost. The notion that the oppressed have no significant history or culture is commonly accepted. Lisa Lowe writes that "the forgetting of violent encounter is naturalized."[27] In this way, systems of oppression are reinforced, in the process aiming to destroy groups of people through genocide, maiming of spirits, erasure of memories, and breaking the will to maintain systems of thought and cultural practices. Epistemicide is enacted in the deliberate destruction or dislocation of entire bodies of knowledge. In another formulation, Patricia J. Williams identifies "spirit-murder" as "a system of formalized distortions of thought" that comprises racism and cultural obliteration, "a disregard for others whose lives qualitatively depend on our regard."[28]

In fact, Africans in America came from long-established and rich cultures. Those with oral traditions produced sons and daughters who were taught at an early age the importance of ancestors and were adept with memory and its uses, with rhythm, rhyme, and mnemonics for keeping alive the lives and cultures of those who had gone before. These skills were particularly useful for those who had been abducted, since in the harsh, abrupt rending of souls from their homelands, written traditions would be useless and physical artifacts would be lost. In contrast, memory can be secret, invisible to those who might wish to destroy the recollection and re-creation of the past. Those of Maria Miller's parents' generation had the knowledge and history of their villages and cultures inscribed on their souls, something that could not be changed with a new name.

In reconstructing the genealogy of Maria Miller and her parents, the researcher confronts challenges that far exceed those presented to the genealogist, who, for example, might be studying "the Founding Fathers." For Africans and their descendants in the Americas, names were imposed, only first names recorded, personal histories vanished. The concatenation of thousands of lost individual histories combines with level after level, layer after layer of loss: the records of individuals, their stories, the social and cultural histories, the political histories, contributions to wars, to maritime trade, to building and city construction, roads and bridges, families and loves. Some remain in small fragments. Likely, we will never know the lives of Lib and Caesar, yet sometimes those memories surface in odd places.

When she was in her late fifties, as the nation prepared for civil war, Maria W. Stewart née Miller turned her mind to her childhood memories in an essay entitled "The First Stage of Life," a remarkable work that appears to represent her own childhood. Evocatively written and full of details of childhood, the work possesses traces of West African cosmologies, thoughts about the sun, moon, and earth, the natural world, and a child's place in it.[29] These observations and memories provide the only sustained descriptions that might be attributed to Caesar, Lib, and other principal individuals of Miller's formative years and of what her early life might have been like with days full of memorable small things.

Chapter Four

"THE DAY OF SMALL THINGS" [1]

... and we build about them walls so high, and hang between them and the
light a veil so thick, that they shall not even think of breaking through.[2]
—W. E. B. Du Bois, *The Souls of Black Folk*

Maria W. Stewart has been honored as the first Black woman political theorist in the United States.[3] She is surely the first to have left significant writings about race, gender, abolition, and the ethics of racial and gender oppression. Her better-known 1830s writings are magnificent, particularly her speeches and essays, many delivered in the form of the jeremiad, deeply reliant on the exhortation to her audiences to undergo a revolution of spirit and political resolve to counter oppression. Her *Meditations*, also from this period, are less political, more personal, immersed in religious contemplation and drawing extensively from another form discourse found in the Bible, particularly the Lamentations of Jeremiah.[4] Writers such as Lena Ampadu, Dianne Bartlow, Valerie Cooper, Shirley Wilson Logan, Joycelyn Moody, Carla L. Peterson, Marilyn Richardson, Ebony A. Utley, and Teresa Zackodnik take up the rhetoric of Stewart's earlier writings with singular acuity, their analyses providing a good starting place for examining her more well-known works. In contrast, her 1860 essay, "The First Stage of Life," is almost unknown and takes a different rhetorical turn, less burdened and more whimsical. Written later in Stewart's life, the essay casts an entirely new light on her life, her attitudes, and her writing. "The First Stage" also has an altogether different set of rhetorical qualities. It is more like memoir, even reverie, a set of mostly lighthearted personal memories told from the perspective of a very young child.

Records reveal that Maria Miller was born to "Lib and Caesar (Negro)," in 1803, one or both of whom had been enslaved.[5] Many enslaved Africans, including, perhaps, Lib and Caesar overcame obstacles to forge culturally rich memories, "infused with traces of Africanisms," as Carla Peterson notes, cobbled together from the vestigial heritage carried in their minds, bodies, and communities, ones that provided a cord of connection to their homelands.[6] Miller, an orphan deposited with the family of a white minister, had much of her small slate of African cultural memory wiped clean by the separation from her parents and community, but it was far from a *tabula rasa* and, according to Peterson, suggests the "workings of a kind of cultural unconsciousness that insists on recalling the example of Stewart's African foremothers."[7] Unveiling her early life is a matter of carefully retrieving the shimmering fragments she has scattered throughout her writings. Once gathered, the tesserae must be pieced together into a mosaic forming a figure otherwise obscured by an indifferent world. Her story "The First Stage" offers the most evocative elements contributing to a larger picture. In this short piece, Stewart tells the story of a young girl, Letitia (from the Latin meaning "happy"), a story either intended—or disguised—as a didactic text. The essay/story was published in the African Methodist Episcopal (AME) church periodical, *Repository of Religion and Literature and of Science and Art*. Recently unearthed by Eric Gardner, this text and another, "The Proper Training of Children," provide real insight into Stewart's own young life and represent the first evidence that her writing is more extensive than previously thought.

"The First Stage of Life" is a revelatory text. Taken as a conscious effort to record something about herself, a number of motives may have impelled her to write this piece. It may simply be fiction. Alternatively, Stewart may not have wished to write in the first person, considering it inappropriate, too personal, as Joycelyn Moody suggests about her 1830s writings.[8] She takes pains at the opening of the piece to note her obscurity and the degree to which her position has fallen "away from those once loved, once honored, and once revered."[9] Thus, she may have assumed that her audience would not wish to hear about the childhood of one whose life and accomplishments were unknown to them, who had "sunk so far in oblivion's dark shade."[10] She may have been too modest to present an autobiographical essay. Or she may have thought it unlikely to be published if presented as autobiography at a time when the idea of memoir by Black women, while not unknown, was not at all commonplace.[11] The story closely recounts the early years of a child whose life may resemble or mirror that of Maria Miller. Her recollections are vivid and personal, filled with allusions to and descriptions of nature: the sun and the moon, water and rocks, fields and flowers. She admits that she does not know where she spent her early years:

Thus Letitia passed away the guileless hours of infancy, like a butterfly in the sunbeams of a summer's day. Where she first saw the blue sky, the beautiful light of day, the field of tall clover elegantly arrayed in pink and green, or the hand that sustained her *she knew not*, she only knew that it was so.[12]

Letitia's story tells of a very young girl whose mother and father both die and for whom the mother's funeral remains an outstanding early memory. An aunt who at first seems to care for her benevolently takes her up, but later, in sorrow, anger, or frustration becomes mean and abusive. Young Letitia remains throughout an innocent observer as a parade of people, some loving, others dangerous and ill-meaning, enter her life and then depart. The memories of these scenes are so vivid that it is hard to imagine that they would be other than grounded in reality, embellished and burnished over the years, not unlike Frederick Douglass's narratives, which Stewart had undoubtedly read by the time she produced this piece. The tale begins with Letitia's fleeting memory of her father placing her in her mother's embrace.

> [Her] first recollection ... was, of her father taking her up in his arms, in consequence of some little excitement out of doors, and carrying her in the house, and placing her in the lap of her mother, she never saw him more, he was drowned, when and where, *she knows not*.[13]

The report of her father's tragic demise by drowning is matter of fact, almost dreamlike. The phrases "the first time," and "she knows not" function not only as repetitive rhetorical devices; they are like incantations. More than that, they present "The First Stage" as an origins story in which the repetition of "she knows not what," nineteen times in this short piece, lies in contrast with Stewart's developed theory of knowledge, her epistemology, which was sophisticated in her later years. The attributed lack of knowledge functions to underscore several kinds of ignorance. One is the ignorance that signifies innocence, including a lack of knowledge of God and the newness of everything she sees.[14] But another, subtextual meaning runs in the current of her deep knowledge of racism, sexism, and deprivation that she as author suffers, writing this text in the build-up to the Civil War, at a far distance from her few years of joy in her life in Boston, married, living in a vibrant Black community, and slightly later, less happily, when she was able to exercise her intellect and remarkable powers freely, and farther still from the innocent days of her youth.

If we cast Letitia as the blameless infant and the 1860s author, Maria W. Stewart, as the wise crone, then the Stewart of the 1830s, at her full powers as a political philosopher, was "Diana in the leaves green," or more appropriately, Oshun, the Yoruban goddess who is "beneficent and generous, and very kind. She does have a malevolent and tempestuous temper, although it is difficult to anger her."[15] Much of the text provides what Peterson calls "a moment of hybridity in which a 'denied knowledge' from the native culture is allowed to silently enter the text."[16] Thus, "The First Stage" sounds three notes that correspond to the stages of Stewart's life. The young girl's innocent observations of nature are deeply impressed in her mind and are liberally sprinkled throughout the narrative.

> The first time Letitia ever noticed the blue sky, and the light of day, she was sent with another little girl to get a pail of water, she climbed upon a ledge of rocks, she fell, and one of the rocks fell upon one of her limbs, she was wounded, she saw the blood flow.[17]

This scene forecasts the words of the essayist, Maria W. Stewart, no longer innocent, no longer ignorant of racial prejudice, but believing in God's judgment. "O, ye great and mighty men of America, ye rich and powerful ones, many of you will call for the rocks and mountains to fall upon you, and to hide you from the wrath of the Lamb" (Rev. 6:16).[18]

Her youthful purity and shock at the injustice of this unfair injury signifying a loss of innocence lie in contrast with the genuine injustices she witnesses over and over later in life, but in her later years, she has a theological framework that prophesizes the redress of wrongs and portends what will come to the wrongdoers with *the wrath of the Lamb*—such an image! Valerie Cooper notes that "Stewart's use of scripture is performative. Hermeneutics is like the performance of a play where script, performer, audience, and stage are inextricably linked."[19] The anger of the innocents is turned into a terrifying portrayal of the final judgment: "She saw the blood flow." Young children cry in pain from an unexpected hurt and often cry as much from the startling injustice as from the bruises and lacerations. In this passage the blameless child is hurt just as she opens her eyes to the world.

Full of biblical allusions, a different set from those cited in her 1830s writings, this origins story reads at times like a creation narrative. The memories are so sweet and idyllic, paradisiacal, almost improbably so. She recalls the first time she saw the sunlight and her first stars:

> The first flowers she saw, was a field of clover, enclosed by a fence. It was in full bloom, and the colors being pink and green, appeared beautiful to her infant vision. What caused the beautiful light of day, she could not imagine, she had never heard of, or seen the sun, and if she had, she had not enough sense to know it. And the first time Letitia was ever out in the sable orb of night . . . all was dark above, she saw no moon or stars, she knew not what they were.[20]

Repeating and elaborating on a vision from a previous passage, the knowing Mrs. Stewart is riffing on the creation story in Genesis, the formless chaos that precedes the creation of day and night, prior to Adam and Eve coming to knowledge of the world, the wonder at how such a world could come into being. By entwining her own biography with biblical creation, she absorbs to herself, *personalizes*, the wonder of all beginnings, the marvelousness of creation and leads the reader to an appreciation of natural beauty and awe of God's immanent power.

As the work progresses, with priceless wit Stewart relates the guileless child's first encounter with the deity—God as an enormous boot in the cobbler's window. "[P]assing by a shop she saw a monstrous large boot, she was filled with fear, she thought it was God's boot, and walked away very softly. This was the first idea Letitia ever had of God."[21] Stewart moves deftly between allegory and autobiographical narrative, for surely the story of God's boot is not the invention a mature mind, but a memory of a childhood experience. The boot is the physical manifestation of the sound of the footsteps of an angry God who knows that Adam and Eve have disobeyed him: "And they heard the voice of the LORD God walking in the garden in the cool of the day: and Adam and his wife hid themselves from the presence of the LORD God amongst the trees of the garden."[22] The thudding noise of the approaching judgment, the first physical manifestation of God found in scripture, is represented when Stewart conjures the boot that portends the fall from grace. Throughout her life, Stewart wrestled with her love of God and her *fear* of him—fear, apparently preceding even her *knowledge* of a divine being. As Moody asserts, along with her "spiritual sisters" Jarena Lee and Zilpha Elaw, Stewart espouses "sacred doctrine to teach revolutionary redemption."[23]

The narrative continues, weaving in a dizzying array of characters. The text affirms that she lived in a community or at least a neighborhood of Black people and that white faces were unknown to her at an early age. Letitia and her mother are traveling, a stepfather has joined them, and into this idyllic scene comes "a beautiful little baby house" with decorated shelves, and she acquires a playmate, "She was white, the first white face, Letitia ever saw."[24] This recollection rings true, since in racially homogenous communities the initial confrontation with complexional difference may be startling. Letitia/Maria here recalls a community of descendants of Africa, which would mean free Blacks, since enslaved ones would have white masters close at hand. Her little playmate was absent; she returns and "reproves Letitia gently" for "disarranging" the doll house.[25] Her first interaction with a white person—a child at that—is to be scolded by her, an interaction that leaves a life-long impression on the author. In relating this incident, the author engages in what George Yancy identifies as "flipping the script." In contemporary terms, by identifying—calling out—the race and actions of her companion she is saying, "Look, a White!" And while innocent Letitia would not be skilled at subverting the text by examining whiteness, the author, Stewart, had more than enough experience to understand the power of this innocently framed and brief observation.[26] Yancy notes that socially in the United States "whiteness is the transcendent norm" but that "by marking whiteness black people can locate whiteness as a specific historical and ideological configuration."[27] For Stewart, this counteracts "the unreflective imposition of a culture," something her essays do unflinchingly. Following the work of W. E. B. Du Bois, bell hooks, and Sara Ahmed, Yancy articulates the necessity of "a black countergaze," which is precisely what Stewart endows Letitia with when she identifies her playmate.[28] Still, the power of reversing the gaze has little impact on the nature of the dominant/subordinate relations that structure most black/white interactions. Letitia may name but cannot change the fact that when her playmate returns, she "reproves Letitia gently."[29] Maria W. Stewart will be less gentle when reproving the actions of whites almost three decades later.

As with all her knowledge, Letitia learns through contrast with what she did not know: "For by the light of Letitia's vision she must have been in the country, but the word country she had never heard, she knew not what it meant." What is a city? That which is not the country. A moment of happiness "in front of an old brown house, with a flight of old brown steps," is disrupted when she is called inside to

> . . . the foot of the [dying] mother's bed. She jumps, she screams, she cries, Oh! Mother, what shall I do, I shall have no one to take care of me. Her mother extends her hand, the last breath is departing, she dies, and poor little Letitia is left an orphan.[30]

This brief passage reverts to the more conventional forms of sentimental literature in which emotions are dramatic and explicitly painted, and the ramifications of the tragedy are spelled out bluntly: "Letitia is left an orphan." In contrast, the following passage more subtly conveys the young girl's emotional state and her attempt to use her agency to change the course of events. The most moving portion of this account comes as the protagonist is face-to-face with her deceased mother: "She steals into the room, uncovers her mother's face, takes the cents from her eyes, opens the lids, to try to bring her to life, sees they won't stay open, replaces the cents, kisses her clay-cold cheek, then leaves the room."[31] While the passage conforms in some ways with the conventions of the period: affective relationships and sentimental reactions to injustice, there is something fresh, real, and compelling about Stewart's tale. In contrast with the emotionality of the previous deathbed scene, this heartbreaking moment, told simply and well, conveys the innocence of childhood almost without emotion and with a grim acceptance of one's fate.

A later passage describes the funeral, where her stepfather takes her to a room cramped with women and men dressed in black and a tall man, the minister, in front. They inter her mother and leave her "until Gabriel shall step one foot upon the earth and the other about the water."[32] A child who suffers traumatic early loss and utter displacement is likely to fix those early notions and images in her mind and perhaps even touch them up more brightly through the constant recollection that may serve as solace in her later isolation: memories recalled, lying awake at night, rising in the morning, or undertaking some tedious and repetitive task during the day. She speculates about whether her mother will be one of heaven's elect, here finally revealing the standpoint of the author's current state. The child Letitia lacks a theological framework; the author of the story is saturated with religious beliefs, including those of elect and damned, heaven and hell.

Stewart is wonderfully adept in the range and choices of scriptural passages and cites in the text a perfect example of her own situation as she is writing in 1860: "Thou shalt by no means afflict my fatherless child. If you afflict them, and they cry unto me, I will surely hear their cry." She tells us that God's early command to Moses was to care for "the forlorn and helpless condition of the widow and the orphan."[33] Maria W. Stewart was both a widow and an orphan. This passage, a stern warning against indifference to this particular kind of suffering, poses God's threat to those who would harm her. She makes herself the site of pity, a skill she drew upon later in life, justly, to solicit shelter and money when she was destitute, as described in her autobiographical "Sufferings During the War."[34]

With both parents gone, Letitia falls into the care of Aunt Sally, of whom she has early memories. She recalls Sally bathing her, "but not without the threat of rubbing all the skin off from her arms, if she did not behave herself, and the first sweet potato she ever saw, her aunt gave her, it was red." Her aunt protects her from the "distinguished man of God," a cousin, who comes for her for some unspoken nefarious purpose, by hiding her in the barn where she "slept in the box under the manger," a thin reference to herself in relation to Christ, an analogy adopted more than once in her political writings.[35] We are told that "Aunt Sally became housekeeper for Letitia's step-father" who then died. Sally took her away, and for a time they lived an itinerant life: "She taught Letitia all kinds of naughtiness, and became very unkind and cruel to her, and went away and left her in the street, without home and without friends ... thus Letitia was cast upon the cold charities of the world." She was then placed in a family where a son terrified her with stories of the devil and led her into youthful transgressions, stealing fruit from the neighbor's trees, but the author observes that at that time "her intellect began to unfold and ripen." It is curiously noteworthy that the mature Mrs. Stewart attributes a "ripening intellect" to this young child, an indication that she was aware of her own precociousness from a very young age, *a desert flower blooming ... unseen.* In her later years, when Stewart counsels, "*The force of precept and example at home has a more powerful influence over the mind of children and youth than all the instruction that teachers can impart to them in Christendom*," she may be reflecting on the precarity of her own young life.[36]

The final part of this phase of her life is itinerant, with Aunt Sally leading her into small sins, we know not what, where she became, again, "almost a wandering gypsy."[37] Ultimately abandoned by Aunt Sally, she

> did not cry unto God in her distress; she did not know who he was; . . . But God knew who Letitia was and directed her steps to an old man called Uncle Pete, and he told her to call upon a certain lady and gentleman . . . [who] took the little stranger under their charge . . . She was taught about God, to read, to pray, and was catechized.[38]

The story develops an epistemic counterpoint between the artless observations of Letitia and the intensely deep knowledge of the author. Throughout, Stewart resists analyzing events from the perspective of maturity, allowing the story to flow and focus on simple daily occurrences, choosing to allow whatever judgment there might be to emerge from the readers' interpretations of the narrative. This preserves the innocence of the young girl and the freshness of the story for the reader. The only reflexive analytic is the insistence on an epistemic frame, not through claiming knowledge, but through its opposite, by reiterating instances of ignorance in variations on the phrase "she knows not."

Were the "lady and gentleman" who took her in and who taught her about God the clergyman and his wife she was to reference regarding her indenture in her 1830s text? If so, at least some of her early days with them held fond memories: "Letitia spent her summers in working about the house, weeding the flower beds, and in going over the hedge, when her work was done, to pick strawberries, blackberries and whortleberries, and in the short summer evening used to sing and dance, and play till bed-time."[39]

Stewart makes a notable observation:

> And in the fall she used to ramble in the woods during the leisure hours, to pick up chestnuts and walnuts, and in winter her time was employed in knitting, spinning, and sliding on the ice—*so much of a boy girl was she,* that she used to try to make sleds to slide on.[40]

Without speculating too deeply about the importance of this comment, it should be observed that gender identity is a strongly recurrent theme during her years of political writing. Stewart vigorously argues that in at least some areas—political thought, religious preaching, and social activism—gender distinctions are not just misplaced but are contrary to God's wishes for the world. In pursuing these roles, Maria W. Stewart is a "boy girl," and more than in any other section of the essay, her pursuits are described with relish and project a level of happiness and freedom that indicates a moving on from the "I know not what" phase of this writing, during which she seems constantly startled by the events around her to a place of greater self-efficacy, a happy "boy girl," gathering nuts and berries in the woods and fashioning sleds.

I imagine that writing this story provided solace to Maria Stewart during the cruel days preceding the Civil War. Her final, instructional message is clear: "We must never despise the day of small things."[41]

> For who hath despised the day of small things? for they shall rejoice, and shall see the plummet in the hand of Zerubbabel with those seven; they are the eyes of the LORD, which run to and fro through the whole earth (Zachariah 4:10).[42]

In the fifth vision of the prophet Zachariah, a golden candlestick is fed with oil from two live olive trees, and the hand of God fuels the building of the Temple. The humblest deeds, picking berries, feeling for the first time the warmth of the sun, and seeing the sparkle of the stars—all these small things help to build the temple of the Lord. Stewart is unfolding the meaning of the lesson to be found in the story of Letitia. She exhorts the reader likewise to find joy in God's natural world, His gift to us. Our appreciation and wonder are prayers that bring the kingdom of God closer. Letitia becomes

> one of the most caressed and loved among her associates . . . like a tree planted in the house of my God, towering like some of the tall cedars of Lebanon, considering all things as loss compared to the excellency of Jesus Christ—soaring aloft, as it were, on eagles' wings, amid the stars, to a city out of sight.

Chapter Five

"BOUND OUT IN A CLERGYMAN'S FAMILY"[1]

The proper training of the young is a subject that ought to excite the religious attention of the community at large.
—Mrs. Mariah W. Stewart, "The Proper Training of Children," 1861[2]

In "Religion and the Pure Principles of Morality," Maria Stewart recalls, "I . . . was left an orphan at five years of age; was bound out in a clergyman's family . . ." At the time of her indenture, relatively few Black people suffered the indignity of enslavement in Connecticut; more were indentured or apprenticed. Alone among the New England states, Connecticut and Rhode Island still practiced enslavement when Maria Miller, a free Black, was bound out to service. In addition to the 6453 "free, non-whites," there were 310 who were still in bondage in Connecticut.[3] The small number and late dates for full emancipation in these states, up to the 1840s—more than fifty years after abolition in the states to their north—shows a callous indifference to those who remained in chains. Indenture was less harsh, if only because the bonded persons found hope in their eventual release from servitude. My search for the indenture papers of Maria Miller was among the most frustrating portions of this research. The court records at the Connecticut State Library for that period of time failed to reveal the sought-after document. Many scholars and researchers offered assistance: Joanne Pope Melish, Richard Boles, Barbara Beeching, Ruth Wallace Herndon, Peter Hinks, and Samantha Boardman. Lists of indentures, or apprenticeships have been catalogued, for example, by Kathy A. Ritter; however, many of these record training to a trade such as blacksmith, cooper, joiner, tinker, or roper, assignments typically given to young white boys who were either orphaned or otherwise in need of a trade. Girls were trained to be servants or housewives. I have not abandoned hope that a record of Maria Miller's indenture might be found some day. In the absence of documentation, I have adopted a strategy of researching all the Hartford churches at the time to uncover the most likely location of her indenture given the decade span of time and the activities of the ministers.[4]

The process of discovering which clergyman's family indentured Miller requires some detective work along with knowledge of the region's history. Religious and civil histories of European settlers in Connecticut originate with Thomas Hooker, an early Puritan arrival in the Bay Colony. It did not take long for the tiny village of Newtowne (now Cambridge, Massachusetts) to fall into religious acrimony. In 1636 Hooker left Cambridge due to theological disagreements with other Puritans when he advocated for relatively broader and more democratic participation in church and civic affairs. Spurned in Newtowne, he moved on to settle Hartford establishing the venerable First Church of Christ (Congregational). Church historian Edwin Pond Parker writes that the Second Church of Hartford was established after Hooker's death because of quarrels about the road to salvation that led to "fire from the altar" and sent "thunderings and lightenings and earthquakes throughout the colony." Cotton Mather wrote that "the true original of the misunderstanding . . . has been rendered almost as obscure as the rise of the Connecticut River."[5]

By the early part of the nineteenth century, four churches served the faithful: the two well-established Congregational churches, a Baptist church, and an Episcopal one. Among possible placements for Maria Miller, the Episcopal Church in Hartford is unlikely. This newer parish faced an icy reception from those who resented the presence of a faith so tied to Anglicanism. The Reverend Menzies Raynor's term as minister, 1801–1811, does not coincide with Miller's decade of indenture, from 1808–1818.[6] Similarly, the tenure and temperament of Pastor Henry Grew (1807–1811) of the marginalized Baptist Church, accord neither with Miller's period of indenture nor her later disposition. Grew was drummed out of town for his unconventional views, ones he may have shared with his brother, who was a congregant at William Ellery Channing's Federal Street Church in Boston. Grew is said to have "adopted sentiments and assuages different from those of the church." With civil and religious affairs so enmeshed, theological disputes were central to daily life across denominations throughout New England.[7]

Ratification of the 1789 United States Constitution and the First Amendment guaranteeing separation of church and state had no effect in Connecticut, where Congregationalism reigned as the established religion with the two Congregational churches dominating the religious landscape in Hartford. By the 1790s their acrimonious historical differences were reconciled, and a strong relationship developed between the Reverend Nathan Strong of the First (Center) Church and the Reverend Abel Flint of the Second (South) Congregational church. Reverend Strong had two children with his second wife, Anna McCurdy of Lyme, both of whom were much older by the time of

Miller's indenture. In addition to leading the spiritual life of his flock, Strong provided them with another kind of spirit. He was in the distilling business and was known for his coarse "sledge-hammer jokes." Replaced as pastor in 1812, Strong died in 1816. Miller mentions only "a clergyman"—presumably just one—to whom she was indentured. Since her release from service in 1818 was six years after Strong's retirement, it seems unlikely that she would have served in the Strong household.

Of the two Congregational ministers, only Abel Flint and his family were at a parish for the full decade of Maria Miller's indenture. Ordained in 1791, Flint led the church until 1824, shortly before his death. When he arrived, newly ordained, the parish repaired the meeting house and parsonage, procured a bell, and threw him a great ordination party with gallons of wine, brandy, cherry rum, and cider, a quarter of veal, one turkey, three hams, and a dozen fowls. Someone was also paid four shillings to clean up after the event. A placement in the household of Reverend Flint presents an enticing possibility. Reverend Flint had a young wife, Amelia Bissell, the daughter of Hezekiah of East Windsor, and small children who needed tending. An intelligent, capable young girl like Maria Miller would have provided a much-desired helping hand.[8] Flint was said to be a decent man, affable and gracious, educated at Yale. In the year of Miller's indenture, the town voted to no longer favor the Congregational churches by sweeping them out at taxpayers' expense and providing for the regular ringing of bells. Who would do the sweeping now? And if a small child were to be assigned to this task, in addition to the drudgery, what private glory of God might she experience in the quiet corners of the nave?

Maria Miller loved the hymns. The pastor had a "remarkable musical voice" and was musically sophisticated, as evidenced by his arranging for a performance of Handel's *Messiah* in 1808. His admirers recall Reverend Flint as "every inch a gentleman," "famous for his excellency as a reader," and a man whose presence in the pulpit was "impressive and commanding." At first, children were not allowed at the Sunday services, but Reverend Flint had created a choir and singing school that practiced frequently at the meeting house where preparations for services also took place, an opportunity not open to Maria Miller as a participant, though perhaps as an onlooker. Another opportunity to absorb the education and erudition around her, Reverend Flint may have written and practiced his sermons and readings at home, within earshot of the servants; his own conversation would have been peppered with biblical quotations and injunctions, providing a second-hand education in biblical exegesis.[9]

The religious revival of 1808 favored both Congregational churches with more individual religious awakenings than had been experienced in fifty years—twenty "new persons" just from May to December—many of them young people who gathered at the church on weekday evenings for meetings.

The revival had begun the previous winter and progressed with a series of "showers of divine grace." These "new trophies of his victorious grace" were in contrast to "those who are yet secure in sin to taste the fruit of their own misdoings." The happy writer of this reflection was relieved that the young converts were well-behaved, not rowdy, eschewing "improper excesses . . . enthusiastic flights and imaginary impulses." The writer, likely Flint or Strong, exhibits his enthusiasm when he exclaims, "[M]ay all the friends of Zion among us be as animated to renewed zeal and fervor! May they wrestle like Jacob, and prevail like Israel!" At either Congregational church, this environment would have saturated the experience of five-year-old Maria Miller as a young orphan.[10]

The parsonage was plain enough, perhaps decorated with wallpaper and carpets. After the War of Independence, the style of women's clothes was for "close-fitting, short-waisted gowns of silk, muslin or gingham with a kerchief over the shoulders and breast. Girls wore a large vandyke, the younger ones low neck and short sleeve." Unlike the clergyman's daughters, Miller's dress would have been very plain indeed. Whether at the First Church or Second, her life would have been much the same except in the care of young children, at which she became adept, and in the liveliness of the thriving Second Church.[11]

The Great Awakenings encouraged parishioners to go beyond the rational exploration of the spirit and to explore the emotional stirrings that contemplation of the divine may bring, something Miller did later in her life. Despite the differences that had separated the First and Second Churches before the War of Independence, the Reverends Strong and Flint had mended the rift and worked together to shepherd their flocks. In 1797 they co-published the *Hartford Selection of Hymns*, mostly by Isaac Watts, the famous English hymnodist, some penned by Flint, to coincide with the revival that led to the formation of the singing school and choir.[12] Since Miller's service began at the same time as the powerful revival that swept across the city, with many "refreshings" and great joy among the congregants as they received the word of God, for a destitute, abandoned young child, the communal religious fervor may have been welcoming because she certainly retained the flavor of spiritual rapture in her writings years later. In her *Meditations* she wrote:

> Never did I realize, till I was forced, that it was from God that I derived every earthly blessing, and that it was God who had a right to take them away. . . . It is now one year since Christ first spoke peace to my troubled soul. Soon after I presented myself before the Lord in the holy ordinance of baptism, my soul became filled with holy meditations and sublime ideas.[13]

Valerie Cooper affirms, "Although [Stewart's] work has been widely categorized as political speech, it also rings with evangelical religious fervor . . . when Stewart inserts biblical verses into her writing, they are not just stylistic flourishes; they are the heart and soul of her message."[14] Stewart observes that she "had the seeds of piety and virtue early sown in my mind," from the connections with scripture and the church that she experienced as a child laborer and young woman.[15]

In keeping with the spirit of missionizing, a movement tainted with genocidal impact, Flint and Strong had established *The Missionary Society of Connecticut* "for the purpose of Christianizing the heathens in North America, and to promote Christian knowledge in the new settlements of the United States."[16] As the church developed its theological goals, it also stressed the importance of conversion and identified those considered to be potentially promising converts and geographical locations. The Great Awakening brought theological changes. In place of the strict Calvinist Doctrine of the Elect, according to which certain souls were designated from birth for salvation, the new dissenting orders preached the potential for universal salvation. The possibility that all could be saved introduced a new notion of individual agency in which both accepting God's grace and doing good works could in principle result in redemption for all. *For all.* From the Reverends' point of view, the culturally genocidal practice of missionizing Indigenous peoples meant potentially thousands more souls that could be bound for heaven. For those who were "missionized," it meant radical loss of culture, and sometimes, death. Saving souls as catalysts for salvation would not hurt the ministers' chances either. But missionizing remote or "exotic" populations was one thing. Closer to home, converting African Americans carried with it a load of special considerations and problems. Still, the religious education of one small servant, or even a host of poorly educated children was too tempting to turn away from. By 1809 the Missionary Society was doing its work in Hartford.

SABBATH EVENING

According to S. G. Goodrich, in 1811,

> Hartford was then a small commercial town of four thousand inhabitants, dealing in lumber, and smelling of molasses and old Jamaica, for it had still some trade with the West Indies. There was a high tone of general intelligence and social respectability about the place; but it had not a single institution, a single monument that marked it as even a

provincial metropolis of taste in literature, art, or refinement. Though the semi-capital of the State, it was strongly impressed with a plodding, mercantile, and mechanical character.[17]

The Reverend Abel Flint embodied the "high tone of intelligence" in the home and church, while the mercantile atmosphere pervaded in the streets. Maria Miller inhaled the smells "of molasses and old Jamaica" as she carried produce and sundries back from the market accompanied by her psychological and spiritual burdens. Life as an enslaved or indentured African American New Englander may not have carried the same trials and brutality as plantation slavery in the Deep South, Brazil, Jamaica, and elsewhere in the Caribbean, but physical and emotional harms were inflicted no less. Recalling her early life as a servant, Nancy Gardner Prince writes in her autobiography:

Sabbath evening I had to prepare for the wash; soak the clothes and put them into the steamer, set the kettle of water to boiling, and then close in the steam, and let the pipe from the boiler into the steam box that held the clothes . . . Hard labor and unkindness was to [too] much for me; in three months, my health and strength were gone. I often looked at my employers, and thought to myself, is this your religion? [18]

Some apologists still argue the benignity of the practices, citing the "almost paternal nature" and noting that in Connecticut few children were torn from their parents, as though this somehow ameliorates the pain of profound familial and geographical disruption.[19] In later years, abolitionist William Lloyd Garrison called Connecticut "the Georgia of New England," so entrenched were the hierarchies of racial privilege.[20] Exposing the myth of kindly Northern slavery, Connecticut researcher Katherine J. Harris notes that "the abuse of the African custom of axial loading—carrying loads on the head—led to fractured bones and caused enthesopathies, acute tears of muscles, tendons, and ligaments from the bones due to excessive lifting of heavy loads."[21] Add to this dislocation from communities, the sexual exploitation, the unfreedom, the denial of dignity and humanity, as well as the trauma, direct and witnessed, to gather a sense of harms to individual, social, and cultural development in servitude. Domestic labor ruined the health of Nancy Gardner Prince in short order, as she attests: "*Hard labor and unkindness was too much for me; in three months, my health and strength were gone.*"[22] Likewise, in 1831, Maria W. Stewart wrote:

How long shall the fair daughters of Africa be compelled to bury their mind and talents beneath a load of iron pots and kettles? . . . How long shall a mean set of men flatter us with their smiles, enrich themselves with our hard earnings; their wives' fingers sparkling with rings, and they themselves laughing at our folly?[23]

Prince and Maria Miller were contemporaries, both New Englanders and both in service to a clergyman. The two had parallel sacramental experiences when later in life they were married just a year apart in the same Boston church by the same pastor.

Drawing on her account in "The First Stage," we may surmise that in her very early life Maria Miller experienced some familial love and care. Despite hardship, her formative years were immersed in a largely Black community where overt anti-Black racism operated on the periphery, and she was not subjected to labor exploitation. She recalls the oddity of seeing a white child and describes a racially homogenous community, suggesting an early childhood of acceptance and affirmation. Once in servitude, Maria Miller's domestic labors may or may not have entailed lasting physical damage, but there can be no doubt that the labor was severe and demanding, including long hours, likely rising well before family members, carrying wood or coal and water from the pump in pails that could weigh as much as thirty pounds or more. The water for washing clothes and linens was boiling hot and filled with toxic substances from the harsh ingredients. In his widely read volume, *The House-servant's Directory*, Robert Roberts advises: "Washing the linens—putting soda in a jar to dissolve it, in the water to soften it, pour into tubs of boiling water—sometimes soak overnight. Cut the soap with a wire."[24] At a young age, her hands would have been calloused and rough; her body may have ached like that of a much older person. Roberts's detailed descriptions paint a portrait of the life of a domestic servant.

> Now, my young friends, I shall here give you some instructions how to proceed with your morning's work, in winter time. In the first place, make it your business to have plenty of wood, coal, or whatever fuel you burn, in its proper place over night, as it will save you a great deal of time in the morning, as the mornings are so short at this season of the year, . . . where perhaps you have three or four fires to make, and grates and fire irons to clean before the family rises . . . have your fires made and rooms warm before you clean yourself for breakfast.[25]

Miller may have slept in a cellar, an airless attic room, or possibly in an outbuilding designed for slaves and servants with little or no heat and poor circulation. She so hated her time as a servant that in later years she reflected:

Few white persons of either sex, who are calculated for anything else, are willing to spend their lives and bury their talents in performing mean, servile labor. And such is the horrible idea that I entertain respecting a life of servitude, that if I conceived of their [sic] being no possibility of my rising above the condition of servant, I would gladly hail death as a welcome messenger.[26]

In her later years, Maria W. Stewart and Robert Roberts crossed paths. Roberts's domestic advice was a standard instructional manual that would have been familiar to Stewart in her years in Boston, not because she was in need of his counsel regarding domestic chores, but because he, like Stewart, published his abolitionist thoughts in the *Liberator*. In the March 12, 1831, edition of William Lloyd Garrison's abolitionist newspaper, Roberts wrote:

O ye schemers! why do ye undertake to impose on the free people of color by telling them that Africa is their native soil, when our fathers fought for liberty, and received nothing for it, and laid their bones here? We claim this as our native soil, and not Africa; for we are sensible that if the land flowed with milk and honey, you would not send a colored person to it; for it is evident some of you would go to the uttermost parts of the world for one dollar's gain: therefore we know that it is not through pure love you want to send us to Africa.

Lydia Maria Child, another of Stewart's contemporaries during the Boston years, was a powerful advocate for abolition who also wrote a book of household advice. Contrast her recommendations for the life of a healthy white family with the conditions endured by someone of Maria Miller's station. Child recommends: "Have your bed-chamber well aired; and have fresh bed linen every week. Never have the wind blowing directly upon you from open windows during the night. It is not healthy to sleep in heated rooms."[27]

In a well-heated house, warm air rises from convection and is fresh from the servants' airing out of the rooms. In contrast, the domestic workers' quarters sweltered in the summer months and were brutally cold in the winter, with no heat except that radiating from a nearby chimney. Child paints a beautiful vision of the Sabbath for white children:

In his family, Sunday was a happy day; for it was made a day of religious instruction, without any unnatural constraint upon the gayety of the young. The Bible was the text book; the places mentioned in it were traced on maps; the manners and customs of different nations were explained; curious phenomena in the natural history of those countries were read; in a word, everything was done to cherish a spirit of humble, yet earnest inquiry.[28]

Reverend Flint's children, Anne and James, only slightly older than Miller, may have enjoyed the kinds of privileges described by Child. Flint and his wife, Amelia Bissell, had lost their first child, Henry, at age three months, and a fourth child, Royal, died of "tussis" (whooping cough) at two years old, not unusual at the time. Given the length of time between the birth of her first child in 1792 and the second in 1797, she may have miscarried several times, as was commonplace.[29]

Sunday may have brought some release for Maria Miller within the constraints of her duties. Still, someone had to help prepare the midday meal. Her time in the rectory may have had some small compensations. It was a literate household with a highly educated master whose children may have had a tutor, so while she longed for education, she absorbed some of the intellectual atmosphere around her. As a spirited child drawn to the physical world, she may have appreciated tasks that took her outdoors. Roberts writes: "[I]n the summer, you must put your butter and cream to cool sometime before you have set the table."[30] A task like this, performed out of doors or in a barn may have lent itself to reflection. Miller saw God in nature. The flowers, insects, water, and heavens were vivid; her finely tuned senses were part and parcel of the vast canvas of the universe that spoke to her directly. With biblical inspiration, she later became the artist who translated through her words visions from the Bible that others could not read. She spoke their words and projected their images and meanings. In "The First Stage," she recalls the pleasure of harvesting berries, a labor that Nancy Prince also describes.

> My brother and myself stayed at home that Summer. We gathered berries and sold them in Gloucester; strawberries, raspberries, blackberries and whortleberries, were in abundance, in the stony environs, growing spontaneously. With the sale of these fruits, my brother and myself nearly supported my mother and her children, that Summer.[31]

There may have been a kitchen garden to tend and some domestic animals to care for: chickens for eggs, a cow or goat for milk, perhaps a pig. In addition to weeding, watering, and harvesting, early mornings may have included milking and then carrying the milk to the house. Imagining her life of servitude, weighing and balancing the contributing factors of her life in domestic bondage, her own view is clear. In her 1832 Franklin Hall lecture Stewart said,

I have heard much respecting the horrors of slavery, but may heaven forbid that the generality of my color throughout these United States should experience any more of its horrors than to be a servant of servants, or hewers of woods, and drawers of water! Tell us no more of southern slavery; for with few exceptions, although I may be very erroneous in my opinion, yet I consider our condition but little better than that.[32]

Maria Miller had no family of her own. Angela Y. Davis illuminated an aspect of life in communities of enslaved persons, the relatively nonappropriative character of personal domestic undertakings: "In the infinite anguish of ministering to the needs of men and children around her (who were not necessarily members of her immediate family), she was performing the *only* labor of the slave community that could not be directly and immediately claimed by the oppressor."

This was not true for domestic servants forced to live with white families. All their labor was appropriated, and any attempt to engage in self-care might meet with harsh retaliation.[33] Stewart's writings reference the sexual exploitation of Black women and girls for whom opportunities were so limited, including those who were "forced to commit whoredoms."[34] Silvia, Nancy Gardner Prince's sister, was one who suffered this fate and who was rescued by her determined and resourceful sibling. Prince writes:

My sister I found seated with a number of others around a fire, the mother of harlots at the head. My sister did not see me until I clasped her around the neck. The old woman flew at me, and bid me take my hands off of her . . . Mr. Brown defended me with his cane; there were many men and girls there, and all was confusion. When my sister came to herself, she looked upon me and said: "Nancy, O Nancy, I am ruined!" I said, "Silvia, my dear sister, what are you here for? Will you not go with me." She seemed thankful to get away.[35]

The religiosity of the settler class was far from a guarantee against sexual exploitation, abuse, and violence, as we have seen from our exploration of slavery in Greenwich, Connecticut.[36] Young girls in particular were targets for exploitation from every direction. Years later, Maria W. Stewart was to observe, "O that my head were waters and mine eyes a fountain of tears, that I might weep day and night for the transgressions of the daughters of my people." At a time when these practices were commonplace but often went unspoken, both Prince and Stewart put their condemnations into words.[37]

On January 19, 1810, Reverend Flint's wife, Amelia, passed away. Flint recorded her death in the church records: "Amelia. Wife of Rev. Abel Flint. Consumption." Their two surviving children, Anne Amelia and James Hezekiah, were twelve and ten, respectively, but Maria Miller was only seven years old, and Amelia's death may have significantly increased Miller's burdens, possibly ameliorated by her increasing independence.[38] Interface with the local Black community was occasioned mainly when she ran errands for the family. The Great Bridge over the Little River had been repaired in 1807, so walking to market was easier; the construction of a new market to replace open air vendors took place in 1810. Still, wagons were a traffic hazard, the river was as important for transport as were the main streets. Her daily life may or may not have brought much association with others of her race, but festival days were a different matter and while the haranguing difficulties of domestic labor may have worn down Maria Miller, there were compensations nonetheless. Miller and other servants would have welcomed the days off allotted to servants, and reveled in special events and celebrations such as Pinkster, Training Day, and Black Election Day.

Chapter Six

"LAUGH AN' SING UNTIL TOMORROW"

NOT a veritable, constitutional, black Governor for the whites, Reader—
no—but a chief executive black officer, among the blacks, for themselves!
—"Scæva" 1853[1]

Growing older and perhaps more trusted, Maria Miller accessed additional freedom of movement, securing provisions for the household, delivering messages, sharing or exchanging produce and goods with neighbors. Heavy burdens and isolation left her with little to distract, entertain, solace, or comfort her. Relief came in the form of walks to the market joining other servants who mingled as they inspected the onions, carrots, cabbages, berries, fish, meats, notions, and textiles at the stalls adjacent to the State House. Wandering down to the river, they watched as the cargo disgorged from barges that made their way upriver from Saybrook. Liveried men assisted fatted town fathers from their horse-drawn carriages while enslaved workers struggled wheeling carts laden with goods. Absorbing Hartford's civic and commercial life, Miller expanded her knowledge of local customs, a consolation and distraction from her daily grind. Organized sociality and public, communal revelry brought welcome relief from the industry required of all able hands and from the constricting ideologies of religion. Military parades, Fourth of July celebrations, and elections offered a chance to celebrate, a change from dull, daily life. The citizens honored their release from the rigid, Old World hierarchies of entailed aristocracy and class-bound peasantry with the not-so-solemn recognition of democratic electoral systems born of the new liberal ideologies. Festive occasions marked their enhanced freedom and equality. Public events were not confined to the settler class. Despite wrenching restrictions, some African Americans had a small degree of freedom of movement and association within the requirements of their servitude. Dating back to the Revolutionary era, they were accustomed to enacting military musters with guns furnished by their masters as a part of regular defense exercises. Throughout the colonies,

African Americans had fought in the War of Independence and trained with weapons, including firearms, in musters and on Training Days. Black historian William C. Nell (1816–1874) writes:

> During the Revolutionary War, and after the sufferings of a protracted contest had rendered it difficult to procure recruits for the army, the Colony of Connecticut adopted the expedient of forming a core of colored soldiers. A battalion of blacks soon enlisted, and throughout the war, conducted themselves with fidelity and efficiency.[2]

Nell's detailed account of the Revolutionary War lists the names of all known Black soldiers in the colonies along with a number of anecdotes about their service including demands for emancipation. In celebrations such as Training Day, Black participants were permitted by their enslavers to brandish weapons and engage in buoyant, self-affirming celebrations with intricate meanings, ones that bore the markings of African historical memory.

ELECTION DAY

For nearly seventy-five years, between about 1750 and 1820, Connecticut's African descendants elected leaders in a complexly orchestrated social and political process. The democratic election of a Black magistrate or "governor" was a longstanding and common practice among free and enslaved Blacks in New England and entailed a day-long ceremony of deep significance known as Black Election Day or 'Lection Day. A hodgepodge of sources ranging from local histories to contemporary scholarship paint a portrait of this ritual, but general knowledge of it is obscured, fostering an impoverished current understanding of the dimensions of Black life, historically. The collection *African American Connecticut Explored* provides an exception to this rule. In a tapestry of short pieces based on knowledge of both West Africa and Connecticut, Katherine Harris and others reconfigure a little-understood and socially vital component of Black life in Connecticut, the election of their governors, a process by which African Americans selected a liaison between Black and white communities.[3] Most public events attracted significant numbers of Hartford's residents. An event as spectacular as the governor's election would have drawn a large gathering of participants and onlookers, Maria Miller and other servants and slaves among them. The history of the Black governors of New England provides a rare line of vision into the lives of African Americans in the late colonial and early years of the Republic and provides a finger-hold for lifting the veil that obscures Black community life.

Writing in the 1850s, the historian Isaac Williams Stuart, writing under the pen name "Scæva," describes the festival:

> For many years previous to the American Revolution, throughout this event, and long after—down nearly to 1820, and perhaps a little later—it was the custom of the negroes of Connecticut, in imitation of the whites, to elect a Governor for themselves. This they generally effected on some day, usually the Saturday next succeeding the Election Day of the whites, and they called it their "Lection Day." At this time they were generally assembled in unusual numbers, with their masters, in one of the capitals of the State. They of course made their election to a large extent, deputatively, as all could not be present, but uniformly yielded to it their assent—and their confidence was at times so unlimited, that without any choice by themselves, they readily permitted their existing Governor to assign his office over to another one of his color.[4]

In 1760 an enslaved man, London, was elected governor in Wethersfield; in 1780 Peter Freeman was elected in Farmington; and between 1755 and 1800 London, Quaw, Cuff, John Anderson, Peleg Nott, and Boston were elected king or governor in Hartford. The elections were ongoing during Maria Miller's time there. In 1810 Quash Freeman and 1815 Tobias were elected in Derby and in 1820 Caesar held the position in Durham "in remembrance of their Kings of Guinea."[5] Some white interpreters cast this as a comic event, using ridicule to portray the participants, but this interpretation fails to grasp the acuity with which Black Americans folded multifaceted meanings into the rituals.

Ignoring the evidence, some scholars downplay or deny these crucial cultural events, while others approach them with derision. One historian writes that "politically, blacks were non-entities," making the astonishing claim that "beyond their families, there is virtually no other data on slave social structure and, in fact, there may have been no such social structure at all."[6] Historical, anthropological, and sociological research as well as common sense underscore the absurdity of this damaging claim. In contrast, leveraging a shift in cultural perspective, drawing on a variety of sources, and providing a detailed account of ties to African traditions, Harris affirms Black "political empowerment" and argues that practices "emerged within the context of the political discourse in colonial society, the exclusion of small numbers of free Africans from the political process, and African agency that asserted a right to freedom using their own political culture."[7] The fact that the election of Black governors in the late eighteenth and early nineteenth centuries remains one of the most obscured historical practices, in keeping with the general idea of epistemicide, shows that the erasure of agentive Black history is alive and well today.[8]

On Black Election Day, participants were "ceremonially armed with guns and swards" and in what William Pierson identifies as "African style"; the sound of gunshots from weapons pointed at the sky punctuated the proceedings, adding to the astonishment of onlookers and revelers.[9] A detailed description of the proceedings provides a sense of the day:

> The elections themselves generally took place the second Saturday in May, a week after the election of the colony's [white] governor. A large parade and festive celebration for the newly elected official would follow. The person chosen was most often a strong, respected, and influential member of the African American community. He was also, in many cases, a servant to a wealthy and influential family. Sam Huntington, who was a black governor in the town of Norwich, was a servant of Samuel Huntington, who was governor of the State of Connecticut at the same time. A black governor could be called on to perform important functions within his community, and the position commanded respect from both black and white residents. In many towns, the governor meted out punishments and upheld law and order among the African American inhabitants. He also acted as a mediator between the black and white communities. Black governors often appointed a lieutenant governor and deputies to help carry out these tasks.
>
> Despite these functions, most of the men who were selected to be black governors were still enslaved.[10]

And despite their unfreedom, African Americans participating in or watching the proceedings on Election Day witnessed a remarkable expression of Black agency and cultural control.

MARIA MILLER AT ELECTION DAY

Given the opportunity, Maria Miller was not the sort of person to be restrained from experiencing Black election days. If Miller was allowed to look on or even join the festivities, perhaps with an older chaperone, she must have wondered at both the celebrations and the seeming license with which the Black population overtook the city.

> On the morning of election day, the beating of drums and an occasional random gunshot quickened black pulses and announced the impending festivities. Although there was little if any work to be done, no one tarried; across New England the bondsmen hurriedly put on the best out-

fits they owned or could borrow, for many faced a long walk to reach the scene of the holiday festivities. Most slaves received their special holiday clothes as hand-me-downs from their masters: nonetheless, once the garments were cleaned up and matched with an African eye for color, they became ensembles of real style and flair. Looking their best, the bondsmen gathered into a procession to escort their incumbent kind of governor to the polls.[11]

Similarly festive were the Training Days.

> His parade days were marked by much that was showy, and by some things that were ludicrous. A troop of blacks, sometimes an hundred in number, marching sometimes two and two on foot, sometimes mounted in true military style and dress on horseback, escorted him through the streets, with drums beating, colors flying, and fifes, fiddles, clarionets, and every "sonorous metal" that could be found, "uttering martial sound."[12]

Miller may have joined a group of revelers as they made their way to a suitable green and shaded location near the Old North Cemetery Ground. Unlike Puritan elections that were held in the confines of their meetinghouses, Black Election Days were more like certain African rituals, held in open fields. Pierson writes that after politicking and the election, "the new governor rode through the town on one of his master's horses, adorned with plaited gear, his aides on each side *al la militaire* . . . moving with a slow majestic pace."[13]

GOVERNOR BOSTON AND THE REVEREND ABEL FLINT

One governor, Boston, was a highly respected leader in the Black community who also commanded admiration among whites. Boston, who lived in Cole Street, ". . . was a genuine African. He used to boast that the real Guinea negro never stole, but only negroes born in this country. All who remember him, and there are many, concur in giving him the character of 'a stable, respectable man.'"[14]

This claim echoes a sentiment expressed by David Walker, who makes a regular incantation of his assertion that whites are murderers of Black people who, in contrast, will not engage in homicide, an act that produces "a solemn awe" in their hearts.[15] Isaac William Stuart tells us that Boston "held his office for many years." Since records show he was first elected in 1800, and Stuart suggests that he died around 1811, his term of office would have coincided with

Miller's early years of indenture. Boston was a well-known figure about town, so she certainly would have recognized him locally and been aware of his death and funeral at which Abel Flint delivered a eulogy: "With his cocked hat and sword upon his coffin, and followed by a numerous train, he was carried into the South Congregational Church, and there Dr. Flint pronounced a sort of funeral eulogy over his remains, which were afterwards deposited in the Centre Burying Ground."[16]

This source relates a further story about Governor Boston's family interactions with Dr. Strong regarding Boston's son Roman, who suffered from mental illness.

> He has a son named Roman, who was crazy, and in his craziness was intolerably filthy ... [Dr. Strong] once employed Roman to hive a swarm of bees. When within about twenty feet of the swarm it suddenly formed in a solid battalion of about six inches deep and three feet long, and it in poured directly towards Roman with such impetuosity that Dr. Strong thought the poor fellow would certainly be killed. But the swarm, soon as it approached within two feet of him abruptly turned off in another direction and left him undisturbed. "The bees couldn't stand Roman."[17]

As much as this passage calls into question Roman's psychological stability, it also calls into question the ethics and judgment of Dr. Strong for employing him in this way. Certainly, a discussion of this event would have taken place in the households of the Congregational ministers, among both privileged and serving classes. This source, dating from the mid-nineteenth century, within memory of the practice of Black governorships, provides a wealth of intriguing material.

JUDICIAL FUNCTIONS

Tensions may have surfaced around the judicial functions of the governors and the occasional spectacle of a Black governor punishing another Black person who has been judged by whites to have transgressed. Some of the punishments were exceedingly cruel. It is common for oppressive social structures to employ surrogates to mete out punishment, deflecting attention away from genuine sources of power.[18] And since quelling insurrection was often on the minds of those with political power, the "bread and circuses" aspect of Election Day served as a steam-release valve eliciting a sense of agency for Black residents amid the festive atmosphere. As surrogate magistrate, the governor served a variety of complex functions, creating a sense of pride and self-governance within the harshest system of popular restriction—enslavement—while moderating unrest.

> The office of Black Governor originated in Massachusetts and then appeared in Connecticut and Rhode Island. These officials served as mediators between the white establishment and the communities of blacks. As such they could appear in ceremonies as heads of their communities or carry out various judicial and religious functions. While they might be elected, this does not imply that they were agents of the blacks who elected them, but only that they commanded enough respect to be heeded.[19]

Some Black governors had assistants and sheriffs, which shows that they had substantial responsibilities and were not mere figureheads. A more comprehensive study of Black governors would be a welcome addition to the existing scholarship.

CULTURAL MEANINGS AND TRANSGRESSIVE BEHAVIOR

White observers developed narratives of ridicule, a common tool of dominance, to undermine respect for and the dignity of their subjects. Scaeva writes:

> When elected Governor, a curious accident befell him [Peleg]. The place of the election was on the Neck, near the north burying yard. Peleg, after he was chosen, had no sooner mounted his horse, booted and spurred, than his impatient and fiery steed started at once for a pond which then lay a little to the south of the cemetery mentioned, and plunging headlong into it, bespattered his excellency head to toe.[20]

Undeterred by this misfortune, Peleg Nott emerged from the pond and took the occasion *to ask for and receive his freedom*—an act that reveals the subversive use of power (tomfoolery?) to gain freedom and autonomy. Enslaved and marginally free Black people became expert at syncretizing white cultural events in ways that on the surface appropriated (mimicked?) Euro-American practices while disguising the actual cultural continuities with African rites and beliefs.[21] Such was Election Day. While the US origins are murky, by the midseventeenth century, enslaved Africans had figured out how to transmute elections to create structures and social events that allowed not just for much-needed revelries, but also social organization, power-sharing, and a measure of internal community control over punishment.

Across many cultures, public festivals such as fairs and carnivals present and are created to provide opportunities for transgressive behavior, and Election Day is no exception. Carnival celebrations may be loosely compared with Election Day to tease out cultural meanings and behavior. Peter Stallybrass and Allon White provide an analysis of transgression based in part on the theories of Mikhail Bakhtin. They note that "Carnival, for Bakhtin, is both a populist utopian vision of the world seen from below and a festive critique, through the inversion of hierarchy, of the 'high' culture." They explain that according to Bakhtin, the fête " . . . celebrates the temporary liberation from the prevailing truth of the established order; it marks the suspension of hierarchical rank, privileges, norms and prohibitions . . ."[22] Analyses of the widespread phenomenon of carnival resonate with historical Black celebrations in the United States. Certainly, it is in keeping with the idea of an inverted hierarchy in which the oppressed for some brief moments are cast as the social leaders, governors and kings, while those with power become mere onlookers. Stallybrass and White go on to note that "[Carnival] may be a stable and cyclical ritual with no noticeable politically transformative effects but that, given the presence of sharpened political antagonism, it may often act as *catalyst* and *site of actual and symbolic struggle*."[23]

As with Training Days, even more so, the election of Black governors would have been understood by major participants to be an enactment of a larger struggle for emancipation. The performance of political power and control provide hope, a vision for the future, through the Black magistrate's performance of judicial functions as well as executive and legislative ones. In fact, in merging West African and Euro-American rituals of choosing leaders and then endowing them with the authority to negotiate, delegate, enforce, and rule, Election Day events provided a central stage for the struggle against oppression.

Note that ridicule from authorities also represents a desire to participate or share in the festivities, a kind of longing for the freedom of expression evidenced in the celebration that is, in fact, unavailable to those in authority. Laughter helps to break down difference. Stewart's "The First Stage of Life" shows that from a very young age, the protagonist had a deeply complex set of experiences across race and culture. Later in life, she attributes to herself precocity and an astute comprehension diverse phenomena. As such, her youthfulness would not have prevented her from absorbing and evaluating the proceedings of festival days. Like so much great theater, the performances encompassed both satire and solemnity. The governors, their deputies and justices were serious in adopting the duties doled out to them. Miller may have absorbed that while Black Election Day was to some degree an imitation of its white counterpart, the levels and layers of meaning endowed participants and viewers with political insight and a modicum of power. Some aspects of

Election Day provide continuity with present-day political satire: elaborate behavior, pantomimes, caricatures that whites so readily assume personify lack of virtue or culture, or that they are poor imitations of the more noble of the species, in fact are sophisticated lampoons of white behavior/posture/ attitudes.[24] A central theme of African American theory and practice in North America affirms that well before the revolution of 1776, Euro-Americans were hypocritical in their application of political principles, in cruel denial about the nature of humanity, and willfully ignorant about the varieties of human culture and society. From the beginning, those who were enslaved, when they had a moment to indulge in the laughter necessary to ease the pain, must have looked at their captors in mock wonder at the righteous posturing with which one member or group of the species lorded over another, all the while, as an act of self-preservation, feigning a form of acceptance. Maria W. Stewart asked, "Then why should one worm say to another, 'Keep you down there, while I sit up yonder; for I am I better than thou?'"[25] In Election Day, the enfranchised of society supplied the guns, the musical instruments and drums, the finery, the time, the food, and the drink that Black participants used to forge a pleasurable, celebratory experience, to invert and reclaim political hierarchies, to facilitate social organization, and, simultaneously, to ridicule their masters' hubris. This would not have been lost on the wondering eyes of Maria Miller. The erasure of knowledge about these long-standing historical events from current research and teaching is in keeping with the theme of epistemicide—the obliteration of knowledge created by and of oppressed groups. The paucity of information reinforces the notion that Africans and their descendants lacked agency and produced little of cultural significance from this time period, and therefore are not worthy of study. But nothing could be further from the truth.

HARTFORD AND THE WAR OF 1812

As the century wore on, foreign policy conflicts escalated in ways that directly affected the citizens of Hartford. The rectory thrummed with talk of conflict and the state of the young nation. When word of a new war against England reached Connecticut midway through the year, Miller was old enough to realize that war could not be a good thing. The declaration of war magnified the widespread atmosphere of dismay. As a center of commerce and trade with Europe and a Federalist stronghold, the overwhelming sense was that the war was a disaster. The state refused to send troops. Others were more willing to serve. In contrast with the brutal constraints of the slave/servant society in which measures of freedom were taken in the smallest increments, under a different set of constraints, on the sea, free African Americans acquired a wider worldview and direct knowledge of other cultures in which oppression of Africans *qua* African did not exist. When Maria Miller was just nine years old, her future husband, in his thirties, was enlisting to fight in the War of 1812.

Chapter Seven

"IN SAUCY DEFIANCE"

A single Frigate lording over the Pacific, roving about the ocean, in saucy defiance of their thousand ships; reveling in the spoils of boundless wealth, and almost banishing the British flag from those regions, where it had so long waved proudly Predominate
—Washington Irving, on the Frigate USS *Essex.*[1]

Maria W. Stewart's 1879 Pension claim attests:

She is the widow of James W. Stewart who served . . . as a seaman and in other capacities on one or more ships or vessels of war in the service of the United States commanded by officers of the U.S. Navy in the war of 1812–1815.[2]

By the time he was thirty years old, James W. Stewart had already served six years as a merchant seaman prior to enlisting in the US Navy.[3] A longstanding pattern emerged. African Americans were not entirely welcome to fight for the United States in its wars, and sometimes they were legally excluded. Nonetheless, regardless of law or policy, their service was solicited, valued, and even praised. In the War of 1812, the service of African Americans was decisive in the outcome.

Despite the legal barriers, as much as 29% of the US Navy was African American, perhaps because while life on the sea was rough, it had long provided a place where individuals were valued for their skills in a setting where expertise tipped an expedition in the right direction as it teetered between disaster from weather, war, or mutiny, and success in plunder, victory, or just plain survival.[4]

Other estimates are slightly lower, between 15% and 25% depending on recruiting locations and methods, still a high percentage of the fighting force. The Black

Jacks, as they were called, encountered abuse and racial slurs all the while gaining esteem in merchant marine and military naval operations. Relative to the social and legal barriers on land, the high stakes at sea created a fierce but attenuated meritocracy. Perhaps this is why James W. Stewart volunteered. Stewart was well suited to the task and found adventure far beyond what the docks of New York offered. From the perspective of the navy, Stewart's racial status may have been ambiguous. Knowing his origins, he counted himself as Black, but when the official who processed his enlistment gave him a quick once-over, he saw a strong, broad man well-suited to the sea and marked him down as "swarthy," a term that cut a wide swathe between "Negro," and "White." Stewart may have used that ambiguity to maneuver more readily among the different factions aboard ship, and all indications are that he did this well. Stewart was a *free* Black man; however, many who were enslaved also chose to fight on the side of the United States, while others threw in their lot with the British. Charles Ball was an escaped slave and self-declared "free man of color" who volunteered to serve in the US Navy and fought in the Chesapeake Bay. His autobiography, *Slavery in the United States: A Narrative of the Life and Adventures of Charles Ball, A Black Man,* provides a rich source of information about life in slavery, as a free man, and about the African religious beliefs he learned from his grandfather.[5] At one point, he found himself aboard a British naval vessel where he

> . . . *was obliged to content myself the best way I could, in my confinement on shipboard; and I amused myself by talking to the sailors, and giving them an account of the way in which I had passed my life on the tobacco and cotton plantations; in return for which, the seamen gave many long stories of their adventures at sea, and of the battles they had been engaged in.*[6]

Many believed that their chances for emancipation in the United States were good. Old-timers recalled the efforts of African Americans to gain political freedom through individual manumissions following the War of Independence as well as through the petition movement since in both Massachusetts and Connecticut, the constitutional Right of Petition was exercised frequently by African Americans at the time.[7] In 1788, "Africa's blacks that are now in chain bondage" in New Haven argued:

> [A]ll our wishes are that your Honours would grant us a Liberation. We are all determined we can toil as long as there is Labor; we would wish no more to be in Slavery to Sin Since Christ has made us free and our tenants to the Cross and Brought our Liberty.[8]

In addition to personal petitions to enslavers, private acts of resistance, public revolts, and insurrections, those who were enslaved used legal, constitutional means to press for freedom. While the petition movement waned in the early nineteenth century, the memory of these political actions and the hope of reversing the despised practice of enslavement remained alive, especially in the minds of those who chose not to join the British. The hopes of those entering the War of 1812 must have also been based on a conviction of US victory and subsequent emancipation, possibly in keeping with the general naval slogan of the conflict: "Free trade and sailors' rights."

The British Empire that impressively ruled the waves infuriatingly hampered commercial success for the emerging nation. Blockades thwarted maritime trade, and the despised British pressgangs boarded US ships to force crew members into service for the Royal Navy. In response, President James Madison made the case for war to Congress. He may have imagined a rerun of the successful ground war of the Revolution, but instead he became embroiled in a naval war against a significantly more powerful foe. For New Englanders, the war was yet another example of disastrous Virginian national leadership; they argued unsuccessfully that commercial success would be more readily promoted by friendship not antagonism. Prepared for a sea engagement, Captain David Porter embraced the opportunity to ply his skills in charge of the frigate USS *Essex*, even though he was dissatisfied with its armaments.[9] The *Essex* had been dry docked at the Brooklyn Naval Yards for repairs when barely two weeks after the declaration of war she sailed out of New York harbor with James W. Stewart aboard.[10] After a period of working the docks, to be once again on a ship out of the harbor may have meant for him a longing fulfilled. The seasoned sailor appreciated the towering magnificence of the masts and miles and miles of ropes and sail. He "knew the ropes," that is, could name every rope and sail. The ship was the thing, the leviathan itself, to be soothed and managed by the ropes and sails and the dozens of hands that caressed them.

Captain Porter left a detailed journal making it possible to piece together significant events in the lives of his crew members.[11] Within this framework, it is possible to trace quite specifically the life of the man who would become Maria W. Stewart's husband. James W. Stewart had substantial influence on her thought, conveying to her the ideas framed by his experiences, at a time when she was emerging from provincial restrictions and the confines of indenture. Jeffrey Bolster writes: "Seamen wrote the first six autobiographies of blacks published in English before 1800. Finding their voices in the swirling currents of international maritime labor, seafaring men fired the opening salvo of the black abolitionist attack and fostered creation of a black corporate identity."[12]

This idea is further developed by Julius S. Scott, who, in *The Common Wind: Afro-American Currents in the Age of the Haitian Revolution*, chronicles how on the sea masterless men and women found ways to move about and evade the authorities, . . . [T]hese people embodied submerged traditions of popular resistance which could burst into the open at any time. Examining the rich world these mobile fugitives inhabited—the complex (and largely invisible) underground which the "mariners, renegades, and castaways" . . . created . . . is crucial to understanding how news, ideas, and social excitement traveled in the electric political environment.[13]

While Scott focuses on the Haitian Revolution, this atmosphere continued to prevail in maritime settings for decades. James W. Stewart's early days at sea were coextensive with the end of the Haitian Revolution in 1804.While acknowledging racism and racial hierarchies on board ships, Gerald T. Altoff affirms that "harmony among ship's crews was essentially a product of the sea environment . . . a ship at sea was an independent and isolated community whose very survival was entirely reliant on the crew that served her." As a corrective to the idea that sailing vessels were all-male environments, Altoff observes that, while rare, "some black women served on merchant ships in regular capacities, usually as stewardesses, cooks, or seamstresses."[14] Through her husband and many other sources, Maria W. Stewart would absorb the complex developments in the politics of the African diaspora.

In the early weeks of the *Essex*'s foray into the war, with Stewart aboard, the ship had "captured a military troop transport, the *Samuel and Sarah*, headed for Quebec, the rum brig *Lamprey* and then the *Leander*, which was carrying a cargo of coal and salt . . . and five more merchant vessels."[15] Shortly after, the frigate, its commander, and its crew did the unthinkable, upending international opinion about the invincibility of the British navy and the almost comically miniscule US one. Porter had expertly maneuvered in battle to capture the much more formidable HMS *Alert*, a British warship, and emerged unscathed. The glory and rewards accorded to the underdog buoyed the spirits of the *Essex* crew.[16]

In balance with the solidarity he may have felt in victory at sea, James Stewart was also well acquainted with virulent, entrenched racism pervading all Euro-American-dominated spaces. Even as a free Black, his interest would have been captured, and sense of justice stung when at seventeen years old, in 1799, he learned that New York State passed the "Gradual Emancipation Act." What should have been a boon to equality instead pushed full abolition far into the future, to 1829, underscoring the tension between recognizing that slavery was morally wrong and the cowardice of legislators who refused to banish this evil within their lifetimes. Making matters worse, despite the federal Constitutional and statutory abolition of the importation of enslaved persons beginning in 1807, illegal transport and commerce were alive and well in the North Atlantic. The docks of New York were diverse spaces designed for "fast living, serious drinking, womanizing, gambling, and carousing," and like active ports the world over, racial and ethnic diversity was common, but so were the offences ranging from slights to violence and police brutality based on racial prejudice.[17] Through his experiences as a merchant seaman, Stewart displayed considerable wisdom. He defied the stereotype of the Jack Tar—drunken, dissipated, wanton—and the sailors under David Porter's command learned discipline on board the ship. More disciplined than the typical sailor, Stewart was highly intelligent and frugal, with a mind for business. When he served as a merchant mariner, his pay was merely that which had been pre-established when he shipped out, based on his time aboard ship and his contracted service with the commercial shipping companies. Typically, discipline was harsh, geared for compliance and not for enlightenment. Not so aboard the *Essex*. Naval crews shared in the bounty captured at sea, an incentive to perform well and undertake risk. Military service to the young country bred self-respect, as did ship-based hierarchies as enforced by an enlightened master such as Porter.

Within six weeks of shipping out, Stewart had experienced firsthand the skill of a capable commander and crew against a larger and better-equipped enemy and a sense of accomplishment issuing from a string of successful captures. The prize money for these successes might have enriched his imagination about possibilities for an entrepreneurial future, one surpassing traditional race and class barriers, but do not think for a minute that life aboard the *Essex* provided a prime example of Enlightenment rationality. After regrouping in Baltimore and setting out for a prearranged rendezvous with other naval vessels, the *Essex* first sailed to Cape Verde, where the crew took on provisions, including tropical fruits and animals, and then approached the equator. Long known for gender creativity, the crews of seafaring vessels devised many clever and provocative traditions. On November 23, 1812, continuing south across the Equator, the crew conducted the traditional gender-bending, "Line Crossing" ceremony that involved costuming, pantomime, play-acting, and song to mark the crossing of the equator and to haze the novice sailors. Porter writes:

> On the 23rd we were honored by a visit from the god of the ocean [Neptune], accompanied by Amphitrite [his wife] and a numerous retinue of imps, barbers, &c. in his usual style of visiting, and in the course of the afternoon all the novices of the ship's company were initiated into his mysteries. Neptune, however, and most of his suite, paid their devotions so frequently to Bacchus that before the ceremony of christening was half gone through, their godships were unable to stand; the business was therefore entrusted to the subordinate agents, who performed both the shaving and washing with as little regard to tenderness as his majesty would have done. On the whole, however, they got through the

business with less disorder and more good humour than I expected; and although some were most unmercifully scraped, the only satisfaction sought was that of shaving others in turn with new invented tortures.[18]

Just as racial categories carried different meanings on board ship, so did gender categories, promoting comfort with gender fluidity and wider tolerance for difference. A shrewd captain, Porter doled out leisure and entertainment just as he did rum and refreshment to induce a sense of camaraderie among the crew.

Porter's attempts to meet with his sister ships in the South Atlantic proved futile, so off the southern tip of the South American continent he was left with the singular decision regarding whether to continue seeking his rendezvous or to strike out in a different direction. Reasoning that a substantial part of Britain's wealth and naval power was bound up in its Pacific whaling fleet, Porter hit upon the idea of rounding Cape Horn, heading to resupply in Concepción, Chile, and mounting his own theater of operation in the South Pacific.[19]

When the African American seaman James W. Stewart signed on to serve in the US Navy in the War of 1812, little did it occur to him that he would be pirating British whalers. Other naval vessels were battling the British in the Chesapeake Bay and the Great Lakes, bombarded by cannon from the enemy: British and loyalists in Canada, with support from Abenaki, Kickapoo, and some members of the Iroquois confederacy. There was a total US military naval force of merely six ships designed for the purpose. The trajectory of the frigate *Essex* defied the conventional plan. But would Porter's crew be willing to undertake the venture? He posted a notice promising the spoils of pillage. Along the Pacific coastline of South America and at sea *Essex* would find "many friendly ports," and, "the unprotected British commerce . . . will give you an abundant supply of wealth; and the girls of the Sandwich Islands, shall reward you for your sufferings during the passage around Cape Horn."[20] Stewart and other crew members read the notice and embraced the idea. The South Pacific offered distinct possibilities, including the potential annexation of territory for future exploitation. Porter believed he would be able to safely resupply in Concepción with captured British loot providing his expense money. Refortified, he set his aim on British whaling ships, seeing in the Pacific both a chance to do serious damage to enemy commerce and an opportunity to earn prize money and personal glory. He kept the sailors occupied with work and training, holding daily boarding and small-arms exercises. Call it piracy or good naval war strategy, the *Essex* often posed as a merchant ship and flew the colors of other countries to lure the British close and ensnare them. Captain Porter earned the admiration of his crew for running a good ship, orderly, and without the cruelty that some captains seemed to relish, yet he was crafty in his dealings with the British.

Past successes, healthy discipline, and a mutually sympathetic crew and command made this a promising sail. Posing as a friendly vessel, the *Essex* approached and captured the packet ship *Nocton*. Porter issued the orders, and fifteen seamen boarded the *Nocton* and subdued their shocked crew. Porter writes: "One of our first victims was a mail packet, the Nocton, an easy target that held a marvelous prize for us $55,000 in gold bullion."[21] Perhaps, if Stewart was able to personally gaze at the massive treasure trove of gold in the hold of ship, a tiny but significant portion of which would be his share, he allowed himself to reflect on his future. Seafaring was hard, physical work, and an able body did not stay young forever, but in this world, a man with the right sort of knowledge and skills could make an excellent go of it selling maritime supplies and equipment. The oceans were the hearts of commerce and war, and money flowed from that direction. Still, proprietorship was risky for free Blacks. Many whites had contempt for Black businessmen and would as soon find a legal way to steal one's stock as to pay for it. The trick would be to find a place with a free Black community that had at least a small amount of political clout, a place far from slavery with a growing maritime trade. Perhaps when the war was over, he could find a home in Boston.

Chapter Eight

"SERVED AS A SEAMAN" [1]

My ship was now totally unmanageable, yet, as her head was toward the
enemy, and to leeward of me, I still hoped to board him.
—Journal of Captain David Porter [2]

SEAMAN STEWART

While Maria Miller was still a child forced to labor at work more suited for
an adult, her future husband continued his wartime service, with additional
chapters of conflict ahead of him. James W. Stewart's experiences aboard the
USS *Essex* extended well beyond the discovery of gold aboard the *Nocton*.
While British ships in the Great Lakes and the Chesapeake were bombarding
US naval forces close to home, Captain David Porter's frigate continued its
piratical tactics, capturing several British whalers, including the *Georgiana*,
near the Galapagos Islands. Porter ordered Lieutenant John Downes and some
of the *Essex* crew to take control of the captured ship; among them, Seaman
Stewart. Maria Stewart attested many years later,

> From the best of her knowledge and belief, [James W. Stewart] served
> under Captain David Porter on the U.S.S. vessel Essex in 1812, and also
> under Lieut. J. Dow [sic] on the vessel Georgiana in 1813, and under
> Commodore or Capt. Stephen Decatur and Commandant W. Lewis on
> the Guerriere in 1815. And in addition . . . she believes that he served as
> a coxswain on the Eperrier in 1815. "served under Lieut. J. Dow [sic] on
> the vessel *Georgiana* in 1813." [3]

The *Georgiana* was commandeered under US control to harry other British vessels. When the two warships met again in Tumbes, Peru, Stewart either rejoined
the *Essex* or stayed with the *Georgiana*. Porter then steered the *Essex* to ride the

"The *Essex* and her prizes in Massachusetts Bay in Nooaheevha." When Captain Porter and the *Essex,* with James W. Stewart among the crew, arrived at Nuku Hiva, the largest of the Marquesas Islands, he claimed the territory for the United States and renamed the harbor "Massachusetts Bay." Pictorial Field Book of the War of 1812, Benson Lossing, 1815.

Humboldt current to the Marquesas Islands, where he claimed the large island of Nuku Hiva for the United States in a colonial grab that was never enforced.

Although James Stewart's immediate fate remains unknown, novelist Herman Melville fashioned a ghost story about the fate of ships like the *Essex* and the *Georgiana.*

> [I]n 1813, the U.S. frigate *Essex,* [under] Captain David Porter, came near leaving her bones. Lying becalmed one morning with a strong current setting her rapidly towards the rock, a strange sail was descried, which—not out of keeping with alleged enchantments of the neighborhood—seemed to be staggering under a violent wind, while the frigate lay lifeless as if spellbound. But a light air springing up, all sail was made by the frigate in chase of the enemy, as supposed—he being deemed an English whale-ship—but the rapidity of the current was so great that soon all sight was lost of him, and, at meridian, the *Essex,* spite of her drags, was driven so close under the foam-lashed cliffs of Rodondo that, for a time, all hands gave her up. A smart breeze, however, at last helped her off, though the escape was so critical as to seem almost miraculous.[4]

Melville conjures the experiences of *Essex* and her crew, the close calls and near catastrophes, as she returned to the waters near Peru, where they came under heavy attack at Valparaiso, so much so that some of the crew jumped ship and swam ashore. Shortly thereafter, Porter surrendered. The *Georgiana* fared no better. The vessel had been captured and sent to Bermuda. While it is difficult to determine James Stewart's exact whereabouts between March 1814 and May 1815—whether he was serving then on the *Essex* or the *Georgiana*—both were captured by the British. In either case, he would have been carried to British-controlled Bermuda and exchanged for British prisoners of war.[5] Remarkably, Maria Stewart recounted some of these details sixty-four years later, in 1879, so familiar was she with her husband's travels.

Meanwhile, in New England, Harrison Gray Otis led a delegation of disgruntled New Englanders to a convention in Hartford to craft a regional response to the war. A little more than ten years later, Mrs. James W. Stewart would live a few short steps away from Otis's by-then-discarded Bulfinch-designed mansion. Now she was just a poor, precocious child with little personal freedom, but possessing powers of intellect and observation that absorbed the animated political discourse in the home of the prominent Hartford citizen to whom she was indentured. A sense of urgency dominated the meeting, attended by delegates from Connecticut, Massachusetts, and Rhode Island, determined to put into action their fierce complaints about federal interference with the region's commercial interests exacerbated by the war. After twelve years of presidents from Virginia, New Englanders were fed up with Southern political domination. One historian opined that, through Jefferson's enduring influence, "the President and his followers were little more than blind followers of Napoleonic France and the inveterate foes of New England commercial interests."[6] The delegates considered the radical action of seceding from the Union, ultimately settling on a more moderate list of demands to be delivered to President Madison and the Republicans.

The political wheeling and dealing of the 1787 Constitutional Convention set the stage for this power struggle. Then, the Three-Fifths Compromise, the devil's deal that handed crucial political power to the South, had designated those who were enslaved as 3/5 of a person for the purposes of taxation and allocating representatives to the US Congress, all the while denying them any civil rights or general liberties, institutionalizing chattel slavery into the founding document and swelling the ranks of Southern congressmen to enforce and protect this inhumanity. At the Hartford Convention, twenty-five years after Constitutional ratification, the most radical among those gathered favored secession from the Union, or at least a repeal of the Three-Fifths Compromise—for political and economic, not moral, reasons.[7] Intellectually, commercially, and dispositionally, many New England citizens seemed closer to the Mother Country, England, and loathed the idea of seeing their profits disrupted by war. The tense discussions at the Hartford Convention took place behind locked doors. Details of the political machinations going on around her may have escaped Maria Miller's understanding, but the clergyman to whom she was in service would have known a good deal. Congregationalists and Federalists ran the state and promoted their common interests, distilled into the convention's resolutions. Once they had settled on the demands, the delegation made its way to Washington DC to make them known. Secession had been dropped from the agenda; nonetheless, their proposals were unlikely to achieve much traction in the Capitol. The war was not going well, so the sudden signing of the Treaty of Ghent to end the War of 1812 caught delegates by surprise and sent them scurrying back home without revealing their intentions. The failure of the Hartford Convention and the outcome of the war had the effect of further entrenching the slavocracy.

THE SECOND BARBARY WAR

When the war abruptly ended, James W. Stewart continued his term of service with the US Navy. Assigned to the USS *Guerriere*, he was put under the command of the highly regarded and much-decorated war hero, Captain Stephen Decatur.[8] The fledgling US Navy had developed into a more skilled fighting force during the war, and her commanders, still feeling belligerent, turned to ongoing conflicts on the Barbary Coast. North Africans in Algiers, Morocco, Tripoli, and Tunis had long imposed a tribute on ships sailing near their shores for commerce in the Mediterranean, a practice the United States labeled as piracy as they determined to end it.

Considered in historical and geographical context, the expulsion of Muslims and Jews from Al-Andalus by Christian armies in the fifteenth century corresponded with the origins of European global expansion. Counterpressure came from North Africa and other locations under control of the Ottoman Empire. The former al-Andalusian Muslims and the Amazighs (Berbers) occupied a region with a small but significant Jewish population, many of whom had fled along with the Moors during the *Reconquista*.[9] The War of 1812 and the Barbary Wars were crucial in furthering the ambitions of global capital through securing trade routes and exploring areas for future expansion. They mark the origins of US global political hegemony and the accompanying narrative of a benevolent, liberal democratic colonial power bringing civilization to the barbarians, a narrative soundly contested today by decolonial theorists. Thus, the role of subduing the Barbary Coast has largely unrecognized importance for current Western power dynamics. It was the first North American conquest of the "Old World," one of the last strongholds of Muslim domination in close proximity to Western Europe, one that wielded significant power over European and US commerce and control of the Mediterranean and West Asia.

While the events are largely forgotten, the first US land battle in this region is memorialized in the *Marines' Hymn* as a victorious engagement on "the shores of Tripoli" in an anthem that signifies US military might.

The determination to Westernize this geographical region resonates with Frantz Fanon's argument, based primarily on his experiences in North Africa, that the sociogenesis of oppression grounded in colonialism is at its heart a change in society, not simply a facet of the individual. In this light, the attempted conquest of the region represented an initial foray into creating an imaginary in which Muslims, Arabs, and other occupants of West Asia were claimed to be naturally inferior to Northern Europeans and their colonizing settlers.[10] For Fanon, the intent of colonization was to be a totalizing experience encompassing language, custom, racial hierarchy, and psychological disposition. Even the Western nomenclature "Barbary" derives from the ideas of "strange" and "foreign," of "barbarism," in contrast with the "civilized" Europeans and Americans who would benevolently tame them. Among the many flashpoints of colonialism, imperialism, expansion, and political and economic control, North Africa continues to be a critical intersection, a collision point in the ideological struggle for the humanity of Africans and non-Christians. The Barbary Wars increased Western control of trade in that part of the Mediterranean and left a weakened region ripe for French colonization in the 1830s, a condition that persisted until and beyond the bloody Algerian War of 1954–1962, one of the starkest examples of brutal repression as it came to a head in the twentieth century.

What may we say about groups of people who are drawn together for shorter or longer periods of time, compacted in close quarters aboard ship, whose cooperation is required and necessary for survival? And beyond the single crews, the legions of mostly men who sailed the ships that littered the seas for centuries? May we think of them, and their ideas, as "creolized," participating in what Jeffrey Bolster calls a "corporate black identity"?[11] The company of sailors such as those described in Scott's *The Common Wind* may be viewed as *creolized* in the senses developed by Jane Gordon, Neil Roberts, Michael Monahan, Drucilla Cornell, and others. In its first meaning, "creolization" describes communities in which "opposed, unequal groups forged mutually instantiating practices in contexts of radical historical rupture." In this case, racialized groups of disparate power were brought together by the exigencies of war and commerce.[12] In a second sense, constituent of these "mutually instantiating practices" was the development of a theoretical analysis of aggressive US foreign policies implemented in conjunction with domestic policies of enslavement and oppression.

For the Black Jacks, deep, personal lived experiences created an epistemic standpoint sharply diverging from that of their commanding officers. Significant numbers of sailors of African descent or their ancestors endured forced residencies in the West Indies during the Middle Passage before being installed on continental North America. Experiential and intellectual similarities between Black sailors bridged cultural differences inherited from diverse European, West African, and West Indian backgrounds to create a degree of unification of thought and purpose—a creolization—that emerged in the naval war and in peacetime contexts. Intensifying this communion, deep associations with the Haitian conflicts produced a shared knowledge that informed their worldviews for years to come. Creolization as a methodological approach describes finding "a different way of narrating the situations that produced what are considered historic moments in the development of political theory."[13] The Haitian Revolution represents one of these moments of rupture.[14] Less than through a single historical disruption, rather, by longstanding political exigency, a disparate group of outsiders—Black sailors—sought spaces in which an amalgam of outliers could come together for shared purposes. The theoretical perspectives of this creolized cohort are typically passed over in favor of the official land- and nation-based metanarratives. For example, the War of 1812 is sometimes called the "Second Revolutionary War," glorifying the US victory and the subsequent defeat of African "piracy"—a negative ascription to what was essentially a common tariff—and the subduing of Islamic influence over Euro and American "rights." Monahan writes, "[I]t is, for instance, through the disavowal of 'outside' influences and interactions, and the repetition of the mythology of a *sui generis* European intellectual tradition that the very idea of a non-creolized foundation for our intellectual practices exists in the first place."[15] In this top-down episteme, the knowledge produced by common sailors whose concrete experiences were often more worldly than those of European philosophers has no standing whatsoever. It may as well not exist. Alternatively, I would argue, the sophisticated understandings of a Seaman Stewart with his Scots and Black ancestry and other seafaring laborers reveal a different perspective on the events they experienced, ones that would influence future analyses. As Nelson Maldonado-Torres asserts, following Fanon: "Human identity and activity (subjectivity) also produce and unfold within contexts that have precise workings of power, notions of being, and conceptions of knowledge."[16]

Such conceptions of knowledge, years later, nourished the voracious mind of twenty-three-year-old Maria Miller. These ideas would go a considerable distance to comprise one element of the attraction between two commanding intellects, Miller and Stewart, as a source of her sophisticated global understanding from one who never left the United States.

A series of sea engagements left the United States in a position to press its advantage. It is distinctly possible that Seaman James Stewart was aboard the *Guerriere* during peace negotiations when the treaty between Omar Agha, the Dey of Algiers, Captain Decatur, and US emissary William Shaler was signed. It is worth noting that in addition to shipping rights, a point of contention was the Americans' demand to end the enslavement of white Christians, while a short distance away, US trafficking in Africans flourished despite its legal prohibition. How James Stewart may have viewed the tenuous triumph of the US Navy over representatives of the Ottoman Empire remains in question. As a member of the US Navy, his loyalties would have been with his commander and crew, but as a man of color and an observer of a broad spectrum of racial and cultural differences, he may have adopted a more circumspect view, even a two-layered one. The typical sense of "double consciousness" developed from a core idea by W. E. B. Du Bois is that of a negative psychological disruption caused by the difficulties in reconciling one's Blackness and Americanness under the defining scrutiny of a racist dominant white gaze. And yet as Lewis Gordon and Paget Henry observe, this form of consciousness may be potentiated into a "second sight"—a critical reflective insight that allows for multilevel analyses unavailable to the oppressors, so thoroughly immersed in the dominant narrative that they cannot see beyond it.[17] Thus, James W. Stewart may be viewed as what Henry calls a "knowing subject," expanding "who is involved in the theoretical dimensions of . . . the structure of what counts as evidential."[18] His evidence—his experiences ranging from the Pacific Islands, the coastal cities of Chile, his knowledge of events on the island of Saint Domingue, and naval service along Barbary Coast—had taught Stewart, in contrast with the myth of naturalized inferiority, that the imaginary of inevitable white domination that prevailed in the United States was just that—a useful, concocted piece of ideology serving to maintain and further entrench existing power relations.

The Barbary treaty may have tilted the balance of power for the time being, but the Ottoman official overseeing the agreement soon became contemptuous of the penury and ineffectuality of the US forces. In counterpoint, the diplomat Shaler advised a friend back home that "the only way to deal with these people [the North Africans] is to treat them as you would plantation Negroes."[19] Aimé Césaire identifies colonization as a "bridgehead in a campaign to civilize barbarism, from which there may emerge at any moment the negation of civilization, pure and simple"—the barbarism of coloniality.[20] In an inversion of the desired outcome—"civilization," the ascription of inhumanity to colonized people is a primary step in crumbling the edifice of everything that is thought of as "civilized" and dehumanizes the colonizer. Writing in the mid-twentieth century, Césaire observes that the distress of Euro-American antifascists of his time arose from the fact that the fascists were applying to *white* people (antifascists, European Jews, homosexuals, and others) the colonialism which, in the words of Robin D. G. Kelley, had "until then had been reserved exclusively for the Arabs of Algeria, the 'coolies' of India, and *the 'n******' of* Africa."[21] Shaler's letter provides one data point in the construction of whiteness that facilitated dehumanization of racial, ethnic, cultural, or religious groups in ways that gave rise to fascism.

Seaman Stewart's experiences are constitutive of the radical alternative epistemologies that are both subterranean and central to oppositional philosophies found in the writings of Maria W. Stewart. In *The Common Wind*, Scott details the ways in which sailors "whispered" historical events of resistance ". . . out again as subversive stories, to circulate with velocity and force around the Atlantic."[22] James Stewart was a part of the mobile labor community composed in part of free Blacks operating liminally in relation to state power and who participated in "how news, ideas, and social excitement traveled in the electric political environment." Profoundly influenced by the Haitian revolution, for Black sailors "the most important item of exchange which was constantly changing hands [was] information" a truth that Scott argues is often forgotten in the historical studies of trade among and between Euro-colonial powers.[23]

Constant resistance to anti-Black laws and practices in the United States and West Indies met with efforts to impose more control over outlaws, maroons, free Blacks, and the self-liberated. The traffic of contraband knowledge met with new restrictions, such as regulations forcing Black sailors to stay aboard ship while docked in Southern US harbors. The practices of storytelling, reading aloud to groups of sailors, smuggling newspapers and pamphlets (such as David Walker's *Appeal*), and sending messages contributed to the ground-up knowledge projects designed to increase degrees of freedom at a time when even free Blacks were in constant danger of being captured and enslaved.[24] As knowledge-producers, communities of creolized sailors produced creolized theories that stood in contrast with and had the potential to subvert the official accounts.[25] The knowledge that James Stewart imparted to Maria Miller bolstered and added a level of complexity to her understanding of colonizing power and the implementation of white supremacy. If we see James Stewart as an ordinary sailor who developed a business sense later in life, we will overlook him as a rich source of inspiration and knowledge for his future wife.

The exploits of Captains Porter, Decatur, and others whose naval adventurism ranged around the globe, far from the principal battle engagements of the War of 1812, functioned as early reconnaissance for future US imperial and colonial activities, initial forays noted and saved for future exploitation.[26] Indigenous eradication and the conquest of the continental West, not global expansion, were the current areas of focus for the United States. Eventually, the United States would move to colonization in the Caribbean, Asia and the Pacific, and elsewhere in Africa.

The *Guerriere* returned to New York on November 12, 1815, and was laid up in the Boston Navy Yard for repairs on March 4, 1816, dates that correspond with Maria W. Stewart's 1879 recollection of the dates her husband fixed as the time of his arrival there. North Slope resident John Brown claims to have seen James Stewart in a navy uniform in 1818, but it may have been earlier since he likely had ended his service by then.[27] Once discharged from the US Navy, James Stewart embarked upon his ambitious entrepreneurial designs.

BLACK MARITIME ENTREPRENEURSHIP IN NEW ENGLAND

James W. Stewart understood that life on land would present obstacles different from the dangers of seafaring life. He was in his late thirties and no longer in the prime condition required for physically demanding labor at sea. Boston offered several attractions, including its distance from plantation-based slavocracy, where the threat and terror of enslavement for free Blacks was more acute than in New England. Boston boasted a vibrant commercial maritime industry, a place ripe with possibility. Stewart had no illusions about the racism he would face in the North and took this in stride, relying on decades of experience before the mast to help him enact his plan to launch a business as shipping agent, eventually a multipronged venture as shipping master, ship broker, and investor in whaling ventures. He would first establish himself in the city and earn trust serving as an intermediary, connecting sailors seeking commercial vessels in need of their service with ship owners in search of a crew. His decades of experience allowed him to build relationships both with sailors and with shipping companies. Officially identified as a shipping agent in archival documents, Stewart may also have masterminded the arrangements between manufacturers and ship owners for the transfer of cargo from places of production to storage in the hold. All this required significant business acumen, self-assurance, and skill.

Stewart found inspiration and a model for his enterprises in a renowned businessman, Paul Cuffe (also Kofi or Cuffee) (1759–1817). A Quaker and a proponent of emigration for Blacks, Cuffe was the scion of a highly successful commercial maritime business. Cuffe's father was of Ashanti heritage, "a poor African, whom the hand of unfeeling avarice had dragged from home and connexions," and his mother was Aquinnah Wampanoag.[28] He was legendary in the community, becoming the wealthiest person of color in the United States at the time, someone whom Manisha Sinha describes as having an "abiding concern for black economic autonomy," a central feature of what I have called Black revolutionary liberalism, the prevailing political philosophy among Northern Blacks from the 1760s to the 1830s, a theory that I argue was promulgated by Maria Stewart.[29] Starting with a small coastal shipping concern near New Bedford, Massachusetts, Cuffe built successively larger schooners with his earnings. He was also someone who in the twentieth century would

Captain Paul Cuffee. An advocate for the rights of African Americans, Cuffee (or Cuffe), built a great shipping empire becoming one of the wealthiest African Americans in the United States in the early 1800s. Cuffee was of mixed Ashanti and Aquinnah Wampanoag heritage. His entrepreneurial success may have inspired James W. Stewart. Schomburg Center for Research in Black Culture, Photographs and Prints Division, The New York Public Library, Digital Collections. Accessed October 16, 2020. http://digitalcollections.nypl.org/items/510d47dc-8f45-a3d9-e040 -e00a18064a99.

have been called a "race man," a pan-Africanist who championed the rights of Africans in America and everywhere. In 1811 when Cuffe brought his ship, the *Traveller*, into Liverpool, its entire crew was either African or of direct African descent.

As an activist for equality like his contemporary, Prince Hall, a founder of the Black Masonic movement, at age twenty-one, Cuffe refused to pay taxes because free Blacks did not have the right to vote. In 1780, he petitioned the council of Bristol County, Massachusetts, to end such taxation without representation. The petition was denied, but his suit may have influenced the 1783 legislation granting voting rights to all free male citizens of the state. Cuffe actively worked to facilitate the emigration of African Americans from the United States to Sierra Leone, addressing Boston's African Sierra Leone

Benevolent Society. His emigrationist efforts were distinct from those promulgated later by the American Colonization Society (ACS), a predominantly
white organization advocating for the removal of African descendants from the
United States to Africa. Cuffe's principles and motivation were to create agency
and prosperity for African Americans, while the ACS viewed free Blacks as a
pernicious influence on enslaved ones, offering migration as a way to mitigate
this influence. It is possible that when James Stewart settled in Boston, he met
Cuffe, as their time there seems to have briefly overlapped before Cuffe's death.
Given his interests, he certainly would have been immersed in the legend of
this extraordinary entrepreneur and freedom advocate. Stewart came to know
the Reverend Thomas Paul, Cuffe's close friend, when he took up residence just
a stone's throw from the African Baptist Church. "October 1, Thursday," Friend
[Quaker] Stephen Wanton Gould wrote in his journal:

> 5th day 1st of 10th M 1818 / I feel better this morning, but am not quite
> smart enough to sit in meeting & attend a committee which meets at
> the breaking up of it to investigate the pecuniary concerns of society.—
> While meeting was sitting had a very interesting call from Thomas Paull
> a man of colour from Boston, a preacher among the Baptists & also an
> intimate friend of our late friend & brother Paul Cuffee, he appears to be
> a religious man & desirous of doing good to all mankind & in particular
> to the people of his colour.—After dinner went up to set a little while
> with the committee at the meeting house.[30]

The connections between the Black mariners, religious leaders, and political
activists fueled the struggle for civil rights and liberty. When James W. Stewart
settled in Boston around 1816, it would be another decade before his future
spouse would arrive. Throughout that time, he strengthened his commercial
prospects and grew his businesses, until as Maria W. Stewart reflected decades
later, "My husband [became] . . . a shipping master or shipping agent and . . .
was engaged and concerned in fitting out whaling and fishing vessels . . ." [31]
Yet while he was exercising his entrepreneurship, she remained in Hartford
studying religion, improving her literacy, and plotting her next step.

The revolutionary hopes of liberation and civil equality for Blacks in the late
eighteenth century faltered in the new century. The petitions of Prince Hall,
Paul Cuffe, Felix, and others had been spurned by the authorities.[32] Recognition
of African American service in the War of Independence that once had ener-
gized hopes for freedom and equality seemed a relic of the more distant past.
By authorizing enslavement, the United States Constitution had broken the
revolutionary promise. The legislative abolition of the slave trade in 1807 had
neither abolished the trade nor softened conditions throughout the country.

On the contrary, economic dependency on slavery became more entrenched, and resistance was taking ever more militant forms.

In *American Negro Slave Revolts*, Herbert Aptheker chronicles hundreds of uprisings and acts of resistance, some inspired by the success of the Haitian revolution.[33] The first decades of the nineteenth century brought rebellions and planned revolts in Virginia, the Carolinas, Kentucky, New Orleans, Florida, and Mississippi. Maroon settlers in the Great Dismal Swamp and elsewhere conducted raids on white communities and met with armed responses. Individual acts of resistance were too common to be enumerated—they were the stuff of everyday life.

JAMES STEWART AND DAVID WALKER AS KNOWLEDGE-PRODUCERS

I have laid the foundation for the case that James W. Stewart would become a transformative source of knowledge for Maria Miller's intellectual and political understanding, a role previously unexplored. Another major source of intellectual fodder for her ready mind was "the undaunted David Walker." While James Stewart's education took place at sea, Walker's development took place on the coast of Wilmington, North Carolina, and its southern neighbor, Charleston, South Carolina, during the most incendiary period of that city's history.[34] So while James Stewart's actions may have been attenuated by his military service and business ventures, Walker experienced events that could not but radicalize a young person exposed to extremely brutal oppression and injustice forged in one of the hottest cauldrons in the heart of American slavery.

Historically, slave resistance and rebellion began on the ships even before the first kidnapped Africans landed in North America in the 1500s, and captives fiercely defied their oppression, steadily over time, in ongoing acts of individual and group rebellion. This may be the first and single most important—as well as partially hidden—fact of African American history—the steady, constant, individual, and organized resistance and struggle. Knowledge passed through orality from families and communities that nurtured and maintained these accounts over decades and centuries; a culture of resistance was bred in the bone. Resistance was subversive, sometimes subtle, involving small acts to foil and undermine the goals of the oppressors while furthering the goals of the oppressed: more freedom, better resources, education, access to transportation, increased ability to socialize, to nurture and care for family and community along with ways of lessening the oppressors' power—psychologically, through means ranging from obeisance to insolence, defiance, and assertion of greater psychological or physical strength. Acts of resistance often drew on the positive exercise of double consciousness and the epistemological advantage of know-ing two cultures—Black and white—while the oppressor arrogantly mistook his own narrow vision for universal knowledge. Another great influence on Maria W. Stewart, David Walker eventually knew the longer history of resis-tance. In his youth, he experienced it, and the repression that accompanied it, firsthand.

Chapter Nine

PARTUS SEQUITUR VENTREM

Partus sequitur ventrem—"that which is brought forth follows the womb."

The classical ideals of ancient Greece and Rome captured the imaginations of early Euro-Americans: republican government, harmony in architecture and art, the idea of a common good, reason and tolerance, and slavery. Slavery was everywhere, from Maine to Georgia, until economic conditions made it anachronistic in the New England states. In the South, more than a million and a half humans were enslaved by 1820, but some Blacks, such as David Walker, had averted the reins of slavery and were born legally free. His status derived from the classical doctrine of *partus sequitur ventrem*, "that which is brought forth follows the womb," a legal rule decreeing a free mother's children to be free, even though the father might be enslaved. In this, he was one of a select few in Wilmington, North Carolina. In his later life, his trenchant philosophy served as the most profound of all influences on the thought of Maria W. Stewart.

Walker's Wilmington was a city run by industrious, skilled, mobile, and confident African Americans, as historian Peter P. Hinks articulates in his careful account of Walker and his milieu. It was the Age of Sail when shipbuilding cities reigned supreme, wealthy, bustling, and productive, on the threshold of global commerce, with ships fanning out from the harbor in every direction and arriving from distant shores. African Americans in Wilmington served as maritime architects, master and apprentice carpenters, draftsmen, laborers, messengers and chefs, cargo haulers and day laborers. These same workers were also enslaved. The sight of a New World metropolis so dominated by Black efficiency and production startled European visitors. It was difficult to comprehend. Still, if one took the time to look into the shadows and recesses, under the awnings, sipping sweet tea, cooled by human fans, white overseers, masters, mistresses, and managers were barely visible through the subtropical haze, counting dollars, issuing general orders, assenting to a proposal here, signing a purchase order there, as presented by their Black underlings and factotums.[1]

Old World observers noted the indolent behavior of white overseers and marveled in a moderately concerned way about the laziness that washed over the white population while Black workers performed every productive aspect of life. Laziness—that great inversion myth—the myth that inverts attributes of character or agency to divert, to blame, to distract. What I call "inversion myths" were popular in the Old South—for instance, "Black men rape white women," when of course the rape of Black women by white men was so endemic as to barely arouse notice from those in power. Yet, in later years, the rape myth became the basis for extrajudicial torture and killing in the form of lynching that for decades fueled the transition from institutional control through slavery to institutional control through mass incarceration. The inversion myth of the lazy Black deflected the reality of the lazy white person. Black women and men built the United States, not just with their scarred backs, but also through their ingenuity and intelligence, their design and execution, and their management skills. But see how "the lazy Black" myth functions: not only does it obscure and malign the remarkable achievements of an intensely productive population, but it also obscures the corpulent overseer (who is also distorted and mythologized), numbed by the absence of necessity, dulled by lassitude, distracted by the executive challenges of maintaining a slave culture, anxious about rebellion, and morally bereft from intimacy, both with people of the slave class and with the nagging lie that undergirded a practice that was bankrupt of principle but also—from the typical white perspective—inescapable. Observers including Jefferson had opined that the hot, humid climate was not well suited to physical industriousness. These entrepreneurs concluded that gaining an economic perch on the edge of the North American continent would best be achieved through the genocidal extermination of the original inhabitants and by compelling others to work through slave labor, a conscious decision in the spread of capitalism and colonialism.

Wilmington, city of tall ships, imports and exports, in the Age of Sail. The USS *Essex*, built in Salem, Massachusetts in 1799, resembled the vessels built in Wilmington, the three-masted ships used for war and commerce manned by the likes of James W. Stewart.[2] A youthful David Walker would have been accustomed to the sight of the magnificent sails towering over the low-lying town, one devoted to their creation and to producing, packing, crating, and loading goods such as cotton, rice, and indigo that filled their holds. Someday he might sail one of these ships away from the South; first he would see more of his native terrain.

Hinks suggests that Walker's father may have been Anthony Walker, "an Ibo of Nigeria" enslaved, while his mother was a free woman of color. David Walker may have received some education through his religious training or possibly listening to sermons such as those delivered in an earlier time by the great Harry Hosier, a Methodist circuit rider traveling through the region. By the early nineteenth century, Methodism had gained a foothold among African Americans in Wilmington. Its appeal was obvious. The denomination rejected the Calvinistic notion of divine election of earthly souls through which the wealthy and privileged justified their good fortune and the misfortune of others. English theologian John Wesley, whose Methodism greatly influenced religious thought in the colonies, had preached that salvation was offered to all. The appeal of this doctrine beckoned to Walker, who adhered to Methodism throughout his life.

Even the lives of great figures in African American history, such as David Walker, emerge as shadows, so few had the privilege of leaving recorded facts and memories. As one of only several dozen free Black people in Wilmington, Walker lived cheek by jowl with those who were enslaved, witnessing the indignities at close range, viscerally feeling the injustice both of slavery and of the liminal status held by those who were not enslaved, but were tightly restricted and widely despised by those in power. Brilliant and curious, in his young life, Walker's range of possibilities was narrowly circumscribed. There were few social organizations and families of free Blacks to create the kind of community he desired since for free people color in Wilmington, "Black" was functionally synonymous with "slave." Free, but not free. Rejecting these conditions, Walker slipped away to Charleston, a short distance to the south, as soon as he was of an age to do so, younger than twenty years. With so little promise at home, he left his native city, "not only with the plan of improving his employment prospects in a city with hundreds more free blacks, but also with the desire to clarify the meaning of his blackness and freedom in a world dominated by slavery." [3]

Charleston was a place where Walker's condition was less of an anomaly, where he could find a home in a community of those with a similar legal and social status. In Charleston, free and enslaved lived close together, but the numbers of free Black people were sufficient to constitute a community of souls, an aggregate brought together in families, benevolent societies, and commercial enterprises as carpenters, coopers, shoemakers, bricklayers, tailors, boatmen, tanners, farmers, blacksmiths, and, of course, teachers and preachers. Methodist icons John Wesley and George Whitfield had visited South Carolina on several occasions in the previous century, establishing a strong following, particularly among Black worshipers. As C. Eric Lincoln and Laurence H. Mumiya observe:

> The Black Church has no challenger as the cultural womb of the black community. Not only did it give birth to new institutions such as schools, banks, insurance companies, and low income housing, it also provided an academy and arena for political activities, and it nurtured young talent for musical, dramatic, and artistic development. [4]

Partus sequitur ventrem, following the womb—a free mother giving birth to free children and the womb of the church giving birth to freedom, spiritually but also here on the face of the earth, through human agency and action. Both enslaved and free flocked to Sunday services in Charleston, some journeying from the countryside and others from coastal islands by boat. Sunday activities resembled small mass migrations, a day free of work for the enslaved, who vastly outnumbered whites in Charleston. "Church bells disturbed the slumber of the port, as drowsy white Charlestonians hastened to dress for Sunday services. For a small city, Charleston was home to numerous churches and temples, all them erected with the money earned from the sweat of Africans."[5]

Initially, there were no official Black churches, although African-Christian syncretic religious practices took place in the forests and fields. As elsewhere, anxious to escape a secondhand place in the house of the Lord, Black places of worship emerged in public. Those who flocked to the African churches in Charleston displayed their finery: plain Linsey-woolsey (linen and wool) gowns embellished with fine stitchery and collars designed to transform the ordinary into the exceptional, *tignons* and headdresses topped with bright feathers or hats made of woven grasses and adorned with bands of salvaged gingham or colorful trade cloth. Walker may have dressed plainly, while some men donned a vest and coat, adorned with a cravat and pocket handkerchief. The attire that one white observer dubbed excessive and grotesque another described as elegant. The costume certainly functioned to subvert the social hierarchy, to uplift the spirit in preparation for receiving the message of the Lord, and to offer a presentation of self worthy of the Lord's attention.

THE GROWTH OF AFRICAN AMERICAN METHODISM

Peter Hinks's study of antebellum slave resistance reveals:

> Before 1815 black Methodists in Charleston, both slave and free, had conducted their affairs with a good deal of autonomy. Although formally under control of the stationed preacher, black stewards, exhorters, and class leaders actually preached, taught classes, oversaw love feasts, and collected and dispersed funds.[6]

Charleston's Black residents reflected with pride and amazement that an independent African American church had been formed in Philadelphia thirty years earlier. In 1787 Richard Allen and Absalom Jones had broken with the white Methodist church over blatant discrimination to establish the first formal Black religio-political organization in the country, the Free African Society. A period of antagonism between the two—white and Black—branches of the church took the form of direct action, litigation, and appeals to church authority that culminated in the first consecrated African Methodist Church with Allen ordained as its bishop in 1816. But that was Philadelphia, Pennsylvania, where the importation of slaves had long since been abolished, and the continuation of slavery was circumscribed. It was also home to many Quakers, whose longstanding antislavery sentiments held attenuated but powerful sway. Would it be possible to have independent AME churches in Charleston, the heart of Southern slavery?

Chilled by the rising prospects of African American organizing through religious institutions, white church leaders sought to reassert control over every aspect of Charleston's Black religious life, an effort that created an underground resistance movement. Black church leaders quietly traveled to Philadelphia to meet with Richard Allen, who ordained them and gave his blessing for separate AME congregations in Charleston. On their return, they found that white church leaders were attempting to usurp control of the revenues, meetings, and congregations of Black religious gatherings. In response, in excess of four thousand Black churchgoers abandoned the local white parishes in protest and turned to constructing an independent African church.[7]

Douglas Egerton reports that, apocryphal or true, a Reverend Drayton opined that "Whites wanted nothing . . . but a good spanking with a sword."[8] Following a dispute about consecrated burial grounds and separate worship, hundreds were arrested for disorderly conduct while a service was in progress. African American church leaders then petitioned the state legislature to build an autonomous church, and when denied, they defied the state's order. One hundred and forty people were arrested and their leaders imprisoned. The determination to continue building churches met with harassment, intimidation, and arrest for doing so. It is possible but unlikely that David Walker was among those rounded up in this sweep since he was a newcomer, not fully integrated within the community. In any case, he was certainly dropped into this heated, even violent political mayhem. Hinks suggests that Walker may have met Richard Allen at some point and heard him preach. Walker wrote:

> . . . [Allen] has under God planted a Church among us which will be as durable as the foundation of the earth on which it stands. Richard Allen! O my God! The bare recollection of the labors of this man, and his ministers among his deplorable wretched brethren (rendered so by the whites) to bring them to a knowledge of God of Heaven, fills my soul with . . . high emotions . . . When the Lord shall raise up coloured historians in succeeding generations, to present the crimes of this nation, to the then gazing world, the Holy Ghost will make them do justice to the name of Bishop Allen.[9]

The familiarity of the service from his Wilmington days may have been a comfort to young David Walker, new to Charleston and perhaps adrift. As the processional directed clergy and congregation alike to enter and praise, the words of Isaac Watts's well-known hymn may have beckoned him to join in.

> From all that dwell below the skies,
> Let the Creator's praise arise;
> Let the Redeemer's Name be sung,
> Through every land by every tongue.
> In every land begin the song;
> To every land the strains belong;
> In cheerful sounds all voices raise,
> And fill the world with loudest praise.[10]

These thoughts ran through the minds of the parishioners. "Through every land by every tongue . . . in every land begin the song." The teachings of Jesus of Nazareth have long been considered to be revolutionary, perhaps never more so than in Charleston at that time. The Lord's message applied to Africans, Haitians, and other Caribbean nations, and to Euro-Americans alike. The rules of logic applied, moving from general to particular and back again, from the possibility of universal salvation *for all people* to the idea of *equality for each individual*, regardless of race.

The places and times for regular weekday religious study meetings were announced at the end of the service. Making a mental note of the information, Walker would know where to meet like-minded folks in his new community and how to continue his spiritual and intellectual development. Select class leaders taught the weekday sessions that were not tied to the stricter Sunday liturgy. At the evening lessons, David Walker learned more than biblical stories; the exhorters branched into more recent history, local events, and current happenings. Evidence suggests that among the exhorters was Denmark Vesey, a formerly enslaved African previously known as Telemaque.[11] Leaving Sunday services, Walker may have felt uplifted by the experience and even more so had he heard the teachings of Denmark Vesey. From his years as a slave-lieutenant, translator, and cultural interpreter for the slave trader Captain Joseph Vesey, Telemaque gained knowledge of the watery terrain he traversed: the archipelagos, ports, and trading centers. Like James W. Stewart's education on the seas, Telemaque acquired knowledge of vastly different cultures and practices. He had been enslaved in 1781 at age fourteen, and in his time at sea, he learned of slave conspiracies or rebellions in Barbados, Jamaica, and Tobago. Telemaque spent time enslaved by Captain Vesey and then was sold to a planter in Saint-Domingue.[12] When the enslaved man seemed to suffer from epilepsy, the commercial exchange between the enslavers was rescinded in what Patricia J. Williams notes is a contract law involving a redhibitory vice, that is to say, a defect in a product. In the case Williams discusses, the "vice" is "craziness" as evidenced by the "product," an enslaved woman named Kate, said to be defective because she continually runs away. This leads Williams to explore the situational contexts for declaring someone "crazy" or "rational." What makes sense to an enslaved person—seeking freedom—is not coextensive with what makes sense to a slaver.[13] Douglas Egerton argues that Telemaque may have feigned epileptic fits in order to escape the horrors of the plantation in favor of life aboard the ship serving Captain Vesey. A wide-ranging study of oppression identifies the myriad strategies employed to reclaim a measure of freedom. Neil Roberts develops the idea of "freedom as marronage," propelled by the imperative of seeking freedom through flight, by individuals as "fugitive acts of truancy," or collectives, exemplified by the maroons of San Domingue, Jamaica, and elsewhere, who form separate communities and social structures.[14] An example of what Roberts identifies as *petit marronage* is found in Kenneth Marshall's finely articulated account of Yombo, enslaved in New Jersey to Aaron Melick, and others who were similarly situated, who reappropriated their time by running away temporarily, claiming their time to themselves, even if just for a few days.[15] Telemaque's strategy, if indeed it was one, was successful. Captain Vesey returned the purchase price in exchange for Telemaque who spent more time aboard ship acquiring languages and skills. When the captain retired, he settled in Charleston. Remarkably, Telemaque won a lottery enabling him to purchase his freedom, taking up the name of Denmark Vesey as a free man.[16]

David Walker, the man who became Maria Stewart's most important mentor, had his political education nurtured in weekly religious meetings that may have been led by Denmark Vesey. Less formal than Sunday services, weekday sessions provided a wider palette for the individual expression of church exhorters such as Vesey. These assemblies provided an opportunity to craft the distinctive African American thought so closely tied to political action. With his arrival in Charleston, Walker found himself at the center of a political, social, and theological war that spanned a decade or, perhaps, centuries, one that had experienced battles, triumphs, retreats, reversals, and disasters. In the words of the great African American poet Langston Hughes:

> *The folks with no titles in front of their names*
> *all over the world*
> *are raring up and talking back*
> *to the folks called Mister.* [17]

In the ebb and flow of resistance movements, ordinary people subjected to oppression organize and respond, often facing severe backlash from the racist establishment and their foot soldiers. Evidence of this may be witnessed by attending to the attacks by white supremacists on Black churches and church-goers that continue today, two hundred years later. Even more alarmingly, these attacks are accelerating. Targeting the very same historic congregation subjected to attack in the 1800s, the neo-Nazi Dylann Roof entered the Charleston Emanuel AME church in 2015 with a Glock handgun and murdered nine worshippers, including the pastor, Clementa C. Pinckney. A week later, President Barack Obama delivered the eulogy for those who died, singing the 220-year-old hymn "Amazing Grace," a song that may have been raised to the heavens by the ancestors of those who struggle for equal regard and dignity.[18] In the time of Denmark Vesey, every engaged African American in the region, like Walker, would have known the details of the magnificent and brutal struggle between the African Methodist Episcopal movement championed by Reverend Richard Allen and his followers in combat with white authorities in an age of determined resistance.

THE VESEY CONSPIRACY

Historians have had a heyday in a controversy over what happened next. The straightforward account holds that in 1821, when David Walker resided in Charleston, Denmark Vesey, capable carpenter and former mariner, took a leadership role in planning what could have been the largest slave revolt in the history of North America. Intricately designed and inspired in part by the Haitian Revolution, the plan is estimated to have encompassed as many as nine thousand free and enslaved people. Over many months, the leaders strategized a military-style takeover and escape. Weapons were procured or manufactured, roles assigned, and arrangements devised. The orders of the day were to seize and secure the Charleston Meeting Street Arsenal, distribute the weapons, neutralize the opposition, secure the harbor, commandeer boats, and escape to Haiti, but not without first liberating all who were locally enslaved. Vesey was suspicious of those who performed domestic roles, fearing that some would be too closely associated with their slave masters. His suspicions were justi-fied. Before the uprising could take place, indications of the plot were leaked to certain plantation owners and political officials. In response, white militias were formed, and surveillance of Black citizens became excruciatingly intense. Several were taken in for questioning. Among those detained for engineer-ing the plan or being associated with it were Peter Poyas, Rolla Bennett, and Mingo Harth. Some were brutalized in the gruesome and infamous Charleston Workhouse, a torture chamber that included a rack designed to keep to heel recalcitrant slaves who were sent there for an education in white supremacy. Tensions surrounding the planned insurrection grew for weeks on both sides, whites nervously anticipating being slaughtered in their sleep, Blacks waiting for death or the rack. Eventually, tortured testimony revealed the name of Denmark Vesey. Once the crisis came to a head, a "Court of Magistrates and Freeholders" was assembled in the Workhouse, according to the *Official Report*: "For the trial of sundry Negroes apprehended and charged *with attempting to raise an Insurrection amongst the Blacks against the Whites (June 22, 1822)*."[19]

Over one hundred persons were accused. By the time the first set of proceedings concluded, thirty-five accused conspirators were hung, two succumbed in the Workhouse, and another forty or so were deported. Testimony implicated the role of the AME churches, which were swiftly destroyed. Among those sent to the gallows—the African Telemaque—Denmark Vesey.[20] The anti-Black racial violence and executions continued through the summer and beyond. Thus, this particular war ended abruptly with a white victory and the execution of Black leaders, along with the demolition of Black churches and meeting places marking the suppression of a revolutionary plan to liberate South Carolina's beleaguered African Americans. Walker would have witnessed and may have participated in some of the fronts of this battle: confrontations, skirmishes, clashes, direct action protests, ideological disputes, physical and legal attacks. It was clear throughout that religious belief had become the surrogate for political engagement. The underlying terrain for Black political activism was the growing body of systematized thought that comprised Black political theory.

Over the years, some historians have argued that there was no Vesey conspiracy, but rather a conspiracy of the planter class to purge unreliable or potentially dangerous insurgents from their ranks. In the case of the Vesey conspiracy, painstaking documentation and evaluation support the contention that a broad insurrection was planned.[21]

POLITICS AND REBELLION

Whites, especially those in positions of power, were often confounded on the issue of Black Christianity. Black congregants complicated white churches, and full integration was not desirable. Separate Black churches had the advantage of "out of sight, out of mind," but allowing Black worshippers to congregate together outside of white supervision and control could be dangerous. Black churches developed intricate original structures and doctrines. They were tolerated, raided, burned, prohibited, and tolerated again, only to have the cycle start all over. In Charleston and across the South, economic as well as religious understanding influenced views on the Bible. Planters, wealthy entrepreneurs, and all those on the commercial side knew about universal brotherhood, but their universe was attenuated. Christian salvation for Blacks implied the possession of souls, those troublingly disembodied ontological essences that, not being physical, could not have a race or color. One did not need to be a theologian, or even a deep thinker, to see the problem. If Black people were to be "saved," then they had to have souls worthy of salvation, and all souls are created equal unless or until sinfulness makes them otherwise. In opposition to this view, South Carolinian ministers developed "the biblical defense of slavery while pleading for the proper religious instruction of the slaves."[22]

Richard Allen and Absalom Jones had founded the Free African Society in 1787 with both religious and political aims in mind: mutual aid, education, freedom of religious practice, and "from a love of the people of their complexion."[23] Foreshadowing the philosophies of David Walker and Maria W. Stewart, a daily practice of righteousness was part and parcel of their theology, hand in hand with the struggle for political freedom and equality. In fact, throughout African American religious thought, the two spheres have often been thought to be inseparable. Perhaps the most well-articulated version is developed in Reverend James H. Cone's Black liberation theology, the seeds of which are explicitly attributed to the work of David Walker, and so, by extension, to Maria W. Stewart.[24] A central theological tenet holds that the Christian God is first and foremost dedicated to rectifying the lives of the oppressed in the here and now; a theology of hope and action. In the late nineteenth century, Anna Julia Cooper articulated a Black womanist theology. Cooper, for whom God is "a singing something," connects the idea of God with music, a concept threaded through Black theology and political theory.[25]

David Walker, who would become an extraordinary political theorist of the nineteenth century, received his revolutionary education in this cauldron of racial conflict. Drawing on the raw materials of prior centuries of Black thought, Methodist religious teachings, biblical inspiration, experiential knowledge, and his own original ideas, Walker creatively fashioned a distinctive liberation theology and revolutionary political theory leaving a profound impact on the thought of Maria W. Stewart, who credited him explicitly when she wrote:

> Many will suffer for pleading the cause of oppressed Africa, and I shall glory in being one of her martyrs; for I am firmly persuaded that the God in whom I trust is able to protect me from the rage and malice of mine enemies, and from them that will rise up against me; and if there is no other way for me to escape, He is able to take me to himself, as He did the most noble, fearless, and undaunted David Walker.[26]

Stewart underscored the profound importance of Walker's thought with the prophetic statement that "God hath raised you up a Walker and a Garrison. Though Walker sleeps, yet he lives, and his name shall be held in everlasting remembrance."[27] Infused with this liberation theology, Black revolutionary liberalism transformed the radical ideals of John Locke and Thomas Jefferson,

applied perversely in colonial and republican America, into a truly consistent
and universal set of ideas.[28] From a phenomenological standpoint, lived experience plays a crucial role in theory development. Enlightenment philosophies
moved from the particular experiential subject positions of a Locke, Jefferson,
or Paine to abstract principles asserting the *rights of man*. Once established,
liberal theory shed the personal historical framework in favor of what was
then posited as abstract universal law, but which in fact was derived from the
perspective of a narrow, privileged experiential frame. No room was left, then,
for the experiences of others, or Others, one might say. Thus, the rights of man
that fueled eighteenth-century revolutions, once abstracted, left no room for
the experiences of the truly oppressed, failing to embrace three-quarters of
humankind. In contrast, the liberation theologies of Reverend Cone, Anna Julia
Cooper, Stewart, Walker, and others take *as a starting point* the experiences
of the oppressed and in doing so radicalize the liberal principles on which
eighteenth- and nineteenth-century political revolutions were based. These
standpoint epistemologies/phenomenologies expose the epistemic lacunae
created by the experiences and knowledge projects of the privileged.[29]

Egerton writes: "When Walker made his way north for Boston in 1821, Vesey's
message of divinely-inspired revolution sailed with him in a warning to those
modern scholars who tend to exclude slave rebels from the roster of leading
abolitionists."[30] Years later, Walker declared that he could not "remain where
I must hear slaves' chains continually and where I must encounter the insults
of their hypocritical enslavers," and "As true as God reigns, I will be avenged
for the sorrow which my people have suffered." [31]

The confluence of events that took David Walker, James W. Stewart, and
Maria Miller to Boston narrate not just their journeys, but also the larger
story of inspired resistance against the oppression of Black people in the US.
Richard Allen had stirred the religious and revolutionary fervor that blanketed
the country from Philadelphia to Charleston and beyond; likewise, in New
York and New England, the Paul family preached radical equality, agency, and
action on the part of African Americans in the cause of self-liberation. The
brothers, Nathaniel Paul in Albany, Benjamin Paul in New York, and Thomas
Paul in Boston, formed a forward wedge in creating a movement from a mix
of Christian theologies sometimes syncretized in popular practice with African religious beliefs, political awareness, and an ethic of self-reliance that
opened several avenues for Black self-expression. Just as Reverend Allen was
well-known across a wide swathe of states for his work, Maria W. Stewart was
well aware of the Paul brothers, whose activities had either direct or indirect
influence on the daring move she was about to make from provincial Hartford
to a more worldly Boston.

Chapter Ten

"HE REFUSED UNLESS WE WOULD RIDE ON TOP" [1]

Let every female heart become united, and let us raise a fund ourselves; and
at the end of one year and a half, we might be able to lay the corner stone
for the building of a High School, that the higher branches of knowledge
might be enjoyed by us.
—Maria W. Stewart, "Religion and the Pure Principles of Morality" [2]

The Connecticut State Library and Archives reveal little beyond a birth record and offer no further reference to Maria Miller, the most notable absence being documentation of her indenture. Most apprenticeship agreements are contracts for training young, sometimes orphaned white boys to a trade. Indigent black children were more likely to be "taken in" informally.[3] Likewise, the much-desired details of Maria Miller's life just after her indenture are unknown to us; details of her story evade our grasp in the absence of recorded facts at a time when the federal census named only the head of household, usually a man, enumerated age groups, and categorized for race and status: free or slave. Examining the life and work of social justice activist Fannie Barrier Williams (1855–1944), Brittney C. Cooper writes:

> The difficulty in indexing Black women's intellectual progress, [Williams] explained, reflected the fact that "separate facts and figures related to colored women are not easily obtainable," while also revealing a still more fundamental problem, namely, that the "peculiar condition" of Black women rendered them invisible within the intellectual dictates of traditional knowledge production.[4]

We shall see the truth of Cooper and Williams's insights throughout this study, particularly in the quest for knowledge about Black women's roles creating an autonomous church in Boston. The historical record offers bits of data about the drive for independent worship in Hartford, an effort dear to Maria Miller, even as a young woman. When her bound service ended in 1818, she would have continued performing the only work she knew, domestic service, either in the home of the clergyman or in another household. Now she would be paid for her work, not much, making her own way engaged in an activity she loathed:

> O, horrible idea, indeed! To possess noble souls aspiring after high and honorable acquirements, yet confined by the chains of ignorance and poverty to lives of continual drudgery and toil. Neither do I know of any who have enriched themselves by spending their lives as house-domestics, washing windows, shaking carpets, brushing boots, or tending upon gentlemen's tables.[5]

The relegation of so many women to the role of domestic worker and similar service positions make it unsurprising that this theme plays a central role in Black feminist theory. Writing as Maria W. Stewart, she encapsulates the intrinsic connection between coerced domestic labor, "drudgery," and the effort to restrict access to knowledge, leaving women "confined to the chains of ignorance." The hard labor, enforced ignorance, and severe curtailment of leisure time meant that education, intellectual development, and written production were sharply restricted, sometimes entirely out of reach. Yet, as Audre Lorde observes,

> The quality of light by which we scrutinize our lives has direct bearing on the product which we live, and upon the changes we hope to bring about through those lives . . . As we learn to bear the intimacy of scrutiny and to flourish within it, we learn to use the products of that scrutiny for power within our living, those fears which rule our lives and form our silences begin to lose their control over us.[6]

The penetrating analysis that Maria Stewart offers a decade later, once she had matured from life as a nominally free woman in her late teens and early twenties to a published author and intellectual a decade later, reveals the degree to which she has spent that time in what Lorde calls:

> The places of possibility within ourselves [that] are dark because they are ancient and hidden; they have survived and grown strong through that darkness. Within these deep places, each one of us holds an incredible reserve of creativity and power, of unexamined and unrecorded emotion and feeling.[7]

Lorde's observations incisively illuminate the poetic prose of Maria W. Stewart, who is uncomfortably scrutinized and policed in domestic service and who searingly scrutinizes herself, particularly in her *Meditations*. There is no more intimate external scrutiny than that experienced by the domestic worker, matched in Stewart's case by a deep internal self-assessment, creating what Patricia Hill Collins calls an "outsider-within" status, the formation of an epistemic duality, a "unique Black women's standpoint," a part of a critical social theory. "When armed with cultural beliefs honed in Black civil society, many Black women who found themselves doing domestic work often developed distinct views of the contradictions between the dominant group's actions and ideologies."[8]

Stationed within the homes of white employers, assisting with the most intimate forms of care while at the same time being held to the strictest hierarchies of status (race, class, gender), domestic workers develop an ability to perform their duties according to the dictates of the mistress/master/boss overtly with compliance and respect while covertly, or internally, carrying on a near constant evaluation of the features of domination. This means developing a two-ness, what W. E. B. Du Bois calls a "double consciousness," one examining one's own self-representations, and the other, an intimate view of the mechanics of whiteness—how employers view themselves and their servants. This two-ness extends to self-presentation, how those consigned to the serving class present themselves to white people, particularly their employers as well as more broadly, in contrast with the self-presentation within their sympathetic communities.

Absent the leisure of the master to write volumes as he pleases, African Americans were often forced to express the "distillation of experience" in a distillation of words: poetry, song, essays, short prose pieces that make up for what they lack in volume by the density of ideas and expression. There is an economy of intellectual production that would soon be found in Maria W. Stewart's meditations and essays. As she steadily saw to her own intellectual development, her storehouse of ideas grew. Collins provides a comprehensive literature survey of the various intersecting dimensions of Black women's labor, anchoring it thus:

> Maria Stewart's claim that "let our girls possess whatever amiable qualities of soul they may . . . it is impossible for scarce an individual of them to rise above the condition of servants" remains true. U.S. Black women may have migrated out of domestic service in private homes, but as their overrepresentation as nursing home assistants, day-care aides, dry-cleaning workers, and fast-food employees suggests, African American women engaged in low-paid service work is far from a thing of the past.[9]

The small consolation for her continued manual labor after her indenture ended was the opportunity for autonomous engagement in communal spiritual and educational uplift. This tumultuous year in Hartford's history witnessed the displacement of Congregationalism as the established denomination along with the long-overdue creation of a written state constitution. That same year, the missionizing efforts of Congregationalists rebounded from the further reaches of the nation, and the idea came to the ministers to educate their own parish children, that is, ones from the favored race. Sabbath Schools throughout the city soon enrolled five hundred students, but likely none of them was Black, just as the congregations at Sunday services were segregated. The Reverend Jeremiah Asher, who spent time as a servant in Hartford as a young man, wrote: "The practice of excluding people of colour from places of worship or allotting them to separate seats in them, is a most wicked and anti-christian practice, tending more than anything else to perpetuate the feeling of prejudice against them."[10]

Responding to the wave of political change inspired by Richard Allen, the Paul brothers, and the movement for independent black churches:

> In 1819, a group of African Americans in Hartford grew weary of being assigned seats in the galleries and in the rear of churches and decided to begin worshiping on their own in the conference room of the First Church of Christ, now Center Church, in Hartford. This would become the first black Congregational Church in Connecticut, the third oldest in the nation.[11]

The combination of her religious upbringing in service, where she "had the seeds of piety and virtue sown early," her natural spiritual inclinations, and her deepening analysis of racial injustice drew Maria Miller to this new congregation where she studied the Bible, developed her nascent literary skills, and learned the art of exegesis.[12] Having secured space for a Sabbath School, the African Religious Society turned to the idea of building a separate house of worship, a hope that, frustratingly, would have to wait. Miller's desire to learn in this setting allowed for a slightly more formal education in the stuffy schoolroom than she received culling bits of learning in the preacher's home. While it ignited embers of hope for expanding her horizons, she remained resentful, feeling the sting of being "deprived of the advantage of education, though my soul thirsted for knowledge."[13] By the age of twenty, she had exhausted the lessons that the Sabbath School could provide. How liberated would she feel from the confining bonds of domestic service and the provinciality of Hartford if she left her home? Steeped in biblical stories of Moses and the exodus of the Jews overlaid with accounts of Black churches along the Eastern seaboard, she cultivated visions of travel to a city with a proper place for African Americans to worship. It would take three more years before she could realize this dream.

Thomas Paul, founder of the African Baptist Church in Boston. Ordained in New Hampshire in 1805, Reverend Paul soon became the first minister of the African Baptist Church in in Boston. Three of the Paul brothers were moving forces in Black ministries in New York and New England. Reverend Paul officiated at the marriage of Maria Miller and James W. Stewart in 1826. Painting by Thomas Badger (1792–1868) circa 1825. From the Smithsonian National Portrait Gallery. Public Domain.

Venturing out would require a delicate combination of persuasion, practicality, subdued hope, and intense determination. A young woman of Miller's youth and piety may not have been eager to travel alone. By 1825, at age twenty-two, her studies at the African Sabbath School were behind her, and she had been an independent worker for many years. It was time to put her plans into action.

Northern independent Black religious communities stretched from Portsmouth to Philadelphia. Many preachers were peripatetic, traveling frequently, spreading the word, and fighting injustices. As transportation improved, some traveled regularly between Boston, Hartford, New York, Philadelphia, and beyond. In her community, Miller came into contact with preachers, laborers, and dignitaries traveling through Hartford, stopping for a few days to speak with local community members or to attend the African Religious Society meetings. Absorbing this broader worldview and acquiring the skills that resulted from greater independence, Miller formulated an ambitious plan to travel to Boston, where she knew that instead of a room tucked away in the Congregational Church, there was a magnificent meeting house built through the labor of its congregants and overseen by the great minister and organizer, the Reverend Thomas Paul, who was in the *avant-garde* of the movement for Black liberation.

THE PAULS

Four of the six Paul brothers from Exeter, New Hampshire, became prominent Baptist religious leaders. The eldest, Thomas, engaged in groundbreaking religious organizing, initiating his preaching in New Hampshire in the early 1800s, and was soon ordained. A confluence of dedicated and resourceful Black community leaders had converged in Boston, in a fury about discrimination in the local white churches. They formed a committee that would first create a religious society and then commence with the steps required to build an independent church. With alacrity, hard labor, and determination, the edifice was raised with Paul named as pastor in 1805. While "Mother Bethel" in Philadelphia was the oldest Black Methodist Church, having been established in 1794, the church in Boston became the first independent African Baptist church in the North. Word of Thomas Paul's success in the Baptist ministry spread through Northern communities on a par with that of Richard Allen for the Methodists. Paul traveled widely, including to New York City, where there was "[a] colony of colored members from the First Baptist Church, then meeting in Gold Street. It was constituted July 5, 1809. It was a small band at the commencement of only eighteen members, and for several years they had no settled pastor."[14]

According to J. Carleton Hayden: "Such was [Thomas Paul's] prestige as a pastor that some Negroes in New York City who desired a separation from a white Baptist church invited him to establish there a Negro Baptist church."[15] Paul "traveled extensively as a spiritual and social reformer, ministering to blacks in New England and in New York and speaking out for racial justice and freedom." He came through Hartford on his travels to NYC.[16] In 1815 he sailed to England with a contingent of Prince Hall Masons where they met with abolitionist luminaries William Wilberforce and Thomas Clarkson. The movement in England received impetus from the writings and lectures of Black thinkers and activists, including formerly enslaved Africans Olaudah Equiano, who published *The Interesting Narrative of the Life of Olaudah Equiano, or Gustavus Vassa, The African* in 1789, and (Quobna) Ottobah Cugoano, who published *Thoughts and Sentiments on the Evil and Wicked Traffic of Slavery and Commerce of Human Beings* in 1787 and "argued that human beings could flourish naturally and that their dehumanization was caused by pernicious institutions of civil society."[17] The strength of the movement in Great Britain provided hope for the missionaries returning to the United States and resonated from the knowledge that liberated Africans were forwarding the movement. Paul drew on his skills as a social organizer and early proponent of liberation theology, blending the forces of fraternal societies such as the Free Masons, religious organizations such as the African religious societies, and sympathetic white Baptist societies to sponsor his political and religious mission work.

In keeping with the family tradition, in Albany, New York, the Reverend Nathaniel Paul helped to establish the African Church Association in 1820 and became the pastor in 1822, opening a Sunday School and then the Wilberforce School.[18] In 1823, Reverend Paul traveled to Haiti, where he met with President Jean-Pierre Boyer to confer about missionizing efforts and emigration plans, following in the steps of Paul Cuffe in the earnest and not unfounded belief that Africans in America would never achieve full equality. His younger brother, Benjamin, became part of the New York City congregation, and after his ordination, the Rev. Benjamin Paul became its pastor in 1824.[19]

So, in 1824, Paul would have traveled through Hartford to New York City for his brother's installation as the minister of the First Baptist Church. It would not have been unusual, then, to spend time with members of the Black community in Connecticut. For dedicated listeners, Paul's stories about his visits to England and Haiti would have relegated the universe that was Hartford to a much smaller, satellite status. He told of places across the ocean: the rejected motherland, England, its determined abolitionists, and the free Black nation of Haiti governed by former slaves. For Miller, her possibilities seemed greater and more real than ever, and she may have there and then hatched a plan for a move to Boston to be executed as soon as possible. What once had been a world that stretched from the parlor to the slop heap and at the outer reaches the market and the great Connecticut riverside, her imagination now encompassed a globe of immense proportions containing lands in Africa where Black people reigned supreme, to Great Britain, a powerful empire with a strong abolition movement, and to Haiti, a country where African slaves had overthrown their oppressors to become a self-determining nation. It provided an opportunity for her to follow Audre Lorde's injunction to "respect those hidden sources of power from where true knowledge, and therefore, lasting action comes."[20]

DEPARTING FOR BOSTON

Maria Miller was simply too thoughtful, rational, and planful to rush away on her own to an unknown city with no employment or living arrangements. The idea to set out on her own formed in her mind months or even years before she executed her plan. She would need an occupation, and while she clearly loathed domestic service, this was the skill she had to trade and was something for which she could provide a reference. Suppose, then, that her plans were developed over the course of several visits from her Virgilian transporter, perhaps Reverend Paul, or someone else who was reliable, connected, and sufficiently virtuous to be trusted in this way, someone spending days in Hartford, discussing recent developments: African Societies, independent churches, Masonic Lodges, an entire community, long-formed but now expanding, coalescing into organizations, each appealing to slightly different audiences but all with the overriding goal of improving the lot of African Americans. She may have found assistance from someone who was passing through and then returning to Hartford at some later time. Spinning her plans, she found the prick and sting of continued domestic labor soothed by the prospect of change. Letters were written, introductions made, a position secured with a family that desired service from someone long-trained, polite, and pious. She would need housing, and Miller may have secured live-in service, or she may have used one of the many boarding houses in Belknap Street on Beacon Hill, Boston. She had saved—frugality in her nature—to pay for transportation and resettlement. Miller's contemporary Nancy Prince recalls the indignity and discomfort when she and her sister wished to take a stagecoach, but the driver, "refused unless we would ride on top. It was very cold and we had never rode in that way; his inhumanity grieves me even now." Prince records her experience of being refused entrance to the carriage cab:

> It was very cold; I had sent my mother my wages the week before, and what money I had, I had taken in advance, of my employers. We were greatly embarrassed when a colored man, unknown to us, penetrated our difficulty, and asked us if we had two dollars; we told him we had; he very kindly took us to the stage office, and we bargained for a horse and sleigh to carry us to Salem, where we arrived safely in about two hours and a half.[21]

Could Maria Miller afford a separate carriage, or was she forced to ride on top in the bitter weather? It is doubtful that Miller could afford a private conveyance for this longer journey. In a public conveyance would she be *refused unless we would ride upon the top*?[22] Fortunately, turnpike and carriage improvements had shortened the distance to Boston from an entire week to a mere day and a half. Timing was everything. Unless other passengers were inordinately tolerant, she would be forced to ride on the outside of the carriage. Good weather was devoutly to be wished. Still, roadways were generally so terrible that at certain times of year they were nearly impassable. Winter travel was good because the roads were frozen—but even with heating pans, the carriage was frigid, particularly if one was seated outside. Late spring could be muddy and treacherous. By May, the sun may have dried the roads, but by my calculations, she must have arrived at least by April.[23] What was the nature of Miller's good-byes to acquaintances in Hartford? Some may have found inspiration from her example; others may have feared for her safety. Did she visit the reverend and his family, or had her new community of fellows entirely supplanted the acquaintances of her youth? When Maria Miller left Hartford, the edifice of an independent African Church destined to become the African American Talcott Street Church in Hartford was close to fruition. When she arrived on Beacon Hill and made her way to the African Meeting House, she would enter a structure that was youthful, but not in its infancy—almost twenty years old—still sparkling like new from the care lavished by its proud parishioners, but also a real *established* African American church.

Chapter Eleven

"THE SUN HAS RISEN GLORIOUSLY UPON THE EARTH"[1]

Around the time that Maria Miller moved to Boston in 1826, the center of activity for prominent and middle-class whites had shifted away from the seediness of the harbor, favoring instead the inland side of the three hills. The Old State House had been abandoned in favor of Bulfinch's more commanding new construction atop Beacon Hill. Miller had walked past the Connecticut State House many times as a young girl, but the Hartford building, also designed by Bulfinch, did nothing to prepare her for the grander new State House poised on the rise with its Revere-made gleaming copper dome. One day she would live in its shadow and reflected light where she could look away from the original Otis Federal mansion and view the imposing red-brick structure perched atop the flattened hilltop, lifting her head and craning her neck to see its copper sphere. But of all the grand and humble places in this great city on a hill, only one caused her pulse to quicken.

The coach's uncomfortable journey ended, and its passenger, Maria Miller, may have had a lonely walk to her planned destination or, more reassuringly, she may have been met by someone, perhaps Catherine Waterhouse Paul, wife of the Reverend Thomas Paul, to welcome her and inquire about her journey: cold and disquieting, her arrival full of promise. Once her lodgings were settled, she sought out the true destination of her journey. Exhilarated by the very thought of a church built by and for people of African descent, Maria Miller hastened in that direction. I imagine her, heels clicking on the cobblestone, rounding the corner from Belknap Street into Smith Court, the crisp spring air and elevation on the hill carrying away the foul smells of rotting fish and sewage from the river.[2] Glancing up at the brick edifice, she may have been emotionally overwhelmed. Is this what it feels like to enter heaven? The humble brick structure seemed grand, her people resembling the angels themselves, streaming through the double doors. Children wearing awkward suits of piety. As a newcomer, she may have taken a place in the balcony gazing down at the nave, flooded with light from the clerestory windows. It was crowded with regular congregants. Brightly painted walls gleamed, and the polished cherry wood rails shone. The altar and pulpit were simple, as befitted the faith. For Miller it was a communion of her people. Did she raise her hand to her brow, shielding her face from the Lord's view, so swelled was she from that worst of sins, the one that sent the holiest Lucifer to become an original inhabitant of the abyss? Still, can pride in the Lord, His people, His house be such a terrible thing?

The sanctuary may have been where she first met her husband-to-be, the aging mariner, James W. Stewart. Maria Miller longed for few things in life: steady religious devotion, a small measure of comfort, and a release from servitude. Beyond that she prayed for justice in this world and the next and sought knowledge of the world beyond the cooking hearths and pantries, the washtubs and sooty grates of those whom she was forced to serve. Worldly knowledge was etched into the physical being of James W. Stewart—his weathered face, his uneven gait, his dark eyes and worn smile. He was attracted by her pleasing appearance but also by the defiant independence she displayed even as a young woman willing to set out on her own and by her crystalline intelligence. Their courtship may have consisted of a series of walks, well within the public eye, perhaps in groups of others enjoying the spring air. Their conversations would have been intense, moving from their personal stories to observations about the city and its history as well as current events. His decade in Boston gave James W. Stewart knowledge of the city's proud revolutionary and maritime history, as well as revealing its less savory underbelly.

BOSTON IN THE LATE SEVENTEENTH AND EARLY EIGHTEENTH CENTURIES

In the decades prior to Maria Miller's and James Stewart's arrivals in Boston, the land rising away from the harbor formed a pastoral sweep revealing little of the city's urban character. Not so for the waterfront. The bucolic scene ended well before the harbor, which thrummed with the commotion of the seaport, a nerve center of commerce and trade. The city had grown up around the Massachusetts State House, the brick edifice in Dock Square that overlooked the schooners, packet boats, and the dinghies that shuttled back and forth between the anchored ships and the piers. Every form of humanity swarmed the harbor, from seamen to stevedores, hucksters, and titans of commerce, all a part of James Stewart's sphere of operation. The land had first been occupied by the thriving Indigenous settlements of the Massachusett, soon decimated by disease and colonial aggression, then by European traders and religious refugees,

Crispus Attucks, the first martyr of the American Revolution, King (now State) Street, Boston, March 5th, 1770. Schomburg Center for Research in Black Culture, Manuscripts, Archives and Rare Books Division, The New York Public Library, Digital Collections. Accessed October 16, 2020. http://digitalcollections.nypl.org/items/510d47db -e3a9-a3d9-e040-e00a18064a99.

eventually becoming the seat of the British royal government. The harborside State House was the platform for James Otis, whose speech sowed the seeds of revolution and who, according the revered Black historian William G. Nell, "boldly asserted the rights, not only of the white, but of the black man," radical words that, once manifested in the reality of the revolution, promoted only the rights of privileged white men rebelling against British colonial rule. Nearby, Otis's sister, Mercy Otis Warren had entertained the Sons of Liberty, written plays and political tracts, and penned the first history of the revolution, another person lost to history despite her considerable contributions.[3]

In the street below the Old State House, Crispus Attucks, "the noble colored man, who fell in King street before the muskets of tyranny, way in the dawn of our Revolution," became the first casualty of the War of Independence when he was shot and killed by British soldiers in the Boston Massacre. Here also, in July 1776, a "Son of Liberty," Colonel Thomas Crafts read the Declaration of Independence from the balcony to a crowd gathered below. For many of the Black activists of the day who supported independence, the document had profound implications about freedom and equal rights, a work later examined so eloquently by Maria W. Stewart, who urged her audiences to "possess the spirit of independence," declaring "WE CLAIM OUR RIGHTS," just as David Walker argued for the rights of man.[4] In the period just prior to Maria Miller's arrival in Boston, while the docks and harbor were throbbing with activity, the Boston Common was an outpost for farms and grazing. John Hancock and the artist John Singleton Copley had laid claim to most of the farmland on and around the hill that for decades boasted a beacon, a light that could be seen far out into Cape Cod Bay. In the geography of the city, the "Tremont" or three "mountains" were in truth just large hills dominating the early landscape on the Boston side of the Charles River. These geological landmarks suffered the ongoing indignity of having their tops sliced off and their gravelly peaks unceremoniously dumped into the river, filling in the Shawmut peninsula to create more space for urban growth. In time, the village-like character of the city vanished in a frenzy of construction propelled by gentleman-architect Charles Bulfinch and the ambitious developers who were his partners. It was Bulfinch whose skill was in "transforming an eighteenth-century town into a nineteenth century city."[5] By 1805 Bulfinch had redesigned Faneuil Hall, nicknamed "the Cradle of Liberty," with its great chamber above an arcade of markets and stalls below, the city fathers apparently "undaunted by proximity of sausage on the rack."[6] It had been built as a gift for the city by wealthy trader Peter Faneuil, owner of the *Jolly Batchelor* and *Merchant Prince* vessels. Faneuil made his fortune in the Triangle Trade that transported manufactured goods from Europe to Africa, carried bound and tortured humans to the Americas, and completed its neat, geometrical figure by taking tobacco, sugar, and cotton to Europe. In his landmark 1944 study of slave ship mutinies, Lorenzo J. Greene writes of "desperate attempts by the slaves to regain their liberty."

> A more celebrated case was that of the Jolly Bachelor, a slave ship belonging to Peter Fanueil, his brother-in-law, John Jones, and Captain Cutler of Boston. While taking on slaves in the Sierra Leone River in March 1742, the vessel, according to George Burchall, was attacked and captured by the natives. In the fight Captain Cutler and two of his men were killed. The Negroes stripped the vessel of its rigging and sails, freed the slaves in the hold, then abandoned the ship.[7]

A heroic insurrection, this early revolt by West Africans resisting the Middle Passage is but one example of the constant, fierce struggle against enslavement. Yet this case underscores the profitability of human trafficking even in the face of such setbacks, along with the role played by still-revered Bostonians. Greene notes, "Seldom has there been a more lucrative commerce" as Faneuil was able to recover the vessel, refit it, and sell it for a substantial sum. A flood of historical cases reveals the determination of those who were kidnapped to exercise their agency in remaining free and independent people whatever the cost. In the face of such wrongs, Maria Stewart sometimes counsels action and at other times counsels patience because of her firm belief in ultimate divine retribution.

> I have seen the wicked in great power, spreading himself like a green bay tree . . . and it is God alone that has inspired my heart to feel for Afric's woes. Then fret not yourselves because of the evil doers. Fret not yourselves because of the men who bring evil devices to pass: for they shall be cut down as the grass, and wither as the green herb.[8]

Like the other colonies-become-states, Massachusetts bore a lengthy and disgraceful history of slavery and the trade, one that is only beginning to be recovered in the twenty-first century as pressure is brought to bear on cities and universities to acknowledge their roots.

THE SLAVE TRADE IN BOSTON

As Maria Miller and James W. Stewart gazed out at the harbor filled with seafaring vessels, he may have recounted to her some of the stories from his time as a merchant mariner prior to the War of 1812 and then his astounding exploits during and after the war. The affidavits and other documents from the end of her long life reveal that she was quite familiar with James Stewart's history—a lifetime of experiences that would take a multitude of conversations to cover, on topics and with analyses utterly new to her. Pacific Islands known for cultures, flora, and fauna barely dreamed of in New England. Life and death battles on the sea. Countries where Christianity was virtually unknown. Deserts stretching up to the shores. Islands where enslaved Africans overthrew their European masters. Viewing the bay crowded with ships of designs she had never seen in Hartford, they may have imagined the arrival of the first Europeans and Africans, and the myriad actions and reactions of Indigenous peoples, Wampanoag, Nipmuc, Nauset, and Massachusett, who made their homes in this harsh climate.

Even prior to Peter Faneuil's lucrative exploits, the first slave ship, the *Desire*, sailed into Boston harbor in 1638, only eight years after John Winthrop's *Arabella* carried Puritans to shore, inspired by Jesus's words from the Sermon on the Mount that they shall build a Christian "City upon a Hill." The slave ship *Desire*. Desire for what, one wonders. Wealth? Labor? Domination? Cruelty? The name perfectly evokes the imaginations of those who were saturated with visions of New World prosperity, rich in natural resources, but lacking the ready labor forces supplied in the homeland by the English working classes. In Europe, labor could be easily exploited. In the New World, particularly after the

View of Boston in 1848 from East Boston. Print. Edwin Whitfield (1816–1892). Boston Public Library. *Digital Commonwealth*, https://ark.digitalcommonwealth.org/ark:/50959/000003203 (accessed October 16, 2020).

devastation of native populations, cheap—in fact free—labor was imported in the form of stolen and tortured human souls. The *Desire* is a perfect emblem of Christian coloniality: it transported native Pequot "prisoners of war" to the West Indies in exchange for captured West Africans to be brought to the North American continent.

In *Stamped from the Beginning: The Definitive History of Racist Ideas in America*, Ibram X. Kendi encapsulates the political thought of the colonizers. "The first generation of Puritans began rationalizing the enslavement of these 'Negroes' without skipping a beat . . . [S]ome British settlers of colonial America carried across the sea Puritan, biblical, scientific, and Aristotelian rationalizations of slavery and human hierarchy."[9]

A poem attributed to a writer called "Africus" that was printed in the March 14, 1828, edition of the Black newspaper *Freedom's Journal* captures the sentiment expressed by Kendi:

> Can a land of Christians so pure!
> Let demons of slavery rave!
> Can the angel of mercy endure,
> The pitiless—tears of a SLAVE!

By 1687, a report from a French Protestant refugee in Boston relates:

> Among others we met a Ship belonging in La Rochelle [France] which was coming from Martinique laden with sugar, and which had previously made a voyage to Guinea, when it had brought one hundred and fifty Negroes, and two Capuchin Fathers who had been obliged to abandon their Post in Guinea, In View of the little Progress they made there.

Evidently, given the abduction and slaughter of their countrymen, the religious message of the French missionaries had not been well received. Forsaking their charge, the priests were forced to witness firsthand the contradiction inherent in swapping out their Christianizing mission for another European practice, conveying humans into slavery. The foreign visitor blithely observed the degree to which seventeenth-century settlers relied upon enslaved labor: "You can bring with you hired Help in any Vocation whatever; there is absolute need of them to till the Land. You may also own Negroes and Negresses; there is not a House in Boston, however small may be its Means, that has not one or two."[10]

The imposed unfreedom of the Africans was a boon for the wealthy and even for poorer farmers and simple merchants who had access to the kind of labor never dreamed of in England. Early Boston was thus domestically integrated while maintaining strict racial hierarchies. The Faneuil family was one among many who became wealthy from the Triangle Trade, exporting rum, lumber, and other local products to traders in West Africa who ensnared those unfortunate enough to be captured and transported in return. Those who survived the tortuous transatlantic journey were often taken to the West Indies and "seasoned"—tortured and "trained" for enslavement—and later transported to the American continents or left for brutal labor on plantations in the Caribbean. Trade vessels such as Faneuil's were loaded with sugar to be distilled in New England's rum factories. Feeding the public's insatiable desire for liquor and sugar for their tea, Faneuil's marketplace and Great Hall lay opposite granite blocks rising from the dust just as Maria Miller arrived in Boston. The newly minted construction of the Quincy Market was a massive and impressive pile designed to dazzle both merchants and buyers, one that failed to impress Bostonians, who were jaded even then, many of whom mocked it as a folly sprouted from the fertile imagination of their mayor, Josiah Quincy. And Faneuil Hall stands today, its name a disturbing memorial to the systematic oppression wrought by its namesake and his brethren.[11]

ECONOMICS, RELIGION, AND RACIAL UPLIFT

From the formation of the African Society in 1796 to the construction and opening of the African Baptist Church in 1806; from the education of children in his home by Primus Hall to the education of children in the basement schoolroom of the church; from economic growth to the growth of the congregation and increased social cohesion, Boston's Black community was becoming stronger, more stable, and more middle class. No longer were residents confined to waterfront boarding houses where many of the sailors lived only briefly before shipping out again. Prior to the construction of the church, discrimination and reprehensible treatment had led many of Boston's Black residents to worship either in their homes or, on certain weekdays, in Faneuil Hall. An accumulation of incidents studded the systematic racism that pervaded white religious practice, evidenced by that endured by Revolutionary War veteran James Easton. Easton owned an iron works factory and was known for his virtue and intelligence. And yet, as William C. Nell relates:

> Mr. Easton [and his] family were victims however, to the spirit of color-phobia, then rampant in New England, and were persecuted even to the dragging out of some of the family from the Orthodox [Bridgewater] church, in which, on its enlargement, a porch had been erected, exclusively for colored people. After this disgraceful occurrence, the Easton's left the church. They afterwards purchased a pew in the Baptist Church at Stoughton Corner, which excited a great deal of indignation. Not succeeding in their attempt to have the bargain cancelled, the people tarred the pew. The next Sunday the family carried seats in the waggon. The pew was then pulled down; but the family sat in the aisle.[12]

The painfully aggressive racism wounded and scarred members of the community while building an attitude of resistance that became instilled in the culture, a stubborn refusal to accept the blatant hypocrisy, a desire to meet bigoted ignorance with steadfast moral superiority, an inner knowledge of righteousness and indignation, akin to what W. E. B. Du Bois a century later termed double consciousness—an awareness of self and simultaneously an awareness of the disapprobation of others, in this case converted into a steady determination to confront injustice.

No doubt affected by this treatment, in later years, James Easton's son, the Reverend Hosea Easton, published *A Treatise on the Intellectual Character, and Civil and Political Condition of the Colored People of the U. States: and with the Prejudice Exercised Towards Them: With a Sermon on the Duty of the Church to Them* (1837).[13] In their remarkable series, *History of Philosophy without Any Gaps*, Peter Adamson and Chike Jeffers call Easton "an uncommonly systematic thinker, one who opposed slavery and racial division with creative and challenging arguments about the nature of racial prejudice."[14] Exploring the nature of causality in human thought, Easton argues that slavery is itself the cause of prejudice, not African ancestry.

> Legal codes, however oppressive, have never as yet been able to crush the aspiring principles of human nature. The real monster, slavery, cannot long exist, where it is sustained by legal codes only . . . When public sentiment, therefore, has become so morally, civilly, and politically cor-

rupted by the principles of slavery, as to be determined in crushing the objects of its malignity, it is under the necessity of calling prejudice to its aid, as an auxiliary to its adopted formal code of wickedness, clothed like a semi-devil, with all the innate principles of the old dragon itself.

Both inspired and discouraged by his father's experiences, Hosea Easton became a philosopher of race; yet the roots of prejudice were as often economic as they were metaphysical. Nell describes the long-term economic enterprise of James Easton's manufacturing firm:

> [I]ntent were the parties in carrying out the principle of intelligent, active freemen, that they sacrificed every thought of comfort and ease to the object. The most rigid economy was adhered to, at home and abroad. A regular school was established for youth connected with the factory; the rules of morality were supported with surprising assiduity, and ardent spirits found no place in the establishment.

But "the enterprise ended in a total failure ... by reason of the repeated surges of the tide of prejudice," which in various ways deliberately destroyed his efforts.[15] Economic attacks on the advancement of Black people were identified perhaps most forcefully by Ida B. Wells a hundred years later as she lifted the veil on false reports of Black sexual assault against white women, the most prominent excuse for lynching as a punishing extrajudicial method of maintaining an iron grip of control over Black people.[16] Wells exposed the economic motivations for violence, enacted under the pretense of protecting white women's virtue. In a crucial dimension, often underappreciated except in antiracist socialist analyses, racism became a means for white economic advancement, a way of eliminating competition both in market/capitalist ventures and in the labor force. James Easton's self-reliant entrepreneurship was denied success, as is often the case today, by the deliberate actions of those who controlled a political, economic, and judicial system structured on the basis of race, gender, and class.
Maria Stewart writes:

> ... [L]ook at many of the most worthy and most interesting of us doomed to spend our lives in gentleman's kitchen's. Look at our young men, smart, active and energetic, with souls fueled with ambitious fire; as they look forward, alas! What are their prospects? They can be nothing but the humblest laborers.[17]

As she made acquaintances in the community, newly arrived in Boston, Maria Miller built her knowledge base about the mechanisms of exploitation. She eagerly queried those whom she met about economics, religion, and law and who just as eagerly filled her in about the Easton family and others, tragic and heroic. Orality was a currency of the day. For those who had familiarity and a sense of the community, a new ear increased the opportunity to teach, inform, and weave a history of the past with an eye to the future.

Chapter Twelve

"THE CIRCLE OF YOUR ACQUAINTANCE"

O woman, woman! Upon you I call; for upon your exertions almost
entirely depends whether the rising generation shall be any thing more
we have been or not. O woman, woman! Your example is powerful, your
influence great: it extends over your husbands and your children, and
throughout the circle of your acquaintance.
—Maria W. Stewart, *An Address Delivered Before The Afric-American Female Intelligence Society of America* (1832) [1]

In the spirit of the dialectic, my research for this project has brought me to two
conflicting and equally true conclusions. First, the state of the records about
the lives and history of African Americans—or lack thereof—is abominable,
and that a surprising number of records, research papers, books and journal
articles have been produced, if only one digs deeply enough and casts a wide-
enough net to find them.[2] Census records, city directories, church records,
firsthand histories, minutes of meetings, published pamphlets, organizational
charters and by-laws, sermons and religious writings join with the many excellent secondary sources ranging across more than two hundred years of history.
Nineteenth-century accounts like those from Maria W. Stewart and William
Cooper Nell join with more recent materials such as James and Lois Horton's
Black Bostonians and the meticulous Historic Resource Study of the Boston
African American National Historic Site to name just a few. Some secondary
sources have different political agendas and ideological frames. The challenge
for the researcher is to negotiate the gaps with an eye to filling some of them
with carefully constructed narratives. Undertaking the research to uncover
Maria Miller's circle of acquaintances is a step towards reconstructing a dedicated community of political activists at one of the most important periods of
autonomous Black organizing in the history of the nation.

Entering the fold of the African American community, Maria Miller met the
family of the Reverend Thomas Paul, minister of the African Baptist Church; his

wife, Catherine Waterhouse Paul; and their children, Ann Catherine, Thomas Jr., and Susan, who was a few years younger than Miller, nearly her contemporary. Exploring their shared love of music, Miller may have mentioned the Hartford clergymen who had compiled and published a collection of the hymns she learned as a child, the two women comparing the merits of various melodies or the poetic beauty of the psalms. Her musical aptitude and leadership skills destined Susan Paul for a remarkable career as an author and choirmaster of the Juvenile Choir of Boston, a group of children who performed at antislavery events around the city.[3] For many in this religious tradition, music provided a pathway to salvation and a medium for closeness to the deity. In the words of Anna Julia Cooper writing later in the century, it felt as though God might be "a singing something." Karen Baker-Fletcher has undertaken a reclamation project of Black women's intellectual traditions reviving the work of Maria W. Stewart, Jarena Lee, Anna Berry Smith, and Anna Julia Cooper, preachers and philosophers who developed a theology, or, following Reinhold Niebuhr, a theographia, that animates vocality and related forms of expression with divine power. Baker-Fletcher's "womanist reflection," aims "to construct an ethics of virtue or *power*," citing the Latin notion of virtue not as passive but as *active* engagement.[4] "Womanism" is another term for Black feminism, described by Alice Walker:

> 1. Womanism, from womanish . . . usually referring to outrageous, audacious, courageous, of *willful* behavior . . . 2 . . . a woman who loves other women, sexually and/or non/sexually . . . Committed to survival and wholeness of entire people, male and female . . . 3. Loves music . . . Loves the spirit . . . Loves struggle . . . Womanist is to feminist as purple is to lavender.[5]

Baker-Fletcher attributes to Anna Julia Cooper's biblical interpretations an affirmation of "the equality of the races and nations and of women with men" and connects womanist theology with Toni Morrison's concepts of power as "making do," as "tar"—the ability to hold things together, as the power of memory, and as the power of regeneration. In her writings and speeches, Maria Stewart will draw upon creative engagement, the memory of past accomplishments of Blacks and women, and the regenerative power of religious commitment as ways of seeking justice. She will use hymns heuristically and as prayerful pauses between her reflections to exemplify themes of spiritual development. Like Maria Stewart and Anna Julia Cooper, a significant number of contemporary Black feminists such as Angela Y. Davis, Morrison, Baker-Fletcher, and Valerie C. Cooper take music to be central to their theorizing as do other Black feminists in contemporary scholarly and popular realms.[6]

Delving into this vibrant community, Miller's life was enriched by her acquaintance with Catherine Paul, who was a source of knowledge about local history. Catherine Waterhouse was seventeen when she married Thomas Paul, shortly after his ordination in 1805 in Exeter, New Hampshire, and just before the consecration of the African Baptist Church. A stone set in the brick edifice announced that the African Meeting House had been completed by members of the community, "A Gift to Cato Gardner. First Promoter of this Building, 1806." The church was

> . . . officially constituted on 8 August 1805 with twenty-four members, fifteen of whom were women. It is not yet clear whether all available sources have been consulted, but to date only the names of the male members—Scipio Dalton, Abraham Fairfield, James Broomfield, Charles Bailey, Richard Winslow, John Basset, Obediah Robbins, Thomas Paul, and Cato Gardner—have been identified.[7]

In their efficacy supporting church construction, women outnumbered men; however, in keeping with general practices of erasure, their names were not recorded, the occlusion emblemizing the tendency in historic documentation to elevate, as Brittney Cooper says, "the study of Great Race Men as the primary paradigmatic frame through which scholars understand African American history and African American knowledge production."[8] This observation is not intended to diminish the contributions of the men named here; on the contrary, we should know more about all the contributors and are fortunate to have this record; however, although more women than men contributed to the church's founding, we do not know with any certainty who these women were. The story that comes to us of this period—the late eighteenth century and early nineteenth century—is that a constellation of activists consolidated their efforts to fashion the core institutions of their rising community beginning with the Prince Hall Masons in the 1780s and the Boston African Society, a mutual aid group formed in 1796, but both groups—for which there are extant records—excluded women. As ongoing social and political organizing led to building the church, a key step in creating a space where members could safely express their full humanity along with their ideas and desires for the future. Women were central to that effort. We are left to tease out what we can from the resources available.

From her growing group of acquaintances, Miller learned the genealogies of local families. Among church founders and their spouses, some of whom may be among the unnamed original supporters, Catherine Paul had met Rosanna Haven Dalton when she first moved to Boston. Rosanna's husband had helped to form the African Baptist Society. Grover and da Silva note that

"Scipio Dalton, freed by Isaac Smith in 1783, was one of the forty-four founding members of the African Society in 1796 and had married Rosanna Haven in 1797."[9] Rosanna and Scipio Dalton were married by Reverend Thatcher in the Brattle Street Church. When Rosanna passed at a young age, Dalton married Sylvia Lathrop. Many women did not survive the process of giving birth, and many infants died with their mothers or survived to be raised by sisters, grandmothers, even daughters, already burdened. Rosanna Dalton may have been one of the fifteen unnamed women who were charter members of this groundbreaking place of worship.[10] Among the other founders, James Bromfield (Broomfield), who passed away the year Miller arrived, had married Susy Mitchel (or Susey Mitchell), who may have been another of the church founders, along with Mary Bassett (1781–1831), whose husband, John Hingham, was a seaman out of Marblehead. There was also Sally Allen, who married Abraham Fairfield in March 1805, Reverend Thomas Baldwin officiating. Another charter member, Richard Winslow married Mary Miles in 1806. While no records have been found indicating that these women were among the initial builders and members of the church, some were wives of the founders and, assuming the efficacy of coordinated effort, some or several may well have been instrumental in raising funds, organizing, planning, and even outfitting the establishment. The women contributed to the loftier dreams such as increased civil liberties as well as to the more traditional domestic concerns such as sewing curtains, selecting pearlware, stoneware, and porcelain for the downstairs kitchen and furniture for the common rooms, generally outfitting the space. Cloth was dear, mending important, and even needles and thread were scarce and precious. Sometimes clothes and household items were handed down from the great households, but accepting them was not without its perils, accusations of stealing awaiting those who wore something too fine.[11] Proper personal appearance was the outward expression of inner virtue, so it was vital to have one good suit of clothing for the Sabbath, not as a sign of pride, but as a sign of self-respect and respect for the Lord.

When the miracle that is the still-standing African Meeting House on Beacon Hill, the oldest standing Black church in America, the one that centered Maria Miller's spiritual life, was finished and put to full use, women of the congregation met in the ground-floor common room to discuss the particulars of their roles, perhaps bringing with them their evening projects such as mending, since time was precious, and the demands of labor were exacting. Children may have played on the wooden floor or under tables as their mothers, sisters, and aunts doled out the regular duties of maintenance and upkeep, sweeping the sanctuary, arranging flowers for the small altar, polishing the cherrywood arms of the pews, cleaning soot from the glass globes covering the light fixtures, purchasing provisions for the pantry. Patricia Hill Collins observes that

... for Black women, new knowledge claims are rarely worked out in isolation from other individuals and are usually developed through dialogues with other members of a community. A primary epistemological assumption underlying the use of dialogue in assessing knowledge claims is that connectedness rather than separation is an essential component of the knowledge validation process.[12]

Unfortunately, we have no access to the conversations that took place in that basement room, no minutes of meetings or rosters of attendance, yet they would have helped to form Maria Miller's evolving political thought. We can with some assurance know that those conversations—that *dialogue*—did take place, and that while the ideas emanating from them often lack attribution in political theory, they are present nonetheless, one reason why Stewart's writings are so valuable. Marilyn Richardson remarks on the

... dialectic between the way in which one perceives the development and unfolding of one's identity, and the way that self is defined by the larger society; what W. E. B. DuBois spoke of in his discussion of the "double consciousness" inherent in any act of black self-definition ... [in Maria Stewart's case] indeed a triple consciousness, as she demonstrates the creative struggle of a women attempting to establish both a literary voice and an historical mirror for her experience as "an American, a Negro," and a woman. [13]

Her ideas were not shaped in a vacuum, and while we may trace the influences of James W. Stewart or David Walker, the influences of her women friends and sisters are more obscure but equally important. Extrapolating from Stewart's writing, we find an expression of a core theme of Black feminist theory that would have been widely shared through the women's gatherings: a raced and gendered conception of ethics, an affirmation of Black women's roles as educators and moral guides.[14] As Stewart asserts: "O woman, woman! Your example is powerful, your influence great: it extends over your husbands and your children, and throughout the circle of your acquaintance," a sentiment echoed and developed in the work of Black feminists throughout the nineteenth century, particularly Anna Julia Cooper, Mary Church Terrell, Harriet Tubman, Frances Ellen Watkins Harper, Fannie Barrier Williams, Ida B. Wells, and the Black women's club movement. While the invocation of women's traditional roles may seem conservative, in the hands of Black women intellectuals, activism demanded both respectability and what Brittney Cooper invokes as a move "beyond respectability," to what Mary Church Terrell termed "dignified agitation." The Black women of Beacon Hill and the West End neighborhood exercised their influence, disseminating ideas generated through dialogues about their daily lives, a gendered and raced analysis of the needs of the community, using strategies devised in these settings, honed and refined in conversation with each other.[15]

NAMING WOMEN/INTERSECTING VISIONS

Then, as now, historical records reflect the entrenched methods that place obstacles in the way of the researcher seeking to reconstruct *who* and *what* specifically contributed to theory-building among marginalized groups. Without records, it is difficult to flesh out the nature of the relationships between Maria Miller, Catherine Paul, and other local women who contributed at this strikingly fertile period for social and political thought as African Americans fashioned an autonomous movement for increased freedom and civil liberties. The triple burden, the intersectionality, the triple consciousness of gender, race, and class oppression may complicate and enrich the effort to excavate and disaggregate data about the roles of Black women. The experiences of race, gender, and class oppression, while creating an intense burden, also create a privileged epistemic standpoint, one that integrates an understanding of complex power dynamics. Instead of narratives of women's dependence, we may uncover a truer and fuller story of myriad contributions and fierce resistance designed to build a better society. In her theorizing about intersectionality, legal theorist Kimberlé Crenshaw articulated the ways that multiple oppressions hinder Black women; and Patricia Hill Collins and Kristie Dotson highlight potential insights when "oppressive hegemonic narratives [are] . . . resisted with alternative standpoints and subjugated knowledges." In several publications over the years, I have traced a genealogy of intersectionality back to Maria W. Stewart and forward again through other nineteenth- and twentieth-century Black women writers.[16] The legacy of hidden social relations means that reclamation work must simultaneously seek to recover the *names and lives* of women who were intellectuals and activists in the community and to reconstruct the social and intellectual milieu that was mutually informed and created by the community women, including those who remain nameless. As Crenshaw insists, we must "Say Her Name."[17]

Others among those whose lives were not entirely obliterated from the record are Lavinia M. Ames Hilton, a contemporary of Miller who belonged to this constellation of leaders. She married John Telemachus Hilton, both of them esteemed for their activism.[18] Her ancestor Prince Ames had fought at Lexington, Concord, and Bunker Hill. The Hiltons briefly lived at 73 Belknap Street around the corner from the meetinghouse in a structure that was built in the year of Miller's arrival, 1826. John Hilton was a hairdresser and musician, highly regarded, and a founder of Massachusetts General Colored Association (MGCA). Lavinia Hilton, a friend of Susan Paul, was known for her intellectual rigor, apparently not impeded by giving birth to five children.[19] Miller would also have known Louisa Marshall Nell, married to William Guion Nell, who lived in Belknap Street and worked as a tailor. Their son, William Cooper Nell, became a much-respected historian and author of *The Coloured Patriots of the American Revolution* (1855), among other works. William G. Nell was originally from Charleston, South Carolina, and while he moved to Boston prior to the Vesey freedom fight and massacre, he may have found this geographical commonality to be a bond with his neighbor, David Walker, whom he certainly would have known.

Patience Young Dalton was another member of the circle introduced to Miller. The first wife of Thomas Dalton, they were married 1818 in the newly opened Methodist Church of Reverend Samuel Snowden, a church known for its appeal to mariners. It is remarkable to consider that the community of several hundred Black residents by then supported *two* independent Black churches, the original Baptist church and the Methodist, more closely associated with the work of the Reverend Richard Allen in Philadelphia and other communities on the East Coast.[20] According to the 1826 City Directory, Thomas Dalton was a bootblack. He and Patience lived in Pierce Alley off South Russell behind the African Baptist Church. While many of the original founders had passed away by the time Maria Miller arrived, succeeding generations of families welcomed her. The family and descendants of Abel Barbadoes (a friend of Prince Hall) and Chloe Holloday were prominent in the community, particularly their son, James G. Barbadoes, who was slightly older than Miller, along with his siblings, and his wives, Almira Long (m. 1818), Mary Ann Willis (m. 1821), and Rebecca Brint (m. 1829) who together produced eleven children. The early deaths of so many women speak to the perils of pregnancy and childbirth, especially in a community not well-served by the local medical establishments. His daughter, Catherine, was a dressmaker. In an extraordinary interview from 1883, Chloe Thomas describes how the church was built:

> I heard from the lips of some of our most honored fathers, Cato Gardner, Father Primus Hall, Hamlet Earl, Scipio Dalton, Peter G. Smith, G. H. Holmes, that George Holmes made the first hod to carry bricks and mortar that was ever used in Boston. He invented it for the purpose of carrying bricks and mortar to build our meeting house with as he was a mason and calculated to do his part to the best of his ability. And Boston Smith, father of P. G. Smith, with the rest of his devoted brothers, was anxious to do all in his power. As Boston Smith was a master builder,

he led the carpentry department . . . Abel Barbadoes, being a master mason also assisted. He was the father of Mrs. Catherine Barbadoes at 27 Myrtle Street.[21]

Another of Miller's contemporaries, Elizabeth Lovejoy Lewis was born in 1804 and married (Kwaku) Walker Lewis in either 1825 or 1826 in Cambridge. She was the daughter of a Black man, Peter Lovejoy, and a white woman, Lydia Greenleaf Bradford. Walker Lewis was a nephew of Quock (Kwaku) Walker, known for his role in the judicial ruling that abolished slavery in the state. Walker Lewis's unusual life included his activism in the community and later joining the Church of Latter-Day Saints (Mormon).

Writing and saying the names and the known facts about these women opens a space for envisioning a community of women, woven together through friendship, common purpose, labor, and family. The women clustered around a table in the church basement, in laundry rooms, or finding a moment of leisure, strolling the streets or gathering around a hearth, to talk and plan, to engage in political action and the quietly subversive process of creating a racially separate religious community in a proud physical structure with space for worship and community use: meals and celebrations, a small living space, meetings, classes, and lessons. Efforts such as these arise not just from daily tasks but from the ideas that animate their actions. Social and political theories are always present and are being spun as individuals in relation with each other formulate the concepts and create the ideas that give shape to their thoughts about what has happened in the past and what the future should look like. The externally imposed prevailing social ideas issue from what Karl Marx would later identify as the superstructure of religion, law, economics, and education, perpetrated by a dominating force. The oppositional narratives, the local stories, self-generated and intricately woven, make sense to those who create them, are closer to describing lived realities, and better explain their lives at the same time motivating action for change and social justice.

THE CULT OF TRUE WOMANHOOD

Certain rigid ideologies shape behavior for all of us. At this time, the notion of the ideal lady, what is sometimes known as the cult of domesticity or true womanhood that governed white women, operated in full force.[22] This prevalent ideology, "the standard by which women were judged" at the time, generated a controlling set of dictates that held for middle and upper-class white women in the eighteenth and nineteenth centuries and even to some degree have carried over to the present. Accordingly, the virtues demanded of white women were

1) purity, 2) piety, 3) obedience, and 4) domesticity.[23] These women must be "pure" in every respect, particularly in their sexual morality, "pure" meaning they must be either virgins, virtuous wives, or mothers. In this ideology, purity is synonymous with whiteness. So entrenched is the association of whiteness and purity that Maria W. Stewart, immersed in this ideological metaphor, urges her readers to

> Show forth your powers of mind. Prove to the world that
> Though black your skins as shades of night,
> Your hearts are pure, your souls are white.[24]

Citing Stewart, Lewis Gordon invites us to "call this theme of revealing a white soul in a black body worthy of recognition by the white world the dialectics of white recognition."[25] The prevalence of the whiteness-as-purity trope compelled Stewart to use it as a metaphor for purity of the soul as she reminds the reader that spirits are neither embodied nor melanated, but they are disembodied and judged only by their virtue and character. Brittney Cooper underscores that "the ideology of true womanhood undergirded the racial nationalism at the heart of white gender role ideology, which demanded that white women reproduce white citizens fit to propagate ideologies of white dominance in service of leading the nation."[26]

In keeping with this analysis, "piety," or religious devotion, for white women meant the steady posture of religiosity. For African American women, piety meant something different—not the passive, silent acceptance of God's will, but active engagement in a seamless continuum of community uplift and resistance to oppression in contrast with the white ideology in which "obedience" for Black women and men referenced not a deity but a relationship to some *person* wielding greater social power. To counter this raced and gendered social requirement, we find that often, while the outward performance of obedience to the master conformed to his or her expectations, history and literature are replete with examples of subversive behavior, as we found through examining the social performances in the election of Black governors in Connecticut. The occasional comedic or ironic compliance with the masters' demands by those who were enslaved could be converted to extract liberating concessions, including, in the case of Peleg Nott, a request for freedom that was granted. For those in subjugated groups, it is clear that obedience is a behavior commanded not by God but by the master/oppressor. In defiance, Black people, then, often performed obedience to the master and mistress in a set of coded behaviors designed to conform to expectations while embodying irony, scorn, resistance, or strategically employed to extract greater autonomy. In her analysis of the raced dimensions of the domesticity ideology, Valerie Cooper argues that

"Black women subverted these idealized race and gender roles . . . even as they appropriated them in their efforts to create and project alternate identities for themselves."[27] The women of the African Baptist and the African Methodist churches were freed from the requirement to perform piety and obedience according to white rules in a predominantly white religious setting, liberating them to do important community work while shedding the necessity of artifice.

Domesticity becomes perhaps the most bitterly risible feature of the Cult as applied to Black women, since so many were obstructed from devoting the kind of care to hearth and home they may have wished to give as they were required instead to perform those services for white families. Among other things, Black "domestics" were restricted from having the full measure of time to give loving care to their own families, while those white women who only ritualistically performed domestic chores wrapped themselves in the mantle of domestic virtue.[28] In contrast, Black women found inventive ways of achieving their goals, as Patricia Hill Collins articulates, by creating avenues for assuring that their families received sufficient loving domestic attention through "organized, resilient, woman-centered networks."[29] It is worth noting that the ideology of the cult was also out of reach for working class white women, who were cast as lacking virtue (purity) and were prevented by their work from performing the full panoply of domestic labor in their own families.

Along with Brittney Cooper, Patricia Hill Collins, Evelyn Brooks Higginbotham, Valerie Cooper, and several others, Angela Y. Davis unpacks the ideology of the cult of true womanhood in relation to race and gender. Davis restructures the concept to reflect realistically Black women's creative responses. In contrast with the exalted cult that shaped the myths about respectable white women, she argues that a different code of conduct, self-generated and created from necessity, governed Black women. Hard work, perseverance, tenacity, and self-reliance are features of Black feminism's answer to the cult throughout the ages, according to Davis.[30] Within this praxeological framework, self-reliance is viewed as an attribute, not of individuals as in classical liberalism, but of communities, a gender-inflected one designed to create mutually supportive families, schools, businesses, and institutions in an environment that nurtured and cared for its members. In this, the theoretical tilt moves away from individualism as posited by Enlightenment liberal theory and towards a more historically accurate construction of society generally. Liberal individualism, along with capitalism, property rights, negative freedom (freedom from state interference), and an odd but pervasive view of rationality as self-interest and mutual disinterest, provides a cornerstone of Locke and Jefferson's classic theory that comprises what Charles Mills identifies as the racial contract in which "whites 'contract' to regard one another as moral equals who are superior to nonwhites and who create, accordingly, governments, legal systems, and economic structures that privilege them at the expense of people of color."[31] The liberal individualistic view holds that collections of individuals emerge from the earth like mushrooms, each seemingly able to survive on their own. No hidden networks of mycelium nurtured these Sons of Liberty. No propertied fathers, grandparents, or uncles supplied the rich loam. No mothers, sisters, aunts, or communities nurtured them. Just their own innate ability, grit, intelligence, and ingenuity created white liberal society, according to this account that has dominated the Western political landscape for the last three hundred years. Thus, by surviving on the fruits and nuts of the forest and the land cultivated with his bare hands, *Agaricus Americanus* is able to singlehandedly make his way to liberty and prosperity.

A long line of writers and activists stretching from Maria W. Stewart and the many nineteenth- and twentieth-century feminists of color to the present with the work of Anita Allen, Kathryn Sophia Belle, Patricia Hill Collins, Angela Davis, Kristie Dotson, and Falguni A. Sheth, to name just a few, have directly or indirectly challenged the basic tenets of classic liberalism. Belle, for example, cites Stewart as identifying "the unequal treatment of women, the paternalism of men and inconsistent constructions of femininity." Sheth argues that across a variety of Western nations, "Their self-understandings are that they are societies that have traditionally operated on the principles of rule of law, individual freedom and equality, and they insist upon a secular public sphere. The narrative of liberalism, in which these concepts are the hallmarks, still hold a dominant currency in these societies."[32]

Alison Jaggar critiques the abstract individualism of classic liberal theory, the notion that able-bodied men acting on their own created a productive, individualistic society, an idea that flies in the face of what we know about human society and, we may surmise, *writ small* about the community on and around Beacon Hill in Boston. Jaggar identifies the flaws in arguing, as liberalism does, that essential human characteristics are properties of individuals independent of social contexts. Margaret McLaren argues that "this priority of the individual obscures the background situation that these collective social movements are struggling against."[33] The ideology of individualism serves to obscure the work of women by erasing childcare and domestic labor, especially for poor and Black women's own families and communities.[34] As Stewart writes, "O, ye mothers ... it is you that must create in the minds of your little girls and boys a thirst for knowledge, the love of virtue, the abhorrence of vice, and the cultivation of a pure heart."[35]

Collins provides an empirically based sociological study of economically exploited and politically disenfranchised Black families and communities. She enumerates the ways that the capitalist political economy of liberalism creates unnecessary dichotomies between public and private, individuals, families, and communities, as well as race and gender divisions of labor in contrast with precolonial African societies that "combined work and family without seeing much conflict." Her insights about enslaved women may apply to nominally free women as well, as Stewart always contended. Just as Davis identifies hard work, perseverance, and tenacity as virtues for Black women, Collins observes that "unlike African precolonial political economies, when women's labor benefitted their lineage group and their children, under slavery, neither men nor women got to keep what they produced." In Marxist terms, they were alienated from their labor, a fact that required them to work even harder, with more perseverance and tenacity and with less reward. Prevented from practicing "individualized maternal care . . . women as a group felt accountable for one another's children" and, indeed, for a range of domestic chores. This is reflected in the sociological and archeological studies about Black residents of Boston, so important for refining our understanding of gender relations and gendered labor in the community. Collins argues that their "subjugated knowledge . . . led African American women to use music, literature, daily conversations, and everyday behavior as important locations" for constructing consciousness and knowledge. For this reason, examining the daily lives of women in community provides pieces of knowledge from which we may reconstruct not just their daily activities, but also their thoughts and ideas.[36]

MARIA MILLER'S LODGING

Examining the living arrangements that structured the community, the types of gatherings, employment patterns, and religious affiliations allows us to fill in some details of daily lives and demonstrate the importance of connectedness in the community, even when the names of individuals—particularly of women— are absent. It seems likely that on her arrival, Miller would have lodged at a boarding house. Several rooming houses were within a short walking distance of the African Baptist Church. Women also roomed with family members or in the households of other families. Almost thirty women listed as "coloured" appear in the 1826 City Directory as living on the few short blocks of Belknap Street, many of them widows, including one at the rooming house on 44 Joy Street, adjacent to the church. "Ann Collins, a white spinster, constructed a building on the lot around 1811. Collins apparently made her living as a landlady, renting to black tenants in the 1820s and 1830s according to tax records."[37]

Of the many tenants there, in 1826, only two were women: Elinor Augustus and Jane Jefferson, a widow. James and Lois Horton note:

> Boarding was especially common for young single adults who were
> not yet financially independent . . . Boarders did more than pay rent.
> Sometimes a boarders' income was pooled with that of other members
> of the household . . . [T]hey undoubtedly provided household and child-
> care services.[38]

Communal meals in the boarding houses nourished the tenants, some of whom
took in white women's wash, trudging to the back doors of the finer houses
to retrieve the linens and haul them back home and then carrying the jugs of
water drawn from the spring, building fires to heat the water in the large vats
in the basement, mixing it with lye, their hands raw with chilblains and taking
the sodden linens up to the attic drying rooms—perhaps the most demanding
part—and then returning it only to collect another load.

Childcare was a shared task. From scouring available records, James and
Lois Horton report that

> . . . taking in the homeless was a civic duty not limited to the finan-
> cially stable. Blacks of all occupational levels, including the unemployed,
> were likely to take in children. The practice was important among blacks
> since Boston's institutions for homeless children admitted only whites.[39]

Responses to oppressive social pressures encompass the creation of cultures of
resistance that rejected the privatization of childcare and resisted white control
of sexuality, reproduction, and motherhood. Collins observes that enforced
segregation, while heinous, meant that children could be taught resistance in
racially segregated spaces and that throughout the community organized resistance could occur out of sight of oppressive authorities, "in a private sphere . . ."
where "children can trust their own self-definitions and value themselves" in
contrast with the whiteness that was all around them.[40] The meeting house
provided a central space for developing strategies of resistance.

THE AFRICAN MEETING HOUSE

For officiating at religious services, the sanctuary of the African Meeting House
was the realm of men, yet it was also a space in which women like Maria
Miller spent time on various purposes and missions. Below the sanctuary at
the ground level was (and is) a multipurpose space that has been carefully
explored by archeologists and historians.

> The Meeting House functioned as a school, a church, and the largest
> meeting place controlled by the black community in the first 30 years

of the nineteenth century. As such, this institution was a space for the creation of a sense of community, a distinct group identity, and emotional immunity from the negativity seen in white-dominated spaces.[41]

The ground floor room of the African Meeting House was in almost constant use for celebrations, dinners, meetings, and Bible study classes. Kathryn Grover and Janine V. da Silva conducted crucial research about the Meeting House and other locations in the Black community on the North Slope, drawing in part on earlier research conducted by Michael Terranova along with Horace Seldon.[42] The space had been used as a school at least since 1812 when a small subsidy for that purpose was provided by the City of Boston, with classes taught by Prince Saunders, a founder of Abiel Smith school, who had sailed to Haiti with Reverend Paul and who was well-connected, having corresponded with both Paul Cuffe, the wealthy Black shipping magnate, and Robert Roberts, the esteemed butler and author of a book on refined domestic labor. The space below the sanctuary also contained a small apartment occupied by Domingo Williams, who was a caterer, producing many community meals in the space. Research has uncovered all manner of crockery at the site: "pearlware, creamware, and redware."

> Williams might have helped arrange some of these church dinners, and many of the ceramics are also likely the trash from his successful business. . . . In his obituary his job is described as "the post of Attendant General to fashionable parties, assemblies and social entertainments, both public and private." [43]

In keeping with the theme of virtuous living, very few containers for alcoholic beverages or patent medicines were uncovered in archeological studies, the medicinal practices and personal dress of the people who used these spaces embodying values of respectability. However, a few remnants from folk practices—cowries and beads—were found. George A. Levesque underscores the distinct character of the African Church in Boston. He suggests that African churches were centers of spiritual celebration, standing in contrast to the drier ceremonies at white churches. African churches offered a spirituality and sense of belonging that fostered community pride and perhaps emotional immunity in an oppressive and racist society.[44] Painting a picture of what the African American community in Boston may have looked like is a study in contrast with depictions of the white community of the time: the "City upon a Hill," the "Athens of America," the "Hub of the universe" or "solar system," as Oliver Wendell Holmes put it—as a gleaming example of white literary social, political, and historic accomplishment. What other stories lie hidden about Boston and Beacon Hill?

PLAYING IN THE DARK—HISTORIOGRAPHY

In *Playing in the Dark*, a work that unflinchingly exposes the nature of whiteness, Toni Morrison reflects:

> For some time now I have been thinking about the validity or vulnerability of a certain set of assumptions conventionally accepted among literary historians and critics circulated as "knowledge." This knowledge holds that traditional, canonical American literature is free of, uninformed by and unshaped by the four-hundred-year-old presence of, first, Africans, and then African Americans in the United States. It assumes that this presence—which shaped the body politic, the Constitution, and the entire history of the culture—has no significant place or consequence in the origin and development of that culture's literature.

Morrison's epistemological analysis exposes the vast terrain of canonical literature for what it is—an elaborate mythology by and about white society. In the standard world of American literature, there are few dark faces. But in the gestalt shift proposed by Morrison, "the overwhelming presence of black people in the United States, . . . is central to any understanding of our—literature [or history] and should not be allowed to hover at the margins of the . . . imagination." Among mainstream scholars, one successful means of keeping Black thought obscured is through keeping both primary and secondary literature in the dark. Primary sources such as Hosea Easton's treatise are hidden. Further, academic and popular recognition are achieved through the creation of a body of commentary. No work, no matter how brilliant, achieves notice without a scaffolding of critical recognition and analysis. Here are Morrison's musings about literature and the "national identity" and for which I invite readers to substitute "philosophy," "history," or "political science" for "literature":

> These speculations have led me to wonder whether the major and championed characteristic of our national literature—individualism, masculinity, social engagement versus historic isolation; acute and ambiguous moral problematics; the thematics of innocence coupled with an obsession with figurations of death and hell—are not in fact responses to a dark, abiding, signing Africanist presence.[45]

The narrative of the signing Africanist presence on the North Slope, the harbor, and across the river, must expand, gain substance and solidity, and push against the weight and whiteness of the Hill.

In her life as well as in her essays and speeches, Maria W. Stewart navigated the demands of the white cult of true womanhood—purity, piety, obedience, and domesticity—while also embodying Angela Davis's "creative responses" to the cult when she describes Black women as those who engage in *hard work, perseverance, tenacity, and self-reliance.* It is no surprise that Black women often speak of feeling weary in the face of the expectations imposed on them. A new generation of scholars and activists simply rejects the ideology of respectability and the social control it carries with it. For Stewart, it was in her nature to be pious. It was part of her personal story to be "pure," even in the face of the contradiction of the "pure Black woman"—as in the dizzying assertion that Black people's souls could be white. As for the next requirement, obedience to expected norms was not in her character. All her life she defied exhortations to be silent, to be withdrawing, to "know her place." As for domesticity, she hated it and said so. And while she was all too familiar with hard work, perseverance, tenacity, and self-reliance, she longed to be in a position to work less hard, to be less hypervigilant, perhaps even to have some leisure and to be reliant on someone else. Within a few months of her arrival, these opportunities arose when she made the acquaintance of a man who had the means and the desire to lighten her load.

Chapter Thirteen

"THE GREAT DAY HAS ARRIVED"[1]

They make us here but food for gunpowder.
—Attributed to a British soldier at the Battle of Bunker Hill, derived from Shakespeare's *Henry IV*, according to historian Nathaniel Philbrick[2]

Emerging from their cocoons once the coverings of snow and ice had melted away, Bostonians reveled in the fine spring weather through communal celebrations that punctuated the season. The first on the calendar in 1826 introduced Maria Miller to a distinctly regional holiday, Bunker Hill Day, marking a signal battle in the War of Independence. Holidays brought her opportunities to become better acquainted with her new friends and a chance to absorb the local history as told by Black Bostonians who had carefully stored their knowledge of their past. Proud of their history, they spoke in detail about events and heroes: Crispus Attucks, Peter Salem, Prince Hall, Cato Gardiner. It resembled nothing so much as a large extended family in which the ancestors were alive in the minds of the present-day visitors to this almost-holy battleground. The Bunker Hill narrative that emerged from local Black keepers-of-the-history at times converged with and at times departed from the triumphal account issuing from Mayor Josiah Quincy and other dignitaries representing the city, the state, and the military. In these entwined versions, the Black community highlighted the roles their families and ancestors played in pivotal confrontations: Prince Hall, who prepared five leather drumheads for the Boston Regiment of Artillery, Crispus Attucks's courage facing British soldiers, the first to die at the Boston Massacre, the hosts of African volunteers in the War of Independence, men such as Peter Salem who shot British commander Major Pitcairn at Bunker Hill.

Depending on one's race and social location, the meanings of those events were endowed with radically different interpretations. The dominant discourse often stripped the African American Crispus Attucks of his race, making him simply an American patriot. Colonial soldiers were said to have fought for freedom from tyranny—little acknowledging that those freedoms were not

"Brave colored artillerist; Peter Salem, the colored American, at Bunker Hill." Many Black Americans fought in the War of Independence in support of the colonists' efforts to be free from British rule, and in the hope that the new country would abolish slavery or, at the very least, manumit the soldiers who supported independence. Schomburg Center for Research in Black Culture, Manuscripts, Archives and Rare Books Division, The New York Public Library, Digital Collections. Accessed October 16, 2020. http://digitalcollections.nypl.org/items/510d47df -962c-a3d9-e040-e00a18064a99.

extended to the underclasses. One dominant account held that Black places of worship resulted, not from discrimination, but from "a desire to be with their own community." As residents of the North Slope and the West End scrambled up the hill for the commemoration on Bunker Hill Day, they separated into affinity groups: mariners and their families, laborers, community leaders, Baptists, and Methodists. Maria Miller may have ascended with her circle of friends, the Hiltons, the Walkers, perhaps linking arms with Susan Paul as they listened to the stories told by the old-timers: the Barbadoes, the Nells, and the Daltons. She may have conversed with Eliza Butler, who was her age, recently married to David Walker.

Part of the excitement of a communal holiday lies in the mingling of different groups, the chance to make new connections and deepen old ones. Such

American abolitionist William Cooper Nell (1816–1874). At the time of the 1826 Bunker Hill Day celebration, Maria Miller's first in Boston, Nell was just ten years old, but events such as this one left an impression. He was to become the most prominent Black historian of the nineteenth century, recording the names and histories of each African American who fought in the Revolutionary War. http://www.theliberatorfiles.com/liberator-photo-gallery/.

may have been the case with James W. Stewart and Maria Miller, as the revelers reached the summit, dispersed, and regrouped to listen to the speeches and the presentation of honors. A deep thinker attracted to intelligence and wide experience, she may have found—or, more likely, been found by—James W. Stewart. The decade James Stewart spent building a lucrative shipping office earned him the respect of local residents. A veteran of the War of 1812, Stewart developed close relationships with other veterans and community leaders. One might imagine their courtship, which for the sake of propriety would have been conducted under the watchful eyes of senior community members. In time-honored fashion, she would have recounted her past to him, her indenture, coming of age in Hartford, her journey to Boston. For his part, he had many intriguing stories to tell. Imagine her keen focus as she learned about his military naval battles, languages and cultures on the coast of Chile and the Pacific islands, the geopolitics of Europe and North Africa, the revolution in Haiti. Later, when Maria W. Stewart wrote: "O, ye great and mighty men of America, ye rich and powerful ones . . . you have acknowledged all nations of the world except Hayti," she may have been thinking of the lessons in world history and politics that James Stewart had taught her—harrying British whalers, trade agreements made on ships along the Barbary Coast, battles fought after the war had ended, race relations among the mariners. [3]

In the setting of Bunker Hill Day, William Guion Nell and Louisa Cooper Nell would have followed the tradition of climbing to the top of Charlestown's promontory along with multitudes of Bostonians for the ceremonies of honor and celebrations of the day, the Nell's ten-year-old son, William Cooper, listening intently to the proceedings, captivated by the stories of Black patriots, accumulating and mentally storing the accounts, the seeds of his historical tour-de-force, *Colored Patriots of the Revolution*, published in 1855.[4] As others scrambled up the hill, they may have recalled the scene the previous year, recollecting details, interrupting and filling in each other's memories, partly for themselves and partly for newcomers like Miller, whose presence may have spurred on storytelling as her companions competed with each other to recount the best tales of Bunker Hill Days past.

The city had been brought to a frenzy the previous year, 1825, by an official visit from one of the nation's most beloved foreign dignitaries. The Marquis de Lafayette was a symbol of French support for the Revolutionary War, securing financial backing from France, and in battle, where he fought in the decisive victory at Yorktown, contributions recalled in 1832 by Maria W. Stewart when she wrote, "God raised up those illustrious patriots, WASHINGTON and LAFAYETTE."[5] A monument to victory was to be constructed, visible from land and sea, a marker of determination and triumph and of God's grace in bringing victory to the far smaller and less-well-equipped colonial forces. Lafayette's placement of the cornerstone of the monument marked the centerpiece of a grand event. Feminist and abolitionist Margaret Fuller had attended.[6] Popular novelist Catharine Sedgwick describes the celebration in a letter to her brother, Charles, "Boston, June 17, 1825."

> The great day has arrived, and is as beautiful as if heaven smiled on our patriotic celebration. The city was never so full, half so full, the people say. There are hundreds vainly inquiring for a lodging. The Common is spread with tents to shelter the militia of the adjacent towns. It is expected that a hundred thousand people will be present. Mr. Webster expects to make 15,000 people hear him. He and his wife sent me an invitation to go in their party, so that I think I shall be sure to be among the hearers–the select few.[7]

Echoes of the previous year sounded when Miller joined the 1826 festivities, mounting the hill with others who would not have been on the guest list for the Webster fete. Instead, armies of people of color waited on guests, performed livery services, and labored, unrecognized, to create sumptuous meals for the hordes of privileged attendees. Domingo Williams's services as a caterer were no doubt called into action. Mrs. Sedgwick partook of the parties and their celebrities:

> I was last evening at a party at Mrs. Quincy's to meet the general; t'was twice introduced to him, and twice shook his well-shaken hand. It is a pleasure certainly to grasp a hand that has been the instrument of so noble a heart, but the pleasure is scarcely individual, for the hand is extended with as little personal feeling as the eyes of a picture are directed.

Celebrity or indifference cloaked Lafayette that evening. The next day she clambered up Breed's Hill (the true name of Bunker Hill) for the speaking and laying of the cornerstone for the monument. She reports:

> Saturday. I am "one of the survivors who fought, bled, and died on Bunker Hill." I can only give you generals. The oration was in Mr. Webster's best style of manly eloquence. It was all fine, and there were some very fine strokes of genius in it; but you will see it and judge for yourselves. You will find from the papers that all the world was there, some say 75,000, some 100,000. We went at nine, and did not get home till after four.[8]

There were household servants in Boston who drove coaches, cooked the dinners, and made preparations in the wealthier homes. While it is unlikely that Sedgwick was known to them, part of her story formed a cornerstone of Black liberation.

ELIZABETH FREEMAN AND THE ABOLITION OF SLAVERY IN MASSACHUSETTS

In Connecticut, emancipation had been haphazard, mainly conducted through gradual change in practice through the 1790s and early 1800s, as may have the case with Maria Miller's parents. In Massachusetts, the abolition of slavery was accomplished through a series of judicial decisions. Catharine Sedgwick had a close and crucial connection with the principal catalyst for emancipation in Massachusetts: Elizabeth Freeman. Sedgwick's father, Theodore, had argued the case of "a chattel slave" known as Mum Bett, the first in a series of court rulings that effectively abolished slavery in Massachusetts. Catharine Sedgwick documented the case in "Slavery in New England" in which a cruel mistress finds

Elizabeth Freeman [miniature portrait] by Susan Anne Ridley Livingston Sedgwick (1788–1867). Also known as "Mum Bett," Freeman sued for her freedom from enslavement. The court case granting her freedom was prior to the more well-known case of Quock Walker that led to the abolition of slavery in Massachusetts in 1783. Courtesy of the Massachusetts Historical Society.

. . . a wheaten cake, made by Lizzy, [Bett's] sister, for herself, from the scrapings of the great oaken bowl in which the family batch had been kneaded. Enraged at the "thief," as she branded her, she seized a large iron shovel red hot from clearing the oven, and raised it over the terrified girl. Bet interposed her brawny arm, and took the blow. It cut quite across to the bone, "but," she would say afterwards in concluding the story of the frightful scar she carried to her grave, "Madam never again laid her hand on Lizzy. I had a bad arm, but Madam had the worst of it. I never covered the wound, and when people said to me before Madam,––'Why Betty!, what ails your arm?' ask missis !" Which was the slave and which was the real mistress?[9]

Bett remained defiant through her suffering. As with the storied case of Frederick Douglass in his confrontation with the slave breaker Covey years later, the offender never undertook to strike a "subordinate" again.[10] In the face of a brutal act, Bett, as she was called then, defiantly asserted love and protection, dignity and humanity, at significant personal cost.

Sedgwick relates that sometime after the violent assault, Bett chanced to hear a declaration read at the Sheffield village meeting house, and thereafter approached the law offices of Catherine's father, Theodore Sedgwick, inquiring why she was enslaved if "all men are born equal and, . . . every man has a right to freedom."[11] Upon consideration, Sedgwick and his law partner argued the case, representing Bett and an enslaved man, Brom. *Brom and Bett v. Ashley*, in County Court in 1781, received a favorable ruling gaining freedom for Bett, who thereafter identified herself as Elizabeth Freeman and for Brom, about whom little is known. The case, examined in greater detail in Christopher Cameron's *To Plead Our Own Cause*, was a precursor and precedent for the better-known case of Quock (Kwaku) Walker in 1783 in which William Cushing, chief justice of the Massachusetts Supreme Judicial Court, wrote that slavery violated the 1780 Massachusetts Constitution.[12] These cases explicitly underlie the landmark 2004 decision written by Chief Justice Margaret Marshall in favor of marriage equality in *Goodridge v. Department of Public Health*.

Thus, liberated after a fashion, Freeman found more sympathetic service in Attorney Sedgwick's home, caring for Catharine and her siblings. In the case of Catharine Sedgwick, her race and class privilege positioned her to write a memoir, a rich source of information about Elizabeth Freeman. She recalls that

> Mum-Bett's character was composed of few but strong elements. Action was the law of her nature, and conscious of superiority to all around her, she felt servitude intolerable. It was not the work—work was play to her. Her power of execution was marvelous. Nor was it awe of her kind master, or fear of her despotic mistress but it was the galling of the harness, the irresistible longing for liberty.

Sedgwick heard Freeman say:

> Any time, any time while I was a slave, if one minute's freedom had been offered to me, and I had been told I must die at the end of that minute, I would have taken it—just to stand one minute on God's *airth* [sic] a free woman—I would.[13]

For Elizabeth Freeman and so many others, the harness of slavery was intolerable. Like Stewart, she viewed death as preferable to enslavement. And yet, as Adrienne Rich observes, "many white women have been mothered by black women, a connection which we sentimentalize at our peril."[14] Catherine Sedgwick and Maria Miller's stories are thus entwined in telling sympathies of spirit and contrasts of perspective. Sedgwick provides a rare and lengthy account of the life of the great, steely, towering and yet obscure figure of Elizabeth Freeman, who in some ways represents the Black women of her day—the hard work, tenacity, self-reliance, and perseverance—whose lives, triumphs, and hardships *were not recorded*, but for whom the memory is embodied in their descendants. Miller would have traveled the same ground on Bunker Hill Day, across the Charles River and up the incline, as had Sedgwick the previous year—who *knew* Mum Bett, was raised and nurtured by her. They saw the same sights, both deeply disturbed about slavery and racial oppression. Both discerned meaning in the founding documents. And yet Sedgwick remains an apologist for whom most enslaved people were "treated with almost parental kindness" and who "shared in the luxuries of rich houses." Miller knew better.

Once atop the hill, the dignitaries and attendees remembered the veterans, living and dead, among them the Africans and African Americans. Nell lists "Titus Coburn, Alexander Ames, Barzilai Lew, all of Andover; and also Cato Howe, of Plymouth—each of them received a pension, Lew was a fifer. His daughter, Mrs. Dalton, now lives within a few rods of the battle field." Caesar Brown, Prince Estabrook, Grant Cooper, and Prince Hall were among those whose service was honored. Peter Salem and Salem Poor were particularly noted as heroes. Brown and Estabrook had died in the war. Peter Salem was credited with shooting the British commander Major Pitcairn and forcing the British troops to regroup, giving the smaller colonial force time to retreat rather than surrender. George Middleton led an all-Black company called "the Bucks of America," which, according to the *Liberator*, was presented with a company banner by John Hancock after the battle.[15] It was not only men among those who served. According to the *Resolves of the General Court of Massachusetts, 1791*, "Deborah Gannett . . . did actually perform the duty of a soldier . . . exhibited an extraordinary instance of female heroism . . . preserving the chastity of her sex," for which she was granted a pension. Nell writes that enslaved men "were induced to enter the service in consequence of a law passed by Congress, by which, on condition of their serving in the ranks of the war, they were made freeman," a promise legislated in Rhode Island, but probably not honored elsewhere.[16] Nell's history of the war is brimming with information, naming every African American in every colony who, as far as he could establish, fought in the war: Joshua B. Smith, Charles Bowles and Primus Hall who went on to become the first teacher in the children's school at the Meeting House. Among Nell's abundant stories is one about Primus Hall's time as a body servant to Colonel Pickering, who often consulted with General George Washington about wartime strategies. On a cold night, he is said to have shared a blanket with Washington, "and on the same straw, under the same blanket, the general and the negro servant slept until morning." Writing in 1852 in the buildup to the Civil War, Nell expresses nostalgia for the liberatory hopes of the Revolutionary Era, when at least in some quarters there was a shared imagining of a land of freedom.[17]

Amidst this immersion in the contributions of Black patriots, in their courtship James W. Stewart and Maria Miller may have walked together discussing the contributions of their compatriots, ascending or descending the hill or along the river where young boys with rough lines and no poles fished off the end of the pier. More gentile strolls in the Public Garden would be off-limits, as Black residents were generally forbidden access to the "public" space. Wherever their courtship took place, lively and intense discourse animated their exchanges. She was deeply curious; he had an abundant cache of information to relate. Sharing their autobiographies, each augmented personal details with ideas about race, culture, politics, and religion. He was taken with the "comely" young woman with the penetrating intelligence, and she, with the charismatic businessman whose knowledge of the world etched lines upon his weathered face.

CELEBRATING REVOLUTIONS

SQUEAK the fife, and beat the drum,
Independence day is come!!
—Country Ode for the Fourth of July by Royall Tyler[1]

"FESTIVALS, AND REMARKABLE DAYS"—JULY 4TH, 1826 [2]

Barely had the denizens of the Tremont and Charlestown recovered from
Bunker Hill Day festivities when the national holiday was upon them—the
fiftieth anniversary of the Declaration of Independence, the Jubilee of Freedom.
Impossible, it seemed, that an event so seared in the minds of the people could
have happened fifty years ago. Over the course of two wars, a multitude of
hardships, and a union sharply divided about issues of governance, the general
feeling among white folks was that the nation was on surer footing. Despite
shaky market conditions, the rising economy had brought them increased
wealth. Canals and railroads were being built. In short, the world was changing, and for those with race and class privilege, prosperity seemed to seal the
verdict on the War of Independence. It was a resounding success.

Black Bostonians were at best ambivalent about Independence Day. To
some degree any day of celebration was welcome, but the irony of the holiday
was not lost on the Black community. The hopes harbored and occasionally
fulfilled for manumitted Revolutionary War veterans had long since vanished
as it became clear that a general abolition and emancipation were not in the
offing. Readings of the Declaration and recitations on its meaning did more
to sear into their minds the hypocrisy of the liberal polity that enslaved and
denied civil rights to multitudes of its population. Elizabeth Freeman had
wondered in the past as Frederick Douglass inquired in the future, "Are the
great principles of political freedom and of natural justice, embodied in that
Declaration of Independence, extended to us?" In his 1852 speech, "What, to

the American slave, is your Fourth of July?" Douglass reflected on the meaning of the celebration:

> I answer: a day that reveals to him, more than all other days in the year, the gross injustice and cruelty to which he is the constant victim. To him, your celebration is a sham; your boasted liberty, an unholy license; your national greatness, swelling vanity; your sounds of rejoicing are empty and heartless; your denunciation of tyrants, brass-fronted impudence; your shouts of liberty and equality, hollow mockery; your prayers and hymns, your sermons and thanksgivings, with all your religious parade and solemnity, are, to Him, mere bombast, fraud, deception, impiety, and hypocrisy.[3]

In Albany, Thomas Paul's brother, Nathaniel, pastor of the Hamilton Street Church, spoke on the Fourth of July, 1827—the occasion of legal abolition in New York State. He reminded those assembled that two million human beings in the US remained in chains:

> Slavery, with its concomitants and consequences, in the best attire in which it can possibly be presented, is but a hateful monster, the very demon of avarice and oppression, from its first introduction to the present time; it has been among all nations the scourge of heaven and the curse of the earth.[4]

Nonetheless, across the nation, picnics were held, pies baked and eaten, music played, and dances danced. For those who were privileged enough to attend, Boston mayor Josiah Quincy gave his Fourth of July address at the Old South Church. For the masses, fiddles and flutes played and revelers sang:

> Sambo, play and dance with quality;
> This is the day of blest equality;
> Father and mother are but men,
> And Sambo—is a citizen.[5]

The muddled sentiments expressed in slaveholder Royall Tyler's ode invoke a brief moment, a day of celebration, when in the white imaginary the universal and generic form of the term "men" is endowed with a gendered application to women, or at least to Republican mothers, while another generous political offer is extended, in verse only, to Black Bostonians, for we can be sure that the policing of Black residents was as strict and disciplined, if not more so, on this day as on every other. At her most eloquent and forceful on the subject of

Frederick Douglass, frontispiece, *Narrative of an American Slave*, Written by Himself. Unknown engraver. 1846. Douglass was the most photographed person of the nineteenth century. As was the case with Sojourner Truth, many who were formerly enslaved understood the power inherent in controlling one's image through the use of photographs. From the Alan Sussman Rare Book Collection. Courtesy of Bard College, *Stevenson Library Digital Collections*, accessed October 14, 2020, https://omekalib.bard.edu/items/show/2898. With thanks to Helene Tieger and Debra Klein.

independence, Maria W. Stewart developed her Black revolutionary politics when she wrote in 1831,

> We will not come out against you with swords and staves, as against a thief; but we will tell you that our souls are fired with the same love of liberty and independence with which your souls are fired. We will tell you that too much of your blood flows in our veins, and too much of your color in our skins, for us not to possess your spirits. We will tell you that it is our gold that clothes you in fine linen and purple, and causes you to fare sumptuously every day; and it is the blood of our fathers and the tears of our brethren that have enriched your soils. AND WE CLAIM OUR RIGHTS.[6]

In a direct blow, Stewart uses this passage to predict the violence that could result from the grave inequities, avowing that the rights of Africans in America will be claimed and achieved in one way or another. In contrast, a different day of celebration and a different revolution were more suited to the political ideologies of African Americans.

COMMEMORATING THE ABOLITION OF THE SLAVE TRADE—JULY 14, 1826

If the Fourth of July represented a cruel irony for African Americans, the summer brought an unhypocritical, ideologically consistent, and more deeply joyful celebration a few weeks later, with July 14 marking the abolition of the slave trade, "Abolition," or "African Day."[7] This celebration both recalled and was markedly different from the festivals that Maria Miller had experienced in Hartford's election of Black governors—symbolic leaders and liaisons between Black and white communities. Public holidays such as Pinkster, Training Days, and Election Days had a long and interesting history in the Northeast, but African Day was distinct. In past festivals, slave masters had employed public celebrations as the Romans had used bread and circuses, to control and manipulate the underclasses, providing distractions and escape valves for pent-up frustration, anger, and resentment under the auspices and watchful eyes of the masters. African Day, organized, supervised, and controlled by those for whom it was intended, was sponsored by the African Society. Since 1808 Black Bostonians had celebrated with picnics, games for the children, speeches, both solemn and joyful, and a parade leading to the African Meeting House, followed by a dinner. Women labored to prepare the feast. Patience Dalton's husband, Thomas, is known to have been one of the marshals in 1820, as she may have recalled for the group of women who were engaged in the preparations. African Day combined a commemoration of the successful slave revolution and independence in Haiti in 1804 and the abolition of the slave trade in the United States and England in 1807, a symbolic representation and a tangible physical expression of the movement for Black liberation.

STEWART, COOPER, JAMES, AND WILLIAMS—ANALYSIS OF THE HAITIAN REVOLUTION

In 1826 slavery was terrifyingly real for the more than two million people in the United States who endured this "hateful monster." A corollary of enslavement and deprivation of freedom was the oppressors' well-founded fear of slave rebellions, particularly in the South, where a long, persistent history of resistance stretched from before the Natchez Uprising of 1730 and the Stono rebellion in South Carolina of 1739, to frequent uprisings in Virginia, including in 1764, to early revolts in Louisiana in 1792 and 1793, to Gabriel's planned uprising in Richmond in 1800, to the German Coast uprising near New Orleans in 1811, and the Denmark Vesey/Telemaque planned insurrection in 1823, to name just a few.[8] It is impossible to overstate the influence of the Haitian Revolution (1791–1804) on the political thought of Black Americans. In 1797, the Boston civil rights leader Prince Hall delivered "A Charge" about racism and the need for unity to oppose it. Hall wrote,

> My brethren, let us remember what a dark day it was with our African brethren six years ago [at the beginning of the Haitian Revolution], in the West Indies. Nothing but the snap of the whip was heard from morning to evening; hanging, broken on the wheel, burning, and all manner of tortures inflicted on those unhappy people for nothing else but to gratify their masters pride, wantonness, and cruelty.[9]

In the Northeast, two decades later, intense frustration with broken revolutionary promises and the hypocrisy of the nation's leaders led to the conclusion that either whites would have to abolish slavery or face revolution and retribution.[10] The most prominent twentieth-century analyses of the Haitian Revolution are those of Trinidadian scholars C. L. R. James, who published *The Black Jacobins* in 1938, and Eric Williams, who published *Capitalism and Slavery* in 1944, justly admired accounts.[11]

More recently, an analysis by Nathifa Greene shifts the epistemic trajectory. Her research provides a much needed corrective by considering the major critics together with Anna Julia Cooper's 1925 work, *Slavery and the French and Haitian Revolutionists; Attitude de la France à l'égard de l'esclavage pendant la revolution*, written while she was a doctoral candidate at the Sorbonne and based on primary source materials from archives in Paris, cited by neither James nor Williams.[12] Cooper is best known for her 1892 publication, *A Voice From the South*, a groundbreaking text in Black feminist thought that has had wide influence, including with the Black Women's Club Movement. Her work addressed white women's racism, womanist theology, education, suffrage, the value of labor, literature and image, and more. Until recently, Cooper's treatise on the Haitian Revolution was widely ignored as a scholarly source. Add to this that as a historical event, the Haitian Revolution has been met with a thundering silence in mainstream curricula and scholarship while the American and French Revolutions—both occurring in slaveholding nations—are intensely studied and widely portrayed as expressions of Enlightenment ideals.[13] The works of James and Williams incorporate the Haitian Revolution into the historical perspective, yet both of these accounts omit a crucial critical source. Enriching the discourse, Greene shows that Cooper's ". . . insights reject the commonplace assumptions that the French and American revolutions of colonial slave owners are the only significant manifestations of human freedom through political struggle."

Almost one hundred years earlier, Maria W. Stewart had made a similar observation:

> We know that you are raising contributions to aid the gallant Poles; we know that you have befriended Greece and Ireland; and you have rejoiced with France for her heroic deeds of valor. You have acknowledged all the nations of the earth, except Hayti; and you may publish, as far as the East is from the West, that you have two millions of negroes, who aspire no higher than to bow at your feet and to court your smiles. You may kill, tyrannize, and oppress as much as you choose, until our cry shall come before the throne of God; for I am firmly persuaded, that he will not suffer you to quell the proud, fearless and undaunted spirits of the Africans forever; for in his own time, he is able to plead our cause against you and to pour out the ten plagues of Egypt.[14]

Stewart identifies the inherent hypocrisy of US foreign policy towards Haiti and asserts that it will be recognized by a higher power as well. In a similar fashion, Greene elucidates Cooper's argument against colonialism as the institution "whose foundations ran counter to the ideals of liberty and equality." Asserting that the Haitian Revolution was "the most significant rebellion . . ." of the Enlightenment era, Greene makes the case that "when read together, these three approaches [those of Cooper, James, and Williams] demonstrate the signal importance of the Haitian uprising as the defining struggle for liberty in the revolutionary era."[15] In the same vein, Stewart implores public and private entities supporting global freedom struggles not to shun, but to include Haiti when setting their sights on global struggles for liberty. Cooper ends her dissertation with the cogent insight that colonialism is a form of suicide in which the subversion of stated ideals through practices of enslavement ensures the ultimate failure of the enterprise, an observation later echoed by Martinican philosopher Aimé Césaire.[16] Taken together, Stewart, Cooper, James, Williams, and Greene, in keeping with contemporary decolonial theorists, underscore the twisted hypocrisy of Enlightenment philosophy.

JAMES W. STEWART AND MARIA MILLER

Informing her views of slavery, culture, and revolution, Maria Miller had found someone with considerable knowledge of the world. By now she knew that her future was entwined with that of James W. Stewart. In 1848 African American theologian Richard R. Wright wrote: "Marriage should be encouraged, yet before marriage due caution should be used. Hasty marriage should always be discouraged, for marriage should be sacred, and a contract, not alone civil, but divine, not to be broken except for reasons specifically given in Scripture.[17]"

They were set to be married in less than a month. Meeting with Reverend Paul, they would have asked for his blessing and for him to perform the service, setting the date of August 10, and reviewing the nature of the ceremony and the meaning of the vows. A general sense of propriety meant that they would not spend time together unchaperoned, but while many activities were gender segregated, there was also free discourse and communion between the sexes, especially on celebration days, during which time the history and practices, for example, of African Day dominated discussion, sermons, and speeches. James W. Stewart had joined the merchant marines as a young man and was an experienced seaman when he enlisted in the navy in 1812. He had a good memory of the events of the Haitian Revolution as retold aboard ship and quite possibly from firsthand contact with Haiti. He would have told Maria Miller about the slave revolt of 1791 that stretched into a more than decade-long struggle for independence and emancipation. His merchant ships may have been forced to maneuver around the British, French, and Spanish warships that for years contested control of Haiti's lucrative trade in sugar. He may have related the history of the slave uprisings, the unspeakable cruelty suffered by those enslaved in San Domingue, and the leadership of Toussaint L'Ouverture and Jean-Jacques Dessalines on a small island that had almost half a million enslaved souls.

On that African Day or other days during their courtship she in turn spoke of her more prosaic early life in the clergyman's home, the intensity of the labor, the indignity of the office, her determination to assert her humanity, to educate herself, and to commune with others of her race in pursuit of wider knowledge. She may have told him of the Black Election Days, the death of the mistress and the distress of the young children, of leaving service and going to Sabbath School. She may have recounted the self-liberating antics of the governor Peleg and the dignity of Boston, who had been called "a genuine African." We know she took particular pleasure in church hymns, and she may also have discussed with him thornier philosophical problems, ones on which she would take a stand a few years later, as they walked among the elms, lindens, and horse chestnuts that dominated the landscape in the Beacon Hill neighborhoods.[18]

James Stewart spoke to her of an easier life. No more domestic work aside from caring for her own household, as she wished. He respected her. He found her to be beautiful. Another benefit of married life—her range of permissible movement and interaction would significantly increase within the acceptable expression of Black womanhood. She would be no longer a maiden, but a matron, the need for constant chaperoning gone. She could speak with others, including men, in addition to Reverend Paul, with less fear of being deemed unrespectable. The gravest dangers, as always, came not from within her community but from outside of it.

Most African Americans knew something of the Haitian Revolution. Reverend Paul had recently returned from Haiti, and many local mariners had visited there. At first, the African Day celebrations were tolerated by the dominant social and racial classes, but over time, whites became more hostile, and in the media war against Black liberation some printed materials invited racist and violent responses encouraged by satirical "Bobolition Day" broadsides, part of ongoing propaganda wars and precursors to the mocking practices of minstrelsy. The Massachusetts History Society explains:

> It is in this milieu that "Bobolition" broadsides like the two held by the Society fit. Written in stereotypical "black dialect" and occasionally featuring grotesque caricatures, these broadsides mocked African Americans and what whites considered black pretensions to literacy, respectability, and upward mobility. Clearly intended to provoke whites, especially those whom Prince Hall called out years earlier as "shameless, low-lived, envious, spiteful persons, some of them not long since servants in gentlemen's kitchings, scouring knives, tending horses and driving chaise," these broadsides would have been, according to Shane White, "plastered all over Boston in advance of the event."[19]

The broadsides had their intended effect. If whites were suspicious of the meaning of African Day to Blacks, they may have had reason to worry about its revolutionary implications, but the Black residents faced far more immediate danger. In 1826, when Maria Miller attended her first celebration, unruly white residents attacked the solemn celebrants. Maria and James may have witnessed that day, or they certainly would have heard immediately about the ugly turn of events.

William C. Nell printed a description of events from abolitionist Lydia Maria Child:

> Our negroes, for many years, were allowed peaceably to celebrate the abolition of the slave trade; but it became a frolic with the white boys to

deride them on this day, and finally, they determined to drive them, on these occasions, from the Common. The colored people became greatly incensed by this mockery of their festival, and this infringement of their liberty, and a rumor reached us, on one of these anniversaries, that they were determined to resist the whites, and were going armed, with this intention. About three o'clock in the afternoon, a shout of a beginning fray reached us. Soon, terrified children and women ran down Belknap street, pursued by white boys, who enjoyed their fright. The sounds of battle approached; clubs and brickbats were flying in all directions. At this crisis, Col. Middleton opened his door, armed with a loaded musket, and, in a loud voice, shrieked death to the first white who should approach. Hundreds of human beings, white and black, were pouring down the street, the blacks making but a feeble resistance, the odds in numbers and spirit being against them. Col. Middleton's voice could be heard above every other, urging his party to turn and resist to the last. His appearance was terrific, his musket was levelled, ready to sacrifice the first white man that came within its range. The colored party, shamed by his reproaches, and fired by his example, rallied, and made a short show of resistance. Capt. Winslow Lewis and my father determined to try and quell this tumult. Capt. Lewis valiantly grappled with the ringleaders of the whites, and my father coolly surveyed the scene from his own door, and instantly determined what to do. He calmly approached Col. Middleton, who called to him to stop, or he was a dead man! I can see my father at this distance of time, and never can forget the feelings his family expressed, as they saw him still approach this armed man. He put aside his musket, and, with his countenance all serenity, said a few soothing words to the colonel, who burst into tears, put up his musket, and, with great emotion, exclaimed, loud enough for us to hear across the street, "I will do it for you, for you have always been kind to me," and retired into his own house, and shut his door upon the scene.

Not surprisingly, even a sympathetic white observer such as Child conveys a version of the events that portrays Blacks as "*our* negroes" and relates a white savior story with her father as the hero. A deeper reading will note the violence which met Boston's Black population daily as well as at important events. Colonel Middleton, a Revolutionary War hero, determined to resist racist violence and to model for the younger generation what it means to confront it head on, even if, then as now, the authorities would likely have sided with the aggressors. "A crowd in blackface carrying pitchforks and noisemakers mobbed that district's black section," so just as today, Black residents had reason to fear for their safety, even in their own neighborhoods.[20] In this environment, James W.

Stewart courted Maria Miller, who had ample reason for concern for herself and her community as she went about her daily activities.

William Gravely discerns an aspect of DuBoisian double consciousness in these celebrations folded into the tension of trying to rectify the meaning of being "African" (or "colored") and "American," especially, for free Blacks, knowing that they lived in a nation with millions of enslaved people. Gravely also describes a sort of phenomenological account regarding the propriety of having white abolitionists speak on these days, citing AME Zion pastor Jahiel C. Beman, who "insisted that the colored man, as he was the injured party, could alone *feel* on this occasion . . . [F]reely acknowledging all the sympathies of our white friends, he considered they could not, having never been placed in the same circumstances with the colored people, feel as they do in celebrating this great event." Important recent work by George Yancy explores this concept in depth. Gravely writes, "Certain features of the form of freedom celebration remained constant . . . [and] had its roots in the black church's style of worship, using choirs, congregational singing, prayers, readings, and sermons . . ."[21] The celebrations provided a rare opportunity for a fuller self-expression, even in the face of harassment and violence, immersed as the revelers were in the public, communal performance of racial pride.

Sometime before the African Day celebration, the news of the July 4 deaths of John Adams and Thomas Jefferson reached the public. A few weeks later, Daniel Webster delivered their eulogies at Faneuil Hall, but Maria Miller was not concentrating at that moment on the loss of these leaders. She was eight days away from marrying James W. Stewart.[22]

Chapter Fifteen

HOLY VOWS

The author, as it were ... basked in the sunshine of prosperity.
—Maria W. Stewart, *Meditations*[1]

THE MARRIAGE OF MARIA MILLER AND JAMES STEWART—
AUGUST 10, 1826

Four notable marriages marked the years 1824–1826 uniting the world travelers Nancy Gardner and Nero Prince, the community organizers Lavinia Ames and John Telemachus Hilton, the revolutionary David Walker with young Bostonian Eliza Butler, and the nascent political theorist Maria Miller with the seafarer and commercial businessman James W. Stewart. The Princes' marriage generated the most sensation on the North Slope, West End, and waterfront communities. Her 1853 memoir, *A Narrative of the Life and Travels of Mrs. Nancy Prince*, documents Nancy Gardner Prince's extraordinary journey from abuse as a domestic servant, to her marriage in Reverend Thomas Paul's African Baptist church, to the court of Czars Alexander I and Nicholas I in Russia and back again to Boston. Skillful narration and her analytic intelligence make the memoir important reading as it chronicles the ordinary and the unusual in a life that resonates in certain ways with that of Maria Miller. Recalling their younger days, both women take time to record their vivid childhood memories of picking berries—Gardner as a paid laborer, Miller indulging in a stolen pleasure—memories associated with the harvest from the perspective of a youthful mind's eye. Less happily, both endured the unreasonable demands of coerced menial labor on young children. As a girl, Nancy Prince was in domestic service, "determined to get more for my labor," as one who "enjoyed the happy privilege of religious instruction" while questioning the hypocritical religious practices of the families she served. Her account reveals the drudgery that would have been shared by other domestic laborers:

I often looked at my employers and thought to myself, "Is this your religion?" I did not wonder that the girl who had lived there previous to
myself had gone home to die. They had family prayers morning and
evening. Oh! yes they were sanctimonious . . . Sabbath evening I had to
prepare for the wash . . . I was called up at two o'clock in the morning
and what embittered my heavy task, I was not spoken to kindly, but was
blamed for being slow, and for not performing my work well. Hard labor
and unkindness were too much for me, and in three months my health
and strength were gone.[2]

Reflecting on her youth, Stewart was also perturbed by the inequities and
burdens of labor so irrationally distributed and the astonishing contradictions within the Christian principles of loving kindness. Presaging the words
of Reverend Dr. Martin Luther King Jr., she mused: "It is not the color of the
skin that makes the man, but it is the principles formed with in the soul." Oppressive conditions including Jim Crow-style segregation extended beyond the
domestic sphere. Both had endured the humiliation of "being refused unless
we would ride on top," outside the cabin of the stagecoach. For both, marriage
provided a brighter future.[3]

The early life of Nancy Gardner took a dramatic turn upon meeting Nero
Prince in 1823, a New Englander who had served in the court of the Russian
Czar and taken a leave to return to Boston. Gardner's account of their meeting
and marriage is brief, stating only, "I made up my mind to leave this country.
September 1, 1823, Mr. Prince arrived from Russia; February 15 I was married;
April 14th, embarked in brig Romulus." Together they traveled to Denmark,
where they "visited the King's palace," and onward to Russia where Nancy
Prince avers, "there was no prejudice against color; there were all casts, and
the people of all nations, all in their place." Her husband was one of twenty
footmen to the Czars Alexander and Nicholas who nervously witnessed the
failed Decembrist revolt for liberal reforms.[4]

Mrs. Prince's descriptions of culturally varied approaches to race challenged
the naturalized racial hierarchies promulgated in the United States by Christian
proslavery advocates. Locally, the story of Nancy Gardner and Nero Prince
expanded horizons both geographically and intellectually. From humble beginnings to her adult baptism by Reverend Thomas Paul, "our then beloved
pastor," in the African Baptist Church where their ceremony of matrimony also
took place, to her experiences in Czarist Russia, Nancy Prince's life rides the
troughs and swells of subjugation and privilege. She shared with the Stewarts
the time period and place of their wedding and the presiding minister. Maria
W. Stewart assuredly knew the story of the Princes' wedding and their European
travels. Nancy Gardner Prince was whisked away to Russia, while Maria Miller
remained in her adopted city. Both felt the warm sunshine of prosperity.

MARRIAGE OF MARIA MILLER AND JAMES STEWART

Marilyn Richardson, the scholar most responsible for recovering the life and works of Maria W. Stewart, opens her landmark work with this description:

> In Boston, Massachusetts, on August 10th, 1826, little more than a month after the July 4th deaths of both John Adams and Thomas Jefferson, Maria Miller and James W. Stewart stood before the Reverend Thomas Paul and exchanged their vows. The bride, a young woman of twenty-three, [was] "one of the most beautiful and loveliest of women."[5]

They were an impressive couple. James W. Stewart is described as a "tolerably stout well built man; a light, bright mulatto."[6] Although financially strapped, Maria Miller may have worn a dress fashioned by a dressmaker among the several African American seamstresses singled out for their skill, someone like Catherine Barbadoes, who may have created something for her in the high-waisted empire style still popular at the time. The caterer, Domingo Williams, who lived in and ran his business out of the ground floor of the African Meeting House may have prepared a meal for the celebrants and friends. Members of Reverend Paul's family, Catherine and Susan, and possibly her friend Elizabeth Williams, who years later recalled knowing her before her marriage, may have all been in attendance. On the groom's side, James's friend John Brown, with whom he had shared a flat on South Russell Street, may have attended along with others of his closer business and maritime acquaintances. Newly married, Maria W. Stewart experienced unadulterated joy as she contemplated a life full of "the sunshine of prosperity." Having taken the middle initial of "W" at her husband's request, she tried out the sound of "Mrs. Maria W. Stewart, wife of James W. Stewart," no longer a working class woman, a "domestic," but a middle-class matron, truly even more than that for her husband was one of the wealthier members of the community.[7] In rapid succession, she was transformed from a domestic worker forced into service for others into a person of high social position as the wife of a prominent and successful businessman. Her courage and willingness to risk traveling away from her native state was repaid; it rewarded her with a sisterhood of women who, instead of being compelled to "bury their talents beneath a load of iron pots and kettles," exercised their intellects, and participated in efforts to improve the lot of their communities and of all African descendants in America.[8]

By early 1827 the Stewarts were living in a rear apartment at 38 South Russell Street, according to tax records.[9] Mrs. Stewart left domestic work behind for good and set about arranging the dwelling to her own tastes with a proper bedstead, tables, cupboards, and other furnishings. Her husband's wealth meant she would not need outside employment at all. Her days may have been spent with other, similarly situated women, attending church as often as she wished, and with her industrious nature, engaging in community service wherever it was needed. Some may have bristled at her new-found social ascendance in a city where Blacks and whites alike claimed separate but crucial "Brahmin" status. It is likely that regular employment in her husband's office was beneath her new station; still, she may have spent time there and occupied herself in various ways. She later argued that such work was perfectly proper for young girls who had been provided with "the most satisfactory references," but this break with social norms would not be well received.[10]

South Russell was a short street laid out just thirty years earlier, when "the pasture lay up along the hillside for about six hundred feet above Cambridge Street." Their apartment was near a calico printing factory and quite near one of the older homes, the Ditson house, a brick building with shuttered windows and a "cavernous" hearth in the basement kitchen. The racially integrated neighborhood was home to sailors, ship captains, traders, and a baker. Some buildings were used as "investment property," including as rentals to such as the Stewarts.[11]

As a shipping agent, James W. Stewart engaged in fitting and outfitting whaling and fishing vessels sailing out of Boston, the only shop of its kind run by an African American. Marilyn Richardson writes, "Stewart's business was at a choice location in the newly built-up commercial area near India Wharf, not far from the Custom-house, developed under the auspices of the Broad Street Association."[12] Broad Street had been created in 1807 from landfill designed to straighten the harbor, "by filling in various coves that gave her so jagged a shoreline." Many coves remained and began to be addressed in 1825 when they were filled at Liberty and Dock Squares. "A few yards away was State Street, rapidly becoming lined with new banks and insurance offices that commercial expansion required."[13] The commercial expansion of the 1820s was accompanied by a feeling of urgency that something must be done both about the expanding enslavement of African Americans and the utter failure to significantly lessen the oppression of Blacks in the North. Richardson writes, "As they were joined in marriage, Maria Miller and James W. Stewart, in their choice of locale and officiant for their wedding ceremony, suggested a sympathy for black social and political causes."[14] The couple chose to be wed in the crucible of northeastern Black political organizing, setting themselves squarely within the movement and associating with the luminaries of local activism.

LAVINIA AMES AND JOHN TELEMACHUS HILTON

At the center of organized resistance efforts, John Telemachus Hilton and Lavinia F. Ames had been married in the African Baptist Church the previous year. The couple were known, not just to the Stewarts, but also to everyone who cared about the cause of African American freedom. John T. Hilton had moved to Boston from Pennsylvania as a young man and soon became one of the most prominent of the Prince Hall masons. His primary profession was as a barber and hairdresser. Energetic and entrepreneurial, he was soon at the center of activity in the North Slope community. "[At] Hilton's shop, in addition to getting a haircut, a customer could purchase tickets for a local event, look for a job through Hilton's employment agency, or purchase specialty items like fine soap. He also sold new and used furniture on a commission basis."[15]

Lavinia Ames Hilton was part of the circle of acquaintances that included Maria Miller and Susan Paul. Her family lineage was well known in the city; an ancestor, Alexander, had fought at Bunker Hill and received a pension for his war service. Smart and engaged in local happenings, apparently unhampered in her activism by giving birth to two daughters and three sons, she is portrayed as an intellectual and active abolitionist along with Susan Paul, both of whom would be among the founding members of the Boston Female Anti-Slavery Society. While the Hiltons were known for their influence in the community, no one among the strong numbers of Black activists was to have a wider reach than the Stewarts' friend, David Walker.

DAVID WALKER AND ELIZA BUTLER—FEBRUARY 23, 1826

Earlier in the year of the Stewarts' union, on February 23, David Walker and Eliza Butler were married by the Reverend Isaac Bonney. Peter Hinks reports that Eliza's

> father, Jonas Butler, had also been born in Boston, but whether as a slave or a free man is not known. Walker had married into a well-established black Boston family. This liaison gave him entrance into black community, which he would have lacked as a single, unconnected male from the South.[16]

Walker had made his way from Wilmington, North Carolina, to Charleston, South Carolina, during the time of the Vesey conspiracy, an occasion of Black rebellion and brutal white retribution. He had witnessed the worst of what could be wrought in the name of maintaining the institution of chattel slavery. Traveling through the southern states and slightly west, Walker gained a damning appreciation of the racially motivated cruelties that prevailed there, whereupon, according to abolitionist minister Henry Highland Garnet, he "travelled rapidly towards the North, shaking off the dust of his feet, and breathing curses upon the system of human slavery, America's darling institution." Once in Boston, Walker set about establishing himself in the community. He "was prepossessing, being six feet in height, slender and well proportioned. His hair was loose, and his complexion was dark." According to Garnet, "he possessed a noble and a courageous spirit, and . . . he was ardently attached to the cause of liberty." Establishing a used clothing store in Brattle Street, not far from James Stewart's office, "he prospered; and had it not been for his great liberality and hospitality, he would have become wealthy." Walker was a Methodist who worshipped at the May Street Church of Reverend Samuel Snowden. In the same month as the Stewarts' marriage and the white mob violence against African Day, David Walker was initiated into the deep and secret heart of the resistance—the Prince Hall masons.[17] In the next few years autonomous Black organizing in the region achieved its apex.

The Hiltons, the Walkers, and the Stewarts were more than just acquaintances. Walker and Hilton were fraternal brothers in the order of Masons; the Walkers and the Stewarts lived within a few blocks of each other. James Stewart and David Walker may have had subversive connections as well as commercial ones. In his work, Stewart was a sort of general contractor preparing commercial ships for sea in addition to holding stock in whaling companies. His work facilitated the procurement of marine hardware, rope. and sails. He also assembled a full roster of seamen and skilled mariners for the ships he was contracted to outfit. Those sailors needed clean, suitable attire. The "slop shops" such as those run by Walker acquired their clothing inventory through a variety of sources, including buying their work clothes from disembarking sailors in exchange for money and civilian clothing. Walker's business encompassed washing and mending the intake and preparing it for the next crew to ship out in transaction with outfitters such as James W. Stewart. Many scholars have speculated that, since copies of Walker's *Appeal* were smuggled into the South through their port cities, copies of his pamphlet may have been sewn into the sailors' uniforms at Walker's establishment and then transmitted to James Stewart's office for outfitting sailors. Renowned for their activism, Black women such as Maria Stewart and Lavinia Hilton, who were already acquainted through the church and mutual friends such as Susan Paul, may have been aware or a part of this dissemination of Black revolutionary literature.

Chapter Sixteen

BLACK FOUNDERS AND THE ROOTS OF BLACK POLITICAL THOUGHT [1]

What was the reason that our African kings and princes have plunged themselves and their peaceable kingdoms into bloody wars, to the destroying of towns and kingdoms, but the fear of the report of a great gun or the glittering arms and swords, which struck these kings near the seaports with such a panic of fear, as not only to destroy the peace and happiness of their inland brethren, but plunged millions of their fellow countrymen into slavery and cruel bondage.

—Prince Hall, "A Charge"

A FREEDOM TRAIL

Just as the contemporary reader may be startled to discover a lengthy history of Black activism, Maria W. Stewart was awed learning about resistance by a vast array of people and actions that preceded her. The ever-widening embrace of the community brought daily revelations in the form of narratives related by friends as well as by religious and community leaders. By 1827, James's and Maria Stewart's lives revolved around two geographically close but strikingly different urban areas. At one pole was the largely residential, racially diverse North Slope of Beacon Hill, and at the other lay the new commercial district around Broad Street near the wharves and the harbor. They lived "at the head of Smith Court, rear of 38 South Russell Street," a few steps away from the African Meeting House, a ten-minute walk from James's shipping office near the heart of the harbor's international business hub.[2] Shops near the Meeting House lodged the piano forte maker Jonas Pickering, a "fancy painter" and a tin plate worker, a baker and a bonnet shop. Silas Wright stabled horses nearby, and a hackman lived close at hand. James Barbadoes lived with his mother, a widow, on Belknap St. The abolitionist minister Reverend Samuel Snowden of the May Street Methodist church lived at 5 Belknap, across from Eliza and David Walker. Among other residents, James Cassel, a ship captain, lived just houses away from the mariners and laborers who were the engines of the maritime industry, some of whom were Black. Wealth and station in life seemingly made little difference for proximity of living spaces in a city where access to employment and civic affairs trumped the desire for exclusivity. Not counting, of course, the Brahmins who occupied the grand houses perched atop the hill.

Walking to her husband's shipping office, Maria W. Stewart made her way down Holmes Alley to Smith Court, past the Nell family home and the African Meeting House, humming with action—church meetings, the catering business, and the schoolroom filled with children under the instruction of their teacher, William Bascom. Choosing her route, she may have skirted the hill by heading down to Cambridge Street, past the home of David and Eliza Walker, the new African Masonic Hall, the grocers, barbers, and shops across the street from Governor Otis's discarded mansion and the West Church next door. Or she may have decided to ascend a short distance to the massive Bulfinch State House, turning sharply at Beacon Street toward the harbor. If she took this route, she would have passed the courthouse where David Walker and John Scarlett were brought up on charges of receiving stolen property at their used clothing store, possibly in an attempt to deter their growing activism. Both were acquitted after "a crowd of witnesses . . . testified to their integrity and fairness in their dealings, and moral character *to be envied by some of a fair complexion.*"[3]

She could hear the cacophony of bells from the churches, the change ringing from the Old North, bells cast and rung by Paul Revere, who had recently passed away. She skirted the shops that printed the local papers, past the Old State House, as the area quickly became associated with the maritime trades. She may have nodded to David Walker in his used clothing shop at 20 Brattle or peered in the windows of William G. Nell's tailor shop, and the hairdressing establishment of James Barbadoes's nearby. As she made her way towards James Stewart's ship outfitter's office on Broad Street, she walked by the crowded Custom House, the paper warehouses, and the shop that declared "Books and Fancy Printing," past a "victualler," a grocer, the cooper Augustus Adams, a druggist, an apothecary, a housewright, Bird's dry goods, the homes of a number of widows, and a handful of laborers, stevedores, provisioners, riggers, mariners, and a hatter. Stewart's shop was at 83 Broad. Next door, at 85, was John Williams. At the rear of 85 was Jane Bence and Alexander Taylor, a mariner. As she closed the distance to his office, she walked past the residence of a white man, Daniel B. Badger, an acquaintance of her husband who ran a tailor shop and may have been one among many who had commerce with James. Badger was also the ward officer for the Third District. She passed the shipping office of Ephraim Titcomb at 16 Custom House Street. As she neared the wharves, Fosters, Long

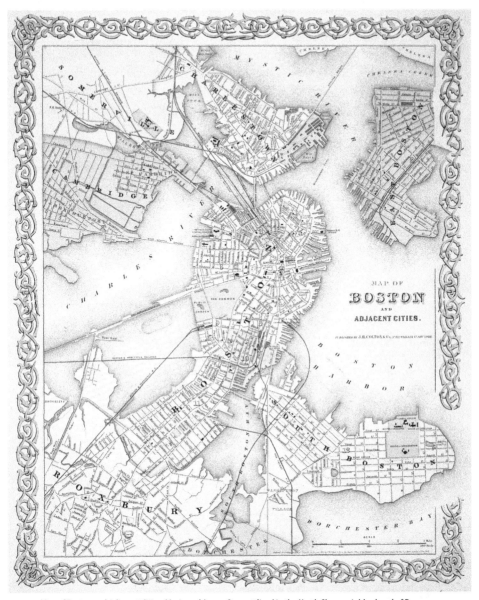

Map of Boston and Adjacent Cities. Maria and James Stewart lived in the North Slope neighborhood of Beacon Hill, just north of the Common. Charlestown and Bunker Hill were directly to the north across the Charles River with the City of Cambridge slightly to the west. The body of water between Boston and Roxbury was later filled in to form the Back Bay neighborhood. Norman B. Leventhal Map and Education Center at the Boston Public Library.

Wharf, and Rowes, she could see the earthen mound, the rise of Fort Hill, once a strategic bulwark, now becoming a gentrified neighborhood. She may have marveled at the new horse-drawn bus line that took workers to and from the city center. Once at Broad Street, the smells of the harbor and cries of the gulls told her she was near. Feeling increasingly secure in her new role, she became familiar with this tightly settled part of Boston, so near to her own residence, but worlds away in purpose and international commercial importance.[4]

Good fortune, ingenuity, and courage had propelled Maria W. Stewart from near-slavery, isolation, and low social standing to a place of love, learning, and prosperity. Acutely conscious of her blessings, she carried with her the knowledge that, like most African Americans, she and others were denied access to a full measure of the primary social goods offered in this city, state, and country. Her very act of leaving Hartford animated her understanding of the raced/gendered/classed—the intersectional—disadvantages of her social position and the obstacles to advancement. Boston was different. In fact, it was more overtly racist than the more gentile city of Hartford, less well-regulated, more rough-and-tumble. In response, the larger activist community devoted itself to abolishing slavery and securing rights as citizens, but the city was volatile, and random acts of racism were common, despite the fact that many prominent Bostonians viewed their city as "the legendary torchbearer carrying the light of Western civilization from the Old World to the New."[5] As Maria Stewart witnessed the activism blossoming before her very eyes, she was also learning the history lessons about the roots of Black political thought in North America, of Black heroes and Black struggle. She read Phillis Wheatley's poems, perplexed by the counterpoint of her enslavement and her international literary acclaim. She heard the names of Black revolutionary war soldiers who had fought in the hope that the Enlightenment ideals of freedom and equality would apply to them, a dream denied. Most impressively, she learned about the most admired and revered Black founder, the freed slave Prince Hall and the cluster of activists who walked with him along these same streets fifty years earlier, from the base of Belknap Street, along Cambridge to the Dock Square State House to deliver petitions demanding civil liberties, and she learned of their determination to charter a Masonic lodge for themselves.

WAVES OF RESISTANCE

Sparring about the origins of abolitionism, some scholars identify the 1830s as the beginning of a white-led movement exemplified by the work of William Lloyd Garrison. I count myself among others who instead identify a first wave starting in the Revolutionary War era, while acknowledging that antislavery resistance began long before then when race enslavement first began.[6] In a comprehensive account that adopts the earlier first wave timeline, Manisha Sinha, "centers African Americans" in " . . . a radical, interracial movement, one which addressed the entrenched problems of exploitation and disenfranchisement in a liberal democracy and anticipated debates of race, labor, and empire."[7]

I consider the first wave to span approximately from the last quarter of the 1700s to the early 1830s, placing David Walker and Maria W. Stewart's work as a pivotal point at the end of the first wave of African American organized resistance and the beginning of a more interracial movement often reductively perceived as white, with Garrison as the most prominent figure.

In the early days of the initial wave, a petition movement, encouraged by Revolutionary War era rhetoric and armed resistance against Great Britain, propelled Black efforts to gain civil liberties. At the same time, Black freemasonry led by Prince Hall earned some hard-won victories securing a crucial avenue for private organizing. Not to be neglected, artistic accomplishments of social and political importance, long practiced in the form of craft and artisanal endeavors, song, poetry, and stories, find written expression in the writings of Phillis Wheatley, whom I take as an example of artistic resistance. This chapter examines the ideas that came out of the early part of this wave of activism: particular concepts of freedom, equality, property, individualism, community, and the social contract, from the first rumblings of the Age of Revolution.

Current practitioners of "Founders Chic," the hundreds and more writers who have capitalized on the popular appetite for stories about the founding of the country, have valorized the traditionally recognized "founding fathers" while making little effort towards writing inclusive histories that record the actions and thought of women, African Americans, and Indigenous peoples. Traditionally, the grand metanarrative of US intellectual history holds that the founding fathers adapted a republican (antimonarchical) ideology based on classic European liberal ideas enhanced by the writings of Madison, Jefferson, Franklin, Washington, Adams, Hamilton, and Jay and some other contributing voices such as Thomas Paine's. Their narratives hold that at the birth of the republic, while there may have been isolated instances of Black protest across the previous hundred and fifty or so years of slavery and oppression, none of these amounted to systematic thought or action.[8] Most whites considered slavery to be either a "necessary evil" or a positive good with enslavement taken as a minor human failing on the part of the heroic but flawed white men who institutionalized and enacted the practice. A handful of scholars have offered a counternarrative of agency harkening back to Black founders, luminaries of the Black intellectual and activist traditions: Richard Allen, James Forten, Prince Hall, Absalom Jones, John Marrant, Phillis Wheatley, to name a few, shifting the trajectory of canonical knowledge from a stream that either excludes Black voices or hears them in a supporting role, to one that is suffused with the voices of Black praxis. A "less partial and perverse" account of US history replaces the tired, traditional versions with ones that acknowledge the centrality of Black thought and actions in our nation's history since colonial times, ones that are distinctly critical of the Founders' duplicitous embrace of liberalism's concepts of freedom and equality and simultaneous promulgation of race-based discrimination and slavocracy.[9] To gain a foothold in socially acceptable forms of resistance, Black activists needed a home.

THE PRINCE HALL MASONS

Alongside the creation of distinct religious denominations, Black Freemasonry represents one of the first examples of institutional resistance to race oppression in the United States. Prince Hall, the lion of African American civil rights in the late eighteenth century, possessed the stature of a Reverend Dr. Martin Luther King Jr. or Malcolm X, known for his oratory, moral leadership, fearless strategies, and lasting accomplishments forwarding the goal of Black civil rights. Hall was a tanner, once enslaved in the household of William Hall, a leather-dresser, from whom he learned the intricacies of this lucrative trade. Some years after his initial bondage, Hall married, but the circumstances of his family life are not clear.[10] Hall keenly felt the violent oppression at the hands of slave masters, local law enforcement, and white mobs seeking amusement in the blood sport of beating other human beings. He wrote about

> [t]he daily insults you meet with in the streets of Boston; much more on public days of recreation, how you are shamefully abus'd, and that at such a degree that you may truly be said to carry your lives in your hands, and the arrows of death are flying about your heads.[11]

William Hall manumitted Prince Hall in 1770 when the high-sounding rhetoric of independence was in the air, the newspapers, and on the lips of English colonists such as James Otis in his State House address excoriating the unfreedom of his settler-countrymen under British rule.[12] Thus, Hall was freed with a trade, a family, and a religious affiliation, with his enslaver's self-deluding declaration that Hall, "has been always accounted a free man by us."[13]

The colonists' intellectual machinery adopted English theorist John Locke's language of natural law, rights, freedoms, and revolution. Locke had written that all men are born "in a state of perfect freedom" and "a state of equality . . . without subordination or subjection." He had written, "Tyranny is the exercise of Power beyond Right, which no Body can have a Right to," and argued for the justness of revolution.[14] Lockean political philosophy, translated across the Atlantic by James Otis, Mercy Otis Warren, Thomas Paine, Thomas Jefferson in the *Declaration of Independence*, and many others, conveyed in the press, pulpit, and other platforms, fueled the American Revolution[15] As the revolutionary theories of the Enlightenment seeped into the culture and colonial resistance inexorably ground towards emancipation from British rule, Black Americans developed a parallel but radically different counternarrative of Black liberation, one through which Maria W. Stewart would a few years later encourage her people to "possess the spirit of independence."[16] I have argued that "Black revolutionary liberalism" is the most apt descriptive term for the school of thought that Prince Hall and early Black organizers along with theorists such as Stewart and Walker helped to create. This term identifies and refines a set of ideas that in the past has been identified narrowly as "Black abolitionism" or loosely as "the Black protest tradition," neither term capturing the range or specificity of this political theory. Further, this identification indicates a continuum of thought spanning decades and crossing centuries. As we shall see, the political philosophy of Black revolutionary (or radical) liberalism is distinguished from Black nationalism while containing elements of this better known and for the most part chronologically later theory.[17] It clearly connects Prince Hall, David Walker, and Maria Stewart's conceptualizations to the European ideas that fueled the American Revolution and yet separates in ways that modify and correct the racialist ideology that accompanied the founding of colonial America.[18] The continuity of thought from Hall to Maria W. Stewart is evident. In "A Charge" (1797), Hall writes about his brothers "dragg'd from their native country by the iron hand of tyranny and oppression," insisting that "all men are free and are brethren."[19] Stewart writes: "All the nations of the earth are crying out for liberty and equality. Away, away with tyranny and oppression! Shall Afric's sons be silent any longer?" With the colonists' success in the American Revolution still in mind, she asks, "Why should man any longer deprive his fellow-man of equal rights and privileges?"[20]

Finally freed, Prince Hall and his cohort set about appropriating one of the most powerful organizations supporting the advancement of white men, the fraternal organization of freemasonry, secretive brotherhoods of certain elites including the nation's traditionally recognized founders that launched men such as Washington, Franklin, John Hancock, and James Monroe into prominence. Hall reasoned that freemasonry could provide an institutional organization for Africans in America to launch their own bid for rights, civil standing, and the abolition of the slavery that surrounded them, beyond the watchful eyes of the overseers. The initial approaches by Hall and his comrades to the colonial Orders of Masons were rebuffed. Undeterred, and despite his general inclination to cast his lot with the land where he had lived for twenty-five years, Hall and more than ten others approached the British Army Lodge No. 441 shortly before war broke out and were initiated into the Fraternal Order of Free and Accepted Masons, soon becoming African Lodge No. 1 with Hall elected as Grand Master. Within a matter of a few years, they were fully chartered as African Lodge No 459.[21] The years-long quest for an African Masonic Lodge represents part of a multipronged approach to civil rights in which Black Americans skillfully used the War of Independence and its underlying political philosophy to fight for their rights.

This chapter and the next ones explore major writers and components of classic liberal theory: concepts of freedom, equality, social contract, property, individualism, capitalism, and independence, but the connections with the birth of liberalism should in no way preclude a critique of this theory from other conceptual perspectives. Philosophers today have a wide range of concepts of freedom to draw on: Marxist or communitarian ones, existential freedom, freedom as marronage, collective ideas of freedom, decolonial ones, libertarian or anarchist ones. My claim that Black philosophers in the age of revolution used the language of the Enlightenment does not foreclose on innovations or modifications from different philosophical traditions. So rich is the material from writers of this period, especially Stewart and Walker, that it may be possible to peel back the language of liberalism to reveal, for example, existential underlayments. Robert Birt writes:

> Every struggle for human liberation is invariably a struggle for a liberated identity. A fundamental transformation of society is certainly indispensable. But if the proof (as Fanon says) of the success of a struggle, "lies in a whole social structure being changed from the bottom up," the ultimate goal of this arduous transformation is to "set afoot a new man."[22]

Social change and individual transformation are different facets of the same phenomenon. Seeking liberated identities, writers in the revolutionary liberal tradition use Locke's idea of negative freedom, that is, freedom from government interference, because it is the theory at hand, because they would like to "claim their rights" as Stewart asserts, and because having the chains of state-imposed restrictions removed would create a sphere of freedom that is almost unimaginable. As Charles W. Mills puts it, "the situation of, e.g., blacks in the United States is arguably the result of the historic and current violation of traditional *negative* rights (life, liberty, property.)"[23] As a central figure in Black political thought, in the spirit of the Bill of Rights, Maria W. Stewart wrote, "This is the land of freedom. The press is at liberty. Every man has a right to express his opinion. Many think, because your skins are tinged with a sable hue, that you are an inferior race of beings; but God does not consider you such."

Her declaration is propelled by her own innate sense of the worth of her people and by the influence of those around her.[24] In particular, the constitutional protections guaranteed in the Bill of Rights and undergirded by the general desire to keep the government at bay were nearly meaningless, then and now, as applied to Black people. The rights to speech, assembly, and religion were severely constrained—consider the treatment of Blacks in white churches and white mob violence on African Day. The Fourth, Fifth, Sixth, and Eighth Amendment rights to probable cause, due process, and impartial juries simply did not apply to African Americans.

The revolutionary nature of original political liberalism is often lost in the present-day tendency to associate neoliberalism with classic liberalism. The genealogy of Black political theories in North America originates in a tradition of rebellion. Theory emanates from practice and experience, and every enslaved person understood that enslavement was wrong. Resistance came in every possible form, from individual acts of rebellion and spontaneous self-liberation, as with the maroons who fled to the swamps of the Carolinas, the Everglades of Florida, and the mountains of Jamaica and Haiti. It came in the form of open warfare such as the Stono Rebellion in 1739, Nat Turner's revolt in 1831, and all the uprisings that were mounted before, after, and in between. Kenneth Marshall illustrates the power of small acts of resistance, such as those of Yombo, one whose "inability to escape slavery (he had a clubfoot) compelled him to develop strategies that enabled him to contest his owner's incessant appropriation of his 'time,' a critical means of white control." Marshall's work is a deep exploration of small acts of resistance, in Yombo's case through thievery, meanness, and truancy, that opens up a largely unexplored field of subtle but effective individual resistance.[25] Thus, a major principle of Black political thought has long been a right of rebellion for the cause of freedom.

Leonard Harris identifies what might be called a first principle of Black political thought, an "insurrectionist ethics" that posits an obligation to insurrect in the face of race slavery. He writes that

> Walker's *Appeal* provided a secular and theological basis for insurrection by arguing that racial slavery was the worst form of slavery in history: it made race a marker separating humanity and promoted perpetual servitude for a people as a way of transferring assets from one population to another.[26]

A deeper consideration of insurrectionist ethics undertaken in chapter twenty-one addresses Stewart's first and, in some ways, most substantial political essay. In the rest of this chapter, I will discuss the overarching theory of Black revolutionary liberalism derived from Enlightenment ideals that in hands of Black theorists were converted from an ideology that had chattel slavery at its base to one of human flourishing for all humankind. I will explore the philosophical underpinnings of the Petition Movement, particularly as they pertain to the *Body of Liberties* and Puritan concepts of covenant theology as considered by Christopher Cameron as well as the idea of the "barbaric culture" identified by Stefan Wheelock. I also use the works of Carole Pateman and Charles Mills to discover how early Black petitions employed what Mills identifies as the "racial contact," a perverted component of social contract theory, to expose flaws in the idea of tacit consent.

THE PETITION MOVEMENT

Open, armed rebellion was not always possible or practical. For those who were enslaved, extreme social restrictions presented major obstacles to organizing. For nominally free Blacks, gradations of freedom created a netherland of free/unfree. This included a measure of free association in worship, politics, and social affairs that mitigated the desire for armed rebellion, and in any case, whites vastly outnumbered Blacks in the North, unlike in plantation societies. Other means were available for creating incremental social change: manumission petitions, legislative action, and judicial rulings. The framework of partial integration into the affairs of the wider community meant adopting and fashioning existing institutional remedies to one's own purposes. Churches, clubs, mutual aid societies, and fraternal groups such as the Freemasons created space for organizing. African Americans used these means effectively to improve their situations, even as the state countered with increasingly harsh legal restrictions on advancement.

The masonic movement was neither the first nor the only peaceful means of social improvement. Christopher Cameron details the political and theological justifications and restrictions adopted by early Puritans regarding the enslavement of Pequots and West Africans. He investigates the ways that the *Body of Liberties* (1646) secured a universal right to petition the courts, a right that was used, often to some effect, by enslaved as well as free persons.[27] Petitions provided a legal strategy for adjudicating violations of rights.[28] In 1773 Felix and others who had "every moral Virtue except Patience" urged abolition, arguing on the basis of public economic contributions of those who "if made free, would soon be able as well as willing to bear a Part in the Public Charges." The petitioners lobbied for legislation to end slavery since "We have no Property. We have no Wives. No Children. We have no City. No Country. But we have a Father in Heaven" who takes up their cause. In the absence of effective legislative action, the following year Peter Bestes, Sambo Freeman,

Felix Holbrook, and Chester Joie followed up, noting, "Sir, . . . you will have the same grand object, we mean civil and religious liberty," and "the divine spirit of freedom, seems to fire every humane breast."[29] The rhetoric of souls aflame with the desire for liberty permeates abolitionist literature. Half a century after these petitions were filed, Maria W. Stewart would assert that once women were allowed an education, "[t]heir souls would become fired with a holy zeal for freedom's cause," and in the spirit of Black revolutionary liberalism, she would proclaim, "African rights and liberty is a subject that ought to fire the breast of every free man of color in these United States, and excite in his bosom a lively, deep, decided, and heartfelt interest."[30] Among many other tactics, Stewart encouraged members of her community to create and sign petitions designed to create social change.

PETITIONS AND THE SOCIAL CONTRACT

A 1774 appeal to the royal governor of Massachusetts provides evidence of the exceptional degree of political awareness among colonial African Americans:

> . . . [A]] Grate Number of Blackes of this Province who by divine per-
> mission are held in a state of Slavery within the bowels of a free and
> christian Country . . . [wish] [t]hat your Petitioners apprehind we have
> in common with all other men a naturel right to our freedoms without
> Being depriv'd of them by our fellow men as we are a freeborn Pepel
> and have never forfeited this Blessing by *aney compact or agreement*
> whatever. [31]

Here, the language of Black revolutionary liberalism, of freedom and natural rights, is augmented with a reference to social contract theory, the central jus-tificatory argument used to legitimize political authority in the Enlightenment and beyond. The petition's contractarian language, "have never forfeited . . . by aney compact or agreement," reveals a high level of political sophistication. John Locke composed his *Second Treatise of Government* to answer the press-ing question, "[W]hat is the source of legitimate political power" if it is not the divine right of the monarch? His answer: individuals *agree* to limit some of their natural rights in a tacit social contract or compact among people who come together primarily for the purpose of protection against both internal and external harms and to increase productivity through private property. Locke's *Second Treatise* was the basis for Jefferson's Declaration of Indepen-dence and the idea of such an agreement is mentioned by Thomas Paine in *Common Sense* (1776). Arguing against tyrannical power, Locke claimed that systematic violation of the contract and of natural rights by the state justified revolution, the argument taken up by the colonists in their war of liberation against the British throne and hinted at in these petitions. It is, therefore, not mere chance that the 1774 petition cites "a naturel right to our freedoms" and that the petitioners "never forfeited this Blessing by aney compact or agreement whatever." The justification for the restriction of rights is thereby undermined.

The American philosopher John Rawls revived the social contract argument in his 1971 book, *A Theory of Justice*, one of the most influential books of political philosophy of the twentieth century.[32] Rawls is taken to have provided an elaborate social contract argument for contemporary liberal democracy, but it is one that takes no consideration of racial or gendered dimensions of the state and society. One response to Rawls was Carole Pateman's *The Sexual Contract*, in which she argues that Rawls's version of the original agreement, the social contract, "held to justify the government of women by men," particularly in "marriage and employment," is in fact about "property in the person and create[s] relationships . . . of [gender] subordination."[33] Adapting this line of argument, Charles Mills holds that this same contract bore a racial dimension, such that, "European expansion and the establishment of white/nonwhite relations of domination adopted race as a structure of exclusion," which Pateman and Mills jointly come to call the "domination contract."[34] As evidenced by the 1774 petition, late eighteenth-century Black activists understood the racial contract and used the power of social contract theory to argue for their liberation. This was a contract they were not a party to, never agreed to, and one that explicitly excludes them on multiple dimensions of civil society. It is, therefore, not a binding agreement for those who are excluded. Thus, a critique of what Mills calls "hegemonic liberalism" and of the real-life applications of concepts of freedom, equality, rights, and contract undergird the powerful arguments for liberation made by African Americans employing Black radical political theory from the revolutionary period to the 1830s and beyond.

BELINDA'S PETITION

Another figure obscured through historical neglect is Belinda Sutton of Medford, who was nonetheless recognized and appreciated by US Poet Laureate Rita Dove in her poem, *Belinda's Petition*:

> *I will not take too much of your Time,*
> *but to plead and place my pitiable Life*
> *unto the Fathers of this Nation.*[35]

And since in my analysis family and community are taken to be central, it is important to note that Sutton is known to have had two children, Joseph and Prine, who were baptized in 1768.[36] One of several feminist critiques of liberalism argues that the central concept of individualism, in Locke and moving forward to the present, envisions a world of healthy young persons making their way in the world through their labor and engagement with property. This inaccurate vision erases children, the elderly, the infirm, and all those who care for them, whose obscured labor is appropriated to the seemingly independent men who were and are actually sustained in families and communities, in large part through the unremunerated labor of women. The importance of Belinda's petition is not simply that it comes from a woman, a relatively rare circumstance, but that it foregrounds her children, her parents, her domestic labor for her enslaver, and the need and right to her fair share of remuneration. Some scholars have suggested the Belinda's petition provides an early argument for reparations.[37]

At the time it was incumbent upon the propertied class not to leave a financial burden on the city or town. Belinda's enslaver, Isaac Royall Jr., willed to her a payment of thirty pounds over three years to be delivered after he died. In 1783 she petitioned his estate for a pension to care for herself and her daughter. While the pension was approved, adequate payment was never made, so she went to the courts again in 1787, 1788, and 1793. The petition states:

> That seventy years have rolled away, since she on the banks of the Rio de Valta received her existence—the mountains Covered with spicy forests, the valleys loaded with the richest fruits, spontaneously produced; . . . would have yielded her the most compleat felicity, had not her mind received early impressions of the cruelty of men, whose faces were like the moon, and whose Bows and Arrows were like the thunder and the lightning of the Clouds. . . . She was ravished from the bosom of her Country, from the arms of her friends—while the advanced age of her Parents, rendering them unfit for servitude, cruelly separated her from them forever! . . . Once more her eyes were blest with a Continent [where] the Laws had rendered her incapable of receiving property—and though she was a free moral agent, accountable for her actions, yet she never had a moment at her own disposal![38]

This section of the petition employs a rhetorical strategy that invokes the very place where Belinda lived the first years of her life in happiness and plenty, reminding the legislators of her independent personhood, her place in a family structure, the denial of the right of property—so central to classic liberal theory—and her capacity as a moral agent. The argument underscores the contradiction inherent in enriching oneself by exploiting her unfree labor while the nation engaged in belligerent action in the name of freedom. The passage evokes Stewart's later observation that "the Americans" have as:

> ... their highest aim to excel in political, moral and religious improvement ... but how few are their among them that bestow one thought upon the benighted sons and daughters of Africa, who have enriched the soils of America with their own tears and blood: few to promote their cause, none to encourage their talents.[39]

The petition is signed with "the mark of Belinda." Some speculate that, lacking written literacy, a surrogate, possibly Prince Hall, composed this petition, but this attribution obscures the fact that the description of her homeland must come from Belinda Sutton's lips, since the scribe would not have known the details of her circumstances. The language of the description brings to mind the words of Maria Stewart as an older woman, written almost a hundred years later in "The First Stage," to describe her own youth—language redolent of another place and time, indeed, another cosmic imaginary. Belinda Sutton's petitions and the other records remind us (as if we would require reminding) that those who were enslaved had families, parents, children, and friends, a fact that is sometimes missing from the reports, documents, and records left to us by the others who petitioned, created organizations, and built churches. Like Maria W. Stewart, Belinda Sutton asserts her frustration at restrictions on her moral agency, legal constraints, and the unfreedom of servitude. Like Stewart, she invokes natural rights, the industry that was required for standing in the liberal republic, and her own desire to contribute rather than burden the state.[40]

Pateman argues that the social contract, which is the foundation of liberal theory, is a dangerous fiction created to assert patriarchal control over women. Mills makes a parallel argument about racial control over Blacks in the racial patriarchy. The fact that the writers of these petitions deny ever having been party to a contract reveals that they are also denying having bargained into an agreement that resulted in their own enslavement. In 1833, Maria W. Stewart would write:

> It is of no use for us to wait any longer for a generation of well educated men to arise. We have slumbered and slept too long already; the day is far spent; the night of death approaches; and you have sound sense and good judgment sufficient to begin with, if you feel disposed to make a right use of it. Let every man of color throughout the United States, who possesses the spirit and principles of a man, sign a petition to Congress to abolish slavery in the District of Columbia, and grant

you the rights and privileges of common free citizens; for if you had
had faith as a grain of mustard seed, long before this the mountains of
prejudice might have been removed.[41]

Like Belinda and others, Stewart understood the ways some people were systematically excluded from the social contract and the civil polity.

PHILLIS WHEATLEY (C. 1753–1784)

Prominent in the pantheon of Black founders, those men and women who
strove to create a more consistent and less hypocritical form of liberal democracy in the seventeenth and eighteenth centuries, several figures stand
out: Ottobah Cugoano and Olaudah Equiano in Britain; in the Americas,
Ceasar Sarter, Reverend Lemuel Haynes, John Marrant, Prince Hall, and Phillis
Wheatley. Christopher Cameron places Sarter as well as Haynes, whose sermon
"Liberty Further Extended" was among the first abolitionist works to use the
rhetoric of the Declaration of Independence, in the tradition of Black puritan
republicanism.[42] Cameron, Arlette Frund, Stefan Wheelock and others analyze
the contributions of the poet Phillis Wheatley in recognition that, as Audre
Lorde observes, poetry as well as prose can have philosophical importance.
Born in the region of Africa near the notorious slave trade port of Dakar she
was then taken to Boston, where she was enslaved. In her lifetime, Wheatley's
collection, *Poems on Various Subjects, Religious and Moral*, garnered considerable attention internationally. Stylistically, the poems follow traditional forms,
and some praise the principles of the American republic. Such praise leads
some scholars to fall into the trap of dismissing her poetry as derivative and
imitative. Wheatley's writings, like those of Maria Stewart and other women
writers, have sometimes been interpreted as conservative in analyses that
overlook the ways that stereotypes and social pressures may force women to
develop imaginative strategies to accomplish their aims. Wheatley is not a
supplicant to white supremacy; she instantiates the duality embedded in one
whose creativity is in chains. Frund identifies her practice of writing poetry
as "her attempt to exercise power over social, religious, and political events."
She notes that

Wheatley overcame the boundaries and obstacles of her position as a
slave and a woman and managed to situate herself in this new field of
discursive power. She first developed her strategies of self-representa-
tion within the family by whom she was enslaved and then negotiated
her entrance into the public sphere.[43]

"Phillis Wheatley, Negro servant to Mr. John Wheatley, of Boston." The poet Phillis Wheatley was kidnapped from West Africa and enslaved by a prominent Bostonian family, later achieving international recognition. Scipio Moorhead, Engraver. [London, Archd. Bell, Sept. 1] https://www.loc.gov/item/2002712199/.

Her precarity sometimes meant downplaying or masking her intellectual accomplishments, her mastery of several languages, and her poetry. She was forced to carefully balance her excursions into liberation rhetoric with an appropriate public display of humility.

In *Barbaric Culture and Black Critique*, Stefan Wheelock draws a threadline from the liberated African (Fanti) Ottobah Cugoano's writing in England, through Wheatley, to Walker and Stewart, who together create an "anti-slavery historiography." Wheelock makes the case that "the culturally 'apostate' practices of commercial slavery opened the way to the emergence of a barbaric culture," by which he means that the embrace of slavery and the trade forced a departure from "religious authority and moral precepts" into pervasive barbaric practices.[44] If, as Barbara Christian says, Blacks are "a race for theory," there may also be a predilection for irony, humor, and playfulness that are among the tools of subjugated peoples. As Toni Morrison remarks, it is a matter of "playing in the dark."[45] Earnest critics have suggested that Wheatley was a conservative, not a liberation figure because of her many appreciative nods to her oppressors, including George Washington. In contrast, Wheelock proposes:

> On the underside of the language of innocence and admonition is the poet's early effort to portray how slavery shadows Anglo Protestant Christianity in the cultural catechizing of its black slaves. If the horrors of the slave trade are not explicitly mentioned . . . there is a playful ambiguity in the poet's recollection of her introduction to Christianity . . . a religious and moral redemption she "neither sought nor knew."[46]

Wheatley lyricizes against the "disgrace" in God's eyes of those who "hold in bondage Afric's blameless race," in keeping with Stewart's admonition, "Oh America, America, foul and indelible is thy stain! . . . for thy cruel wrongs and injuries."[47] Christopher Cameron describes how, in a 1774 letter to Samson Occom, Wheatley wrote, "In every human Breast, God has implanted a Principle, which we call Love of Freedom; it is impatient of Oppression, and pants for Deliverance."[48] Wheatley's poem in praise of George Washington prompted a meeting with the Revolutionary War hero—and so, by her embodiment of African American high literary achievement—she forced Washington face-to-face to see what his own slaves might achieve, given the opportunity. She forced him to face the hypocritical instantiation of his revolutionary Enlightenment ideals. This can only be called subversive. Like Wheelock, Cameron's work is exemplary in reclaiming this foundational voice. He demonstrates the ways in which Wheatley's work

> [s]poke to the central political ideologies of the day, especially republicanism and natural rights. But I would argue that her critical importance lies in inaugurating the tradition of "black prophetic witness," to use Cornel West's phrase. Intimately tied to this tradition is the use of the jeremiad. For white Puritan ministers in the colonial era, the jeremiad relied on notions of providentialism and articulated a worldview whereby God was intimately involved in earthly affairs, an outlook that would have accorded well with traditional African cosmology, as scholars have noted a similar lack of distinction between sacred and secular realms in African thought.[49]

The notion of "black Prophetic witness" has deep roots in African American theology, and Maria W. Stewart should be counted among those witnesses. Cameron writes: "Wheatley's application of covenant theology relates to the influence of republicanism on her work and, in turn, the contribution of her work to republican ideology."[50] This is of no small consequence. Joanne Tetlow argues that John Locke adopted a version of "covenant theology" in which he grounds his "law of Nature." She argues that Locke rejects the predestination doctrine of John Calvin, and allows for "the dignity of human freedom" meaning the exercise of free will, although, as we shall see, enslavement presents a troubling theological conundrum, in the philosophical "problem of evil."[51] Cameron's analysis speaks directly to the position taken up by Stewart, who read Wheatley's poetry in *Freedom's Journal*. Among Stewart's many prophesies,

> You may kill, tyrannize, and oppress as much as you choose, until our cry comes before the throne of God; for I am firmly persuaded that he will not suffer you to quell the proud, fearless, and undaunted spirits of Africans forever; for in his own time, he is able to plead our cause against you, and to pour out upon you the ten plagues of Egypt.[52]

Wheatley had lived much her life as a slave and a servant in a wealthy home just a few blocks away from the place of Stewart's own domicile fifty years later. They are not alone among Black women who were prophetic witnesses. Other women who might have become ordained in the Black churches had it not been for the gender discrimination they faced include Jarena Lee, and Zilpha Elaw, who, according to Joycelyn Moody, combine "a secularized protest against injustice with the sacred issues of their evangelicalism as well as an interdenominationalism."[53] Cameron inscribes the thread of connection in the prophetic tradition from Wheatley and Stewart to Douglass, Malcolm X, and Fannie Lou Hamer.[54]

Black political thought, rooted in the seventeenth and eighteenth centuries, pursued the avenues of both reform and revolution. Those who were enslaved employed a wide variety of survival strategies but ultimately understood that their only real alternatives were either quiet escape or armed rebellion as moral imperatives to resist their unjust condition. Those who were nominally free could tap into alternative strategies. A surge of activism in the 1820s was predicated on Black resistance organizing fifty years earlier, just as the inspirational ideas on which their mission was based had taken form in those days of the American Revolution.

Chapter Seventeen

"TO AMELIORATE OUR MISERABLE CONDITION"

The Second Half of the First Wave[1]

> *O, ye great and mighty men of America, ye rich and powerful ones, many*
> *of you will call for the rocks and mountains to fall upon you, and to hide*
> *you from the wrath of the lamb, and from him that sitteth upon the throne;*
> *whilst many of the sable-skinned Africans you now despise, will shine in*
> *the kingdom of heaven as the stars, forever and ever. Charity begins at*
> *home, and those that provide not for their own, are worse than infidels. We*
> *know that you are raising contributions to aid the gallant Poles; we know*
> *that you have befriended Greece and Ireland; and you have rejoiced with*
> *France for her heroic deeds of valor. You have acknowledged all the nations*
> *of the earth, except Hayti; and you may publish, as far as the East is from*
> *the West, that you have two millions of negroes, who aspire no higher than*
> *to bow at your feet and to court your smiles. You may kill, tyrannize and*
> *oppress as much as you choose, until our cry shall come up before the throne*
> *of God; for I am firmly persuaded that he will not suffer you to quell the*
> *proud, fearless and undaunted spirit of the Africans forever; for in his own*
> *time, he is able to plead his own cause against you, and to pour out upon*
> *you the ten plagues of Egypt.*
> —Maria W. Stewart, *"Religion and the Pure Principle of Morality,"* 1831

On January 1, 1804, Jean-Jacques Dessalines, a former slave and revolutionary leader, declared his country's independence from French control and presided over the formation of an independent nation, the Republic of Haiti. Just a few years later, in 1806, the African Baptist Church opened its doors to a proud public of worshippers. In rapid succession, Great Britain passed the Abolition of the Slave Trade Act and the United States passed the Act Prohibiting the Importation of Slaves, measures that slowed but by no means stopped participation in the international trade in humans. Shortly thereafter, the community lost its greatest organizer, Prince Hall, civil rights petitioner and founder of the African American Masonic movement. The mourners who followed Hall's funeral cortège to the Copp's Hill Cemetery reflected that while there was still no general emancipation, free northern Blacks now had places of their own to worship, while organizations such as the Freemasons and the Free African Society actively improved conditions. Children attended school. Following the ground-breaking formation of the Masonic Lodge #459 in Boston, lodges had incorporated in Providence and in Philadelphia, Boston's rival for independent organizing. A spirit of hope prevailed.

Within two decades of the consecration of the African Baptist Church that had created a sense of progress in the community, that sense had dampened, prospects for abolition dimmed, and the general mood was one of alarm fol-lowed by heightened resistance. A confluence of events and political shifts had produced worsening conditions countered through a rise of Black activism. National politics, economics, and growing rancor were closing in on African Americans in new ways. If the period from the Declaration of Independence to the abolition of the slave trade was characterized by the gradual relinquishing of the bonds of slavery in the North, the next few decades signaled a retrench-ment nationally. Recall the fragile but real sense of cross-racial alliance, at least in some quarters, during the Revolutionary War period. That era brought the judicial abolition of slavery in Massachusetts in the 1780s, the wave of manu-missions in Connecticut in the 1790s, and the development of Free African Societies into the early 1800s. In contrast, territorial expansion and increased industrialization in the North, along with the full-speed-ahead move towards the monoculture of cotton in the South, further entrenched racial oppression. Through the Missouri Compromise of 1820, Maine entered the union as a free state and Missouri as one that expanded enslavement nationally, causing many African Americans to abandon hope for a general abolition without fierce, broad, and concerted opposition. Tighter legislative restrictions strangled Black advances. So desperate were the slave states to perpetuate the notion of intellectual inferiority that they legally countenanced whipping even those who *taught* enslaved people to read.

James Brewer Stewart argues that in the North, two developments collided— the rise of Black "respectability" and the spread of populism—resulting in increased anti-Black racism from the white working class, a development that is instructive even today.[2] Improved prospects from institution building, mutual aid, increases in opportunity, and collective effort had narrowed the distance between classes creating a more substantial Black middle class of stature and visibility. Brewer Stewart asserts that concomitant with this development was a respectability politics that led to a class system within Black society, one that encouraged uplift but also tended to lump, intentionally or not, lower class

Blacks and whites together as lacking virtue, creating a desire by many whites to resist both the class structure and Black racial advances. Others challenge this analysis. Jacqueline Bacon argues that among Blacks, "the elite and poor were allied."[3] In either case, working-class whites disdained class association with working-class Blacks and distanced themselves through racist responses that were promoted by populist politicians such as Andrew Jackson. Addressing respectability politics, Brittney C. Cooper reintroduces the term "organized anxiety" drawn from the writings of Fanny Barrier Williams (1855–1944), a leader of the National Association of Colored Women (NACW), to understand the intricacies of race, class, and gender—intersectional—consolidated efforts. Cooper writes, "Black publics are forged—organized—on anxious terms . . . not only in terms of what Black people are *anxious about* but also what they are *anxious for*. It is simultaneously an anxiety of adversity and an anxiety of aspiration."[4] Community-wide, women in particular were hyperaware of the implications of public organizing, work that cast aspersions on their sexual virtue, their class presumptions, their aspirations. Given the degree to which white poor and working classes feared unflattering comparisons with Black social hierarchies, white resentment of Black success had real implications.

In the traditional gendered political economy, the role of women—mainly privileged white women—remained circumscribed. Most early white women's organizing in the United States tended to be neither radical nor feminist, but it comprised primarily elite women operating within established norms: benevolent groups and institutions such as the Boston Female Asylum for orphaned girls and the Female Missionary Society, groups that supported existing race, class, and gender ideologies enforced by existing power structures. African American women put their efforts towards mutual aid societies that would help cushion women and their families in case of increased hardship, but some were eager to create change and challenge parameters restricting middle-class Black women's behavior.

In the latter half of the 1820s, Maria W. Stewart was immersed in a community that fostered men as leaders. As a married woman, Stewart experienced an elevation in status, transformed by personal, financial, religious, and intellectual support. In patriarchal cultures, women are first the property of their fathers, and then the property of their husbands, and in the ideology of white supremacy, slaves and servants are always children. In Stewart's case, no longer a servant, and married, she was now an adult, suddenly a member of the middle class with privileges never before dreamed of. The wife of a prominent businessman, she was financially secure and freed from servitude. As a congregant in good standing, married in Thomas Paul's church, she had respectability. What she still did not have was the gender privilege that would have allowed her to take her place publicly in the burgeoning political institution-building and civil resistance around her. Like similarly situated women, she was relegated to a supporting role, one that nonetheless carried some weight since in the close-knit Black community men generally did not share the patronizing contempt that many white men exhibited towards women, daughters, and wives. Still, powerful forces restricted access to public roles. The scarcity of resources, shared oppression, and respect for the contributions of women often placed women and men on a more equal footing, while the conventions of respect-ability dictated that women maintain a much lower public profile. Public space was male space, so when the explosion of organized resistance took place, com-munity women were present but much less visible. Within the sphere of accept-able behavior, Maria W. Stewart strengthened her standing within the church and entered the community of married women, now included in conversations about the joys and vicissitudes of the marital state, conversations not deemed proper in the company of unmarried women, along with intellectually richer, deeper, and riskier discourse about politics and action. A grounding principle for Stewart was the unhesitating performance of virtue and respectability. Using the term employed by Brittany Cooper and Fannie Barrier Williams, she was anxious—anxious for change and for opportunity—chafing at the restrictions she faced based on her gender and race. For the moment, she only spoke privately with her husband and with other women about her ideas, as was respectable. The time for their public expression was rapidly approaching.

THE PRINCE HALL MASONS AND THE MASSACHUSETTS GENERAL COLORED ASSOCIATION

In 1824, although Andrew Jackson won the popular vote, John Quincy Adams became president through the electoral college, in what became known as the "corrupt bargain." With Jacksonian populism spreading, property requirements for the electoral franchise were being dropped, and the more rigid class system for whites was crumbling. Duplicitous ideologies of white elites feigned toler-ance for class differences while encouraging intraclass and race animosity. Many working-class whites used whatever means at hand to attack, degrade, and oppress all Blacks, including those who were demonstrating signs of re-spectability. The mob reaction to African Day celebrations is one instance of this impulse. In public, elites generally supported colonization—the removal of Blacks to Africa—as a "benign" solution to the "race problem" while indirectly reinforcing mob violence. In response, the Black community displayed a new-found fervor and determination to affirm their political goals.[5]

With the African American Freemasons now well established, a core group could reassert their prerogative towards further political organizing. In this atmosphere, John Telemachus Hilton, the Reverend Thomas Paul, and fellow Freemasons were initiating David Walker in the new Masonic Hall on the corner of Cambridge and Belknap, alarmed at the degree to which conditions were deteriorating and more determined than ever to act. Corey D. B. Walker argues,

> Through certain Masonic rituals, African American Freemasonry serves as a crucial site where a cultural and political identity based on the logics and technologies of the construct of race is produced and reproduced as a part of one's participation and membership in African American Freemason lodges.[6]

At this crucial juncture of autonomous Black resistance, a wave of organizing took place: a declaration of independence by Black Freemasons, the publication of an African American owned and operated newspaper, *Freedom's Journal*, the formation of the Massachusetts General Colored Association, and the publication of David Walker's *Appeal to the Colored Citizens of the World*. Jacqueline Bacon writes,

> Since the Revolution, African Americans had been creating powerful community institutions and arguing forcefully for civil rights, and by the 1820s, black activism was particularly strong. Protesting oppression and asserting their right to determine their own destinies, African Americans developed a national political consciousness that linked citizens throughout the country.[7]

In 1827 the African Grand Lodge declared its independence from all other (i.e., white) Grand Lodges leading to a forceful tradition of independent African American jurisdictions in North America that became known as Prince Hall Freemasonry.[8] Seeking to expand their sphere of influence beyond the restricted membership of their fraternal brotherhood, Reverend Thomas Paul and his fellow Masons sought to embrace a larger number of people and to create an explicitly political organization. To this end, Thomas Dalton, John Scarlett, William G. Nell, James G. Barbadoes, Walker Lewis, and others incorporated the Massachusetts General Colored Association (MGCA) to agitate for the abolition of slavery and the end of discrimination in education, civic affairs, organized religion, marriage, public accommodation, and to provide uplift.[9] John T. Hilton had arrived from Pennsylvania bringing his considerable skills. And David Walker had arrived just a few years after the Denmark Vesey slaughters, enraged at the treatment of Blacks, North and South, determined to do something about it. Hilton's influence was so profound that in later years Garrison declared that Hilton "had never been found to be wanting in intelligent discrimination as to the best course of action … and had ever been ready to do his utmost in behalf of the cause, without compromise or fear."[10] Unlike the Masons, the MGCA became an organization straightforwardly dedicated to the abolition of slavery, one that unleashed a dynamic powerhouse about to press its full exertions in the effort towards equality. Is it just happenstance that David Walker, with detailed personal knowledge of the vicious Southern strategies for enforcing white supremacy, arrived to fuel the impulse to further organizing? In 1828, in a rousing address at a meeting of the MGCA Walker stated:

> The primary object of this institution, is, to unite the colored population, so far, through the United States of America, as may be practicable and expedient; forming societies, opening, extending, and keeping up correspondences, and not withholding any thing which may have the least tendency to meliorate our miserable condition, with the restrictions, however, of not infringing on the articles of its constitution or that of the United States of America.[11]

There can be no doubt that Walker, along with others, inspired his comrades to action. With this address, Walker's writing career was launched, between his work with the Masons and the MGCA, his work for *Freedom's Journal*, and drafting his major philosophical treatise—his *Appeal*.

FREEDOM'S JOURNAL

While abolitionist newspapers had been published in the past, *Freedom's Journal* was the first to be solely in the agency of Black Americans. Prior to its publication, Boston activists were meeting to marshal support. Jacqueline Bacon writes:

> On the evening of Monday, Feb. 20, 1827, a group of prominent African American Bostonians gathered at the home of abolitionist David Walker. Among the guests were John T. Hilton, leader of the black Freemasons in the city; Walker's neighbor George B. Holmes—a hairdresser, musician and Mason—and the Rev. Thomas Paul, pastor of Boston's African Baptist Church. The meeting was convened to consider the Prospectus for the first African American newspaper, Freedom's Journal, which would begin publication the following month in New York. "In the opinion of this meeting," they resolved, "there is reason to believe that great good will result to the People of Colour by the publication of the 'FREEDOM'S JOURNAL.' … [W]e freely and voluntarily agree to give it our aid and support, and to use our utmost exertions to increase its patronage.[12]

It is unlikely that either of the Stewarts attended this meeting; James was a businessperson, not an activist. And Maria was a woman. Still, they would have been aware of and enthusiastic about the meetings taking place just down the street. The publication launched three weeks later, on March 16, in New York City as the first newspaper owned by an African American in the United States, John Russwurm and Samuel Cornish, editors. David Walker became the Boston agent. It would publish 104 issues in two years, from March 1827 through March 1829. While children were by now being educated in the schoolroom of the Meetinghouse, men and women were experiencing a radical and deep weekly education through *Freedom's Journal*. The paper printed news and advertisements, reprinted previously written pieces by the Philadelphia abolitionist James Forten, the poetry of Phillis Wheatley and Lord Byron, editorials, and letters, all designed to educate and motivate. As the local distributor, Walker took subscriptions and may have delivered bundles to local retail shops and barbershops, where conversations about the content took place after hours. Barbers played an important role, "Beyond distributing newspapers, . . . [they] worked actively with abolitionist societies and lent their shop space to the struggle."[13] Published on Saturdays, locals including the Stewarts started reading the paper that evening—silently, to themselves, out loud to each other, in groups of friends or to their families—anywhere they could gather unmolested. They continued reading after church on Sunday and then throughout the week, with discussions, re-readings, and considerations about how to contribute, support, and nurture this crucial resource. Ten years later, abolitionist Theodore Wright called it "a clap of thunder." Bacon writes, "Arguments in the paper shaped the activism of both African-American and white leaders and reformers for generations to come, and the community activism fostered by the periodical catalyzed the abolition movement."[14]

Maria W. Stewart may also have taken her first step into the public arena in *Freedom's Journal* in 1827. Calvin Herndon asserts, and Jocelyn Moody concurs, that she was the author of a letter to the paper published on August 10, 1827, signed "Matilda."[15]

Messrs. EDITORS,

Will you allow a female to offer a few remarks upon a subject that you must allow to be all-important. I don't know that in any of your papers, you have said sufficient upon the education of females. I hope you are not to be classed with those, who think that our mathematical knowledge should be limited to "fathoming the dish-kettle," and that we have acquired enough of history, if we know that our grandfather's father lived and died. 'Tis true the time has been, when to darn a stocking, and

cook a pudding well, was considered the end and aim of a woman's being. *But those were days* when ignorance blinded men's eyes. The diffusion of knowledge has destroyed those degrading opinions, and men of
the present age, allow, that we have minds that are capable and deserving
of culture. There are difficulties, and great difficulties in the way of our
advancement; but that should only stir us to greater efforts. We possess
not the advantages with those of our sex whose skins are not colored
like our own, but we can improve what little we have, and make our
one talent produce two-fold. The influence that we have over the male
sex *demands, that our minds should be instructed and improved with the
principles of education and religion*, in order that this influence should
be properly directed. Ignorant ourselves, how can we be expected to
form the minds of our youth, and conduct them in the paths of knowledge? how can we "teach the young idea how to shoot," if we have none
ourselves? There is a great responsibility resting somewhere, and it is
time for us to be up and doing. I would address myself to all mothers,
and say to them, that while it is necessary to possess a knowledge of
cookery, and the various mysteries of pudding-making, something more
is requisite. It is their bounden duty to store their daughters' minds with
useful learning. They should be made to devote their leisure time to
reading books, whence they would derive valuable information, which
could never be taken from them. I will not longer trespass on your time
and patience. I merely throw out these hints, in order that some more
able pen will take up the subject. *MATILDA*

Whether or not Stewart is the author of this piece, it resonates with themes dear
to her. It is no accident that the first theme here and elsewhere is ignorance and
education, in the same way that epistemic violence resonates today for so many
feminist theorists, for example Linda Alcoff, Patricia Hill Collins, Brittney C.
Cooper, Kristie Dotson, and José Medina, to name just a few. Arguing to enlarge
the sphere of "proper epistemic subjects," Kristie Dotson writes:

> The erasure of Black women's lives, plights, triumphs, and thought is
> a staple realization in US Black feminist thought . . . from Maria W.
> Stewart's call for "head work" to [Frances E. W.] Harper's realization that
> what passes as knowledge and produces ignorance form formidable ad-
> versaries for black women's liberation.

Reaffirming the work of Patricia Hill Collins, Dotson underscores the importance of placing "black feminist thought in the centre of analysis," a recommen-
dation I strongly endorse.[16] In contrast with the present-day tendency to see

intersectionality as a hodgepodge of widely varying dimensions and inclusions, I would argue that the most accurate connotation of the term from Maria W. Stewart to Kimberlé Crenshaw to the most recent scholarship and activism is that Black feminist thought is situated at the center of intersectional analysis.

Epistemic violence, a method of erasure, obliteration, and aggressive racist attack, displays a variety of aspects. One, it is designed to keep individuals and groups in ignorance on a day-to-day basis with the objective of using this powerful tool to control, demean, diminish, and handicap, as a way of preventing or forestalling resistance and insurrection. This is accomplished, for example, through the denial of education, restrictions on freedom of assembly, and excessive demands of labor. African Americans understood that knowledge, from both experience and book-learning, was and is a precious commodity. Quincy T. Mills describes how a Black businessman, William Dabney, recalls his father's advice:

> Never let a white man know how much you really do know about anything except hard work . . . He don't care how superior you are in working, but for Gawd's sake, son, please listen, if you ever expect to get any money or anything worth while out of a white man, always make him feel like he knows more than you and always act as if you think he's the greatest man in the world.[17]

Another manifestation of the epistemic violence we have seen throughout this study is the silencing designed to obliterate all historical knowledge of past events, theories, ideas, and movements by presenting a narrative through which the dominant/hegemonic powers can "demonstrate," using official accounts, that Black people have never accomplished anything of value because they are naturally incapable of doing so. Thus, even today, few people are aware of the intellectual labors, or even the names of those who are studied here.

Matilda's piece from *Freedom's Journal* credits men with taking an enlightened position about women's education: "But those were days when ignorance blinded men's eyes. The diffusion of knowledge has destroyed those degrading opinions, and men of the present age, allow, that we have minds that are capable and deserving of culture."

She makes an argument familiar with women writers from Mary Astell and Mary Wollstonecraft to Sojourner Truth, Frances Ellen Watkins Harper, and Anna Julia Cooper, namely, to be worthy of their husbands, their God, and themselves, and a boon to their children's education: "[O]ur minds should be instructed and improved with the principles of education and religion." She argues that this is a responsibility of women especially, to educate young people. In her 1830s writings, Stewart is emphatic about the revolutionary value of education. In the *Common Wind*, Julius S. Scott brings to light the epistemic importance of information generated from the ground up and transported on currents propelled by word of mouth. Any epistemology of oppression must pay keen attention to these powerful subterranean rivers of information that educate, fuel, and sustain oppositional narratives and lead to struggle and resistance. In the case of *Freedom's Journal* and through its pages, oppositional discourse found the light of day. With *Freedom's Journal*, five months after her marriage, Maria W. Stewart had something compelling to read.

Chapter Eighteen

"THE MOST NOBLE, FEARLESS, AND UNDAUNTED DAVID WALKER"[1]

—MARIA W. STEWART, RELIGION AND THE PURE PRINCIPLES OF MORALITY

The *Historic Resource Study of the African Meeting House* conducted at the Boston African American National Historic Site in 2002 and compiled by Kathryn Grover and Janine V. da Silva condenses findings drawn from a number of sources and is a valuable repository of information. They write that

> . . . as [Peter] Hinks has noted, also living on the east side of Walker's Belknap Street block in 1827 were fellow Prince Hall Masons John B. Pero and George B. Holmes, both of them hairdressers. Next door were Frederick Brimsley and Pitts, who were both, like Walker, members of the Massachusetts General Colored Association, founded just the year before, in 1826. Again like Walker, all of these men had shops near the waterfront, Pero in Dock Square and the rest just west of that square, on Brattle Street. Across the street from Walker's house were Prince Hall Masons John Courreaux, William Vassall, William Brown, and the Methodist minister Samuel Snowden. Courreaux was a mariner, while Vassall and Brown were waiters, or "tenders."[2]

Shortly thereafter, David and Eliza Walker bought a house on Bridge Street, nearby in the West End, and James and Maria W. Stewart moved into the apartment vacated by the Walkers, evidence of the close relationship between the two families. Others joined the Walkers in their move to the West End and away from the crowding on the North Slope, including Aaron Gual, a cofounder of MGCA and the William G. Nell family.

In rapid succession, a number of organizational steps had been taken. The Prince Hall Masons consolidated their power by incorporating as an

David Walker's *Appeal to the Coloured Citizens of the World* (1829) was one of the most widely acclaimed and condemned treatises on the abolition of slavery. Walker, a friend of and inspiration to Maria W. Stewart, died within a year of his book's publication. David Walker, *Walker's Appeal*. Title page and frontispiece showing slave on top of mountain, with his hands raised to paper labeled "libertas Justitia," which appears in sky / Childs, 1848. [Published] Photograph. https://www.loc.gov/item/92513183/.

independent lodge. Emulating Prince Hall and the masonic activists of the previous century, among this new wave of activists, Walker, Hilton, Paul, and others were pushing hard against Northern social and civil restrictions while at the same time railing against Southern slavery. Intellectually, in their vision for the future, this cohort was integrationist, not separatist, but they knew from experience and as a practical matter that agitating for change was often best done in racially separate groups. While the African lodge had been reserved for Black members, it had always been subsumed under the rules and principles of other Grand Lodges, beholden to a hierarchical white organizational structure. Finally, they severed the bonds of allegiance. With their various levels and secrets, the Masonic orders had been effective in creating a core group of loyal and dedicated members, but the rules were too restrictive for broader social organizing. The initiation process was exclusive and time-consuming.

The newcomer, John Hilton, became grand master and in 1828 addressed the lodge in a speech that was then published through the efforts of Dalton and David Walker.[3] To move past the restrictions, members united around the idea of creating a separate organization with a wider embrace and without the confining rules and orders of freemasonry—the Massachusetts General Colored Association (MGCA).

Walker had found common cause in his associations with the Black Methodist Church, the Prince Hall Masons, the MGCA, and the friendships he formed in Boston—likely the first trusted relationships of his often endangered and peripatetic life in North and South Carolina and the travels that followed his departure from Charleston in the wake of the Vesey judicial horrors. He found his public voice in his 1828 address to the MGCA, and while there is no evidence that he wrote for *Freedom's Journal*, through his connections as a reader and an agent he came to appreciate the power of the written word to inform, educate, and inspire. Perhaps one reason he did not contribute is that he was already at work on his own more systematic tract for by this time he was laboring at one of the most important pieces of writing by an African American in the nineteenth century, his *Appeal to the Coloured Citizens of the World*.[4] The community was strong and mostly united in its resistance to oppression, but with the election of Jackson and Calhoun, prospects for the future seemed grim. Walker continued writing furiously. It was in this atmosphere that he published the first edition of his *Appeal* in September 1829, addressing the issues of "Our Wretchedness in Consequence" of slavery, ignorance, religion, and colonization.

ANALYSIS OF THE *APPEAL*

Walker's *Appeal* augments Black revolutionary political thought and insurrectionist ethics, tackling the metaphysics of enslavement. The Enlightenment philosophers John Locke and Immanuel Kant had posited criteria for personhood: possession of reason and the ability to act morally, vaguely claiming that the criteria would apply universally, while excluding the majority of people through race, class, and gender categorization as well as criteria of defectiveness, and pseudoscientific theories of human inferiority. As Lucius Outlaw argues, "in the Western traditions that have been mediated to us as "philosophy," the key conceptual vehicle ... has been ... the idea and ideal of reason, ... the essence of humans," without which one suffers from what Outlaw calls "ontological death."[5] In this school of thought, Black people went from being full members of the human family to being brutes, as David Walker despairs. So it was Walker's first task to establish them as persons—members of the human family. He writes:

But to prove farther that the condition of the Israelites was better under the Egyptians than ours is under the whites, I call upon the professing Christians, I call upon the philanthropist, I call upon the very tyrant himself, to show me a page of history, either sacred or profane, on which a verse can be found, which maintains, that the Egyptians heaped the insupportable insult upon the children of Israel, by telling them that they were not of the human family. Can the whites deny this charge? Have they not, after having reduced us to the deplorable condition of slaves under their feet, held us up as descending originally from the tribes of Monkeys or Orang-Outangs? O! my God! I appeal to every man of feeling—is not this insupportable? Is it not heaping the most gross insult upon our miseries, because they have got us under their feet and we cannot help ourselves?

He lays bare the inconsistencies when he writes:

My beloved brethren:—The Indians of North and South America—the Greeks—the Irish . . . and the Jews . . . , All the inhabitants of the earth, (except, however, the sons of Africa) are called men, and of course are, and ought to be free. But we, [Blacks] and our children are [thought of as] brutes!![6]

Walker has in mind Jefferson in particular. Thomas Jefferson's *Notes on the State of Virginia* clearly articulated his views on naturally inferiority. Jefferson wrote:

Blacks, whether originally a distinct race, or made distinct by time and circumstances, are inferior to the whites in endowments of both body and mind. It is not against experience to suppose, that different species of the same genus, or varieties of the same species, may possess different qualifications. Will not a lover of natural history then, one who views the gradations in all the races of animals with the eye of philosophy, excuse an effort to keep those in the department of man as distinct as nature has formed them? This unfortunate difference of colour, and perhaps of faculty, is a powerful obstacle to the emancipation of these people.[7]

Jefferson was familiar with the burgeoning Enlightenment writings on race; his library contained seminal works by early race theorists, a testimony to his familiarity with all manner of Enlightenment thought, *much of which did not posit the inferiority of Black people.*[8] It was up to Jefferson, the "ambidextrous philosopher," to choose which route he would take. And he chose to mark people of the African diaspora as inferior, a challenge directly taken up by Walker.[9] As refutation of Jefferson, Walker provides a counterargument in several parts. He asserts as an intuitively known fact the claim that Black people are men, issuing a universal declaration that "Man, in all ages, and in all nations of the earth, is the same."[10] In a line of reasoning adopted earlier by Mary Wollstonecraft and later by John Stuart Mill and Harriet Taylor with regard to women, he repeatedly contends that whites specifically deprive Black people of education—keep them in ignorance—in order to disguise the fact that they are rational creatures: "[I]t is the greatest desire and object of the greatest part of the whites, to keep us ignorant." If a creature lacks a certain natural capacity, for example to reason at the higher levels required by civil and political life, then why, Walker asks, would one bother to create social and legal barriers to something that is naturally impossible anyway? Why? Because "[t]hey are so afraid we will learn to read, and enlighten our dark benighted minds." In his *Appeal*, this is joined with a plea to his community to teach reading to young people at the highest level so that they may demonstrate their abilities.[11] Among the many responses to Jefferson's writings found in the *Appeal*, Walker addresses the twin Enlightenment features of morality and rationality seated in the soul. "Have we souls in our bodies? Are we men who have any spirits at all? ... I am after those who know and feel, that we are MEN, as well as other people; to them, I say, that unless we try to refute Mr. Jefferson's arguments respecting us, we will only establish them."

Walker asks, are we moral? Do we have souls? Can we not engage in arguments? Do we have reason? He repeats the question, "Are we men!!—I ask you, O my Brethren, are we MEN?" In doing so, Walker provides rational, moral, and anthropological arguments against Jefferson's view. Indeed, the most radical feature of his text was its very existence, living proof that a Black man not only could reason and behave morally, but that he could write philosophical literature and critique the most revered philosopher in the nation.[12]

EPISTEMOLOGY

Walker's plea and the focus from both sides on issues of manhood in all its meanings underscore the importance of an intersectional race and gender analysis sensitive to the fact that manhood is measured against both a racialized and a gendered concept of "man" and of what it means to be a woman, and a Black woman.[13] In *Black Women's Intellectual Traditions*, I argue that "gender ideologies tied to notions of sexuality and reproduction are possibly the most influential means of maintaining racism and sexism." Hazel Carby holds that according to the prevailing ideology,

Black manhood . . . could not be achieved or maintained because of the
inability of the slave to protect the black woman in the same manner
that convention dictated the inviolability of the body of the white woman. The slave woman, as victim . . . [was] defined in terms of a physical
exploitation resulting from the lack of the assets of white womanhood:
no masculine protector or home and family, the locus of the flowering
of white womanhood.

As a caution, however, Patricia Hill Collins cites as an impediment to African American political equality the pervasiveness of the view that "a reverse,
damaged gender ideology [is] a sign of racial difference" that rests on "flawed
ideas concerning Black masculinity and Black femininity," a topic that was also
familiar to Maria W. Stewart.[14]

COLONIZATION AND EMIGRATION

David Walker and Maria Stewart vehemently opposed colonization, the plan
to "drain off" "mixed race" free African Americans, sending them to Africa,
in order to "to get those of the coloured people, who are said to be free, away
from those among our brethren whom they unjustly hold in bondage, so that
they may be enabled to keep them more secure in ignorance and wretchedness."[15] The issue of colonization may be confusing for the uninitiated since
there were several different "back-to-Africa" movements advocated by different people with vastly different motives, as well as opponents of both. Some
earlier community leaders like Paul Cuffe had harbored hopes that one avenue
away from oppression lay in emigration to Sierra Leone or elsewhere, an idea
appealing particularly to those who still remembered their homeland. Pursuing a similar line of thought, Reverend Thomas Paul had traveled to Haiti in
1823, and returned with a better understanding of the economic and political
conditions there after meeting with President Jean-Pierre Boyer. As a result,
in part because of language barriers, he abandoned the idea of emigration
and redoubled his efforts pressing for increased civil rights at home. These
activists and others represent a coming together of intellect, broad experience,
and determination to take up the mantle of Prince Hall and other founders
of the Black political movement. With a few exceptions, such as *Freedom's
Journal* editor Samuel Cornish, by the late 1820s, Black people did not support
proposals for emigration from the United States—and many, such as Walker
and Stewart, vigorously opposed it. She writes, "If the colonizationists are
real friends of Africa [Black people], let them expend the money which they
collect, in erecting a college to educate her injured sons in this land of gospel,
light, and liberty."[16]

There are several schools of thought and some shifting grounds on the issues; thus, we may distinguish between colonizationists, emigrationists, and anticolonizationists. The first group, exemplified by the American Colonization Society (ACS), wished to address "the race problem" by removing free Blacks to other countries, hoping to eliminate their "interfering influence," advocating on behalf of the enslaved. For Walker, Henry Clay personifies "a white man, and too delicate to work in the hot sun!! Was he not made by his creator to sit in the shade and make the blacks work for him without remuneration for their services to support him and his family!!!"[17]

In contrast, emigrationists such as Cuffe, and Thomas Paul for some period of time, felt that moral defects in the character and intellect of white Americans made them unsuitable as co-citizens. The best expression of this view comes twenty years later from Martin Delany in his book *The Condition, Elevation, Emigration, and Destiny of the Colored People of the United States, Politically Considered* (1852), in which he argues that Black people had no future in the United States as a result of white moral defectiveness.

A third group, the anticolonizationists, were generally in favor of integration even as they practiced strategic separation. Their goal was not segregation; rather, they understood the value of convening Black-only groups for the purposes of organizing and agitating for liberation, with a goal or objective of integration and social equality. These distinctions remain to this day, with white supremacists roughly aligning with the ACS colonizationists, separatists aligning with Black nationalists, and an array of social justice activists embracing both separatist and integrationist strategies to achieve their goals.

1829—GARRISON'S JULY 4 SPEECH

At around this time, support came from a surprising quarter, a Massachusetts native, trained as a printer, with an interest in religion, ethics, and politics. While the printer, editor, and abolitionist William Lloyd Garrison is often characterized as holding colonizationist views early in his career, his biographer, Henry Mayer, provides a more subtle reading of the circumstances surrounding his July 4, 1829, speech at the Park Street church, "his most radical statement yet on the necessity for abolishing slavery in the name of equal rights, not racial separation."[18] Garrison had acquired some of his views working at Benjamin Lundy's newspaper, *Genius of Universal Emancipation* in Baltimore. We may only speculate about the degree to which direct connections with Boston's African American activists persuaded Garrison to embrace the idea of immediate abolition, but I suspect that their influence was significant. In any case, very soon he was to become one of the most instrumental forces in the public dissemination of the political philosophy of Maria W. Stewart.

DISSEMINATING REVOLUTION

Walker was no armchair political philosopher. He immediately set about creating networks for distributing his book. Peter Hinks, whose research uncovered much of this material, writes that Walker relied on "sailors, overland travelers, and the U.S. Postal Service," to deliver his *Appeal* to those who would be "receptive to its message." An extant letter in Walker's handwriting to a friend, Thomas Lewis, in Richmond, Virginia, reveals that he sent thirty copies to be sold at 12 cents apiece. He sent a packet to Henry Cunningham of Georgia, a preacher with the Savannah African Church—which, no doubt fearing to be apprehended with the materials, Cunningham quickly took the police, who alerted the mayor and the governor, who in rapid succession wrote to the "Indendant of Charleston" and the Mayor of Boston so that "the parties concerned . . . may be dealt with properly."[19] That these letters along with the various copies of the *Appeal* found in the South still exist signals a much wider effort by Walker and his comrades to distribute the work and an equally vigorous effort to suppress it. In Virginia, Governor Giles "convened an extraordinary closed-door session" to forge a response to the "encreasing activity in circulating amongst the people of colour incendiary pamphlets and speeches."[20] In response to a letter from authorities in Richmond, Virginia, Massachusetts governor Harrison Gray Otis conducted an investigation and replied that Walker "Does not seem to have violated any of these laws. It is written by a free black man, whose true name it bears. He is a shop keeper and a dealer in old clothes," and in conversation, "he openly avows the sentiments of the book and authorship." And while Otis "abhors" the sentiments expressed in the text, he explains that he has "no power to control the purpose of the author."[21] A white sailor in Charleston who distributed the pamphlet was tortured into giving testimony, sentenced to a year of hard labor, and fined one thousand dollars for his part, however innocent, in distributing the book.

Many have speculated and it would not be at all surprising if James Stewart played a role in distributing the first edition of Walker's *Appeal* in the South. Stewart was listed in tax records as a colored "shipper of sailors," and according to Garrison biographer Henry Mayer, one of the ways Walker smuggled the pamphlet into the southern states was by having the pamphlet stitched "into the linings of jackets he sold to black sailors."[22] James Stewart may have facilitated the transfer of clothing. Through his business, Stewart heard everything that was going on from his customers, wholesalers, vendors, and the people on the street. He was connected with the seamen's community—possibly a member of one of their mutual aid organizations, the military community, the white and Black communities, and the merchant communities. He was discreet and well respected. Information passed freely but also subtly among those who were trusted. While the Stewarts were married in Reverend Paul's church, he may have had a closer affinity to the May Street Methodist Church of Walker and Snowden. Hinks writes:

> Reverend Snowden's antislavery vehemence may well have outpaced the more moderate Paul. He also had a special mission to the black mariners, who favored his church overwhelmingly, and he had helped any number of them who feared kidnapping when they were in Southern ports. Many of these seamen also probably knew Walker, whose shop provided them with wares and hospitality.[23]

The fluidities of the subjugated knowledges generated from Black communities, north and south, free and enslaved, were merging in ways that were intellectually liberating for African Americans and terrifying for those who perpetrated the slavocracy. Walker's writing, including his *Appeal*, is in the tradition of Black revolutionary political theory that draws upon and corrects the inconsistences of Enlightenment philosophy. Walker embodies what Leonard Harris has called insurrectionist ethics, a view that radical action or advocacy thereof is a moral imperative or duty in order to acknowledge full personhood and the flourishing of all humanity, a theory explored in depth in later chapters.[24] Walker and Stewart's words reveal a conscious connection with classical liberal theory in their repeated referencing of Thomas Jefferson, the primary conduit of Lockean liberal ideas in revolutionary America.

There is a crucial trajectory from the past to the present work of one of the central figures of contemporary African American philosophy, Charles W. Mills. Through *The Racial Contract, Contract and Domination, Black Rights/White Wrongs*, and many essays, articles, and lectures, Mills has provided the most sustained analysis and critique of the racialized functions of liberal theory.[25] In his analysis, contract liberalism was initially designed to create and maintain a category of subpersons excluded from the social contract but who sustain the contract's beneficiaries. He argues that in our nonideal society inexorably drenched in the ideologies of liberalism, a wholesale rejection of liberalism such as the one envisioned in Marxist analyses is not practical.[26] Instead, following a line of argument developed by Zillah R. Eisenstein, he argues that radicalizing liberal theory provides the best hope for producing a more egalitarian society in the United States. Mills details how this might happen and what the theoretical components of such a project are in twenty-first-century liberatory discourse. Since philosophical theories gain credibility and prestige in part through their pedigree, discerning a distinct thread of thought from the eighteenth to the twenty-first centuries lends authoritative weight to Black revolutionary liberalism—or, as Mills would say, Black radical liberalism, both as a sustained political theory and as an activist movement. For Maria W. Stewart, all the anticipation, all the anxiety, all the preparation in the fight for greater equality had been building to this moment of excitement and fear surrounding the publication and distribution of Walker's *Appeal*. There was a frisson—sparks were in the air—such was the sense that change was going to come.

Chapter Nineteen

"CUP OF SORROW" [1]

The author, as it were, upon the one hand, has basked in the sunshine of prosperity; and on the other, she has drunk deep in the cup of sorrow.
—Maria W. Stewart, *Meditations*

MID-DECEMBER 1829

James W. Stewart came home short of breath, feeling weak and unwell. His wife sent for Dr. Caleb H. Snow, the son of Captain John and Huldah Snow, originally from Bridgewater and likely a connection through James's business interests there. Shortly thereafter, she had a visit from Dr. Shattuck, who must have provided significant treatment and medication, perhaps digitalis or some other heart remedy, in the hope that the therapeutic properties of the foxglove plant might restore his health. [2] Derived from the roots of a pale pink speckled flower that cloaked the sometimes deadly, sometimes beneficial effects, the restorative powers would deliver a shock to the heart that might either revive or permanently silence him. With no recovery in sight, Maria Stewart sent word to the shipping office to say that her husband was unwell and would not be able to attend to his work. Shortly thereafter, she received a visit from Daniel B. Badger, the tailor, and Ephraim Titcomb, whose shipping office was just two doors away from James's Broad Street shop in the commercial area near the Custom House, possibly accompanied by Herman H. Holcomb and William P. Horst. Disappearing into the sickroom, they stayed for a time having a lengthy, muffled conversation, leaving Maria Stewart to wonder what was transpiring. Ending their conference with the dying man, they left quickly, a sheaf of papers in hand.

DECEMBER 17, 1829

When James W. Stewart died suddenly of heart failure, Maria Stewart was devastated, mirroring a recollection summoned a year later when she wrote:

> "What shall it profit a man if he gain the whole world and lose his own soul?" dropped from the dying lips of the companion of my youth. O God, was not my conscience stung with remorse and horror, was not my soul torn with anguish, and did not my heart bleed when the summons came: "He must die, and not live." Die! Oh, must he die?
> —Maria W. Stewart, *Meditation X.*

Her husband's body would have been laid out in the Belknap Street house for mourning, as was the custom, where visitors came to pay their respects. It was winter; the need for an expedited burial not present, only to keep the fires burning low. To lie in bed while your husband and protector was lying dead in the next room was a profound reckoning. The Reverend Thomas Paul had recently resigned his position at the African Baptist Church, perhaps due to poor health, to internal controversy in the church, or both, but he nonetheless made his way to the Stewarts' lodging, to pray with her and to console her.

Given their friendship, David and Eliza Walker may have paid their respects, to help her mourn and to find meaning in his death, about the cheapness of life for African Americans, a result of discrimination and brutal oppression, and about the glories of God and salvation of the soul. Walker's Methodism gave him a fierce faith to match his sense of justice. The Walkers' daughter, Lydia Ann, was a little more than a year old, and Eliza would have been concerned at the time about the violently repressive responses to the *Appeal* and the danger it placed them in. The *Appeal* had been published a mere two months prior, and its reception was like a burst of sun—or rain, depending upon your point of view. It had quickly gone into three editions. Walker's discussions about the causes of racial oppression were among the few things that distracted Mrs. Stewart, now a widow, from her despair, drawn as she was, irresistibly, to the topic. Perhaps, as they sat in quiet mourning for her deceased husband, she spoke with Walker of James Stewart's travels, recounting the already familiar tales of the sea, the repeated dangers he had faced compared with the mildness for him of life on land. If, as had been speculated, Stewart was a partner in the dissemination of Walker's pamphlet, his passing would have been doubly mourned as a companion of the heart and a subversive political ally. Always the chameleon and apt businessman, James had connections and the powers to put plans into action that few others connected with the Black community possessed. Lines of distribution would be broken. Beyond the personal loss was the crucial political setback.

Her circle of her friends and his joined together for Stewart's funeral service. Maria Stewart, looking suitable for mourning, was in a state of shock and confusion. Although he had recently stepped down as pastor of the African Baptist Church, records show that Reverend Paul performed the service. Catherine and Susan would be in attendance, and the community turned out in strength. James Stewart was well known, established in Boston for thirteen years with connections across race and class in the brotherhood of mariners. Respected among seamen and merchants for his knowledge and stature, both humble seaman and wealthy mariners noted his passing. His experiences on the sea had cast him farther and to more remote corners than many experienced sailors for whom the North Atlantic comprised their entire map and scope of experience. He had served both as a merchant seaman and a military one. His stories were well known. And he had married a brilliant and beautiful woman almost half his age and had cared for her well-being. The community of seafarers and commercial people were joined by those whose lives centered around the African Baptist Church and those, primarily seamen, who were more closely tied to Reverend Snowden's May St. Methodist Church where the Walkers worshipped. Neighbors and boarders were on hand. And her friends in Christ, in service, and in activism joined as well.

Geographically, Boston's tadpole shape, with its head jutting into the sea, the narrow tail forming an isthmus to the inland, created a cinch that squeezed its inhabitants into neighborhoods that left little room for burial grounds. Copp's Hill, where the remains of Prince Hall lay, was full. The Granary and King's Chapel, with their Puritan forefathers and errant theologians, were crowded and inhospitable. The city leaders had ordered a new burying place to be built in the South End in 1810 and construction proceeded apace, in a location neither apt nor welcoming. Did pall bearers endure the long walk from Belknap Street to the Neck bearing a man known for his solid construction? It was common to have two sets of bearers and even then to stop and rest along the way. Maria Stewart, deeply in shock and mourning, made the journey with the funeral procession, possibly torn—cursing God for her ill fate and praying fervently for his salvation and her own.[4]

DECEMBER 21, 1830

Maria Stewart's grief was shattered almost immediately by the stark demands of a legal system infamous for its complications, particularly in matters of death, Blackness, and the requirements of being a woman and wife in mourning, for just days after his death and before the frost had settled on his grave, the estate of James W. Stewart was called for probate. From the beginning, settling James Stewart's estate calls to mind the worst of Charles Dickens's descriptions

of England's Chancery Courts and criminal deception, as well as the names
of his nefarious characters. Just as quickly, goods were taken from her house
by Daniel B. Badger and Isaiah Woods, ingratiating themselves to the stricken
widow—or simply deceiving her—as she found herself emotionally devastated
and without the means to survive. Some household goods were sold to provide
cash for day-to-day sustenance, but even here, the deceit is clear since Woods
later presented a bill to the estate in the form of a note purportedly signed by
Maria W. Stewart indicating that she had agreed to the exchange, but instead of
a signature there appears an "X"—supposedly the sign of an illiterate widow. In
later years, Alexander Crummell suggested that Stewart could not "even pen her
own thoughts ..." Crummell's is a case of a sympathetic romantic notion of a
benighted frail woman—sadly false. In Woods's case, it was simple forgery. Just
a glance at other court documents reveals a beautifully formed and flourished
signature: Maria W. Stewart.[5]

JANUARY 11, 1830

As required by law, notices of James W. Stewart's death were placed in newspapers so that those who had a claim against the estate, those to whom money
might be owed, could submit their claims. A will or perhaps two petitions were
introduced in probate court. At the moment of the reading, Maria W. Stewart
would have felt nearly as much distress as from her husband's untimely death:
the contents were revelatory and shocking. His funeral debts were to be paid
"by my executor herein after named."[6] All fair and good, but who is to be the
executor? Before this person could be named, after barely two sentences, the
will names a daughter, *Fanny Thompson*, as the recipient of "one bed, bedstead,
and bedding." According to an 1879 affidavit signed by Crummell and Wesley
Howard, James Stewart had acknowledged "one or two illegitimate children"
before their marriage, so Maria Stewart presumably had been apprised of the
connection.[7] Jolted back to the reading by mention of her own name, she finds
the bestowal of "one bed, bedstead bedding"—one would hope so, that her
marital bed would come to her. And then the revelations continue, "To Laura
Stuart of Winson [Windsor]," presumably a wife! "in the state of Connecticut,
the sum of five dollars to be paid out of my estate by my executor herein after
named." Again, the mystery.[8]

And then the crushing announcement: "And as to all the residue of my estate
real and personal I do hereby, give, devise & bequeath all the residue of my
said estate, real and personal ... to Daniel B. Badger, my executor" along with
"his heirs, executors, administrators, assign forever ..." Not given to faintness
of mind, heart, or body, Maria Stewart's resilience may nevertheless have failed

her. Badger. The pushy man who brought his friends to James's bedside while his health was failing. A business acquaintance, perhaps, possibly one of many associates in his commercial ventures, but hardly a friend and confidant. She could think of many other trusted friends who would be named before Mr. Badger and his cronies. The meaning of the words drifted into her consciousness while she tried both to comprehend the implications and to listen to what was being read. Net proceeds to be invested in "the public fund or in bank stocks . . ." And more. Property bequeathed to someone purported to be James's mother, Phebe Freeman of Windsor and again Fanny Thompson, and even more to a designee, with any residuals going to Daniel B. Badger Jr., apparently Badger's son. Why on earth him? It was not at all clear why James would have family in Connecticut, particularly the far inland town of Windsor, when he spent his life at sea and near the shore. A curiosity of the Windsor address—a town at a good distance, in another state, subject to different laws—was that it was known to Herman Holcomb, a witness to the will.[9]

The reading of the will continued, designating that "one other third part of the income of said property to my wife Maria W. Stuart, as long as she remain my widow & unmarried." Note—not the *property* itself but the income generated by it, with the principal going to Badger Jr. and *his* heirs. This would mean that it would be up to the younger Badger to distribute the income, as it accrued, to Maria Stewart. And if the principal were spent? The whole of the principal not otherwise dispersed was to go to Badger Sr., which in case of his decease, goes to Badger Junior, and to Fanny's children, should she have any. Signed: Ephraim Titcomb, Herman H. Holcomb, and William P. Horst, also signed J. W. Stewart. Titcomb, from Newburyport, had a shop at 79 Broad, a mere two doors away from the shipping office of James W. Stewart. Herman H. Holcomb's family hailed from an area near Windsor, Connecticut. Awash in a wave of confusion, Maria Stewart's known world faded into streaks of watery gray, dripping across the vivid lines of what a few days ago was her reality—a husband, a home, friends, church, business—blurring them into a vanishing montage replaced by a more hideous picture. Was she a bigamist? Was Laura Stuart his true wife? Had she been deceived? Who was this family, rarely mentioned and never seen, yet who evidently held such a place of honor in James's heart as to precede her in his bequeathals? Who was her tormentor, and how did he bring this about? And finally, did this mean she might be destitute again? These thoughts and more clouded her mind as she made the dismal trek home.

With judicial consideration and investigation, the will was ultimately dismissed due to what Marilyn Richardson describes as "legal measures so blatant and shameless that even the presiding judge found them hard to stomach—at one point a mystery woman was put forth as a competing widow." A measure of relief washed over Maria Stewart.[10] She may then have felt that his estate would come to her after all, but her legal problems had only just begun. Pause for a moment to consider the devastating destruction accomplished by legal systems perverted to the ends of the powerful and privileged. Contrast the need, then and now, for impartial procedural and true substantive justice, and the vast injustices perpetrated by power differentials, structural and personal—truly intersectional—that make the outcomes of judicial proceedings a sham leaving so many in despair.

FEBRUARY 8, 1830

A Petition of Administration was filed along with seven additional motions—eight entries pertaining to "orders of notice," bonds, letters, and a warrant for inventory. Maria Stewart was charged with creating an inventory, which she produced on March 15, along with a list of debts. She petitioned for a widow's allowance, and in court again on March 25, she requested funds for counsel "in opposing the Probate of the will of the deceased" and for other legal services rendered. It appears as though she may also have traveled to New York, possibly in relation to settling the estate, although it is unclear why. At this time, shaken with regret and uncertainty, with the submission of the list of debts before the probate judge, Joseph Hall, Maria W. Stewart filed a petition—a request to declare personal insolvency. She had no personal income and no access to her husband's estate as long as it remained in probate.

Having failed at their initial gambit, Badger and his partners began a campaign to usurp Maria W. Stewart's power as administrator of the estate. The estate still contained plentiful assets. Having been thwarted from using the simpler expediency of a fake will, Badger and company set about to strip the estate of its assets through the more complicated means of producing various claims against it, while Maria Stewart continued her work providing an asset inventory. This must have been an arduous task, as her access to and understanding of his business was not thoroughgoing. She was, however, affirmed as administrator, and Badger was legally excluded as executor. Through the course of time, Badger managed to collect $8.25 for sailing shares and, puzzlingly, $50 for funeral expenses, in addition to funeral expenses of $78.25, as well as a charge for $505.50 for an indeterminate expense, while Mr. Woods, who absconded with items from their flat just a few days after James's passing—the man with the paper supposedly from Maria Stewart marked "X"—submitted a bill for $379.46. And the estate was still not close to being settled. Court proceedings would drag on for two more years.

Fifty years later, Stewart's friend Louise Hatton investigated James's death and wrote:

I was startled at the developments made, and at once understood why she carried such a sad, sorrowful, and mysterious countenance. In having occasion to very often visit the different courts I found her husband had been a gentleman of wealth, and left her amply provided for; but the executors literally robbed and cheated her out of every cent; so she was left entirely alone in the world—without mother, father, sister, or brother—in fact, not a living relative in the world to care for her, and with so much amiability and piety of character that she would have suffered wrong rather than defend her rights.[11] She knew there was a will made, but never heard it read, as one of the executors took it out of the house as soon as it was drawn up—which was two days previous to her husband's death. She never knew the contents of her husband's will until 1879, when I myself informed her. It was made on the 15th of December, 1829.

In investigating her case I made frequent visits to the different courts, to find her marriage record and also his death record. I heard there was a will made. I also visited the Probate Court. I asked for the will; it was given to me; and I spent quite a time in reading it over, with surprise and indignation. I cannot express the horror I felt at the great wrong and injustice done the poor, helpless woman, now far advanced in years; but at that time one of the most beautiful and loveliest of women. O, what a shame—what a dreadful shame—for those robbers to so shamefully cheat her out of all that her husband had left her.[12]

It is not clear what document Hatton read, whether she referred to the disavowed will or some other record, as the court eventually ruled that James W. Stewart had died intestate. In any case, the results were the same. Maria Stewart was widowed, in the process of declaring bankruptcy, and under assault from strenuous efforts to steal from her whatever financial expectations she may have had.

MEDITATIONS

In 1826 was married to James W. Stewart; was left a widow in 1829; was, as I humbly hope and trust, brought to the knowledge of the truth, as it is in Jesus, in 1830, in 1831 made my public profession of my faith in Christ.
—Maria W. Stewart, "Religion and the Pure Principles of Morality"[1]

Wracked with despair, discouraged, and ashamed, Maria Stewart began writing down her thoughts, typically upon returning from Sunday service while reflecting on the sermon. She had begun putting her despair into words, rationally and spiritually working out her grief through her writing. The resulting *Meditations* provides a roadmap of her inner life during this period of time. My reading of the original documents, the published *Meditations*, suggests that the introduction was penned after the rest of the *Meditations* was written, and just before its publication, for reasons that will become clear. She began writing her meditative thoughts shortly after James's death, a set of therapeutic introspections, borrowing from a hymn written by the Reverend Samuel Occom, a member of the Mohegan nation, who became a Presbyterian minister:

Tell me no more of earthly toys
Of sinful mirth and carnal joys.[2]

She was attending church services regularly on Sundays and Thursday evenings, praying alone during the week and taking counsel with friends, the Reverend Paul, Catherine and Susan, possibly the Walkers—David and Eliza. It is possible to trace the events of 1830 using her *Meditations* as clues. During this time, she quietly underwent a personal salvation—a conversion experience—like those souls who were saved in 1808 by the Reverent Abel Flint in Hartford, Connecticut. "Being brought to knowledge of the truth as it is in Jesus" was a mystical experience signifying the process of being "born again" in Christ.

She wrote her *Meditations* as reflections on her inner experiences all the while dealing with James's business affairs. A schism at the church had torn apart the bedrock of her equilibrium and created acrimony among the congregants, so she had to make the journey of her grief at least partly on her own while continuing to raise her political consciousness, following local events by word-of-mouth and national and international ones in newspapers.

1830

In her first *Meditation* she wrote, "I have been sorely troubled in my life," and "I have found that a Christian's life is a life of warfare; for the spirit wars against the flesh, and the flesh wars against the spirit," and like St. Paul, she laments, "I am forced to cry out ... O wretched man that I am! Who shall deliver me from this body of sin and death?" and she *is* warring—with Badger and the courts for her livelihood, frightened that she will be destitute, and possibly also in the African Baptist Church where there is turmoil among the congregation and trying in her deep sorrow to comfort herself with the thought of salvation.[3]

By *Meditation II*, having just returned from church, she is feeling some comfort; "O, may what I have heard prove a rich and lasting blessing to my soul," perhaps indicating an opening made for her conversion experience. *By Meditation III* she is engaging in an imaginary call and response, opening with the salutation, "My friends ..." This moment seals her conversion, and she is grateful that she was not so unlucky as to die before being born again, fortunate "that I have not been consumed ... I am not now in hell lifting my eyes in torments," declaring that she is "a prisoner of hope." "I rejoice that I have been born a rational and accountable creature, and that ever I was born to be born again."

The hopeful portion of her journey through trauma and grief, however, is not sustained in *Meditation IV*. In this writing session, she is "cast down, O my soul ..." " ... [I] have just returned from church-meeting. Didn't perceive that Christian spirit of fellowship which ought to exist."[4] This may have been personal, but just as likely it was a result of the dissension in the church, in which she may well have taken sides. The source of conflict, some scholars have suggested, may have been over the acceptable degree of political activism appropriate to the church. Thomas Paul's magnificent quarter-century reign bringing the church from infancy to maturity had ended in conflict, and he was replaced by Reverend John Peck. We may be assured that Stewart took the side of the more politically radical religious denominations such as the Methodism of Snowden and Walker, and fell on the side of agitation for rights. Like Walker, this would be part and parcel of her system of both political and religious beliefs—that salvation was available to everyone, even white people, and that to be saved, those souls must lead virtuous lives and be cleansed of their racial hatred, a commitment leading to rights and liberties for her people and all people.

Further, if this was March 1830, as is likely, she would have just been forced to file for personal insolvency, still with the hope of gaining from James's estate, for she writes, "[H]ave met with an earthly disappointment. Am somewhat disheartened.—For naked came I forth from my mother's womb, and naked I shall return hither."

> The Lord gave and the Lord hath taken away: blessed be the name of the Lord. O my soul, labor not for the meat that perisheth, but for that which endureth unto life eternal. Lord, thou hast chastened me sore; but though thou hast caused me to fall, thou hast not utterly taken from me thy loving kindness: but thou hast dealt in tender mercy and compassion with me. I adore thee, praise thee, and bless thee, Parent of mercies, for thy patience and forbearance with me; for hadst thou left me to myself, where would my mad career have ended? Parent of mercies, give me calm submission to thy holy will in all things; for thou hast said that as thy day is so shall thy strength be.[5]

Stewart casts about for blame and seeks to understand what has befallen her. With reference to Stewart and her "spiritual sisters," the "sanctified black women" Jarena Lee and Julia Foote, Susan Houchins explains the three-fold nature of the mystical experience of salvation:

> First, during a period of purification, the individual recalls her past life, reviews her autobiographical data—so to speak—attains profound self-knowledge, and is overcome with remorse. Second, along the mystic way, God enlightens her, reveals to her esoteric theological truths, sometimes bestows a gift of deeply erotic visions, which symbolize the depth of their shared mystical love, and promises her eternal salvation. And third, the mystic is profoundly affected and permanently transformed (sanctified) by the experience."[6]

Shortly thereafter, in *Meditation V*, Stewart is comforted by the thought that "if we live pure and virtuous lives here, when we come upon the bed of death, we shall be enabled to lean our head on the bosom of Jesus, and to breathe our souls out sweetly there," a thought that corresponds with the second stage.

GRIEF, DESPAIR, TRAUMA, AND RACISM

In her loneliness and despair and with few friends, Maria W. Stewart turned to her religion for comfort, but the process of understanding her losses and coming to terms was by no means easy. Valerie Cooper remarks on Stewart's near obsession: "[I]n the context of so much personal loss, it is not surprising that Stewart mentions the possibility of her own death so frequently."[7] On the issue of trauma, Linda Martín Alcoff observes,

> I gain self-determination by embracing my emotions and embodiment rather than seeking to transcend them, even emotions caused by the destructive acts of others. Instead of retreating from all others after a traumatic event, my salvation from destructive acts lies in opening myself up to others, even leaning on them.[8]

And yet, although Stewart frequently appeals to her "friends" (and sometimes her "unconverted friends") in her *Meditations*, few people are available to provide her with solace and understanding. Few are there for her to abide by Alcoff's sage advice to open herself up to others. In the circumstance, she uses thought, prayer, and writing to open herself up to Jesus through her *Meditations* and by declaring herself committed to the savior. On the issue of despair, Lewis Gordon observes that "human beings are aware, no matter how fugitive that awareness may be, of their freedom in various situations, that they are consequently responsible for their condition on some level, that they have the power to change at least themselves, through coming to grips with their situations, and that there exist features of their condition which provide rich areas of interpretative investigation."[9] For Stewart, that change may or may not be the existential one that Gordon and Sartre imagine, but in conceptual kinship, she makes a radical leap of faith by accepting the inevitability of death and embracing her own power to act and believe as she will through what Joycelyn Moody calls a "theology of survival."[10]

One of the most systematic accounts of Blackness and trauma is found in George Yancy's *Black Bodies, White Gazes*. Stewart has been immersed in white racist responses to her Blackness throughout her life, but that constant state does not shield her from ever newer forms and expressions of race and gender hatred. The courtroom supplied a new venue, one that is psychologically disruptive under the best of circumstances, for her to be fixed and judged by the white male predatory gaze. According to Yancy, the claims about "white people and their racist gestures" have "empirical content in relationship to the larger history within which they get their purchase, and they are underwritten by white racist brutality" an expression of colonial power, a part of the "epistemic regime of whiteness." The actions of Badger and others like him abide in a historical context in which the idea of "Black property" is anathema, and white appropriation is institutionalized as a practice.[11] David Walker provides a historical context:

> I ask those people who treat us so *well*, Oh! I ask them, where is the most barren spot of land which they have given unto us? Israel had the most fertile land in all Egypt. Need I mention the very notorious fact, that I have known a poor man of colour, who laboured night and day, to acquire a little money, and having acquired it, he vested it in a small piece of land, and got him a house erected thereon, and having paid for the whole, he moved his family into it, where he was suffered to remain but nine months, when he was cheated out of his property by a white man, and driven out of door! And is not this the case generally? Can a man of colour buy a piece of land and keep it peaceably? Will not some white man try to get it from him, even if it is in a *mud hole*? I need not comment any farther on a subject, which all, both black and white, will readily admit. But I must, really, observe that in this very city, when a man of colour dies, if he owned any real estate it most generally falls into the hands of some white person. The wife and children of the deceased may weep and lament if they please, but the estate will be kept snug enough by its white possessor.[12]

Walker thus presciently imagined Maria Stewart's predicament.

Intellectually, Stewart's education in "the cradle of liberty" was an immersion in the hypocrisy of Enlightenment ideologies. She simultaneously came to understand the related tenets of reformed theology, rejecting the notion of a white "elect" while embracing the idea of salvation through religion. Valerie Cooper observes that Stewart seems to be combining "evangelical theology … with the republican rhetoric at the foundation of the United States," particularly in her repeated use of the term "independence," while at the same time she endeavors to make these theories internally and externally consistent with what Yancy calls the "empirical content" of the "larger history."[13] In addition to the daily reminders of the failures of equality promised by classic liberal theory, a barrage of traumatic incidents confirmed the failure of the American promise to Black people. Addressing Du Bois's views on the emotions imposed by double consciousness, Yancy speculates that "the pain and trauma of rejection was probably all the more intense because he thought he (Du Bois) shared certain similarities" in being an American, as promised by republican ideals of equality.[14] The cognitive dissonance generated by the chasm between theory and practice was and is a profound source of pain.

SPRING-SUMMER 1830

In the spring of 1830, the final edition of David Walker's *Appeal* was published. Maria Stewart was shattered by the sudden death of its author, her friend, on August 6. While her shock and sorrow at this event were very real, in this phase of her grieving and her conversion, she may have almost envied him, while mourning the loss of his voice and fervor. Clearly, she thought deeply about the nature of death, and at this point she truly would have welcomed it for herself, declaring forthrightly that she had nothing to fear. Some of her fears were for the unsaved souls. The protectors of the system of slavery had offered a reward for Walker's death, and rumors circulated that this wish had been fulfilled, that he had been poisoned. They were countenanced years later by Henry Highland Garnet in his biographical remarks that introduced a new printing of Walker's *Appeal*.[15] In another view, Walker biographer Peter Hinks writes that "only a few days after his beloved infant daughter, Lydia Ann, died of consumption, David Walker too was carried away by the same dread disease."[16] It would be almost a year before Maria Stewart would write of his death, but its tragic occurrence may have planted in her the seed that grew into a desire to continue his labors.

NEW YEAR 1831

Stewart's moods swing as she records her thoughts. In *Meditation VIII*, she inquires, "Is there *no balm in Gilead?*" and her surprising reply? "Yes there is." Examining the translations of this familiar biblical verse is revealing. Sometimes translated into gender-neutral terms as: "Is there no physician there? Why then is there no healing for the wound of my people?" In the King James Version, it is: "*Is there* no balm in Gilead; *is there* no physician there? why then is not the health of the *daughter* of my people recovered?" The daughter. "Yes there is," Stewart replies.[17] As Valerie Cooper explores in detail, Stewart regularly finds a personal identification with biblical passages, as in the epigraph for in *Meditation XIII*, "The widow and the fatherless, seek for his aid in sharp distress," from *Deuteronomy*.[18] She writes, "Another year past and gone forever," a reflection that brings her hope. While there is still no settlement of her husband's estate, and local and national news are generally bad for the cause of freedom, Stewart writes about hearing words directed towards her "Methinks I hear a voice which says,—Daughter be of good cheer; thy sins be forgiven thee. Consoling thought!"[19]

Maria Stewart may have had yet another source of good cheer, for on that very New Year's Day, William Lloyd Garrison published the first issue of *The*

Liberator.[20] On Saturday, January 1, she had read with joy the motto: "*Our country is the world—our countrymen are mankind,*" and opening salutation:

> To date my being from the opening year,
> I come, a stranger in this busy sphere,
> Where some I meet perchance may pause and ask,
> What is my name, my purpose, or my task?
>
> My name is "LIBERATOR"! I propose
> To hurl my shafts at freedom's deadliest foes!
> My task is hard—for I am charged to save
> *Man from his brother*!—to redeem the slave!

Garrison takes this birthing moment to make amends for his own past wrongs, quite likely spurred on by his new friends in the North Slope community and his reading of Walker's *Appeal*—with its full article devoted to a screed against the American Colonization Society. Garrison writes:

> In Park-street Church on the Fourth of July, 1829, in an address on slavery, I unreflectingly assented to the popular but pernicious doctrine of *gradual* abolition. I seize this opportunity to make a full and unequivocal recantation, and thus publicly to ask pardon of my God, of my country, and of my brethren the poor slaves, for having uttered a sentiment so full of timidity, injustice and absurdity.

Garrison repents his previous sympathies with the ACS. In her sorrow, Stewart must have rejoiced. *Freedom's Journal* had ceased publication in March 1829, and while the *Liberator* was not the product of African American agency, it filled the lacuna created by the previous loss. At about the same time, Stewart wrote the introduction to her *Meditations* and identifies her conversion experience:

> Never did I realize, till I was forced to, that it was from God I derived every earthly blessing, and that it was God who had a right to take them away. I found it almost impossible to say, "Thy will be done." It is now one year since Christ first spoke peace to my troubled soul. Soon after I presented myself before the Lord in the holy ordinance of baptism, my soul became filled with holy meditations and sublime ideas; and my ardent wish and desire have ever been, that I might become a humble instrument in the hands of God, of winning some poor souls to Christ. Though I am sensible that Paul may plant, and Apollos water, but that

God alone giveth the increase, through Christ strengthening me I can do all things; without him I can do nothing.[21]

My contention is that she composed the introduction to her *Meditations* at this time, after the other fourteen meditations were written. The introduction, then, signals the culmination of this form of written expression, and the beginning, at least in her thoughts, of addressing both her religious and her political views more systematically.

The inaugural issue of the *Liberator*, published by Garrison and Isaac Knapp, marked a new beginning for interracial organizing. In January, a meeting took place in the African Meeting House to form the New England Antislavery Society. A few months later, as Christopher Cameron writes, a "meeting occurred in Boston on 12 March 1831 and included the leading African American abolitionists in the state—Reverend Samuel Snowden, Robert Roberts, James G. Barbadoes, Masonic leader John T. Hilton, Reverend Hosea Easton, and Thomas Dalton," vowing to make every effort to oppose the Colonization Society.[22] But 1831 fails to bring her relief from the courts. On February 21 there are more Orders of Notice, and she is forced to petition for yet another allowance. As if this all weren't enough, on April 13, the Reverend Thomas Paul passed away.

The *Liberator* reported:

It is our painful duty, to-day, to insert the death of Rev. Thomas Paul, (for many years Pastor of the African Baptist Church in Belknap street) which took place in this city on Wednesday afternoon, at 5 o'clock. He died of consumption, age 51 years. Few men ever deserved a higher eulogy than Mr. Paul. In his manners, he was dignified, urbane and attractive; his intellect was assiduously cultivated ... As a self-made man, (and, in the present age, every colored man, if made at all, must be self-made) he was a prodigy. His fame, as a preacher, is exceedingly prevalent; for his eloquence charmed the ear, and his piety commended itself to his hearers. Though severely afflicted, by a long and distressing illness, he bore his sufferings with marvelous resignation; not a murmur escaped his lips; death came to him as an angel of light. And truly he might exclaim with an apostle, in view of his ministerial career, "I am now ready to be offered, and the time of my departure is at hand—I have fought a good fight, I have kept the faith; henceforth there is laid up for me a crown of righteousness, which the Lord, the righteous Judge, shall give me at that day."[23]

In her grief for James W. Stewart, David Walker, and Thomas Paul, Stewart also finds not just solace, but something like ecstasy from her conversion experience, and no small amount of astonishment that others are not keen to join her in the saturation of divine happiness. She develops a sense of urgency, a desire to share her born-again experience with her friends and those in her circle. She is driven from both sides by her visceral joy in her acceptance into the arms of the Lord and her stark fear that others will be left behind. Her conversion experience is new—in the front of her mind. In the course of her rapid intellectual and spiritual development, Stewart will experience a number of transformations and developing complexities in her thinking. Along the country's Eastern seaboard, apocalyptic events were taking place.

AUGUST 21–23, 1831

An enslaved man in Virginia was visited by spiritual visions, "a keen, mechanically gifted man whose religion offered him a rationalization for his opposition to the status quo." According to Herbert Aptheker, "six slaves, then, started out, in the evening of August 21, 1831, on their crusade against bondage." The uprising failed but took the lives of many enslavers. "Turner was tried and, though pleading not guilty, since, he said, he did not *feel* guilty, he was condemned to hang."[24] An item in the *Salem Gazette* in Virginia read:

> A fanatic preacher, by the name of Nat. Turner [Gen. Nat. Turner!] who had been taught to read and write and permitted to go about preaching in the country, was at the bottom of this infernal brigandage. He was artful, impudent, and vindictive, without any cause or provocation that could be assigned.[25]

As for cause, like the Vesey plot, and the flood of other rebellions, religious, moral, and political convictions underwrote their actions. Likewise, the rebellion reverberated throughout the nation, especially in the South. In *Incidents in the Life of a Slave Girl*, Harriet Jacobs wrote:

> Not far from this time Nat Turner's insurrection broke out; and the news threw our town into great commotion. Strange that they should be alarmed, when their slaves were so "contented and happy"! But so it was. . . . The next day, the town patrols were commissioned to search colored people that lived out of the city; and the most shocking outrages were committed with perfect impunity. Every day for a fortnight, if I looked out, I saw horsemen with some poor panting negro tied to their saddles, and compelled by the lash to keep up with their speed, till they arrived at the jail yard. Those who had been whipped too unmercifully

to walk were washed with brine, tossed into a cart, and carried to jail. One black man, who had not fortitude to endure scourging, promised to give information about the conspiracy. But it turned out that he knew nothing at all. He had not even heard the name of Nat Turner.[26]

In merciless retribution, Nat Turner was hanged in Virginia in October. Prince Hall Mason and prominent community organizer John Telemachus Hilton called for a fast day in remembrance of Nat Turner for November 11, 1831. In the face of the events of the past year, the deaths and disappointments, the growing national strife, along with the redemption she experienced, Maria Stewart felt compelled to make a life-changing decision.

Chapter Twenty-one

MARIA W. STEWART AND THE PRINCIPLES
OF MORAL AND POLITICAL THEORY

Feeling a deep solemnity of soul, in view of our wretched and debased situ-
ation, and sensible of the gross ignorance that prevails among us, I have
thought it proper thus publicly to express my sentiments before you.
—Maria W. Stewart, "Religion and the Pure Principles of Morality"

And so we come once again to the moment when, feeling less crushed with grief or silenced by the social and psychological barriers imposed by race oppression, elitism, and gender condescension, at age twenty-eight, Maria W. Stewart walked into the office of William Lloyd Garrison and Isaac Knapp with a piece of writing and a request that the foremost white abolitionist of the day put it into print. Maria Stewart was more than inspired. She was on fire with the power of truth behind her and the protection of God all around her. She had little to fear. Garrison recalls:

> . . . you made yourself known to me by coming into my office and put-
> ting into my hands, for criticism and friendly advice, a manuscript
> embodying your devotional thoughts and aspirations, and also various
> essays pertaining to the conditions of that class with which you were
> complexionally identified—a class "peeled, meted out, and trodden un-
> derfoot." You will recollect if not the surprise, at least the satisfaction I
> expressed on examining what you had written.—far more remarkable
> in those early days than it would be now, . . . I not only gave you words
> of encouragement, but in my printing office put your manuscript into
> type, an edition of which was struck off in tract form, subject to your
> order. I was impressed by your intelligence and excellence of character."[1]

Along with her *Meditations*, she handed him an essay, "Religion and the Pure Principles of Morality, The Sure Foundation On Which We Must Build." If this were the only of Stewart's writings, she would justly deserve to be recognized as a great writer and political theorist. The complexity and outpouring of ideas and passion signal an intellect pent up and prepared to let her ideas flow. She might have titled this essay, in Kantian terms, "The Practical Principles of Morality" since in reality it is a handbook for revolutionary practice. Garrison published this work as a tract and advertised it in the October 8, 1831, edition of the *Liberator*. Stewart opens the essay: "Feeling a deep solemnity of soul, in view of our wretched and degraded situation, and sensible of the gross ignorance that prevails among us, I thought it proper to publicly express my sentiments before you." She is calm and clear in the light of truth. She knows what she must do. As is rhetorically conventional, she downplays her abilities and asks for forbearance, exhorting her readers to turn their attention to "knowledge and truth." The next paragraph, the autobiographical one that this book has already closely examined, is perhaps one of the most well known. It is worth reviewing her opening remarks:

> I was born in Hartford, Connecticut, in 1803; was left an orphan at five years of age; was bound out in a clergyman's family; had the seeds of piety and virtue early sown in my mind, but was deprived of the advantages of education, though my soul thirsted for knowledge. Left them at fifteen years of age; attended sabbath schools until I was twenty; in 1826 was married to James W. Stewart; was left a widow in 1829, was, as I humbly hope and trust, brought to the knowledge of the truth, as it is in Jesus in 1830; in 1831 made a public profession of my faith in Christ.

In this beautifully condensed biographical piece, Maria W. Stewart recounts her life as it is inscribed on her spirit, as it makes sense to her. While I have provided evidence, in order to become clearer about her early life, that she was born in Greenwich, Connecticut, it makes little difference for the woman who has a book of memory in which she is writing. In this passage she cites her 1830 "born again" experience as imbuing her with the "spirit of independence" such that "I would willingly sacrifice my life for the cause of God and my brethren."[2] While many commentators underscore the religiosity of her work, and rightly so, it is profoundly significant that her first philosophical claims as the text proceeds are not religious; they are political and made for the sake of her "brethren," adopting a common enough term, but one particularly employed by David Walker and the Prince Hall Masons who have been at the forefront of recent political efforts including *Freedom's Journal*, the Massachusetts General Colored Association, and Walker's *Appeal*. She opens the body of her text, declaring, "All the nations of the earth are crying out for liberty and equality. Away, away with tyranny and oppression! Shall Afric's sons be silent any longer?"[3] Her initial admonition is not for heavenly salvation but for earthly action. The essay adopts language drawn from John Locke's classical liberalism arguing for freedom and equality for African Americans. A few years earlier, David Walker had ended his *Appeal to the Coloured Citizens of the World* reproducing the most radical and inflammatory statement he could find, the "declaration made July 4, 1776:

> When ever any form of government becomes destructive of these ends, it is the right of people to alter or abolish it, and to institute a new government laying its foundation on such principles, and organizing its powers in such form, as to them shall seem most likely to effect their safety and happiness.

He reiterates:

> We hold these truths to be self evident—that ALL MEN ARE CREATED EQUAL!! *that they are endowed by their Creator with certain unalienable rights*; that among these are the right to life, *liberty*, and pursuit of happiness.[4]

In adopting and revising revolutionary language and ideas, David Walker and Maria W. Stewart became political theorists, applying the Enlightenment concepts of liberal political theory to African Americans, diasporic Africans worldwide, and in Stewart's case, to Black women as well. In doing so, they directly engaged with and responded to proslavery ideologies. By identifying the varieties of arguments supporting oppression and providing their own responses, they also enriched and recreated Revolutionary-era political theory developing concepts specific to the African American experience, a *Black revolutionary liberalism*, an original, consistent, and universal application of Enlightenment ideologies. Unlike the classic liberalism of the gendered elite in the early American national period, the theory developed by African Americans in the late eighteenth and early nineteenth centuries retained and expanded the radical character forming a basis for future theories of Black resistance and revealing the shortcomings of traditional liberalism as it was used to further the oppression of African Americans.

GENDER AND AUTHORITY

Stewart goes on to assert, "This is the land of freedom. The Press is at Liberty. Every man has a right to express his opinion," perhaps in part as an inoculation against the criticism she anticipates as a woman entering the public sphere. By adopting the formulation "every man," intended in its universal sense, Stewart asserts her own right to express her opinion. And as with *Adam*, another universalized formulation, she writes,

> God . . . hath formed and fashioned you in his own glorious image, hath bestowed upon you reason and strong powers of intellect. He hath made you to have dominion over the beasts of the fields, the fowls of the air, and the fish of the sea. He has crowned you with glory and honor; hath made you but a little lower than the angels; and according to the Constitution of these United States, he hath made all men free and equal.[5]

The poise of this opening salvo concisely identifies her "as a rational and accountable creature," her self-signification in *Meditation III*. Attuned to the language of discourse, Stefan Wheelock notes Walker's attention to the function of various grammars, including the ways that "violence-knowledge," is often couched in "polite discourse," as in the writings of Thomas Jefferson.[6] Chike Jeffers and Peter Adamson underscore the ways that David Walker uses exclamation points to express his "rage, frustration, and disbelief" at what is occurring in this "republican land of liberty."[7] Yet, what is deemed an acceptable form of expression then and now is also tied to gender. Jefferson engages in polite discourse and the language of science to disseminate his "violence knowledge." Walker uses exclamation points to express outrage. Operating under additional gender constraints, Stewart often adopts more modulated forms of expression to convey ideas that are equally infused with emotionally laden thoughts and ideas since the accusation of excessive passion is a common tactic used to dismiss women's words. Quietly folded into these assertions, she writes, "Far be it from me to recommend to you either to kill, burn, or destroy. But I would strongly recommend to you to improve your talents; let not one lie buried in the earth. Show forth your powers of mind."[8]

Many commentators have taken her at her word that she is not encouraging violent action or the use of force in response to injustices. Is she drawing a distinction between herself and Walker's "incendiary" tract? The view of Stewart as a more peaceful advocate for change is worth reconsideration. The phrase "far be it from me" is and was commonly used to express the opposite of the stated claim. There is an air, almost of sarcasm, attached to the phrase.[9] Given the intense furor over Walker's *Appeal*, it makes sense for Stewart to issue a disclaimer, even one that is meant ironically, in contrast with her polite admonition to "improve your talents." And yet here, I suggest, lies the kernel of her social and political theory, one that prescribes a series of steps to achieve a just state, one that is couched in a complicated moral theory.

The first step for successful political action is found in a *principle of everyday righteousness*, to live a *righteous* life as individuals, families, and community members. This, the most persistent theme in Stewart's writing, underscores the vital importance of righteous living both as a good in itself and as the first step along the path to achieving unity and virtue as a community and ultimately, justice in the wider world. Moral and educational improvement as a theme persists from Walker's moral philosophy through to Stewart's. Later in *Religion* she writes:

> Our young men and maidens are fainting and drooping, as it were, by the wayside, for want of knowledge; when I see how few care to distinguish themselves in either religious or moral improvement, and when I see the greater part of the community following the vain bubbles of life with so much eagerness, which will prove to them like the serpent's sting upon the bed of death, I really think that we are in as wretched and miserable a state as was the house of Israel in the days of Jeremiah.[10]

Stewart's assertions are components of a systematic theory. *Everyday righteousness* is the foundation of moral behavior. As a side effect, of less significance but socially helpful, a righteous Black community might command more respect from whites and pave the way for increased civil, political, and religious rights. Most crucially, a unified community of morally upstanding citizens is a precondition of the successful struggle for political freedom and equality. Stewart's consistent claim exemplifies her *Second Principle, the Struggle for Political Freedom and Equality,* the injunction to engage actively in the political struggle for freedom and equality with the goal of achieving genuinely universal civil, religious, and political rights. The principles of universal brotherhood touted in classic Euro-American liberal theory but never instantiated in practice are consistently promulgated in *Black* or *"African"* Christianity and Black revolutionary liberalism. Stripped of inconsistencies by writers across the centuries ranging from Prince Hall to Charles Mills, these principles converge to prove the justness (righteousness) of freedom and equality for all, the universal equality of humankind.

Reflecting on knowledge gleaned from James W. Stewart, David Walker, and on events occurring since her arrival in the city, certain contributing influences emerge. Her writing reveals the degree to which she is moved by the idea of revolution. The celebration at Bunker Hill in 1826 drew the struggle for American independence, a distant marker, into a present and future vision of magnificent accomplishment. Those wizened men—Black men—inspired by the Declaration of Independence, believed that armed struggle would mean freedom for all. One could see on their faces and in their military demeanor something that made their broken bodies stand proud, that they embodied revolutionary ideals even against the betrayal of having the silken mantle of freedom withheld from African American soldiers. The memory of those speeches and testimonials invigorated the revolutionary ideals and merged with the religious ideas recently reaffirmed, leading to a third principle, the Principle of Justice, a belief that in time God's love of all mankind will bring about justice—along with freedom and equality—for the virtuous and damnation for all others. The ultimate goal of virtuous behavior and political enlightenment is justice on earth as it will be in heaven, the justice of Judgment Day.

The theology developed by early African American writers such as Lemuel Haynes and John Marrant combine theological and republican ideals.[11] For Walker and Stewart, these are claims for a kind of pan-Africanism since worldwide the descendants of Africa have been uniquely oppressed by the Euro-American slave trade. Walker and Stewart in particular returned often to the verse in Psalm 68:31 "Princes shall come out of Egypt; Ethiopia shall soon stretch out her hands unto God." And Stewart tells us, "And were it not that the King Eternal has declared that Ethiopia shall stretch forth her hands unto God, I should indeed despair," an apocalyptic verse. Stewart's conversion experience had occurred in 1830 after the deaths of David Walker, her husband James W. Stewart, and the Reverend Thomas Paul, an experience she describes in her political writings as profoundly transformational.

Jennifer Rycenga observes that a "unity of religious and philosophical thought peaked at this particular time because, for women, as well as for free Black men in the United States, the emotional qualities of the Second Great Awakening and the cooler rationalism of the Enlightenment were not mutually exclusive."[12] Stewart affirms an Enlightenment criterion for personhood—reason or rationality—claiming it for herself and for her community at large and ends the passage declaring her fearlessness, her willingness to be a martyr for the cause, her faith in God's protection, and her admiration for another one who has already joined God: "the most noble, fearless and undaunted David Walker."[13]

Stefan Wheelock argues that David Walker "traced the reprobate character of American politics back to perversions in the nation's historic language of covenant . . . an errant theological belief that that blacks were designed by Heaven to be an 'inheritance' to whites and their children forever," a theology of racial inheritance that drives American exceptionalism.[14] Like Walker, Stewart rejects this errant theology and remains faithful to an idea of covenant theology that holds that both grace and good works are necessary for salvation. The idea of good works signals the outward performance of *everyday virtue*, difficult for those who are oppressed, who labor too hard and are drawn to everyday vice for immediate relief from their pain. Therefore, she holds that the first step towards full access to political freedom and religious salvation is to "improve your talents . . . and show forth the powers of mind."[15] She replaces the errant theology with the invocation of two covenants: God's covenant with Adam and the United States Constitution's covenant with the citizens of the country. This accords with Melvin Rogers's analysis of Walker's use of the terms "appeal" and "citizen," which "exemplify the ways blacks constituted themselves as political actors at the very moment their ability to do so was called into question or denied."[16]

INSURRECTIONIST ETHICS

A theory taking shape in the twenty-first century, one that unites the idea of everyday morality with political struggle, labels the philosophical positions advanced by Walker and Stewart "insurrectionist ethics." In his 2002 essay, "Insurrectionist Ethics: Advocacy, Moral Psychology, and Pragmatism," Leonard Harris argues for a philosophy that makes advocacy "representing, defending, or promoting morally just causes—a seminal, meritorious feature of moral agency," and holds that it is constituent of a moral theory that he calls Insurrectionist Ethics.[17] Harris traces this theory to the work of David Walker's in his *Appeal*. When Walker died in 1830, Stewart's speeches and essays developed Walker's demand for advocacy as an ethical stance. Harris, who calls himself a Walkerite, articulates the *insurrectionist* moral and political theory that he ascribes to Walker and Stewart, the key feature of which is a willingness to engage in and/or advocate for insurrectionist practices when patterns of oppression are such that they deny full humanity to oppressed groups. In other words, Harris is arguing that insurrectionist activities and the advocacy of such are not merely justified on occasion but are *morally required* under certain conditions. Building on the work of Harris, an impressive contingent of scholars are contributing to the project of articulating and fleshing out the theory. Lee McBride describes insurrectionist ethics as "an attempt to work out the types of moral intuitions, character traits, reasoning strategies that culminate in action, and methods required to garner impetus for the liberation of oppressed groups."[18] Most of these scholars agree that among the chief features of this theory of ethics, according to José Medina, is "not only the right but the duty to disobey, resist, and actively fight against social practices and political institutions that perpetuate oppression."[19]

Most significantly, Jacoby Adeshei Carter argues that Maria W. Stewart is "a paradigmatic insurrectionist and black feminist thinker."[20] Medina joins Carter in this claim. Harris, Carter, McBride, Medina, Kristie Dotson, and Paul C. Taylor contribute to the effort of reclaiming and developing the theory. These writers consider the merits of placing this theory in the tradition of American pragmatism developed by Charles Sanders Peirce, John Dewey, William James, Alain Locke, Cornel West, and others and are particularly concerned with whether or not that tradition is sufficiently robust to accommodate the moral requirement for active resistance. According to Lewis Gordon, Alain Locke "defended a form of pluralism through which human beings worked out their differences in active negotiation of political life and cultural creativity."[21] Carter argues that a *feminist* insurrectionist ethics is a cure for pragmatism's shortcomings, drawing in particular upon what several current thinkers have posited as Stewart's concept of "full personhood." He weaves a thread of connection from Stewart through the pragmatism of Alain Locke to Harris's account of Walker and from there to his own analysis of Stewart. Carter holds that Stewart asserts "the humanity of African Americans against the impediments of white supremacy," avows "equal personhood by women against the ingrained constraints of patriarchy," and requires accepting "the existential possibility of death." He demonstrates that Stewart's feminism increases the emancipatory potential of insurrectionist ethics, and therefore pragmatism must incorporate her feminist version and concept of personhood or accept limitations.[22] Medina adds, "Stewart's insurrectionism is an important precursor to womanism or black feminism in arguing for the centrality of the lived experience of black women for full human liberation in the United States," tying it to the pragmatist conception of human flourishing.[23] Writing in a similar vein, Kristie Dotson is concerned to expand the theory to include "a standard that identifies insurrectionist acts as morally relevant where the act is characterized by deep, motivational ambivalence." She draws on the example of Margaret Garner, who "succeeded in killing her 2-year old daughter, Mary Garner, in 1856, before being captured as a fugitive slave," a haunting story retold by Toni Morrison in her novel *Beloved*. Dotson and Medina underscore the importance of lived experience in moral decision making, a feature Stewart struggled to make clear to her audiences, who sometimes tended not to give epistemic weight to her subject position.[24]

EPISTEMIC VIOLENCE, GENDERED VIOLENCE, POLITICAL VIOLENCE

In keeping with the themes of epistemic violence—epistemicide—Medina highlights Stewart's view that epistemic oppression is "at the core of anti-black racism in the United States as resulting from being excluded from access to and participation in knowledge projects (education, research, public deliberation, etc.) and from being confined to manual labor under extreme conditions of exploitation." He argues that Stewart saw "education as a form of self-empowerment and resistance against epistemic oppression . . . for fighting the epistemic side of racial oppression with *epistemic insurrection*" designed, to use the pragmatist's term, to create a society in which human flourishing becomes the norm. The role of excessive labor and lack of education are front and center in Stewart's essay "Why Sit Ye Here and Die?"[25]

GENDERED VIOLENCE

Through Stewart's religious conversion she experienced a profound revelation—a revealed knowledge—an awakening that simultaneously her opened her mind to deep political truths. If all are equal in God's eyes, then, contrary to years of immersion in the psychology of inferiority, and almost treasonously, all races are equal. Stewart had revealed to her the truths of race *and gender* equality for disembodied souls are neither raced nor gendered, and although men and women had certain clearly differentiated roles in society, in some ways, for example in the understanding and grace of the Lord, they are equal. (Or, possibly, women have an advantage, she sometimes argues.) And if religious and political knowledge are one and the same, as she sometimes suggests through her principles of morality, then women may equally access political knowledge. This revelation gave her courage to address the forbidden issues of gender and sexual violence.

In the form of a letter and in language that more closely resembles her *Meditations*, in *Religion*, she writes an exhortation to the women of her community, addressing the sexual violence rained upon women and girls: "I might weep day and night for the transgressions of the daughters of my people," a topic rarely seriously addressed in any literature of the period. She calls upon women to become an army to create change: "O, ye daughters of Africa, awake, Awake, Arise! No longer sleep or slumber, but distinguish yourselves. Show forth to the world that ye are endowed with noble and exalted faculties." Her lengthy admonition that the parents and community are failing to teach children virtuous behavior is both a signature theme for Stewart and a reason why her community did not always warm to her message. She is impatient for revolutionary change and believes that by instilling others with that fervor, "their souls would become fired with a holy zeal for freedom's cause . . . Knowledge would begin to flow, and the sins of slavery and ignorance would melt like wax before the flames."[26]

POLITICAL VIOLENCE

Stewart provided a multipronged plan for the liberation of her community. She laid out clear steps to be taken: virtuous behavior, right education of children, building schools and shops leading to economic responsibility and self-sufficiency. Exhibit the entrepreneurship of a James W. Stewart who went head-to-head with his white competitors and partners to create a small maritime empire. In addition, like Walker, Stewart encouraged the public to engage in whatever actions may be necessary to bring about change. Several scholars have challenged the oft-repeated notion that Stewart was fundamentally pacifistic. In "Sympathetic Violence," Christina Henderson argues that Stewart encouraged "readers to cultivate both Christian love and violent resistance to slavery." She notes that "Stewart looks to biblical examples of God's wrath" and "develops this defense of violence" and that she "goes so far as to urge African Americans to be prepared to carry out this destruction through violent revolution," adding evidence to the rightness of considering Stewart to be an insurrectionist ethicist.[27] Declaring that African Americans "are not an inferior race of beings," Stewart draws on scripture from the book of *Genesis* to argue that Black people are made in God's image, and then she invokes the Declaration of Independence and the preamble to the Constitution of the United States to declare that all men are free and equal.[28]

"WE CLAIM OUR RIGHTS" [29]

The sight of Black heroes of the War of Independence on Bunker Hill Day had evoked a history of promise and betrayal. At the dawn of the revolution, African Americans who lived liminally had to contemplate quickly and choose a path—abandon the country where most of them were born with its cruel restrictions and tortures for an unknown fate with the British or stay loyal, if loyal can be the word, to their native or residential land in the hope that revolutionary ideas would be extended to them. In the heart of slave-holding Maryland, many African Americans risked their lives to escape in a massive flotilla onto the Chesapeake Bay to waiting British vessels. Some drowned, and others were captured and returned. Still others made it to the British enemy ships. Race slavery in much of coastal New England was more individualized, with fewer people enslaved, many living with smaller family groups, laboring at rural farms and in homes. There is little reason to think it was less cruel or deadeningly confining, but lacking a community of familiars, resisters such as Elizabeth Freeman and Quock Walker resorted to individualized approaches to liberation through the court system. Both were ultimately successful. In the second wave of Black resistance in the republic, activists and philosophers such as Walker and Stewart envisioned multiple avenues to liberation, ranging from judicial remedies, to education, to mutual aid, to truancy and marronage, to insurrection.

Maria Stewart had been writing steadily for at least two years and had the notion to speak in public. She had written *Religion* in 1831 in the wake of the deaths of her husband, David Walker, and the Reverend Thomas Paul. Throughout this time, she was regularly called to probate court for the maddeningly slow process of resolving her husband's estate. In the meantime, Northern control of national leadership had passed, to be replaced by the slaveholders and slave defenders Andrew Jackson and John C. Calhoun. Nat Turner's rebellion had hardened feelings on all sides, and, along with Philadelphia, Boston was taking the lead in organizing antislavery societies and publishing abolitionist tracts. Maria W. Stewart offered both her *Meditations* and her essay on religion to Garrison. He responded thus:

> For sale at this office, a tract addressed to the people of color, by Mrs. Maria Steward, a responsible colored lady of this city. Its title is, "Religion and the Pure Principles of Morality, The Sure Foundation On Which We Must Build." The production is most praiseworthy, and confers great credit on the talents and piety of its author. We hope she will have many patrons. Extracts of the paper hereafter. Price 6 cents.[30]

Within a year, a pamphlet with her *Meditations* was in print. Her new test was to see whether or not she could translate the written word into public speech. Accordingly, she helped to form and then gave her first public lecture before the Boston Afric' American Female Literary Society.

Chapter Twenty-two

"A RATIONAL AND ACCOUNTABLE CREATURE"

The Frowns of the world shall never discourage me, nor its smiles flatter me.
—Maria W. Stewart, "An Address Delivered Before the Afric-American Female
Intelligence Society of America

Jacqueline Jones opens *Labor of Love, Labor of Sorrow* with a hermeneutic of
Zora Neale Hurston's novel *Their Eyes Were Watching God* and the character
Nanny,

> . . . who never confused the degrading regimen of slavery with her own
> desires as they related to work, love, and motherhood . . . [T]hroughout
> her life she had sustained a silent faith in herself and her sisters that was
> permitted no expression within the sentimental void of bondage. "Ah
> wanted to preach a great sermon about colored women sittin' on high,
> but thy wasn't no pulpit for me." [1]

We know of several African American women who found their pulpits in
the late eighteenth and early nineteenth centuries, among them, Jarena Lee
and Zipha Elaw, both of whom wrote spiritual narratives about "the peculiar
experiences of African American holy women." Joycelyn Moody describes
their work as combining "a secularized protest against injustice with the sacred
issues of their evangelicalism and the travel details of their respective itinerant ministries." [2] Contemporaries of Maria W. Stewart, Lee published *Religious
Experience and Journal Of Mrs. Jarena Lee: Giving an Account Of Her Call
To Preach the Gospel* in 1836, and Elaw published her *Memoirs Of the Life,
Religious Experience, Ministerial Travels and Labours Of Mrs. Zilpha Elaw: an
American Female Colour* ten years later. Less well-known as public speakers
than Sojourner Truth, Lee and Elaw served as itinerant preachers who were
constrained by the intersectional oppression they faced. [3]

MRᔱ JARENA LEE.

Preacher of the A. M. E. Church.

Zilpha Elaw and Jarena Lee are among those women, "spiritual sisters," who preached the gospel in the early nine-teenth century. Lee and Elaw were itinerate preachers, whereas Maria W. Stewart wrote and delivered her essays and speeches and then became a teacher. Schomburg Center for Research in Black Culture, Manuscripts, Archives and Rare Books Division, The New York Public Library. New York Public Library Digital Collections. Accessed October 16, 2020. http://digitalcollections.nypl.org/items/adeef885-b392-cb33-e040-e00a1806300a.

Among the places for African Americans to preach, perhaps none was so glorious as the brick and wood structure built by their own hands for their own spiritual purposes, not appropriated by others in labor or achievement. Reverend Thomas Paul had stood at that gleaming pulpit gazing into the perfectly proportioned and seemingly soaring rafters over the gallery, towards the curving, mirror-imaged ascending twin staircases, and over the polished cherry arms and backs of the wooden pews. Neither a man nor an ordained minister, Maria W. Stewart was forbidden access to the pulpit in the African Baptist Church to preach about Black women and men sitting on high while white folks hid from the wrath of the lamb. She was instead invited to lecture in the first-floor room of the African Meeting House. Stewart's speech, *An*

Address Delivered Before the Afric-American Female Intelligence Society was printed in the *Liberator* on April 28, 1832. This society, formed late the previous year, wrote a Constitution to govern its practices.

> Whereas the subscribers, women of color of the Commonwealth of Massachusetts, actuated by a natural feeling for the welfare of our friends, have thought fit to associate for the diffusion of knowledge, the suppression of vice and immorality, and for cherishing such virtues as will render us happy and useful to society, sensible of the gross ignorance under which we have too long labored, but trusting by the blessing of God, we shall be able to accomplish the object of our union—we have therefore associated ourselves under the name of the Afric-American Female Intelligence Society.

They were to meet monthly and pay dues for purchasing books and renting meeting space. Members must be "of good moral character" and must not be "obnoxious"; otherwise they would face removal. The group would also function as a mutual aid society in case of illness provided that members "do not rashly sacrifice their own health."[4]

Garrison described the new trend for literary societies in support of higher intellectual achievement in the *Liberator*.

> During His recent sojourn in Philadelphia, (rendered inexpressibly delightful by the kindness of friends,) the Editor of the Liberator had the privilege of visiting and addressing a society of colored ladies called the "Female Literary Association." It was one of the most interesting spectacles he had ever witnessed. If the traducers of the colored race could be acquainted with the moral worth, just refinement, and large intelligence of this association, their mouths would hitherto be dumb. The members assemble together every Tuesday evening, for the purpose of mutual improvement in moral and literary pursuits. Nearly all of them write, almost weekly, original pieces, which are anonymously put into a box, and afterwards criticised by a committee. Having been permitted to bring with him several of these pieces, he ventures to commence their publication, not only for their merit, but in order to induce the colored ladies of other places to go and do likewise.[5]

The Boston society had its own protocols. Stewart's must have been one of the first addresses to the Society and it was her first public speech to what should have been a welcoming audience. It is possible, however, that she may have been more severe than they were expecting. Unaccustomed to speaking in public, Stewart tested her rhetorical and oratorial skills in front of an audience of women and yet, perhaps for that reason, she has only a little to say about gender through much of her talk, a topic that is a standard theme in her other works. More than her other productions, she relies here on the form of the jeremiad, designed to remind the listener of the punishment that awaits the unrepentant as well as the joy of salvation for the deserving few. The argument is a rhetorical descendant of the hellfire-and-brimstone sermons of the early colonial minister Jonathan Edwards.

Stewart's lecture, brilliantly and beautifully written, was not designed to ingratiate the speaker to her audience. It begins by admonishing Black women to be kinder and more helpful to each other in a rhetorical move that may have been intended to seek sympathy and understanding for herself. I think it is fair to say that at the moment when Stewart read this address, she was so discouraged, so deep in sorrow, that she was truly longing for death. She spoke in a place and at a time when levels of dissention were high. Reverend Paul had passed away. The congregation was wracked by disagreement over its direction. Stewart was systematically losing her inheritance in repeated courtroom appearances. She had no kinship ties in Boston—or anywhere that she knew for that matter. She expressed her disappointment with the women in front of her quite frankly. Her origins were distinctly humbler than many of those around her who had firm ties to the area, some of whom were quite prominent. After her general invocation in the style of the jeremiad, she made a few nods to her political themes and launched into a criticism of African Americans generally. "It appears to me that there are no people under the heavens that are so unkind and so unfeeling towards their own as are the descendants of fallen Africa." At one level she was grappling with the problem of theodicy—the puzzle about why an all good, all knowing, and all-powerful God would allow evil in the world. The idea that Africans as a group had done something sinful to deserve God's punishment was common enough among white Christian apologists, but for Stewart it was a real question that pertained both to her people and to her very personal situation. Why was she being punished by God? She had endeavored to be virtuous. She had exhorted those around her to do the same, and still God saw fit to cast upon her—like Job—ever more afflictions. She mourned that "professed followers of Christ would have frowned upon me," noting,

A lady of high distinction among us, observed to me that I might never expect your homage. God forbid! I ask it not. But I beseech you to deal with gentleness and godly sincerity towards me; and there is not one among you, my dear friends, who has given me a cup of cold water in the name of the Lord, or soothed the sorrows of my wounded heart.

After this bitter remonstrance, she tells them that "God is love" and that "God will bless you, not only you, and your children for it. Cruel indeed, are those that indulge such an opinion respecting me as that." This cannot have been what the women sitting before her had expected when they signed up for their literary society—a direct rebuke from a former indentured servant so overwhelmed with grief that she is longing for the Lord to take her. She closes with a passage that foreshadows the writings of Anna Julia Cooper some sixty-two years later. Stewart writes: "O woman, woman! Upon you I call; for upon your exertions almost entirely depends whether the rising generation shall be any thing more than we have been or not. O woman, woman! Your example is powerful, your influence is great." In the 1890s Cooper was a leader in the club women's movement, a group that took as a major theme women's role in the wider project of racial uplift.[6] In *A Voice from the South* (1892), Cooper articulates this commanding role: "Only the BLACK WOMAN can say 'When and where I enter, in the quiet undisputed dignity of my womanhood, without violence and without suing for special patronage, then and there *the whole Negro race enters with me.*'"[7]

One wonders what happened as the group parted from the literary society meeting for the evening. Did some of the women present approach Stewart and try to comfort her? Did they storm out? Were they ashamed or angered? Perhaps some of each. Her lecture must have met with at least some sympathy, otherwise she would not have been invited to speak a few months later at Franklin Hall. Had she been a man and a preacher, a likely vocation for someone with an intellectual affinity such as Maria Stewart's, she might have been in a position to urge her flock to greater virtue, charity, and kindness. As a woman and a former servant, she was subjected to the social norms of obedience and silence and when she violated those norms, the reception was chilly.[8]

Stewart's next foray into the public domain was a short piece published in the *Liberator* on the new Negro Convention Movement. Initially organized in 1830 as the American Society of Free Persons of Colour and held at the Mother Bethel Abyssinian Methodist Episcopal (AME) Church in Philadelphia, the church's founder, Reverend Richard Allen, presided. Emigration to Canada West appeared to be a promising and urgent response to increasing oppression, a strategy later fostered by Abraham Shadd and Mary Ann Shadd Cary.[9] In part, the gathering constituted an effort to ensure that any emigration movement, contra the ACS, would be self-generated by Black leaders to places *they* selected through means *they* supervised, and not something controlled by whites as a step in genocidal removals. Attended by representatives from seven states, no one from Massachusetts made their way to the first convention. The following year produced a plan to establish a college or school for Black students in the New Haven area, a knowledge project thwarted by whites at about the same time Prudence Crandall's interracial school was forced to close. In 1832, Hosea Easton and Nathan Johnson attended from Massachusetts. Garrison had provided extensive coverage of the event, writing: "The question which excited the greatest interest, and elicited the most debate, related to the purchase of lands in Upper Canada, as an asylum for those who may be compelled to remove from the slaveholding states."[10]

Buoyed by the national organizing, Stewart wrote a letter, "Cause for Encouragement Composed Upon Hearing the Editor's Account Of The Late Convention In Philadelphia."[11] Stewart's letter, building on Garrison's article, is less a consideration of the convention movement than it is an occasion to reiterate her themes and to express optimism about the future; "where is the soul among us that is not fired with holy ambition? Has not every one a wish to excel . . . ?"[12]

Stewart is not alone in her optimism. At a July 17 meeting at the African Meeting House Garrison said:

> Last year, I felt as if I were fighting single-handed against the great enemy; now I see around me a host of valiant warriors, armed with weapons of immortal temper, whom nothing can daunt, and who are pledged to the end of the contest. The number is increasing with singular rapidity. The standard which has been lifted up in Boston is attracting the gaze of the nation, and inspiring the drooping hearts of thousands with hope and courage.[13] July 17, 1832

Of course, the "host of valiant warriors" had been there all along. What had changed was Garrison's ability to see them. Stewart's optimism was not long lived, but her despair was converted into an ongoing call to action, as evidenced by the theme of her next public lecture.

Chapter Twenty-three

"WHY SIT YE HERE AND DIE?"

O, horrible idea, indeed! to possess noble souls aspiring after high and honorable acquirement, yet confined by the chains of ignorance and poverty to live lives of continual drudgery and toil.
—Maria W. Stewart, Lecture Delivered at Franklin Hall, 1832[1]

The first-floor room of the Belknap Street African Church was put to good use. A few months before Stewart's lecture to the Afric-American Female Intelligence Society, organizers used this same space to form the New England Anti-Slavery Society (NEASS), the first mixed-race group of its kind. Writing in 1872, Henry Wilson notes that the preamble to the NEAAS Constitution, presented in at a meeting on January 6, 1832, declared:

[E]very person of full age and sane mind had a right to immediate freedom from personal bondage; that man could not, consistently with reason, religion, and the eternal and immutable principles of justice, be the property of man; that whoever retained his fellow-man in bondage was guilty of a grievous wrong; that difference of complexion was no reason why man should be deprived of his natural rights, or subjected to any political disability.[2]

Garrison, Knapp, David Lee Child, Reverend Snowden of the Methodist Church, and Hosea Easton all attended the initial organizational meetings along with some surprising names—Elizabeth Buffam Chace, among white women, an early supporter openly associated with antislavery organizing, and Reverend Henry Grew, one of the clergyman we considered as a possible indenturer of Maria Miller, and rejected since he had been run out of Hartford for his radical views, then joining William Ellery Channing's church in Boston.[3]

Stewart's next lecture, at Franklin Hall, was one of the earliest to be delivered to a race- and gender-inclusive audience. Situated on the north corner of Franklin and Washington Streets, Franklin Hall was the regular meeting place of the NEASS. By the time of this lecture, she had honed her rhetorical skills, having matured quickly in this respect. The speech was more rousing, more determined, and less discouraged, even while employing the kind of life-and-death rhetoric for which she was known. It was designed to animate the audience. She opens with the striking inquiry, a call to arms:

> Why sit ye here and die? If we say we will go to a foreign land, the famine and pestilence are there, and there we shall die. Come let us plead our cause before the whites: if they save us alive, we shall live—and if they kill us we shall but die.[4]

Directed in part against the American Colonization Society members who wished to send free Blacks "to a foreign land," she aims to discourage those who may be tempted to view emigration as a viable alternative to resistance in the United States. Free Blacks are needed here to carry out the fight against oppression, particularly given new avenues for resistance building on recent interracial abolitionist cooperation. She also makes her appeal to whites, highlighting their power to create change. Through influential African American lobbying, allies such as Garrison were coming around to the cause of "immediatism," that is, of immediate, not gradual abolition.

Once more addressing her subject position, she continues: "Methinks I heard a spiritual interrogation—'Who shall go forward, and take off the reproach that is cast upon the people of color? Shall it be a woman?' And my heart made this reply—'If it is thy will, be it even so, Lord Jesus!'" Her bold bid for authority against potential detractors relies on her claim that Jesus has spoken to her directly, that she has been chosen by him for this vocation. Her analysis ties servitude to slavery and extends beyond the concerted efforts towards abolition to the ways that the excessive demands of labor combined with the deprivation of education conspire to naturalize the condition of Black people, making it seem as though Black excellence itself would be a violation of natural law. Institutionalized practices restricting access to resources are particularly effective in undercutting the growth and flourishing of young people, especially girls. In one of the better-known passages from this speech, Stewart recalls surveying members of the community about their willingness to employ what might be called "shopgirls." Her respondents demure, supposing it would be bad for patronage. Subtextually, seeking a practical solution to the thorny dilemma of how to liberate young girls from white women's fearsome control in domestic service, she speculates about alternative forms of employment, seizing upon the expediency of allowing girls to work in shops, something not commonly practiced at that time. The door of opportunity is resoundingly slammed against this proposal in the face of restrictive gender ideologies and "the powerful force of prejudice."

> Let our girls possess whatever amiable qualities of soul they may; let their characters be fair and spotless as innocence itself; let their nature taste and ingenuity be what they may, it is impossible for scarce an individual of them to rise above the condition of servants.

Careful attention to the text of this lecture reveals Stewart's keen awareness of the degree to which the twin oppressors of excessive labor and thwarted education successfully enforce barriers to race, class, and gender excellence. "Neither do I know of any who have enriched themselves by spending their lives as house domestics, washing windows, shaking carpets, brushing boots, or tending upon gentlemen's tables."[5]

Reflecting on her past, she empathically projects her personal experiences onto others, similarly situated: her coming of age as an indentured servant and the obstruction of her intellectual development. In a stark statement of her loathing of forced domestic labor, she asserts that she would "gladly hail death as a welcome messenger" rather than return to servitude, contending that servitude in the North is little better than the slavery of the South.

Stewart undertakes a phenomenology of the experience of domestic labor in contrast with the revolutionary spirit of white Americans who, unfettered by menial labor (since they have slaves and servants to do it for them), are able to excel in the manner dictated by revolutionary ideals.[6] Yet, "ragged as we are," Black people also desire liberty, but are often ineffectual because "continual hard labor deadens our souls." In connecting labor with education, knowledge, and virtue, Stewart ties them together as nearly unattainable under the yoke of bruising labor that "irritates our tempers and sours our dispositions; the whole system becomes worn out with toil and fatigue, nature itself becomes exhausted" under capitalist racial patriarchy. She will not disparage those who, through no fault of their own, labor in domestic servitude. Women and girls are especially afflicted by hard labor. In a penetrating analysis of the embodied experience of domestic labor, and an argumentative challenge to the white women who maintain this tyranny, she asks:

> What literary acquirement can be made, or useful knowledge derived, from either maps, books, or charts, by those who continually drudge from Monday morning until Sunday noon? O, ye fairer sisters, whose hands are never soiled, whose nerves and muscles are never strained, go learn by experience! Had we had the opportunity that you have had, to improve our moral and mental faculties, what would have hindered

our intellects from being as bright, and our manners from being as dignified as yours? Had it been our lot to have been nursed in the lap of
affluence and ease, and to have basked beneath the smiles and sunshine
of fortune, should we not have naturally supposed that we were never
made to toil?[7]

She continues this argument to contrast the embodiments of privilege and
oppression, the white women whose "forms" are "delicate" and "constitutions . . .
slender," and she appeals to white women for solidarity with her cause. The
same is true for "our young men, smart, active and energetic, with souls full
of ambitious fire" who nonetheless have no prospects as evidenced by the
"middle-aged men clad in their rusty plaids and coats," who labor to keep
warm in winter, and their wives who "toil beyond their strength." Beyond the
analytical, Stewart's art is in creating a vivid psychological and visual rendition
of the conditions that surround her, a creative aptitude best experienced by
reading her essays, each one, from start to finish.

THE PHENOMENOLOGY OF LABOR

The gendered aspects of labor affect women's and men's epistemic conditions,
each in different ways. Men's employment often puts them in the public sphere,
where discourse is informed by broader opportunities for interaction. For
those who circulate in public, shifts in employment provide for a wider spectrum of experience and dialogical interaction. Someone who was a seaman,
a carpenter, a dockworker, a bootblack, or a barber may connect with a range
of people conversing about a range of experiences and ideas that might lead
to political action.

Experiences within the domestic sphere—the private sphere—are no less
important as a site of knowledge production. Women typically labor at occupations such seamstress, food worker, house servant, laundress, making purchases
at the market, tending children, planting gardens, . . . and performing the most
intimate services for middle-class and wealthy women. The circumstances of
domestic labor may be claustrophobically oppressive and are often devalued;
however, this subject position can provide a distinct and crucial epistemic
standpoint, one which Stewart has impressively mastered. Patricia Hill Collins
explains the unique angle of vision generated from detailed knowledge of the
most intimate thoughts and actions of white people in their homes.

The distinctive perspectives gained from their outsider-within placement in domestic work provide the material backdrop for a unique

Black women's standpoint. When armed with cultural beliefs honed in Black civil society, many Black women who found themselves doing domestic work developed distinct views of the contradictions between the dominant group's actions and ideologies ... [that may] speak to the power of the dominant group to suppress the knowledge produced by subordinate groups, but it illustrates how being in outside-within locations can foster new angles of vision.[8]

Stewart had long intimately observed the behavior of white folks. Not only did she have embodied knowledge of the immense skilled labor required to keep people alive, to bring children into the world, to nurture them, feed them, clothe them, and cook for them—essential life skills and forms of knowledge systematically devalued by most epistemologies—but she saw clearly how white women with class privilege become dull and soft, suited for a delicate kind of learning, and how white men overestimate their own administrative skills and their value, attributing those achievements to innate superpowers rather than to the privilege that accompanies having a coterie of underlings to advise, inform, and execute their orders. Black feminist epistemologists have long noted that women especially are privy to the "outsider within" status, gaining deep personal knowledge of the oppressor. It is also crucial to note that men are excluded from some of the knowledge acquired in the domestic spheres, inter- and intraracially. The authoritative supposition from a position of gender privilege is often that *there is no knowledge,* or no important knowledge generated from women's spaces. Yet one refutation of this position is the anthropological, literary, sociological, and philosophical evidence of critical, distinct, "women's knowledges" generated in gender segregated communities.

Generally speaking, Stewart is not simply importuning against the *difficulty* of the labor, but against the drudgery, meniality, and unfreedom of being compelled to spend long hours doing certain kinds of work. The awakening that accompanied her transition from the confined milieu of servitude to her experiences as an independent woman in Boston, and increased awareness through her friendships with the Paul family and friends, with the Walkers, and with James Stewart, led her to be truly aghast at what she had missed, lamenting that the Bible, while sustaining, "during the years of childhood and youth ... was the black book that I mostly studied."[9] In addition to the *Liberator* she was likely now reading the major local newspapers, although her access to books was limited. Unlike Lydia Maria Child, she had no access to the library collection at the nearby Boston Athenaeum. Books were a prized commodity in the community, used, borrowed, traded, and discussed, not left to collect dust on shelves—popular books by James Fennimore Cooper, Washington Irving, or Catharine Sedgwick as well as histories and political treatises. The

Pauls and other families may have had libraries and allowed her some access to these scarce commodities.

While she was a severe critic of the distribution of labor in the United States, Stewart was not a critic of capitalism, per se. In fact, in the 1830s, before full industrialization and 18 years before the publication of Karl Marx's *Communist Manifesto*, few writers undertook that criticism.[10] On the whole, market economies were an improvement—equalizers—in comparison with the vast property exclusions of feudal economies. Yet she was sensitive to the ways that colonial economies exploited the labor of enslaved Africans and their descendants to unfairly build capital for Euro-Americans and effectively prevent all but a few (e.g., Paul Cuffe, James Stewart) from gaining any significant wealth.

The Franklin Hall lecture stands out as an acute analysis of the dual strategy of imposing excessive labor while thwarting opportunities for education, along with heavy policing practices, to squeeze African Americans into a position where resistance was nearly impossible without Herculean effort. Understanding that the subordinate groups may mirror the white gender respectability politics that especially restrict Black women, Stewart argues for the strongest possible code of virtue while simultaneously importuning society to open up the public sphere to women, in business, politics, and in religion, creating a new notion of Black women's place in society. She finishes her address with a rallying cry, forecasting rapid change in the future, to raise a WASHINGTON and LAFAYETTE, foreseeing a future in which African Americans will also achieve these heights of accomplishment.

Chapter Twenty-four

"ON AFRICAN RIGHTS AND LIBERTY"

A LECTURE ON AFRICAN RIGHTS AND LIBERTY, will be delivered on
Wednesday Evening next, at the African Masonic Hall, No 28 Cambridge
Street, near Parkman's market, by Mrs. Maria W. Stewart. The Hall is con-
venient to accommodate ladies and gentlemen, and all who feel interested
in the subject are respectfully invited to attend. After the lecture, a collection
will be taken to defray the expenses of the evening.
To commence at 7 o'clock precisely.
—*Liberator*, 2 March 1833 [1]

That the African Masonic Hall, the creation of an exclusively Black and male organization, was the setting for Maria W. Stewart's lecture on African rights and liberty indicates both her ascendance in the community's regard and the degree to which resources were shared. Women and people of all races were welcomed to the lecture hall, curious to hear what this person of local note had to say. In her usual style, Stewart drew upon all her skills: erudition, biblical knowledge, historical knowledge, concepts of gender—womanhood and manhood—and a sense of respect and pride, to spur her audience to increasingly active resistance against violations of republican values and civil rights. An inquiry into the wretched condition of Blacks and a handbook for future achievement, the address lays the blame for current conditions at the feet of people of all races. Whites condescendingly assign a deficient natural inclination towards liberty and the initiative to achieve it, evidenced by the perceived shortage of Black representatives in the annals of science, literature, politics, and more. For Stewart, however, the blame also rests on whites for whom Blacks have "enriched their soil and filled their coffers."[2] The key to liberation is moral and economic improvement along with fearless political action. She puts her considerable talents towards elucidating these arguments.

BLACK AUTONOMY AND FREE WILL

Stewart's lecture in the Masonic Hall represents a progression from the "Ladies Department" of the *Liberator*, to the polite society of the Black women's literary society, to the race and gender mixed audience of Franklin Hall, to the bastion of Black male authority, the African Masonic Hall. The speech is both an inspirational call to arms and a philosophical argument addressing issues of evil, the road to salvation, moral and economic autonomy, free will and virtuous achievement. The contrast between the rousing encouragement of this address and the plaintive cries of her address to Afric-American Female Intelligence Society could not be starker. She opens: "African rights and liberty is a subject that ought to fire the breast of every free man of color in these United States, and excite in his bosom a lively, deep, decided and heart-felt interest."

She asks why people of color have not achieved more. Is it God's punishment for some past transgression or ancient wrong? Is it, as the oppressors claim, a lack of ambition? Whites claim that ". . . our natural abilities are not as good, and our capacities by nature [are] inferior to theirs."[3] She longs to respond and to encourage others to respond to these charges, appealing to the manhood of those in the audience. Her inquiry addresses both metaphysical and theological questions. First, what is the nature of Black autonomy and free will? Second, why would a good God allow the evil of slavery?

In response to the charge that fully human free Blacks would have launched their own republican revolution based on classic liberal ideals, Charles Mills argues that unlike whites, Blacks have been denied "the equal capacity to will, and have been subjected instead to the immoral causal imposition of a racialized *white* will in the founding of the polity."[4] Mills is not denying the moral autonomy of African Americans; he is revealing both the ideological constructions imposed by whites onto Blacks and the actual construction, through the racial contract, of institutions that literally and figuratively shackle African Americans. In *The Racial Contract*, Mills argues that at a global level, the triumphal story of Euro-domination and virtue, even in the present, creates a negative space for non-Euro-American cultures and nations and blames those nations for what is described as their own economic and moral failure. All of these are embedded in a racial contract, in which Europeans are "valorized as unique, inimitable, autonomous," in contrast with other nations that according to the dominant narrative, "for reasons of local folly and geographical blight the inspiring model of the self-sufficient white social contract cannot be followed."[5]

Further articulating Euro-American republican ideology and practice, François Furstenberg takes the philosophical concept of freedom as moral autonomy and applies it to the specific example of the American Revolution. He articulates the central theme of "a mythologized narrative of the American

Revolution" which held that it was: "[A]n act of heroic resistance by a people threatened with slavery. That narrative promoted a liberal-republican ideology that linked freedom to resistance, grounding slavery in an act of individual choice—consent, even—and thereby legitimating slavery on principles consistent with the American Revolution."[6]

The parallel narrative thread was one of Black and slave degeneracy as punishment for sinful behavior. According to this account, morally autonomous, freedom-loving, and virtuous slaves would have successfully challenged their captors and achieved freedom as the American colonists had done. This narrative is accompanied by a series of tactics designed either to deny the existence of the long and deep history of slave resistance or to explain away individual examples, not as evidence of virtuous resistance, but as additional confirming instances of Black mercilessness and moral depravity. Consider for example the white reactions to Gabriel Prosser's revolt, Denmark Vesey's plot, Nat Turner's rebellion, and the thousands of other cases of resistance to bondage.[7] Stewart struggles and vacillates between accepting the dominant narrative and arguing to refute it, "It was our gross sins and abominations that provoked the Almighty to frown thus heavily upon us, and give our glory to others."[8] In counterpoint, long before Mills, Furstenberg, and others put the stamp of current scholarship on this idea, Stewart characterizes the argument of whites who: " . . . boldly assert that did we possess a natural independence of soul; and feel a love of liberty within our breasts, some one of our sable race, long before this, would have testified it, notwithstanding the disadvantages under which we labor."

To counter this, Stewart calls upon past achievements and exhorts her audience to engage in lives and practices that disrupt the narrative. Walker and Stewart both adopted the ideology of moral autonomy, the vital importance for Black people to exhibit moral behavior, and beyond that, intellectual excellence. She encourages her audience to "endeavor to turn their attention to knowledge and improvement, for knowledge is power."[9] Lacking subtlety or a sense of her audience, as she sometimes does, Stewart wonders why Black people have not achieved more, displaying that she also suffers from the epistemic violence of historically obliterated Black attainment. At this point either she does not know of or in any case does not mention the accomplishments of Benjamin Bannister, John Marrant, Olaudah Equiano and Ottobah Cugoano, Briton Hammon or Jupitor Hammon, Crispus Attucks, Phillis Wheatley, Paul Cuffe, Prince Hall, Richard Allen or Absalom Jones, and others. Either way, she makes her message heard: the time for excellence is now.

THEOLOGY, THE PROBLEM OF EVIL, AND MORAL WORTH

Parsing the intricacies of Stewart's theological views presents challenges. Given her precocity and her youth, she would still have been articulating to herself the contours of her theological beliefs. She pursued several lines of thought about the problem of evil, that is, how to reconcile the existence of evils such as slavery with the idea of an all-good (beneficent), all powerful (omnipotent), and all-knowing (omniscient) God who would seemingly not allow such evils to exist. She seeks an explanation, a vindication—a theodicy—for why a good God would so punish her people. Like medieval scholars, she sometimes carries on an internal dialogue of questions and answers. For example, she wonders on the one hand why Black people lack accomplishments and may be themselves responsible for poor treatment as punishment for failings. On the other hand, she recognizes that Black people have been "the principal foundation" of white achievement.

Writing about the problem of evil and citing Stewart, Barbara Omolade muses, "[I]n a twist that suggests divine intervention, the racist and cultur-ally restrictive Protestantism practiced by white British colonists and their American descendants was transformed by African Americans, especially women, into a faith that 'unleashed their silenced tongues' and unfettered their restricted bodies."[10] Throughout her political thought, Stewart constructs a brilliant condemnation of whites, arguing that those African Americans who prepare themselves spiritually and intellectually for the day of reckoning will form a new elite vanguard while white Americans will be punished for their immoral treatment of Blacks. The African American form of this argument provides a racialized analysis of two types of sinners: "American" (white) sin-ners who, without immediate repentance and reform, will surely be damned to hell, and "African" (Black American) sinners who, if they make themselves morally ready for the day of reckoning, will rise to power.[11] Stewart writes:

> O ye great and mighty men of America, ye rich and powerful ones, many of you will call for the rocks and mountains to fall upon you, and to hide you from the wrath of the Lamb and from him that sitteth on the throne; whilst many of the sable-skinned Africans you despise will shine in the kingdom of heaven as stars for ever and ever.[12]

Walker also argues for Black moral superiority:

> I know that the blacks, take them half-enlightened and ignorant, are more humane and merciful than the most enlightened and refined European that can be found in all the earth. AND Let no one say that

I assert this because I am prejudiced on the side of my colour, and against the whites or Europeans. For what I write, I do it candidly, for my God and the good of both parties: Natural observations have taught me these things; there is a solemn awe in the hearts of the blacks, as it respects *murdering* men (which is the reason whites take advantage of us) whereas the whites (though they are great cowards) where they have the advantage, or think that there are any prospects of getting it, they murder them all before them, in order to subject men to wretchedness and degradation under them.[13]

The exceptionalist argument assesses historical and social evidence to expose the moral failure of white Americans and the moral ascendancy of Black Americans, "A God of infinite purity will not regard the prayers of those who hold religion in one hand, and prejudice, sin, and pollution in the other . . ."[14] Walker and Stewart grasp the white exceptionalist argument that sees slavery as God's gift to his chosen people and convert that argument to their own uses, contingent upon the upright moral behavior of Black people. Peter Hinks holds that like other "black proponents of political activism, racial solidarity, and even resistance [Walker] understood the tenets of moral improvement to be central components of their strategies," and "blacks adopted moral improve-ment . . . for their own politically and racially motivated reasons."[15]

Parallel to the Euro-American philosophical argument about moral au-tonomy, an economic autonomy argument further refined the category of full personhood and expressed an "abhorrence of the consequences of personal dependence" equating political identity with economic autonomy. Eric Foner explains that "it was an axiom of eighteenth-century political thought that dependents lacked a will of their own and did not deserve a role in public affairs," citing remarks by James Wilson and by Thomas Jefferson, who wrote, "[D]ependence begets subservience and venality, [and] suffocates the germ of virtue."[16] Stewart endorses a concept of freedom as economic autonomy. She points out that in terms of the oppressors, economically, "in reality we have been their principal foundation."[17] She exhorts her audience to "be diligent in business" and reiterates her pleas for "schools and seminaries of learning for our children and youth." She urges members of the ACS to drop their coloniza-tion scheme and instead use their funds and efforts "in erecting a college" for Africa's descendants in America.[18]

Consistent application of liberal-republican principles regarding equality of opportunity are a cornerstone of Stewart and Walker's writings. Once again, to counter Jefferson, Walker challenges the oppressors at the very least to stop interfering with Black productivity:

Has Mr. Jefferson declared to the world, that we are inferior to the whites, both in the endowments of our bodies and of minds? It is indeed surprising, that a man of such great learning, combined with such excellent natural parts, should speak so of a set of men in chains. I do not know what to compare it to, unless, like putting one wild deer in an iron cage, where it will be secured, and hold another by the side of the same, then let it go, and expect the one in the cage to run as fast as the one at liberty.[19]

Stewart urges "every man of color throughout the United States, who possesses the spirit of and principles of a man, sign a petition to Congress to abolish slavery in the District of Columbia, and grant you the rights and privileges of common citizens."[20] Recently, a cohort of scholars led by Daniel Carpenter examined "a dataset of over 8,500 anti-slavery petitions sent to Congress" that shows high levels of women's activism in a petition movement that encompassed antislavery, temperance, and objections to Cherokee removal from their ancestral lands among other demands, noting the efforts of "the Grimké sisters, Maria Chapman-Weston, and William Lloyd Garrison (who was heavily influenced by the black abolitionist Maria Stewart)." Stewart was not found to have signed any petitions, but in this speech, her mind was on these efforts, encouraging men to sign. Carpenter demonstrates that for women, this was a particularly prominent form of political activism.[21]

In keeping with the petition movement, she urges her compatriots to "be bold and enterprising" and connects commercial enterprise with political rights by directly encouraging people to "sue for your rights and privileges," meaning this literally, as an appeal to legal protections and remedies based on the liberal political system.[22] In 1879 Stewart followed her own advice and sued for her husband's pension from the War of 1812, using the proceeds to republish her written work—one of the reasons we have this work today.

Maria W. Stewart and David Walker's Black revolutionary liberalism self-consciously adopts a theory of freedom as moral and economic independence. The propaganda about Black dependence that provides a river of damaging characterizations into the twenty-first century has its origins in slavery and in dependency arguments against Black civil rights. Stewart cautions her listeners against using prejudice and discrimination as an excuse and an obstacle to achievement. Black radical liberalism did not unthinkingly accept the notions of moral and economic independence as a meaning of freedom. Its practitioners were well aware of the disabilities and institutional barriers to economic success. In a sense, then, theirs was a more consistent application of the liberal concept of negative freedom, freedom from interference, on the part of African American and feminist advocates of economic independence. Stewart ends this speech with a rallying cry: "They would drive us to a strange land. But before I go the bayonet shall pierce me through. African rights and liberty is a subject that ought to fire the breast of every free man of color in these United States, and excite in his bosom a lively, decided, deep, and heartfelt interest." [23]

Chapter Twenty-five

"FAREWELL ADDRESS"

*Farewell. In a few short years from now, we shall meet in those upper
regions where parting will be no more. There shall we sing and shout, and
shout and sing, and make heavens high arches ring.*
—Maria W. Stewart, Speech delivered September 21, 1833, described in the *Liberator*,
September 28, 1833, and signed by her from New York, April 14, 1834[1]

At this fiery time of coordinated African American organizing when the issue
of slavery had once again come to the forefront of national discourse, Maria W.
Stewart chose to leave Boston, perhaps to become even more deeply engaged
in the struggle. Activists defied racial barriers with a single-minded sense of
purpose. Christopher Cameron writes:

> Garrison's 1832 *Thoughts on African Colonization* drew ... heavily from
> the work of blacks, as it reprinted dozens of minutes from anticoloniza-
> tion meetings throughout northern black communities. One such meet-
> ing occurred in Boston on 12 March 1831 including the leading African
> American abolitionists in the state—Reverend Samuel Snowden, Robert
> Roberts, James G. Barbadoes, Masonic leader John T. Hilton, Reverend
> Hosea Easton, and Thomas Dalton.[2]

In 1833 Boston's activist women formed the gender-segregated but racially diverse Boston Female Anti-Slavery society (BFAAS).[3] Among the early members
of the group were Maria Weston Chapman, Lavinia Hilton, Lydia Maria Child,
Susan Paul, and possibly Maria W. Stewart. That same year, the all-Black and
male MGCA merged with the New England Anti-Slavery Society, eventually
becoming the Massachusetts Anti-Slavery Society in 1835, a chapter of the
national American Anti-Slavery Society. Boston was not alone as a vibrant
political scene. In New York, the public-school system incorporated the Free
African Schools, literary and abolitionist societies were formed, and shortly

thereafter, David Ruggles opened the first African American bookstore in the nation.

In September of 1833, Maria W. Stewart returned to the schoolroom of the African Meeting House to deliver her "Farewell Address." Her philosophy of everyday righteousness and political struggle together with an apocalyptic vision of justice had framed her first published work and was refined in subsequent ones. Her theology of salvation provided a powerful motive for others to repent of all sin, lead virtuous lives, and accept the grace of Jesus. The motive of evading eternal damnation provided added incentive, as Stewart reveals, "I was glad when I realized the dangers I had escaped; and then I consecrated my soul and body, and all the powers of my mind to his service." The "Farewell Address" has less of the bitterness found in her earlier thought and of which she "drank to the very dregs" at her lowest points of despair. She laments that she had been misrepresented in the past, "and there was none to help." Badger's accusations had likely gone some distance to discredit her in the community, and certainly his attempt to introduce a wife and daughter for James Stewart in the will who purportedly had prior claim to his wealth, even if discredited by the judiciary, would have been poorly received in an atmosphere where respectability was paramount. The accusations may explain to some degree the vehemence with which she extolled the necessity of virtue.

Abandoning the travails of the past, this speech emanates hope. She "found that religion was full of benevolence; I found there was peace in believing."[4] The reader may find some amusement in the way that, once more defending her public speechifying, she gently corrects St. Paul who, unlike Garrison, fell into mistaken teachings about the subordinate role of women. Paul's fault lay in the fact that he did not *share her experience*, as she once more insists upon an embodied phenomenology. St. Paul, she argues, would change his mind did he "but know of our wrongs and deprivations."[5]

A longstanding argument for the oppression rested on a tenet that Black people exhibited a lack of cultural and historical achievement. Defending unequal treatment in *Sociology for the South*, George Fitzhugh wrote: "The earliest civilization of which history gives account is that of Egypt. The negro was always in contact with the civilization. For four thousand years he has had opportunities of becoming civilized [but did not]. Like the wild horse, he must be caught, tamed, and domesticated."[6]

Walker and Stewart both responded to this type of claim, Walker citing Jefferson's promulgation of the belief. A proto-genitor of the Africana movement, Walker developed many familiar themes also asserted by Stewart: that the origins of humankind are to be found in Africa, that African culture attained magnificent scientific and intellectual heights, that Egyptians were Black and that ancient Greece and Rome owed their achievements to the influence of

African culture.[7] To this Stewart added that women in ancient times and in the Middle Ages rivaled the achievements of men: Was not Deborah both a mother and a judge? Did not Queen Esther save the Jews? She contemplates the notion that women have a more direct connection with God than men do: "a belief, however, that the deity more readily communicates himself to women, has at one time or another prevailed in every corner of the earth." She cites numerous examples across cultures and through time of women's achievements and worthiness of equality with men, asserting that women could "look into futurity," and possessed a "supernatural attraction" to the deity. In defense of her own philosophical teachings she says:

> In the 15th century . . . [we find] women occupying the chairs of Philosophy and Justice; women writing in Greek, and studying Hebrew. Nuns were poetesses, and women of quality Divines; and young girls who had studied Eloquence. . . . The religious spirit which has animated women in all ages, showed itself at this time. It has made them by turns, martyrs, apostles, warriors, and concluded in making them divines and scholars.

She directs her gaze into the future, observing that "the mighty work of reformation has begun . . . the dark clouds of ignorance are dispersing. The light of science is bursting forth. Knowledge is beginning to flow."[8] Her sense of hope and excitement for the future is palpable.

Beyond her protofeminism, Stewart argues that: " . . . poor, despised Africa was once the resort of sages and legislators of other nations, was esteemed the school for learning, and the most illustrious men in Greece flocked thither for instruction."

Stewart's early invocation of the mantra of Black nationalism, "Ethiopia shall again stretch forth her hands unto God," raises the issue of whether or not her political philosophy and Walker's are properly labeled "nationalist."[9] As Lena Ampadu observes, "Historians and other scholars often have gravitated to the ideas of male figures, those of Marcus Garvey, Henry Highland Garnet, and Martin Delany, as central to examining . . . black nationalism to the exclusion of women's ideas" such as Stewart's. Among present-day philosophers, Tommie Shelby's extensive work on Black nationalism designates Delany's mid-nineteenth-century writing as an originating point, but Ampadu urges scholars to reach further back to the writings of a neglected Black woman philosopher. Analyzing Stewart's work, she finds that in addition to endorsing a glorious African past, Stewart "promoted not only race pride and uplift, but other important elements of nationalism such as unity, group consciousness, and self-determination." She argues that Stewart endorses an idea of "systematic nationalism" rather than a nationalism dependent on land acquisition, a vitally important theoretical development in the face of the Colonization Society's attempts to remove Black Americans to Africa.[10] Lucius Outlaw asserts: "There is a long history of efforts by scholars African and of African descent to reclaim Egypt from the intellectual annexation to Europe that was urged by Hegel in his *The Philosophy of History*," a history he documents assiduously.[11] More recently, cutting-edge philosophers have initiated a knowledge project that shifts the authoritative center of gravity away from the canonical stalwarts and towards critiques by Africana philosophers who "creolize the canon." It might be said that Walker and Stewart were early practitioners of this approach.[12]

In a sharp response to colonization efforts by the ACS, Stewart and Walker repeatedly assert their native status and the historic role of Black people in creating the United States of America, all the while highlighting their ancestors' cultural achievements. Their arguments about the significance of Black culture stood upon earlier efforts by Paul Cuffe, Richard Allen, Prince Hall, and others who contributed to the creation of indigenous Black religious and social organizations designed to instill pride and solidarity.[13] The movement's force was such that by the 1820s there were churches, mutual aid societies, and literary societies for men and women that honored Black cultural heritage, as did *Freedom's Journal*, devoted to "everything that related to Africa."[14]

In a deeply emotional revelation, Maria W. Stewart announced her departure from Boston: "I am about to leave you, perhaps never more to return," dipping a final time into the well of pain filled with the anguish she feels at the gender and class prejudice within the community, only to revive herself and her message of hope. Celia Bardwell-Jones explores Gloria Anzaldúa's notions of the tug-and-pull of various social locations, especially when she "criticizes her cultural traditions" as Stewart does in calling out sexism within her community. For Anzaldúa and Bardwell-Jones, this "does not mean that she is disloyal to her cultural community," which she has dedicated herself to defending.[15] Critical dialogue internal to a community has widely different dimensions than externally generated criticism, which does not mean that either are always taken kindly. Stewart's path has taken her through the phases of her philosophical vision: everyday righteousness and political action leading into the realm of redemption. In her vision of the approaching millennium, all that is needed is for her people to prepare themselves, work towards unity within the community "til prejudice becomes extinct at home" and attend to "religion and the pure principles of morality," to "cultivate your own minds and morals," to "turn your attention to industry," and await a glorious future. She thanks those "kind individuals," her friends. She believes that she has fulfilled her personal obligation to "God's ancient covenant."[16]

Based on her "Farewell Address," many scholars accept that Maria W. Stewart fled Boston solely due to the opposition she experienced for lecturing in public as a woman and the discouraging degree of sexism she faced. The full reasons for her departure may be more complex. It may be that after the deaths of James W. Stewart, David Walker, and Thomas Paul, she lost heart for staying in the city, but she was tied up in the courts until 1832, when the case was finally settled, and she was left with very poor prospects for supporting herself. Her life was a journey, wandering and seeking, always moving closer to the centers of activity sometimes in ways that are quite alarming. Later in life, she moved ever closer to the Civil War battlefields. In the 1830s, Boston felt small to her. She had exhausted her possibilities and may also have had a contingent of creditors—real or imagined—eager to find other ways to complicate her life. New York seemed promising. Prospects for a position as a teacher in Williamsburg, New York, as well as the city itself, and closer proximity to Philadelphia—alive with abolitionist action—enticed her. Her head and heart cried out for a larger platform. The people of Boston, most of them anyway, were reserved in their approach to religion. She did not realize what she would lose when she no longer had William Lloyd Garrison as an advocate willing to publish her writing, but in Brooklyn she could teach and would become affiliated with an activist church.

In her life, Stewart had experienced the depths of despair, starting with the loss of her parents in her earliest years. She was subjected to the wrenching separation from her extended family and community at the age of five, when she was forced into manual labor, an occupation that shaped her as she moved from girlhood into adolescence and then young adulthood, when she was finally freed from the legal bonds of indentured labor—not free to change the kind of employment deemed acceptable for her but only to contract her labor on her own terms. The best expression of this measure of her newfound freedom was her attendance at a Sabbath School for African Americans in Hartford, acquiring an education that brought her into a community of like-minded souls that afforded her the opportunity to develop an intellect that was longing for sustenance. It also brought her into contact with travelers passing through the city with news of a wider world, stories that set her dreams on fire and produced a determination that, despite race and gender restrictions, she would chart her own course.

The courage of her move to Boston had been rewarded handsomely when she was accepted into a vibrant activist community of free Blacks rivaled at the time only by Philadelphia. She fell in love with and married a man whose worldly sophistication was unsurpassed. With the influence of James W. Stewart, Thomas Paul, David Walker, William Lloyd Garrison, and the women whose names are more hidden and whose influences are more difficult to trace, she came to intellectual maturity and joined the struggle. Her work was profound then and continues to have profound reverberations now. She set off for New York City full of hope for the future and wisdom about the obstacles she faced, but she carried with her a safety net that, when it was working, banished all fear.

> O Lord . . . cause thy face to shine upon us . . . that there might come a mighty shaking of dry bones . . . there is beauty in the fear of the Lord . . . and we last meet around thy throne, and join in celebrating thy praises.[17]

Maria W. Stewart, born Maria Miller, had loved the music of the church since she was a child. Her inevitable death was real to her and no longer frightening. Instead, it was something to be welcomed in all its glory with its vision of the Lord's shining face and the sound of God's trombones, for "There we shall sing and shout."[18] Until that time, she had other work to do and forty-six more years to do it.

POSTSCRIPT

The New York Society for the Manumission of Slaves established the city's first African Free School in 1817 with Brooklyn's first school opening in the late 1820s. Maria W. Stewart delivered her "Farewell Address" in September of 1833 at the African Meeting House in Boston and sent a written copy to William Lloyd Garrison six months later from her new home in Williamsburg, Brooklyn, where she had taken up a teaching position. Unwavering in her commitment not to be one of "the flowers among us that are 'born to bloom unseen,'" she continued to draw upon her supporters in New England laboring to have a collection of her works, *Productions of Mrs. Maria W. Stewart presented to the First Africa Baptist Church & Society, of the City of Boston*, published by "Friends of Freedom and Virtue" in 1835.[1]

Stewart was as determined as ever to continue working towards abolition and women's rights. In 1837 she reunited with her Boston friend Susan Paul at the *Anti-Slavery Convention of American Women* held in Manhattan. Attended as well by the prominent abolitionists Lydia Maria Child, Angelina Grimké, Sarah Grimké, Lucretia Mott, and another African American from Boston, Julia Williams, who may also have been a friend of Stewart.[2] Held concurrently with the fourth meeting of the American Anti-Slavery Society, the delegates called for immediate emancipation. Writing in the *Proceedings*, Maria Weston Chapman identified the central principles adopted there:

> Every obligation of humanity, of religion, of patriotism, of maternity, of every relation of womanhood is upon us, to leave no labor unper-formed which may hasten the emancipation of our country from its bondage ... [O]nly by feeling, thinking, and acting like human souls can we be fitted for wives and mothers.[3]

Stewart was active in the community, joining a female literary society, the African Dorcus Association, and lectured occasionally over the years.

At the highest levels of Black accomplishment and activism, the Reverend Henry Highland Garnet and the moral philosopher and antislavery activist

Alexander Crummell recognized Stewart's accomplishments. Later in his life, Crummell wrote an endorsement of her work and a reminiscence about her.

> I remember very distinctly the great surprise of both my friends and myself at finding in New York a young woman of my own people full of literary aspiration and ambitious scholarship. In those days, that is at the commencement of the anti-slavery enterprise, the desire for learning was almost exclusively confined to colored young men. There were a few young women in New York who thought of these higher things, and it was a surprise to find another added to their number.[4]

While Crummell's assessment may have underestimated the general desire for education and justice among Black women, he nonetheless honored Stewart as a public-school teacher and member of a female literary society. Sarah Mapps Douglass, a contemporary of Stewart and another prominent writer and abolitionist also taught in New York's African schools, so it is likely that the two knew each other. There is still much to be learned about the circle of women who were active in New York and elsewhere at the time.[5]

Citing a history of Black public schools in Brooklyn, Marilyn Richardson notes that by 1845, Stewart was recorded as having taught more than sixty scholars, and that in 1847, she was appointed assistant to Hezekiah Green, the school's principal.[6] These successes notwithstanding, Stewart conveys that for an unspecified reason she "lost her position" in New York City and that "hearing the colored people were more religious and God-fearing in the South, I wended my way to Baltimore in 1852. But I found that all was not gold that glistened." She again worked as an educator, as she records in the autobiographical work "Sufferings During the War."[7] In Baltimore, she lectured on the topic of "The Proper Training of Children" at the Ladies Literary Festival held at the St. James Protestant Episcopal Church in November 1860 and published the speech in the *Repository of Religion and Literature and of Science and Art* of the African Methodist Episcopal (AME) Church. Eric Garner's excellent sleuthing discovered this and another work,

> . . . a short story entitled "The First Stage of Life" [that] joined Frances Ellen Watkins Harper's "The Two Offers" as one of the earliest examples of short fiction published by a black woman when it was serialized in the April, July, and October issues of the *Repository*.[8]

After almost a decade, her time in Baltimore came to an end. Stewart felt compelled to seek the seat of power at one of the most dangerous times in the history of the capital. She moved to Washington, DC, shortly after President

Abraham Lincoln's inauguration. There, she organized a private school that was favored by prominent citizens of the Black community, including Henry Bailey, pastor of the Abyssinian Baptist Church, who records, "I have seen her going through the streets in the dead of winter looking up the little children who should be attending school; and where their parents could pay or not, she was perfectly willing to give her time and strength in teaching them."[9]

Is it a surprise given the relatively close-knit circle of well-educated African Americans that she had met in Baltimore and in Washington renewed her friendship with Elizabeth Keckley, the seamstress for and confidante of Mary Todd Lincoln? Stewart reveals this connection in "Sufferings During the War," a work that has received little scholarly attention despite providing a rich source of material about her life as well as a rare and heart-breaking account of someone in her social position during the Civil War.

As a flood of emancipated and self-liberated people swelled the capital, the Freedman's Hospital was established in 1862 to provide aid and succor to those seeking sanctuary and assistance during and after the war. Placed under the leadership of Alexander T. Augusta, the hospital was thereby administered by an African American during the period of Reconstruction. Maria W. Stewart gained employment there, eventually becoming Matron, an administrative supervisor.

Legislative acts stipulating pensions for war veterans and their widows were passed in 1871 and 1878, the latter possibly prompting Stewart to investigate whether or not she had a right to a pension resulting from James W. Stewart's service in the US Navy.[10] Amos Hunt, a Notary Public from Washington, DC writes: "The necessary applications and proof were made to the Pension Office for pension and bounty land; and in March, 1879, a pension of $8 per month was granted to Mrs. Maria W. Stewart, commencing with March 9, 1878."[11] While she was not awarded the 160 acres of land, she received the pension that she used to underwrite a republication of her previous writings along with a brief, new autobiographical preface. The book opened with several important letters of commendation, a biographical sketch by her friend, Louise Hatton, and the essay "Sufferings During the War." Notably, in her preface, she charged that her work had been "suppressed for forty six years." Stewart understood language and this choice of terms indicates the sophisticated epistemology that undergirded the knowledge that her ideas, and those of so many others, did not achieve wide currency, not for lack of trenchant analysis or beauty of prose, but because social, legal, and economic institutions coupled with individual practices elevated even the most mundane thoughts of the privileged and smothered the intellectual accomplishments of those who challenged systematic oppression.

Marilyn Richardson's research uncovered a number of details about the Freedman's Hospital, where Stewart lived in the waning years of her life and where she died. She records that, "[f]ollowing a service conducted by the Rev. Alexander Crummell, rector of St. Luke's Episcopal Church, she was buried at Washington's Graceland Cemetery on December 17, fifty years to the day after her husband's death."[12]

Stewart's tenacious character would not permit financial hardship, institutional discrimination, a lack of educational degrees, gender harassment, poverty, or legal restrictions to deter her from believing that what she had to say was worthwhile for others to read, nor from getting her work published. For all we know about her, and considering her substantial body of work, she remains a shadowy figure. Like Prince Hall, Belinda Sutton, Phillis Wheatley, Thomas Paul, David Walker, Susan Paul, and others, her contributions to early Black political theory and activism are undeniable—a bequest worthy of recognition, of further study, and of awesome worship.

ACKNOWLEDGMENTS

A number of years ago, the historian and scholar Marilyn Richardson single-handedly reclaimed a brilliant thinker from obscurity, writing *Maria W. Stewart: America's First Black Woman Political Writer*, a work that compiles Stewart's most notable works along with a wealth of biographical data and a beautiful introductory essay. Since then, she has generously encouraged my endeavor to learn and teach more about Maria W. Stewart and the political milieu of the late eighteenth and early nineteenth centuries. Thank you, Marilyn, for bringing Maria Stewart into my consciousness and for your support. Your work is a gift to generations of readers.

In the years surrounding Richardson's pathbreaking work, diligent research guided by innovative theoretical frameworks made for an infuriating and magical time in the academy—infuriating due to the revelations of "why didn't I know" about the legions of thinkers that emerge when one engages with what Chike Jeffers and Peter Adamson call "the history of philosophy without any gaps" and magical because the remote, abstract theories of entrenched Euro-American traditions were being critiqued, challenged, and even replaced by far more resonant ones born of novel approaches to knowledge-production. To be a young scholar at that moment meant to watch a transformation of the academic world in congress with the social upheavals of the time, ones that still convulse today. I am grateful to those who guided and influenced my intellectual development at that time: at Clark University, Cynthia Enloe, Pamela Wright, Serena Hilsinger, Lois Brynes, Angela Bowen, Beverly Grier, and Jennifer Abod; at the College of the Holy Cross, Diane Bell, Ann Bookman, Bertram Ashe, Deidre Hill Butler, Carol Conaway, Karen Turner, Melissa Weiner; and most profoundly from afar, Patricia Hill Collins, Angela Y. Davis, Toni Morrison, Alice Walker, and other luminaries of Black feminist writing. This awakening inspired what one reviewer called a "canon-busting" edited collection, *Women and Men Political Theorists: Enlightened Conversations*, my effort to produce a novel and inclusive take on primary sources in the history of modern philosophy.

In a departure from the rigid restrictions of traditional academic philosophy, several scholarly groups have served as powerful correctives. Among them are *Philosophy Born of Struggle*, the brainchild of Leonard Harris, where I first became familiar with the work of Charles W. Mills, Anita Allen, and "the most noble, fearless, and undaunted David Walker." While many disciplines were mired in tradition, reproducing themselves and their ideas, a sea- change occurred with the creation of the Caribbean Philosophical Association, an organization dedicated to "shifting the geography of reason" and therefore our way of thinking about all theoretical and activist work produced through the African diaspora. Those founders—George Belle, B. Anthony Bogues, Patrick Goodin, Lewis Gordon, Clevis Headley, Paget Henry, Nelson Maldonado-Torres, Charles Mills, and Supriya Nair—broke new ground and embraced innovative work, in an organization later guided by Neil Roberts, Douglas Ficek, Jane Anna Gordon, Rosario Torres-Guevara, and Michael Monahan. The Collegium of Black Women Philosophers founded by Kathryn Sophia Belle has been transformative.

The revelations born of these transformative movements led Carol B. Conaway and me to create the edited volume *Black Women's Intellectual Traditions: Speaking Their Minds* (2007), a work that insisted that Black women had every bit as much and as valuable to say as the intellectuals traditionally held in high esteem in the nineteenth century. Carol and I were grateful and humbled when this work received the Letitia Woods Brown Memorial Award from the Association of Black Women Historians (ABWH) and extend thanks and appreciation to A'Lelia Bundles and the entire awards committee for this recognition.

A lively set of professional organizations sustains conversation about race, gender, class, sexuality, philosophy, and history: the African American Intellectual History Society (AAIHS) become a reality through the efforts of Christopher Cameron, Ashley D. Farmer, and Keisha N. Blain. At those conferences I learned from conversations with Nneke D. Dennie, Nathifa Greene, and many others who were eager to embrace this new organization. At the Feminist Ethics and Social Theory (FEAST) conferences, I have been particularly nurtured by Celia Bardwell-Jones and Margaret McLaren—although the cross-attendance in this compact and intellectually soaring amalgam of small societies makes it nearly impossible to distinguish which connections were made at which intellectual feast. The California Roundtable on Philosophy and Race (CRPR) has provided a forum, led in recent years by Falguni Sheth and Mickaella Perina. The Radical Philosophy Association (RPA) is currently steered by José Jorge Mendoza and George Fourlas, both of whom are more than colleagues; they are close friends and intellectual sparring partners. And not to be excluded are the more informal study groups where I meet and converse with Ann Ferguson, Karsten Struhl, Richard Schmitt, Nanette Funk, and many other comrades.

At the Museum of African American History-Boston/Nantucket (MAAH), I received guidance from Beverly Morgan-Walsh and L'Merchie Frazier, whose magnificent art honoring nineteenth-century Black women guides the eye to another way of knowing. The Beacon Hill Scholars also keep the flame alive, guided for many years by Horace Seldon's passionate leadership. Michael Terranova and Horace were indefatigable collectors of all things to do with Black Boston and Beacon Hill. Michael's tour of the alleyways, brick facades, and ancient rooftops perfectly conjures the sound of congregants at the African Meeting House as their heels click on the cobblestones.

I am grateful for the help of Hannah Elder at the Massachusetts Historical Society and of the librarians at the Connecticut State Library. Jeffrey Bingham Mead has been particularly clear-eyed in his approach to his family history, and he assisted in connecting me with Maggie Dimock, curator of Collections and Christopher Shields, curator of Library and Archives at the Greenwich Historical Society.

I must be a particular nuisance to colleagues past and present at Worcester State University, considering all those with whom I have conversed or cajoled into reading portions of my work and from whom I've learned about race, gender, and social justice: Nathan Angelo, Laxmi Bissoondial, Frank Boardman, Sonya Connor, Michelle Corbin, Elena Cuffari, Johnathan Flowers, Aldo García Guevara, Charlotte Haller, Ken Marshall, Tanya Mears, Sarah Sharbach, Dan Shartin, Hardeep Sidhu, Richard Schmitt, Henry Theriault, Heather Treseler, Marcela Uribe-Jennings, Karen Woods Weierman, and Amanda Whitman. I have also received support from Dean Russ Pottle, the unflagging encouragement of President Barry Maloney, and research funds from Provost Lois Wims, all of whom deserve thanks.

As a Resident Scholar at the Women's Studies Research Center at Brandeis University, among the many women who have inspired me through their artistic creativity, activism, and intellects are Ann Caldwell, Margaret Morganroth Gullette, Laurie Kahn, Annette Miller, Shula Reinharz, and Janet Freedman. My residency as Visiting Scholar at the American Antiquarian Society in 2017 provided the tranquility, community, and resources that fueled my determination to complete my work. Lisa Boehm, Neil Roberts, Manisha Sinha, and Stefan Wheelock generously offered their services as readers for the initial proposal to publishers and have continued to champion the project along the way. I feel immense gratitude for their support. I would like to also thank the anonymous reviewers for their insights and guidance.

I received editorial guidance from Barbara Grossman and Louise Knight, editorial assistance from Michael Levine, and research assistance from Samantha Boardman, Chelsea Dickhaut, Katie Commerford, and Johanie Rodriguez. Ben Gerhardt has been unfailing in his work contributing very materially to the manuscript, especially his help compiling the bibliography. Kim Noonan provided much-needed assistance preparing the illustrations.

The most enduring support editorial support came from Patsy Baudoin, who carefully read and commented on each chapter, providing encouragement, suggestions, editorial remarks, and the faith in this project that allowed me to move forward during the times when forward movement was most difficult. Among others who provided lengthy close readings, Charles Mills has long been a generous commentator as well as an inspirational philosophical influence. Daniel McLean made heroic contributions. I appreciate the assistance of Craig Gill, Katie Keene, Lisa McMurtray, Laura Strong, and Camille Hale at the University Press of Mississippi.

I've benefitted from the work of Jameliah Shorter-Bourhanou, who is making fine additions to scholarship about Maria W. Stewart. In addition to her excellent book about Stewart, Valerie C. Cooper shared her expertise about certain biblical references. Peter P. Hinks provided a close reading of my article "Crying out for Liberty," one that brought home the necessity of linking political and religious thought, especially among nineteenth century Black writers. In addition, he made numerous suggestions about sources and ideas.

For deep and challenging conversations on race and political theory, I am particularly grateful to Carol Conaway, Aldo García Guevara, Janine Jones, Jean King, Kenneth Marshall, Meredith Roman, Colin O'Reilly, Jiaqi O'Reilly, and Evelyn Simien.

My parents, George and Shirley Waters, fostered an atmosphere of intellectual curiosity in the home that took flight when through an odd twist of fate, I attended Bard College. And because "what goes around comes around," that good fortune returned recently when I was invited by archivist Helene Tieger to curate an exhibition of works drawn from the Alan Sussman Rare Book Collection at the Stevenson Library at Bard, allowing me to hold in my hands first and early editions of books by Olaudah Equiano, Mary Wollstonecraft, Frederick Douglass, Charles Ball, and the magnificent compendium about the Underground Railroad by William Still. The permanent internet version of this exhibition feels like an extension of this book http://omekalib.bard.edu/exhibits/show/abolition-resistance--works-fr. Along with Helene, Debra Klein and Anna Cinquemani were instrumental in creating the exhibit, a material testament to the power of written resistance.

On the "home team," among those not already mentioned are Gloria Abramoff, Larry Abramoff, Lysa Bennett, Lucinda Cowell, Gwen Davis, Gordon Davis, Andrea Dottolo, Debbie Fisher, Ellen Johnson, Dr. Sandy King, Deb Lyons, Sandy McEvoy, Ginger Navickas, Amy Ness, Colin O'Reilly, Ed O'Reilly, Jiaqi O'Reilly, K Soysa, Holland Sutton, Jon Seydl, Melita Tapia, Steve Taviner, Karen Turner, Lihua Wang, Matthias Waschek, and Nancy Waters. If this seems like a host of helpers, it is. My work on Maria W. Stewart has spanned twenty-five years, sweeping in many supporters (and critics). I thank the reader for allowing me to name them.

Of course, the major inspiration was Maria W. Stewart. Every time I read her words, I feel a fire in my soul.

Permissions

African Meeting House is reprinted here by permission of the poet, Regie Gibson.

"Crying Out for Liberty: Maria W. Stewart and David Walker's Black Revolutionary Liberalism." Kristin Waters, *Philosophia Africana* 15, no. 1 (Winter 2013): 35–60. Copyright © 2013. This article is used by permission of The Pennsylvania State University Press.

NOTES

POEM

1. This poem was written for the *Museum of African American History*—Boston/
Nantucket. I would like to thank Regie Gibson, not only for his permission to use the poem,
but also for writing something that captures the essence of the miracle that is the still-
standing African Meeting House, the oldest extant Black church in the United States. https://
www.maah.org/

INTRODUCTION

1. Richardson, Marilyn, ed., *Maria W. Stewart: America's First Black Political Writer*,
(Bloomington: Indiana University Press, 1987), 30.

2. From William Lloyd Garrison's testimonial letter printed in the 1879 edition of the
Meditations from the Pen of Mrs. Maria W. Stewart, reprinted in Richardson, ed., *Stewart*,
89. Unless indicated, all references to the writings of Maria W. Stewart are taken from
Richardson's book. The biblical quote "peeled, meted out . . ." is from Isaiah 18:7.

3. I am very grateful for the assistance of Peter P. Hinks with this portion of my archival
research. I found this listing through Ancestry.com several years prior to my Connecticut
State Library visit but dismissed it due to the birthplace listing of Greenwich, Connecticut, a
location that does not accord with Stewart's own recollection that she was born in Hartford.
Later, Hinks helped to draw it to my attention again. I will argue in this book that the mistaken recollection was natural since she was orphaned as a very young child and spent many
of her early years in Hartford. This issue is taken up in more depth in chapter two. Hinks, the
leading authority on Stewart's friend David Walker, is in no way responsible for any errors I
have made and was helpful at several stages of my research.

4. Mariah W. Stewart, "The First Stage of Life," in "Two Texts on Children and Christian
Education," introduction by Eric Gardner. *Modern Language Association (PMLA)* 123, no.
1 (January 2008): 162–65. "Mariah" is among the variant spellings of her given name, as
"Stuart" is a variant of her surname. In the nineteenth century "Maria" was typically pronounced "Mariah."

5. For a definitive edition, see Peter P. Hinks, ed., *David Walker's Appeal to the Coloured
Citizens of the World* (University Park: Penn State University Press, 2000). For direct access
to *Walker's Appeal*, see the online published version: David Walker, *Walker's Appeal, in Four*

Articles; Together with a Preamble, to the Coloured Citizens of the World, but in Particular, and Very Expressly, to Those of the United States of America, Written in Boston, State of Massachusetts, September 28, 1829, Documenting the American South, University of North Carolina Chapel Hill, 2001, https://docsouth.unc.edu/nc/walker/walker.html, accessed October 13, 2020.

6. Throughout the text, the reader and the author must try to disentangle colonial ideologies adopted from Euro-American cultures from those generated by Indigenous Americans and West Africans. Views of gender would have been significantly different depending on the source. In precolonial African cultures and Indigenous American ones, women had significant roles in governance, suggesting that the diminished status of Black women in the United States, as in the church records, was likely adopted in emulation of Euro-colonial norms and/or imposed as part of the legacy of enslavement.

7. Grover, Kathryn and Janine V. da Silva, "Historic Resource Study Boston African American National Historic Site," 2002, 68. https://www.nps.gov/parkhistory/online_books/bost/hrs.pdf, accessed April 8, 2020.

8. See Patricia Hill Collins, *Black Feminist Thought: Knowledge, Consciousness, and the Politics of Empowerment.* Second edition. New York: Routledge, 2000 and the Bibliography for works by these authors and others.

9. The church built by African Americans in Boston is referred to in a literature spanning more than two hundred years varyingly as the Independent Baptist Church, the African Baptist Church, the African Meetinghouse, and the Belknap Street Church. Note that Belknap Street is now Joy Street, off of which one can find the Meetinghouse, on Smith Court.

10. I first introduced the concept of Black revolutionary liberalism in "Crying Out for Liberty: Maria W. Stewart and David Walker's Black Revolutionary Liberalism," *Philosophia Africana* 15, no. 1 (Winter 2013): 35–60. For a fuller discussion, see several of the later chapters that are devoted to political theory.

11. In this context, the terms liberalism and republicanism are mutually supportive, liberalism designating natural rights theory and republicanism designating a rejection of monarchy, aristocracy and an embrace of liberty. The Enlightenment meanings are quite different from those attached to "liberal" and "republican" today.

12. In *The Racial Contract* (Ithaca: Cornell University Press, 1997), Charles W. Mills introduces the concept of epistemologies of ignorance to designate the willful capacity of whites not to see the raced realities around them. The concept has been significantly developed since Mills's introduction of the term. See *Race and Epistemologies of Ignorance*, ed. Shannon Sullivan and Nancy Tuana (Albany: SUNY Press, 2007). See especially in that volume, Linda Martín Alcoff, "Epistemologies of Ignorance: Three Types." I address the ideas of willful and reflexive ignorance in "A Journey from Willful Ignorance to Liberal Guilt to Black Feminist Thought," *Departures in Critical Qualitative Research* 5, no. 3 (Fall 2016): 108–15.

13. Richardson, *Stewart,* 29.

14. Hinks, *Appeal,* 14.

15. Leonard Harris, "Insurrectionist Ethics: Advocacy, Moral Psychology, and Pragmatism," in *Ethical Issues for a New Millennium,* ed. John Howie (Southern Illinois University Press, 2002). First published as Leonard Harris. *Transactions of the Charles S. Peirce Society* 49, no. 1 (Winter 2013): 93–11.

16. The impressive group of philosophers exploring the idea of insurrectionist ethics, in addition to Harris, includes Jacoby Adeshei Carter, Kristie Dotson, Christina Henderson, Lee McBride, José Medina, and Paul C. Taylor.

17. Richardson, *Stewart*, 37–38.

18. On intersectionality, see Kristin Waters, "Past as Prologue: Intersectional Analysis from the Nineteenth Century to the Twenty-First," in *Why Race and Gender Still Matter*, ed. Namita Goswami, Maeve O'Donovan, and Lisa Yount (London: Pickering and Chatto, 2014), 27–41, in which I provide a genealogy of the concept of intersectionality tracing it back to Maria W. Stewart. In the same volume, see Kathryn T. Gines, (now Kathryn Sophia Belle), "Race Women, Race Men and Early Expressions of Proto-Intersectionality, 1830s-1930s." The term "intersectionality" employed to indicate the interactions of race/gender/class oppression is developed by Kimberlé Crenshaw in "Mapping the Margins: Intersectionality, Identity Politics, and Violence against Women of Color," *Stanford Law Review* 43, no. 1241 (1990–1991), and many other publications. Her current efforts to organizing against intersectional oppression extend to the African American Policy Forum and "Say Her Name" projects, https://aapf.org/, accessed October 5, 2020.

19. The term "epistemicide," is used by Ramón Grosfogel to describe this phenomenon. See "The Structure of Knowledge in Westernized Universities: Epistemic Racism/Sexism and the Four Genocides/Epistemicides of the Long 16th Century," *Human Architecture: Journal of the Sociology of Self-Knowledge* 11, no. 1 (2013): 73–89.

20. My abiding interest in reclamation work has led me to seek out, read, and study the works of many lesser-known writers. I have found this kind of research so compelling that my first edited book was entirely devoted to re-conceiving the canon in political philosophy in *Men and Women Political Theorists: Enlightened Conversations*, published by Blackwell (now Wiley) in 2000. The collection selected readings from canonical writers in the Western tradition of modern philosophy: John Locke, Jean-Jacques Rousseau, Edmund Burke, James Madison, John Stuart Mill, and paired them with those of women and people of color: Mary Astell, Mary Wollstonecraft, Mercy Otis Warren, Frederick Douglass, and Anna Julia Cooper. Maria W. Stewart's essay "On African Rights and Liberty" is paired with a selection from John Stuart Mill's most well-known piece, "On Liberty," a radical defense of human freedom that was inconsistent with his position as a colonial administrator for the East India Company. Two decades later, in the 2020s, the approach of incorporating hitherto marginalized voices into the teaching and scholarship about political theory in the seventeenth to the nineteenth centuries is still not sufficiently practiced, and thus, important voices are still not heard.

21. Collins, *Black Feminist Thought*, 12.

22. Richardson, *Stewart*, 48.

23. Mariana Ortega, *In-Between: Latina Feminist Phenomenology, Multiplicity, and the Self* (Albany: State University of New York Press, 2016), 120.

24. Collins, *Black Feminist Thought* and Richardson, *Stewart*, 82.

25. The notion of "head-work" is used by Stewart and explored by Kristie Dotson in "Inheriting Patricia Hill Collin's *Black Feminist* Epistemology," *Ethnic and Racial Studies* 38, no. 13 (2015): 2322–38.

26. A disturbing example of repetition of misinformation is a photograph that routinely appears in internet searches for Maria W. Stewart and that commonly appears on websites

containing information about her, a photograph of a woman who *is not* Stewart. There is at this time no known photograph of Maria W. Stewart, although I still hold out hope that one might be found.

27. I have addressed this topic in "A Journey from Willful Ignorance to Liberal Guilt," in *Departures in Critical Qualitative Research*. Also see Lewis R. Gordon, *Disciplinary Decadence: Living Thought in Trying Times* (New York: Routledge, 2007) and on the particular issue of the systematic barriers facing black academics, see Jameliah Shorter-Bourhanou, 2017. "Legitimizing Blacks in Philosophy" *Journal of World Philosophies* 2, no. 2. https:// scholarworks.iu.edu/iupjournals/index.php/jwp/article/view/1258.

28. Horace Seldon was an indefatigable advocate for African American rights. http:// www.beaconhillscholars.org/william-lloyd-garrison, accessed September 11, 2020.

29. Kathryn Grover and Janine V. da Silva, "Historic Resource Study Boston African American National Historic Site," 2002. Michael Terranova contributed mightily to this research.

30. William C. Nell, *Colored Patriots of the American Revolution, With Sketches of Several Distinguished Colored Persons, To Which is Added a Brief Survey of the History and Prospects of Colored Americans*, introduction by Harriet Beecher Stowe (Boston: Robert F. Wallcut, 1855); W*illiam Cooper Nell, Nineteenth-century African American Abolitionist, Historian, Integrationist: Selected Writings from 1832–1874*, edited by Dorothy Porter Wesley and Constance Porter Uzelac (Baltimore: Black Classic Press, 2002); James Oliver and Lois E. Horton, *Black Bostonian: Family Life and Community Struggle in the Antebellum North* (New York: Holmes and Meier, 1979); Hinks, *Appeal*; Peter P. Hinks, *To Awaken My Afflicted Brethren: David Walker and the Problem of Antebellum Slave Resistance* (University Park: Penn State University Press, 1997); Manisha Sinha, *The Slave's Cause: A History of Abolition* (New Haven: Yale University Press, 2016).

31. See for example, L. Gordon. *Disciplinary Decadence.*

32. https://www.nytimes.com/2016/07/27/us/politics/michelle-obama-white-house -slavery.html

CHAPTER ONE

1. Richardson, *Stewart*. The quoted verse is adapted from Thomas Grey, *Elegy Written in a Country Churchyard* (Boston: Estes and Lauriat, 1751). As Richardson notes, the actual line is "Full many a flow'r is born to blush unseen, And waste its sweetness on the desert air," 48.

2. Ruthann Robson, "Genealogy," in *Masks*, introduction by Marge Piercy (St. Paul: Leapfrog Press, 1999), 4.

3. Richardson, *Stewart*, 48.

4. A note on nomenclature. For the most part I use the terms "Black" and "African American" interchangeably. In Stewart's day, many Black people felt close to Africa or were in fact African natives. Stewart and others in her time sometimes used the term "African" to denote all Black people in America, as will become evident.

5. Richardson, *Stewart*, 28–29. Some of the essays were titled by William Lloyd Garrison in the *Liberator*. Others were given titles by Marilyn Richardson in her 1987 book.

6. Richardson, *Stewart*, 28.

7. Robert Roberts, *Robert Roberts' Guide for Butlers and Other Household Staff* (1827; repr., Bedford, MA: Applewood Books, 1993).

8. Richardson, *Stewart*, 48.

CHAPTER TWO

1. Birth record from the Barbour Collection at the Connecticut State Library, 1803.

2. Richardson, *Stewart*, 28.

3. See Jeffrey B. Mead, *Chains Unbound: Slave Emancipations in the Town of Greenwich* (Baltimore: Gateway Press, 1995), 14. For a graphic personal account of a similar experience, see Harriet Jacobs, *Incidents in the Life of a Slave Girl* (1861; repr., New York: Dover Publications, 2001).

4. See Linda Kerber, *No Constitutional Right to be Ladies* (New York: Hill and Wang, 1998). The ideology of Republican motherhood held that it was the duty of women to have sons in order to promote liberty and build the nation through public service, while women and girls were to excel in the domestic sphere through virtue and by educating children for their future roles.

5. Barbour Collection, vol. 1 p. 150. "Jared, had formerly negro Lucy, d. Prudence, b. 4 March 1818," Mead, *Chains Unbound*, 14.

6. Kristie Dotson, "Querying Leonard Harris' Insurrectionist Standards," *Transactions of the Charles Peirce Society* 49, no. 1 (Winter 2013): 74–92. See for a discussion of how to conceptualize the anguish of enslaved mothers.

7. Spencer P. Mead, *Ye Historie of Ye Town of Greenwich County of Fairfield and State of Connecticut* (New York: Knickerbocker Press, 1911). See also Daniel M. Mead, *A History of the Town of Greenwich, Fairfield County, Conn., with Many Important Statistics* (New York: Baker & Godwin, 1857).

8. Jeffrey B. Mead, *Chains Unbound*, 33–36.

9. Charles W. Mills, *The Racial Contract* (Ithaca: Cornell University Press, 1997), 27.

10. Mead, *Chains*, 5.

11. Ibid., 6–7. In general, I have chosen not to use "Sic" to indicate misspellings, trusting the reader to sort through differences in spelling.

12. Ibid., 7.

CHAPTER THREE

1. Bob Marley, *Buffalo Soldier*, from the album *Confrontation*, 1983. Lyric is as follows, "Stolen from Africa, brought to America, fighting on arrival, fighting for survival."

2. Enrique Dussel, *The Invention of the Americas: Eclipse of the Other and the Myth of Modernity*, trans. Michael D. Barber (New York: Continuum, 1995).

3. Mills, *The Racial Contract*.

4. Richardson, *Stewart*, 63.

5. The phrase "Founding Fathers" is troubling in many ways. It instantiates the idea of a paternalistic group of men, many of them slaveholders, all of whom participated in denying civil rights and liberties to the majority of the population. I adopt the phrase "Black Founders" as a corrective to describe intellectuals and activists such as Richard Allen, Paul

Cuffe, James Forten, Prince Hall, Lemuel Haynes, John Marrant, Phillis Wheatley, and others. I have argued for a historical re-periodization more amenable to the idea of a Black
founders stretching from around 1750 to 1834 that would include writers such as Stewart
and Walker in the presentation, "Maria Stewart, David Walker and Insurrectionist Ethics"
at the conference, "Black Thought Matters," sponsored by the African American Intellectual
History Society, held at Brandeis University, April 2018. In standard historical periodization
the revolutionary period transitions to the Age of Jackson and does not adequately account
for theoretical developments by African Americans. In 2007 *William and Mary Quarterly*
published an important forum on "Black Founders," 4, no. 1, with many excellent articles. A
comprehensive account of Black abolitionists is in Sinha, *The Slave's Cause.*

6. On the practice of slave owners assigning Africans classical names such as Caesar,
Cato, Pompey, and Scipio, see Gary Nash, *Forging Freedom: The Formation of Philadelphia's
Black Community, 1720–1840* (Cambridge: Harvard University Press, 1988), 81. On naming
patterns among African Americans, see also J. L. Dillard, *Black Names, Contributions to the
Sociology of Language* 13, ed. Joshua A. Fishman (The Hague: Mouton, 1976); John Thornton,
"Central African Names and African-American Naming Patterns," *William and Mary
Quarterly* 50, no. 4 (October 1993): 727–42.; Lorenzo J. Greene, "The New England Negro as
Seen in Advertisements for Runaway Slaves," *Journal of Negro History* 29, no. 2 (April 1944):
125–46, and Henig Cohen, "Slave Names in Colonial South Carolina," *American Speech* 27, no.
2 (May 1952): 102–7, http://www.latinamericanstudies.org/slavery/AS-1952.pdf accessed April
24, 2020.

7. G. M. James Gonzales de Allen, "On 'Captive' Bodies, Hidden 'Flesh' and Colonization,"
in *Existence in Black: An Anthology of Black Existential Philosophy*, ed. Lewis R. Gordon
(New York: Routledge, 1997), 131–32. See also Regis Mann, "Theorizing 'What Could Have
Been': Black Feminism, Historical Memory, and the Politics of Reclamation," *Women's
Studies* 40, no. 5 (2011): 575–99.

8. "Slave Religion," Center for Digital History, Washington Library, accessed February
18, 2019, https://www.mountvernon.org/library/digitalhistory/digital-encyclopedia/article/
slave-religion/#note3, accessed April 12, 2020.

9. Mills, *The Racial Contract*, 45.

10. For an account from analytic philosophy of the performative qualities of speech, see
John Searle, *Speech Acts: An Essay in the Philosophy of Language* (Cambridge: Cambridge
University Press, 1969), but for a feminist analysis see Mary Daly, *Gyn/Ecology, The Meta-
Ethics of Radical Feminism* (Boston: Beacon Press, 1978) and elsewhere on naming as a way
of creating or recreating reality.

11. Katherine J. Harris, "Freedom and Slavery," in *African American Connecticut Explored*,
ed. Elizabeth J. Normen (Middletown: Wesleyan University Press, 2013), 3. See Neil Roberts,
Freedom as Marronage (Chicago: University of Chicago Press, 2015) for an account of marronage as a process of self-emancipation.

12. Linford D. Fisher; "'Why Shall Wee Have Peace to Bee Made Slaves': Indian
Surrenderers during and after King Philip's War," *Ethnohistory* 64, no. 1 (January 2017):
91–114. doi: https://doi.org/10.1215/00141801-3688391.

13. Daniel Cruson, *The Slaves of Central Fairfield County: The Journey from Slave to
Freeman in Nineteenth-Century Connecticut* (Mount Pleasant: History Press, 2007), 13.

14. Hinks, *Appeal*, 37–38.

15. Karl Marx and Frederick Engels, *The Communist Manifesto*, trans. Samuel Moore (London: Penguin Books, 1967).

16. For an account of the historical and cultural arguments for slavery and the rejoinders from Stewart and Walker, see Waters, "Crying Out for Liberty."

17. Ágnes Heller, "Europa, Europa," in *The European Fall: 28 Essays on the European Crisis*, ed. Christoffer Emil Bruun (Copenhagen: Politiken, 2013).

18. Enrique Dussel, *The Invention of the Americas*, trans. by Michael D. Barber, 28.

19. Ramón Grosfogel, "The Structure of Knowledge in Westernized Universities: Epistemic Racism/Sexism and the Four Genocides/Epistemicides of the Long 16th Century," *Human Architecture: Journal of the Sociology of Self-Knowledge* 11, no. 1 (2013): 77.

20. This list is by no means exhaustive, and number of decolonial theorists continue to expand.

21. Richardson, *Stewart*, 65. Keep in mind that in contrast with Northern Europe, Mediterranean cultures of the day were more closely associated with what is now considered to be the Middle East or "Western Asia." Stewart writes, "In the thirteenth century, a young lady of Bologne [Christine de Pizan] devoted herself to the study of the Latin language and of the laws. At the age of twenty-three she pronounced a funeral oration in Latin in the great church of Bologne; and to be admitted as an orator, she had neither need of indulgence on account of her youth or of her sex. At the age of twenty-six she took the degree of doctor of laws, and began publicly to expound the Institutes of Justinian. At the age of thirty, her great reputation raised her to a chair, where she taught the law to a prodigious concourse of scholars from all nations. She joined the charms and accomplishments of a woman to all the knowledge of a man. And such was the power of her eloquence, that her beauty was only admired when her tongue was silent" ("Farewell Adress"). While current scholars may find errors in Stewart's and Walker's historical remarks, the point remains that they were trailblazing in their efforts to reclaim the histories of women and of Black Africans against the even more egregiously error-ridden chronicles of the Europeans, especially regarding marginalized populations.

22. Hinks, *Appeal*, 21.

23. Charles W. Mills and Carole Pateman, *Contract and Domination* (Cambridge: Polity Press, 2007). An account of racial patriarchy is given by Mills, who attributes early formulations to Barbara Omolade, "Hearts of Darkness," in *Words of Fire: An Anthology of African-American Feminist Thought*, ed. Beverly Guy-Sheftall (New York: New Press, 1995), 362–76, and Audre Lorde, "The Master's Tools Will Never Dismantle the Master's House," in *Sister Outsider: Essays and Speeches* (1984; repr., Berkeley: Ten Speed Press, 2007), and to the Combahee River Collective, *The Combahee River Collective Statement* (Boston: Combahee River Collective, 1977), a Black feminist manifesto. See also Pauline E. Schloesser, *The Fair Sex: White Women and Racial Patriarchy in the Early American Republic* (New York: NYU Press, 2005), and Christine Delphy, *Separate and Dominate: Feminism and Racism after the War on Terror*, trans. David Broder (New York: Verso Books, 2015).

24. Examples of enslaved princes include Aphra Behn's fictionalized account in her groundbreaking book *Oroonoko: Or the Royal Slave* (1688), based on her experiences in Surinam. This early novella, largely overlooked, is one of the first written in English, and presents a profound abolitionist argument. Also well worth reading are the biographical accounts about the life of Abdul-Rahman Ibrahim Ibn Sori, a Muslim Emir from Timbo,

West Africa, who was sold into slavery. See, for example, *Prince among Slaves: The True Story of an African Prince Sold into Slavery in the American South,* Terry Alford (Oxford: Oxford University Press, 1977).

25. For Locke's participation in the slave-trading Royal African Company, see Clarence Sholé Johnson, *Cornel West and Philosophy* (New York: Routledge, 2003).

26. "Shifting the Geography of Reason" was adopted as the ongoing conference theme for the Caribbean Philosophical Association, an organization founded in 2003 by George Belle, B. Anthony Bogues, Patrick Goodin, Lewis Gordon, Clevis Headley, Paget Henry, Nelson Maldonado-Torres, Charles Mills, and Supriya Nair.

27. Lisa Lowe, *The Intimacies of Four Continents* (Durham: Duke University Press, 2015). Stewart and Walker both argued for the recognition of African American cultural heritage as one key to humanization. See also Kristin Waters, "Crying Out for Liberty."

28. "I see it as spirit-murder, only one of whose manifestations is racism—cultural obliteration, prostitution, abandonment of the elderly and the homeless, and genocide are some of its other guises. I see spirit-murder as no less than the equivalent of body murder." From Patricia J. Williams, *The Alchemy of Race and Rights: Diary of a Law Professor* (Cambridge: Harvard University Press, 1991). See also Orlando Patterson, *Slavery and Social Death: A Comparative Study* (Cambridge: Harvard University Press, 1982). The concept of reclamation or recovery work, scholarship and activism designed to rediscover and bring to light lost or deliberately suppressed histories and intellectual work is the premise behind, especially, much feminist writing including Black feminist work. It has been a guiding principle for my work, including in Kristin Waters, ed., *Women and Men Political Theorists: Enlightened Conversations* (Malden, MA: Blackwell Publishers, 2000) and Kristin Waters and Carol B. Conway, eds., *Black Women's Intellectual Traditions Speaking Their Minds* (Burlington: University of Vermont, 2007). A more recent example of this sort of work is Mia Bay, Farah J. Griffin, Martha S. Jones, Barbara Savage, eds., *Towards an Intellectual History of Black Women* (Chapel Hill: University of North Carolina Press, 2015).

29. Gardner, "Two Texts," 162–65.

CHAPTER FOUR

1. Eric Gardner, "Two Texts on Children and Christian Education," *PMLA* 123, no. 1 (2008): 65.

2. W. E. B. Du Bois, *The Souls of Black Folk* (1903; repr., New York: Dover Publications, 1994), 41.

3. "The First Black Woman Political Theorist" comes from the title of Marilyn Richardson's ground-breaking book on Stewart that reprints a number of Stewart's writings for the first time in more than one hundred years.

4. To disambiguate, Stewart's 1879 republication of her essays along with new testimonials is titled "Meditations from the Pen of Mrs. Maria Stewart." This title was first used in 1832 to designate a set of religious meditations.

5. Miller entry. Barbour Collection.

6. Carla Peterson, *Doers of the Word: African American Women Speakers and Writers in the North (1830–1880)* (New Brunswick: Rutgers University Press, 1995), 57.

7. Ibid., 57.

8. Joycelyn Moody, *Sentimental Confessions: Spiritual Narratives of Nineteenth-Century African American Women* (Athens: University of Georgia Press, 2003), 27.

9. Gardner, "Two Texts." All references to Gardner's introduction and to the story in *The First Stage* are to the *PMLA* publication by Eric Gardner. This quotation is found on page 162.

10. Ibid., 162.

11. The most well-known autobiography at the time by a Black woman was Nancy Prince, *A Narrative of the Life and Travels of Mrs. Nancy Prince* (Boston: Nancy Prince, 1850). Many editions of this work are available, including https://archive.org/stream/narrativeoflife t1853prin/narrativeoflifet1853prin_djvu.txt accessed April 26, 2020. In this work I have used Nancy Prince, *Narrative of the Life and Travels of Mrs. Nancy Prince*: Nancy Prince, retitled as *A Black Woman's Odyssey through Russia and Jamaica*, in the version with the introduction by Ronald G. Walters; repr. (Princeton: Marcus Wiener Publishers, 1990), 6–7.

12. Gardner, "Two Texts," 163, Emphasis mine.

13. Ibid., 162, Emphasis mine.

14. Mary Wollstonecraft, *A Vindication of the Rights of Woman* (London: Joseph Johnson, 1792). In her work, Mary Wollstonecraft contrasts the innocence of youth with the ideology of innocence that men try to impose on women as a way to keep them ignorant, uneducated, and to bar them from public, civil life.

15. "Diana in the leaves green" is from the poem by John Skelton, quoted in Robert Graves, ed., *The Greek Myths* (1955; repr., London: Penguin Books, 1992), and it refers to one aspect of the Triple Goddess. Oshun is the Mother of the African sweet or fresh waters. While Stewart never bore children, at the time when she was speaking in Boston, she was in her fertile years.

16. Peterson, *Doers of the Word*, 73.

17. Gardner, "Two Texts," 162.

18. Richardson, *Stewart*, 39.

19. Valerie C. Cooper, *Word, Like Fire: Maria Stewart, the Bible, and the Rights of African Americans* (Charlottesville: University of Virginia Press, 2011), 17.

20. Gardner, "Two Texts," 162.

21. Ibid., 163.

22. Gen. 7:8, King James Version (KJV).

23. Joycelyn Moody, *Sentimental Confessions*, xii.

24. Gardner, "Two Texts," 163.

25. Ibid., 163.

26. George Yancy, *Look, a White!: Philosophical Essays on Whiteness*. Philadelphia: Temple University Press, 2012.

27. George Yancy, *Black Bodies, White Gazes* (Lanham: Rowman & Littlefield, 2017), 3.

28. Ibid., 8.

29. Gardner, "Two Texts," 163.

30. Ibid.,163.

31. Ibid.

32. Ibid., 164.

33. Ibid.

34. Richardson, *Stewart*, "Sufferings During the War," 98–109.

35. Gardner, "Two Texts," 162.

36. Ibid., 156.

37. Ibid., 165.

38. Ibid.

39. Ibid.

40. Ibid. Emphasis mine.

41. Ibid.

42. KJV.

CHAPTER FIVE

1. Richardson, *Stewart*, 28–29.

2. Gardner, "Two Texts," 159.

3. "Slave, Free Black, and White Population, 1780–1830," Center for History Education, University of Maryland Baltimore County, accessed February 18, 2019, https://userpages. umbc.edu/~bouton/History407/SlaveStats.htm. The 1810 census recorded a population of about 5% "free, non-whites" in Rhode Island—3609 and 108 enslaved.

4. See Richard Boles, "Documents Relating to African American Experiences of White Congregational Churches in Massachusetts, 1773–1832," *New England Quarterly* 86, no. 2 (June 2013); Barbara Beeching, "African Americans and Native Americans in Hartford 1636–1800: Antecedents of Hartford's Nineteenth Century Black Community," *Hartford Studies Collection: Papers by Students and Faculty* 7 (November 1993): 1–66, http://citeseerx.ist .psu.edu/viewdoc/download?doi=10.1.1.1017.3257&rep=rep1&type=pdf; and Kathy A. Ritter, *Apprentices of Connecticut: 1637–1900* (Salt Lake City: Ancestry Publishing, 1986); Ruth Wallis Herndon and John E. Murray, ed., *Children Bound to Labor: The Pauper Apprentice System in Early* America (Ithaca: Cornell University Press, 2009). Richard Boles was kind enough to share some his research findings with me. He did not find Maria Miller among the records he studied.

5. Edwin Pond Parker, *History of the Second Church of Christ in Hartford* (Hartford: Belknap and Warfield, 1892), 4; Barbara Beeching, "African Americans and Native Americans in Hartford 1636–1800: Antecedents of Hartford's Nineteenth Century Black Community," *Hartford Studies Collection: Papers by Students and Faculty* 7 (November 1993): 1–66, http:// citeseerx.ist.psu.edu/viewdoc/download?doi=10.1.1.1017.3257&rep=rep1&type=pdf. On pages 44 and 45 Nathan Strong's enslaved persons were listed:

Williams, Easter, age 46, free. Nathan Strong (NC 1805). In Hartford 7 yr; former master Rev Nathan Strong

Williams, London, age 56, free. Nathan Strong (NC 1805). In Hartford 7 yr; former master Rev Nathan Strong. (44–45)

6. Stewart worshipped at many different churches throughout her long life, including the African Baptist, AME, and Episcopal. Her decisions about where to worship were based in part on her location, race, the strength and disposition of the ministers and their congregations, and a wide range of religious, personal, and economic needs, more so than an allegiance to a particular version of the Christian faith.

7. Samuel Beckwith, et al., *Centenary Memorial of the First Baptist Church Hartford, Connecticut, March 23d and 24th, 1890* (Hartford: First Baptist Church, 1890), 192, https://

play.google.com/books/reader?id=ToYBAAAAYAAJ&hl=en&pg=GBS.PA14, accessed April 24, 2020. Of the Hartford parish ministers, only Pastor Grew reported a person of color in the household in the 1810 census, but this morsel of information provides insufficient reason to infer that Miller had been indentured in his precarious household. Census reporting of people of color was neither uniform nor necessarily accurate. Still, this association is not impossible. Grew's daughter, Mary, was an abolitionist who attended the 1837 Anti-slavery Convention of American Women, as did Maria W. Stewart.

8. The church was founded 1669–70.

See Asaph Willard, *Plan of the city of Hartford: from a survey made in 1824* (Hartford: Surveyed and published by D. St. John and N. Goodwin, 1824) Map. Library of Congress, Digital Collections: Maps, https://www.loc.gov/resource/g3784h.ct003489/?r=-0.8,0.352,2.601,1.428,0.

9. Parker, *History*, 194, 136.

10. *The Connecticut Evangelical Magazine and Intelligencer* 1, no. 12 (December 1808): 441, and "A brief account of the Origin and Progress of the present Revival of Religion in Hartford," *The Connecticut Evangelical Magazine and Intelligencer* 1, no. 7 (July 1808): 263–67.

11. Parker, *History*, 174.

12. Nathan Strong, Abel Flint, and Joseph Steward, *The Hartford Selection of Hymns* (Hartford: John Babcock, 1799), https://archive.org/details/hartfordselectio0ostro, accessed April 24, 2020.

13. Stewart, *Meditations*, in *Productions of Mrs. Maria W. Stewart, presented to the First African Baptist Church & Society of the City of Boston* (1835), repr. in *Spiritual Narratives*, the Schomburg Library of Nineteenth-Century Black Women Writers, introduction by Susan Houchins (Oxford: Oxford University Press, 1988), 23.

14. Cooper, *Word, Like Fire*, 4.

15. Richardson, *Stewart*, 29.

16. Parker, *History*, 168.

17. *The Memorial History of Hartford County, Connecticut*, 1633–1884, volume 1, ed. James Hammond Trumbull (New York: E. L. Osgood, 1886), 161.

18. Many editions of this work are available, including https://archive.org/stream/narrativeoflife1853prin/narrativeoflife1853prin_djvu.txt, accessed April 26, 2020. In this work I have used Nancy Prince, *Narrative of the Life and Travels of Mrs. Nancy Prince: Nancy Prince*, retitled as *A Black Woman's Odyssey through Russia and Jamaica*, in the version with the introduction by Ronald G. Walters; repr. (Princeton: Marcus Wiener Publishers, 1990), 6–7.

19. Daniel Cruson, in *The Slaves of Central Fairfield County*, 21. In a claim that is bewildering and obviously indefensible, particularly in a relatively recent publication, Cruson argues for the benignity of slavery in Connecticut.

20. Normen, *African American Connecticut*, xvi.

21. Ibid., 8.

22. Prince, *Narrative*, 7.

23. Richardson, *Stewart*, 38.

24. *Roberts' Guide for Butlers and Other Household Staff*, Robert Roberts. Originally published in 1827 (Bedford, MA: Applewood Books, 1993), 174–78.

25. Roberts, *Guide*, 41

26. Richardson, *Stewart*, 46.

27. Lydia Maria Child, *The American Frugal Housewife, Dedicated to Those Who Are Not Ashamed of Economy*, Lydia Maria Child, S. S. & W. Wood, 1838. Originally published in 1832. It is a curiosity that Child, a prolific writer, does not record meeting Maria Stewart in Boston even though it is very likely that Child attended some of Stewart's lectures and wrote voluminously about abolition.

28. Child, *The American Frugal Housewife*, 111.

29. "The Abel Flint Family," from Edwin Pond Parker, *History of the Second Church of Christ in Hartford*, appendix III, with thanks to Samantha Boardman for her research assistance.

30. Roberts, *Guide*, 43.

31. Prince, *Narrative*, 4.

32. Richardson, *Stewart*, 45.

33. Angela Y. Davis, "Reflections on the Black Woman's Role in the Community of Slaves" *Massachusetts Review* 13, no. 1/2 (1972): 81–100, 87.

34. Richardson, *Stewart*, 39.

35. Prince, *Narrative*, 9.

36. See also *Religion and Domestic Violence in Early New England: The Memoirs of Abigail Abbot Bailey*, ed. Anne Taves (Bloomington: Indiana University Press, 1989). Abigail Abbot Bailey reveals in her memoir the abuse her husband inflicted on her as well as his adulteries, incest, and sexual assaults on servants.

37. Ibid., 30.

38. Parker, *History*, 127.

CHAPTER SIX

1. Isaac Williams Stuart, *Hartford in Olden Times: Its First Thirty Years*, ed. W. M. B. Hartley (Hartford: F. A. Brown, 1853), https://archive.org/details/hartfordinoldentoostua/page/n9 /mode/2up/search/Laugh+an'+sing+until, accessed April 24, 2020. Published under the pen name "Scaeva," the chapter of this source dedicated to Black governors opens by citing a popular song of the day, "Laugh an' sing until to-morrow, 'Tis de Darkies holiday!" 37.

2. Nell, *Colored Patriots of the American Revolution*, 133. Nell names 57 blacks who served in Connecticut and recounts some personal histories.

3. This is not to be confused with the election of official white governors. Harris in Normen, *African American Connecticut*. Another source is Patrick Rael, *Black Identity and Black Protest in the Antebellum North* (Chapel Hill: University of North Carolina Press, 2002). See also, "Connecticut's Black Governors," History and Genealogy Unit, Museum of Connecticut History, last modified February 2005, https://museumofcthistory.org/ connecticuts-black-governors/ April 26, 2020.

4. Isaac Williams Stuart, *Hartford in Olden Times*, 37. Framed as they are by white historians, there is much to question about these accounts. The work of Katherine J. Harris and others serves as a partial corrective. Still, some of the language and descriptions provided by white framers is disrespectful at best. I include the material only because with so little written about the practice, every source contributes to our understanding, even when requiring critique.

5. Harris, 35.

6. Cruson, *The Slaves of Central Fairfield County*, 29, 42.

7. Harris, 36.

8. "Emerging from the Shadows, 1775–1819: The Black Governors," Hartford Black History Project, accessed February 18, 2019, http://www.hartford-hwp.com/HBHP/exhibit/03/1.html.

9. Pierson, *Black Yankees*, 122.

10. https://museumofcthistory.org/connecticuts-black-governors/, accessed April 15, 2020.

11. Pierson, *Black Yankees*, 120–21. Some of this language and the characterization are offensive. See my earlier footnotes on this topic addressing my decision to include it as source material.

12. Stuart, *Hartford*, 38.

13. Pierson, *Black Yankees*, 122.

14. Stuart, *Hartford*, 40.

15. Hinks, *Appeal*, 26.

16. Stuart, *Hartford*, 40.

17. Ibid., 40.

18. Among others, Mary Daly discusses the complex role of "token torturers," those who are selected by oppressors to enact punishment or harm on those who are similarly oppressed. See Mary Daly, *Gyn/Ecology: A Metaethics of Radical Feminism* (Boston: Beacon Press, 1978).

19. "Emerging from the Shadows, 1775–1819: The Black Governors," Hartford Black History Project.

20. Stuart, *Hartford*, 40. Peleg Nott is buried in the Hartford Ancient Burial Ground. https://www.africannativeburialsct.org/person/nott-peleg-black-governor/, accessed July 11, 2020.

21. In *Black Identity*, Patrick Rael writes about "a distinctly black manipulation of white election-day celebrations," 55.

22. Peter Stallybrass and Allon White, *The Politics and Poetics of Transgression* (Ithaca: Cornell University Press, 1986), 6. I would like to thank Daniel McLean for leading me to this source and for valuable discussions on the topic. See also Jeroen Dewulf, *The Pinkster King and the King of Kongo: The Forgotten History of America's Dutch-Owned Slaves* (Jackson: University Press of Mississippi, 2017).

23. Stallybrass and White, 14.

24. Contemporary correlatives would be comedians who mock white behavior—Richard Pryor, Dave Chappelle, Key and Peele, Chris Rock, Wanda Sykes, Sarah Cooper, and others too numerous to list.

25. Richardson, *Stewart*, 29.

CHAPTER SEVEN

1. Washington Irving, *The Works of Washington Irving: A Miscellany*, (Vol. 6) 1907, Jenson Society, also quoted in David Porter, "The Pacific Cruise 1813–1814."

2. Richardson, *Stewart*, Appendix C: War of 1812 Claim of Widow for Service Pension, 116.

3. The rank of "Seaman" is above that of "Landman" and "Ordinary Seaman." To achieve this rank, Stewart needed six years of previous service.

4. See also "Black Sailors and Soldiers in the War of 1812," The War of 1812, Public Broadcasting Service (PBS), accessed February 18, 2019, http://www.pbs.org/wned/war-of-1812/essays/black-soldier-and-sailors-war/.

5. https://docsouth.unc.edu/neh/ballslavery/menu.html.

6. Charles Ball, *Slavery in the United States: A Narrative of the Life and Adventures of Charles Ball, a Black Man, Who Lived Forty Years in Maryland, South Carolina and Georgia, as a Slave Under Various Masters, and was One Year in the Navy with Commodore Barney, During the Late War* (New York, John S. Taylor, 1837), Documenting the American South, University of North Carolina Chapel Hill, 1999, https://docsouth.unc.edu/neh/ballslavery/ball.html, accessed April 24, 2020, 474. The reluctance of many who were enslaved to cast their lot with the British in the War of Independence and the War of 1812, while it may be puzzling to some, in some ways is parallel to that of some undocumented residents of the US for whom the prospect of "return" to their "home" countries means deportation to a place where they never lived in the first place. For instance, Ball was offered the opportunity to go to Trinidad.

7. Stephen Higginson, "A Short History of the Right to Petition Government for the Redress of Grievances," *The Yale Law Journal* 96, no. 1 (November 1986): 142–66, https://www.jstor.org/stable/796438?seq=1#page_scan_tab_contents, accessed April 24, 2020. See also "Petitions," The Making of African American Identity: Volume 1, 1500–1865, Primary Resources in U.S. History & Literature, National Humanities Center, last modified March 2007, http://nationalhumanitiescenter.org/pds/maai/community/text4/text4read.htm.

8. *Petition of 1788 by Slaves of New Haven for the Abolition of Slavery in Connecticut*, The Making of African American Identity: Volume 1, 1500–1865, Primary Resources in U.S. History & Literature, National Humanities Center, last modified March 2007, http://www". hartford-hwp.com/archives/45a/023.html.

9. George C. Daughan, *The Shining Sea: David Porter and the Epic Voyage of the U.S.S. Essex during the War of 1812* (New York: Basic Books, 2013).

10. From a distance of 65 years from the time of embarkation, Maria W. Stewart misrecalled the date of departure, which she identifies as August 16, 1811 instead of 1812. Stewart in Richardson, "Appendix C," 117. The document is from the District of Columbia, County of Washington, and is entitled: *War of 1812 Claim of Widow for Service Pension*. It was recorded on February 26, 1879 in Washington D.C.

11. David Porter, *Journal of a cruise made to the Pacific Ocean, by Captain David Porter, in the United States frigate Essex, in the years 1812, 1813, and 1814: containing descriptions of the Cape de Verd island, coasts of Brazil, Patagonia, Chili, and Peru, and of the Gallapagos Islands* (Philadelphia: Bradford and Inskeep, 1815). See second edition online via: https://archive.org/stream/journalacruisemooportgoog?ref=ol#page/n8/mode/2up/search/vol+II, accessed April 24, 2020.

12. W. Jeffrey Bolster, *Black Jacks: African American Seamen in the Age of Sail* (Cambridge: Harvard University Press, 1997), 4.

13. Julius S. Scott, *The Common Wind: Afro-American Currents in the Age of the Haitian Revolution* (London: Verso, 2017), 4.

14. Gerard T. Altoff, *Amonst My Best Men: African Americans and the War of 1812*, intro. by Joseph P. Reidy (Put-in-Bay, Ohio: The Perry Group, 1996), 8, 11.

15. David Porter, *Essex*, 158.

16. Ibid., 159.

17. Paul A. Gilje, "On the Waterfront: Maritime Workers in New York City in the Early Republic, 1800–1850," *New York History* 77, no. 34 (October 1996): 395–426.

18. Porter, *Essex*, 15.

19. Tom Deforest, "War of 1812: Commodore David Porter and the *Essex* in the South Pacific," Historynet LLC, accessed February 18, 2019, https://www.historynet.com/war-of -1812-commodore-david-porter-and-the-essex-in-the-south-pacific.htm.

20. Porter, quoted in George C. Daughton, *Shining Sea: David Porter and the Epic Voyage of the U.S.S. Essex during the War of 1812* (New York: Basic Books, 2013), 88. While there is much to say about gender and colonialism regarding Porter's enticement, I shall leave it to reader to provide an analysis.

21. David Dixon Porter, *Memoir of Commodore David Porter: Of the United States*, originally published 1875, 109.

CHAPTER EIGHT

1. Richardson, *Stewart*, "Appendix E."

2. David Porter, *Essex*, 154.

3. Richardson, *Stewart*, "Appendix E."

4. Herman Melville, *The Encantadas or Enchanted Isles*: "Sketch Fifth: The Frigate, and Ship Flyaway," in *The Encantadas and Other Stories*, ed. Joslyn T. Pine (1854; repr., New York: Dover Publications, 2005). The story was first published in 1854 in *Putnam's Magazine*.

5. James W. Stewart's name does not appear on the list of prisoners to be exchanged found in Porter's diary, so likely he was on the Georgiana at the time.

6. Historian Jack Chatfield made this observation in his introduction to *The Public Records of the State of Connecticut 1812–1813*, vol. 16 (Hartford: Office of the State Historian, 1997); Walter W. Woodward, "The War Connecticut Hated," Connecticut History, June 18, 2019, https://connecticuthistory.org/the-war-connecticut-hated/, accessed April 24, 2020

7. The outcry at the Hartford Convention for removal of this inhuman arrangement was not an antislavery one. On the contrary, attendees felt that slaves should be counted as nothing—as zero rather than 3/5 of a person—a move that would entirely undermine Southern power as enslaved persons in those states comprised a very significant proportion of the population.

8. Richardson, appendix C, 116–17. A supplementary affidavit to Maria W. Stewart's War of 1812 Claim of Widow for Service Pension signed by Stewart and G. S. Palmer, M.D. also identifies the brig *Eperrier* as one on which James W. Stewart served as coxswain. That vessel was assigned to convey a copy of the treaty along with "the 10 US citizens recently liberated from Algerian prisons" to the United States, but the ship was lost at sea. *United States Naval Medical Bulletin*, vol. 16, United States Navy Department, Bureau of Medicine and Surgery, Washington D.C., Government Printing Office, 1907–1949, Series: NAVMED 112, 699–706.

9. For an analysis of colonization in this historical time and place, see L. Gordon, *An Introduction to Africana Philosophy*, 158–59.

10. Michael Monahan, "Reason, Race, and the Human Project: Sylvia Wynter, Sociogenesis and Philosophy in the Americas," in *Philosophizing the Americas: An*

Inter-American Discourse, ed. Jacoby Adeshei Carter and Hernando A. Estévez (New York: Fordham University Press, 2017).

11. Bolster, *Black Jacks*, 4.

12. Jane Anna Gordon, *Creolizing Political Theory: Reading Rousseau through Fanon* (New York: Fordham University Press, 2014), 14–15. Ira Berlin uses the term "creole" "to refer to Black people of native American birth" and "Atlantic creole" to identify especially but not exclusively the people of the "charter generations" "whose experience, knowledge, and attitude were more akin to that of confident, sophisticated natives than of vulnerable newcomers" as they were often portrayed. (253–55) He does this to reveal "some of the processes by which race was constructed and reconstructed in early America."

13. Julius Scott, *The Common Wind: Afro-American Currents in the Age of the Haitian Revolution*, fore. Marcus Rediker (London: Verso, 2018); J. Gordon, *Creolizing Political Theory*, 2–3 and 13.

14. See chapter fifteen for a more in-depth discussion of the Haitian Revolution and the various historical interpretations of events there.

15. Michael Monahan, ed., *Creolizing Hegel* (New York: Rowman and Littlefield, 2017), 5.

16. Nelson Maldonado-Torres, "Outline of Ten Theses on Coloniality and Decoloniality," Foundation Frantz Fanon, Caribbean Studies Association, October 23, 2016, http://carib beanstudiesassociation.org/docs/Maldonado-Torres_Outline_Ten_Theses-10.23.16.pdf , accessed April 24, 2020.

17. L. Gordon, *Africana Philosophy*, 78–79.

18. J. Gordon, *Creolizing*, 14–15.

19. Roy F. Nichols, "Diplomacy in Barbary," *The Pennsylvania Magazine of History and Biography* 74, no. 1 (January 1950): 113–41, 121. This magazine is published by the University of Pennsylvania Press.

20. Aimé Césaire, *Discourse on Colonialism*, intro. Robin D. G. Kelley, trans. Joan Pinkham (New York: Monthly Review Press, 1972), 40.

21. Robin D. G. Kelley, "Introduction," in Aime Césaire, *Discourse*, 36.

22. Scott, *The Common Wind*, from the introduction by Marcus Rediker, ix.

23. Scott, *The Common Wind*. 4

24. Certainly, issues of the newspapers, *Freedom's Journal* and *Liberator*, would have been part of the contraband a decade or more later. So, possibly, Maria W. Stewart's writings published in the *Liberator* or by William Lloyd Garrison's press may have found their way a distance from home.

25. Marcus Rediker, "Foreward," in Julius Scott, *The Common Wind*, 4; Scott, *Common Wind*, 83 and 118.

26. See also, Daniel Immerwhar, *How to Hide an Empire? A History of the Greater United States* (New York: Vintage, 2019).

27. Richardson, *Stewart*, appendix F.

28. Peter Williams, *Discourse Delivered on the Death of Capt. Paul Cuffe, Before The New-York African Institution, In The African Methodist Episcopal Zion Church, October 21, 1817* (London: Darton & Co., 1818), http://paulcuffe.org/wp-content/uploads/2019/03/Discourse -Peter-Williams.pdf, accessed April 24, 2020.

29. Sinha, *The Slave's Cause*, 161, and Waters, "Crying Out for Liberty," 48–50.

30. "'Friend' Paul Cuffe of Westport," Master History of Quakerism, Kouroo Contexture, accessed March 1, 2020, http://www.kouroo.info/kouroo/thumbnails/C/FriendPaulCuffe.pdf.

31. Richardson, appendix D.

32. Chernoh M. Sesay, "The Revolutionary Black Roots of Slavery's Abolition in Massachusetts," *The New England Quarterly* 87, no. 1 (2014): 99–131.

33. Herbert Aptheker, *American Negro Slave Revolts* (New York: Columbia University Press, 1943). Aptheker has been challenged as a source, with comments ranging from calling his book a "seminal masterpiece" to the claim that it does not deserve to be called a "history." It has also, therefore, been overlooked as a source in recent years, which is one reason that I choose to use it here, in the belief that these earlier efforts should not be forgotten. It is a wondrous compendium heavily dependent on primary sources, both useful and stirring.

34. Richardson, *Stewart*, 30.

CHAPTER NINE

1. Peter P. Hinks, *To Awaken My Afflicted Brethren: David Walker and the Problem of Antebellum Slave Resistance* (University Park: Penn State University Press, 1997). This chapter and others relating to David Walker owe considerably to the scholarship of Peter Hinks and to discussions with the author. See also, Peter P. Hinks, ed., *David Walker's Appeal to the Coloured Citizens of the World*.

2. Frances Diane Robotti, *The USS Essex: And the Birth of the American Navy* (Holbrook, MA: Adams Media, 1999).

3. Hinks, *To Awaken*, 12, 21.

4. C. Eric Lincoln and Lawrence H. Mumiya, *The Black Church in the African American Experience* (Durham: Duke University Press, 1990), 8.

5. Douglas R. Egerton, *He Shall Go Out Free: The Lives of Denmark Vesey* (Lanham, MD: Rowman and Littlefield, 1999), 101.

6. Hinks, *To Awaken*, 25.

7. While this number may seem inflated, consider it in perspective. Black residents constituted the majority population in this city of 23,000.

8. In *He Shall Go Out Free*, Egerton cites (110) a version of which may be found here: Lionel Henry Kennedy, and Thomas Parker, eds., *An official report of the trials of sundry Negroes, charged with an attempt to raise an insurrection in the state of South-Carolina: preceded by an introduction and narrative: and, in an appendix, a report of the trials of four white persons on indictments for attempting to excite the slaves to insurrection* (Charleston: James R. Schenck, 1822), 22 and 76, https://www.loc.gov/item/90107205/, accessed April 24, 2020. The complexity of the historiography surrounding the Vesey affair cannot be overstated, and the veracity of certain documents has been challenged. For a recent comprehensive compilation and assessment, see Douglas R. Egerton and Robert L. Paquette, *The Denmark Vesey Affair: A Documentary History* (Gainesville: University Press of Florida, 2017). See also David Robertson, *Denmark Vesey: The Buried Story of America's Largest Slave Rebellion and the Man Who Led It* (New York: Vintage, 1999), 110.

9. Hinks, *Walker's Appeal*, 65–66.

10. See Isaac Watts, *From All That Dwell Below the Skies (1719)*, Hymnary, https://hymnary.org/text/from_all_that_dwell_below_the_skies, accessed March 1, 2020.

11. In private correspondence, editor Patsy Baudoin has pointed out that in Homer's *Odyssey*, Telemachus, spent twenty years in the absence of his father, Odysseus, just as those who were enslaved were torn from their families.

12. For an interesting article on the historiography of this event, see Douglas R. Egerton, "Forgetting Denmark Vesey: Or, Oliver Stone meets Richard Wade," *William and Mary Quarterly* 59, no. 1 (January 2002): 143–52.

13. P. Williams, *Alchemy*.

14. Roberts, *Freedom as Marronage*, 98 ff.

15. Kenneth E. Marshall, *Manhood Enslaved: Bondmen in Eighteenth- and Early Nineteenth-Century New Jersey* (Rochester: University of Rochester Press, 2013).

16. It was the norm at the time for manumitted individuals to take the name of those to whom they were enslaved (consider, for example, Prince Hall). Recent trends in historical writing are reconsidering this practice, especially in cases where the name may have been imposed and not chosen. In relation to Vesey and philosophical theories, Robertson makes reference to doctrine of Negritude, 32, an avenue worth pursuing.

17. See Langston Hughes, "In Explanation of Our Times," *Voetica Poetry Spoken*, accessed March 1, 2020, https://voetica.com/voetica.php?collection=1&poet=23&poem=1912, where you can hear the full poem read. This poem was brought to my attention by Gordon T. Davis of Worcester, Massachusetts, who has a bit of the David Walker in him.

18. https://www.youtube.com/watch?v=IN05jVNBs64, accessed February 10, 2021.

19. John Oliver Killens, ed., *The Trial Record of Denmark Vesey* (Boston: Beacon Press, 1970), 41. The account here has been challenged widely.

20. David Robertson, *Denmark Vesey*, 101. "Rolla Bennett, Batteau Bennett, Ned Bennett, Peter Poyas, Jesse Blackwood hanged between 6–8 am on July 2—attempt to raise an insurrection." Some believed that Vesey would reappear through a supernatural power, so Vesey acquired an almost Christ-like persona.

21. See Douglas R. Egerton and Robert L. Paquette, *The Denmark Vesey Affair: A Documentary History* (Gainesville: University Press of Florida, 2017), for a painstaking look at the primary source documents.

22. See Manisha Sinha, *The Counterrevolution of Slavery: Politics and Ideology in Antebellum South Carolina* (Chapel Hill: University of North Carolina Press, 2000), 15–16.

23. Joanne Grant, ed., "Preamble of the Free African Society," in *Black Protest: History, Documents, and Analyses; 1619 to the Present* (New York: Fawcett, 1986), 53.

24. James H. Cone, *A Black Theology of Liberation* (Maryknoll, NY: Orbis Books, 2010). See also *The Cross and the Lynching Tree* (Maryknoll, NY: Orbis Books, 2013), and others of the many of Cone's writings.

25. Robertson, *Denmark Vesey*, cites Martin R. Delany as connecting the teachings of Vesey to the doctrine of Negritude and also calls him a "prophet of the Enlightenment," 133 ff. See also the womanist theology of Anna Julia Cooper, *A Voice of the South*, ed. Mary Helen Washington (1892; repr., Oxford: Oxford University Press, 1982), including the introduction by Washington and a contemporary articulation of her theology by Karen Baker-Fletcher, *A Singing Something: Womanist Reflections on Anna Julia Cooper* (Chestnut Ridge, NY: Crossroad, 1994), excerpts found in Kristin Waters and Carol B. Conway, eds., *Black Women's Intellectual Traditions Speaking Their Minds*.

26. Richardson, *Stewart*, 30.

27. Ibid. 40.

28. Waters, "Crying Out for Liberty."

29. For a detailed exposition of standpoint epistemologies, see many of the writings by Sandra Harding and Patricia Hill Collins, for example, Sandra Harding, *Science from Below: Feminisms, Post-colonialities, and Modernities* (Durham: Duke University Press, 2008), and Patricia Hill Collins, *Black Feminist Thought*. There is an extensive and important literature on standpoint epistemologies.

30. Egerton, *He Shall Go Out Free*, 117.

31. Hinks, *Appeal*.

CHAPTER TEN

1. Prince, *Narrative*, 10.

2. Richardson, *Stewart*, 37.

3. Melissa Weiner, College of the Holy Cross, who has conducted extensive research on Dutch slaves in colonial New York, considers children who were "indentured" without legal papers to have been "kidnapped" since many such children were stolen from families without any mutual agreement.

4. See Brittney Cooper, *Beyond Respectability: The Intellectual Thought of Race Women* (Urbana: University of Illinois Press, 2017), 38, an excellent work on writings about silencing Black women in US history.

5. Richardson, *Stewart*, 46.

6. Audre Lorde, "Poetry Is Not a Luxury," in *Sister Outsider: Essays and Speeches* (1984; repr., Berkeley: Ten Speed Press, 2007), 36.

7. Ibid., 37.

8. Collins, *Black Feminist*, 13. Special thanks to Patricia Baudoin for reiterating the importance of these theoretical developments.

9. Patricia Hill Collins, *Black Feminist Thought*, 46. For example, considering the power of poetry and essays, the academic insistence on a higher word count as requisite for admission to the canon is one way of gatekeeping to prevent those with limited access (resources such as time, available publication venues, mentors, even paper and pen) from disseminating their ideas, often based on race, class, and gender, just as (pre) Enlightenment writers enforced restrictions not just through access to education but through restricting publication to treatises written in Latin, Greek, and Hebrew, which women were not taught.

10. Jeremiah Asher, *Incidents in the Life of the Rev. J. Asher, Pastor of Shiloh (Coloured) Church, Philadelphia, U.S.: And a Concluding Chapter of Facts Illustrating the Unrighteous Prejudice Existing in the Minds of American Citizens Toward Their Coloured Brethren*, intro. Wilson Armistead (London: Charles Gilpin, 1850), https://archive.org/stream/incidentsinlifeooarmigoog/incidentsinlifeooarmigoog_djvu.txt, accessed April 24, 2020. Asher was born near New Haven (1812–1865) and became "a servant and a coachman" in Hartford when he was fourteen. Thus, Miller may have had occasion to see the young man who would become a well-known preacher at Shiloh Baptist Church in Philadelphia. For Asher's "Protesting the Negro Pew," see Milton C. Sernett, ed., *African American Religious History: A Documentary Witness* (Durham: Duke University Press, 2000).

11. Faith Congregational Church, accessed July 19, 2019, http://faithmatterstoday. org/?page_id=37. Among the early pastors was "Rev. Dr. James W.C. Pennington, who is re-membered as an eloquent orator, preacher, and freedom fighter. A fugitive slave, he escaped from Maryland through the Underground Railroad. For years, Pennington feared that he would be dragged back into slavery, until Harriet Beecher Stowe's brother-in-law, John Hooker, purchased him for $150. Pennington received his freedom papers on June 3, 1851. His Bible remains in the Church's possession."

12. Richardson, *Stewart*, 28–29.

13. Ibid., 29.

14. Jonathan Greenleaf, *History of the Churches of All Denominations in the City of New York from the First Settlement to the Year 1846* (New York: E. French, 1846).

15. Rayford W. Logan and Michael R. Winston, eds., "'Thomas Paul, J.' Carleton Hayden," in *Dictionary of American Negro Biography* (New York: W. W. Norton & Co. 1982), 483.

16. James Oliver and Lois E. Horton, *Black Bostonian: Family Life and Community Struggle in the Antebellum North* (New York: Holmes and Meier, 1979), 46.

17. L. Gordon, *Africana Philosophy*, 42. Ottobah Cuguano, *Thoughts and Sentiments on the Evil and Wicked Traffic of the Slavery and Commerce of the Human Species, Humbly Submitted to the Inhabitants of Great-Britain* (London: Ottobah Cugoano, 1787), https://play.google.com/store/books/details?id=BkUSAQAAMAAJ&rdid=bo ok-BkUSAQAAMAAJ&rdot=1, accessed April 24, 2020. See also Olaudah Equiano, *The Interesting Narrative of the Life of Olaudah Equiano, or Gustavus Vassa, The African* (London: Olaudah Equiano, 1789).

18. Logan and Winston, *Dictionary*, 483.

19. Jonathan Greenleaf, *A History of the Churches of All Denominations in the City of New York*.

20. Audre Lorde, "Poetry Is Not a Luxury," in *Sister/Outsider*, 37.

21. Prince, *Narrative*, 8.

22. Ibid., 10.

23. Maria Miller married James W. Stewart in early August of that year. Someone of her piety and sense of respectability would allow for a courtship of at least several months.

CHAPTER ELEVEN

1. Maria W. Stewart in *Spiritual Narratives*, intro. Susan Houchins, *Meditation II*, 26.

2. Belknap Street on Beacon Hill in Boston is now Joy Street.

3. William C. Nell, *Colored Patriots of the Revolution: With Sketches of Several Distinguished Colored Persons: to which is Added a Brief survey of the Condition and Prospects of Colored Americans* (Boston: Walcutt, 1855), 39. Mercy Otis Warren , another "erased" woman, was active in political circles, wrote plays, poems, and anti-federalist politi-cal essays, as well as a three-volume *A History of the Rise, Progress, and Termination of the American Revolution* (1805), a work that is mostly ignored by historians and popular writers/ researchers today despite its comprehensive account and keen insights. See also Kristin Waters, *Women and Men Political Theorists: Enlightened Conversations* (New York: Wiley, 2000).

4. Richardson, *Stewart*, 40.

5. Walter Muir Whitehill, *Boston: A Topographical History* (Cambridge: Harvard University Press, 1959), 55.

6. Ibid., 68.

7. Lorenzo J. Greene, "Mutiny on the Slave Ships," *Phylon* 5, no.1 (December 1944): 346–54.

8. Richardson, *Stewart*, 40.

9. Ibram X. Kendi, *Stamped from the Beginning: The Definitive History of Racist Ideas in America* (New York: Bold Type Books, 2016), 19.

10. E. T. Fisher, trans., *Report of a French Protestant Refugee, in Boston, 1687* (Brooklyn: Munsell Printer, 1687), https://archive.org/details/reportoffrenchproofish/page/n5/mode/2up, accessed April 25, 2020.

11. Currently several groups, among them the New Democracy Coalition, are calling for renaming Faneuil Hall which memorializes the slave trader and was a site of slave auctions. These efforts are meeting with fierce local resistance. The proposal is to rename the building for Crispus Attucks, the Revolutionary War hero. https://www.thenewdemocracycoalition.org/the-faneuil-hall-race-reconciliation-project/ accessed April 11, 2021.

12. William C. Nell, *Colored Patriots of the Revolution*, 33–34.

13. Hosea Easton, *A Treatise on the Intellectual Character, and Civil and Political Condition of the Colored People of the U States : and the Prejudice Exercised Towards Them : with a Sermon on the Duty of the Church to Them* (Boston: Isaac Knapp, 1837), https://archive.org/details/treatiseonintellooeast, 39.

14. *History of Philosophy Without Any Gaps*, Peter Adamson and Chike Jeffers, https://historyofphilosophy.net/hosea-easton, accessed July 22, 2020.

15. Nell, *Colored Patriots*, 34.

16. On lynching, see Ida B. Wells, *Southern Horrors: Lynch Law in All Its Phases* (1892) and *The Red Record* (1895) as well as Joy James, *Representations of Black Feminist Politics* (New York: St. Martin's Press, 1999*), Paula J. Giddings, Ida: A Sword Among Lion: Ida B. Wells and the Campaign Against Lynching* (New York: Harper Collins, 2009*) and Gender and Lynching: The Politics of Memory*, Evelyn Simien (New York: Palgrave Macmillan, 2011).

17. Richardson, *Stewart*, 48–49.

CHAPTER TWELVE

1. Richardson, *Stewart*, 55.

2. The extensive footnotes and bibliography in this text are intended to provide a set of signposts to the significant resources for future scholars as well as to provide due credit to those who have done this work in the past.

3. Susan Paul wrote *Memoir of James Jackson: The Attentive Obedient Scholar Who Died in Boston, October 31, 1833, Aged Six Years and Eleven Months*, ed. Lois Brown, (Cambridge: Harvard University Press, 2000). See also Lois Brown, "Out of the Mouths of Babes: The Abolitionist Campaign of Susan Paul and the Juvenile Choir of Boston." *The New England Quarterly* (2002): 52–79.

4. Baker-Fletcher, Karen. *A Singing Something* also excerpted in *Black Women's Intellectual Traditions*, ed. Waters and Conaway, 2007.

5. Alice Walker in *In Search of Our Mothers' Gardens: Womanist Prose* (New York: Harcourt Brace Jovanovich, 1983) xi–xii.

6. See Baker-Fletcher, *Singing*, 169, 221–22, Angela Y. Davis, *Blues Legacies and Black Feminism: Gertrude "Ma" Rainey, Bessie Smith, and Billie Holiday*. New York: Pantheon, 1998, and Valerie C. Cooper, *Word, Like Fire*. See also Toni Morrison's novel *Jazz* and the strong strains of theory in popular music from the work of Nina Simone, Queen Latifah, Lauryn Hill, and Beyoncé, to name just a few.

7. Kathryn Grover and Janine da Silva, *Historical Resource Study*, 68.

8. The church was authorized when Thomas Paul and Scipio Dalton "who was then a member of the First Baptist Church, sent the customary letter to the First and Second Baptist Churches asking their aid in constituting a new church." Horton and Horton, *Black Bostonians*, 40–41 and 143n. Brittney Cooper, *Beyond Respectability*, 24.

9. "At the end of March,1799 he had purchased a lot on Holmes Alley from Theodore Phinney, and in 1800 he traded his Holmes Alley lot for the west half of Cromwell Barnes's double house (later identified as 19 Belknap and 60–62 Joy Street). With Thomas Paul, he may have been one of the "colored Baptists" whom William C. Nell described as having "obtained access to a small room in a low wooden building situated on the north corner of Belknap and Pickney [sic] streets . . . this was the same house once occupied by Colonel Middleton," Grover, Kathryn and Janine V. de Silva, "Historic Resource Study Boston African American National Historic Site," 2002, 168–69. Much of the information in this chapter was gleaned from Ancestry.com and from the Boston City Directories.

10. Ibid. "Some months before this formal incorporation, the First Baptist Church had created a committee composed of trustee Daniel Wild, a trader and former auctioneer; bakers William Bentley and Edward Stevens, housewright Ward Jackson, chocolate manufacturer John Wait, and merchant Mitchell Lincoln. On 23 March 1805, this committee purchased from Augustin Raillion a parcel of land forty-eight by fifty-nine feet square on the south side of Smith Court. The parcel, which had a building on it, was part of two larger lots Raillion had acquired from the Carnes estate and Henry Hill. The committee sold the building for $75 and spent $365 on timbers and window frames salvaged from the 1736 Old West Church at Cambridge and Lynde Streets, then being rebuilt." 68.

11. I'm reminded of the political philosopher Jean-Jacques Rousseau, who confesses that as a young man he stole a ribbon of some value then blamed it on a servant girl. See Rousseau's *Confessions*. Rousseau is heralded for his belated honesty; the servant was punished.

12. Collins, *Black Feminist Thought*, 260.

13. Richardson, *Stewart*, 82.

14. Kristin Waters, "Some Core Themes of Black Feminist Theory," in Waters and Conaway, eds., *Black Women's Intellectual Traditions*, 372.

15. Brittney Cooper, *Beyond Respectability*, 29.

16. See especially, Kristin Waters, "Past as Prologue: Intersectional Analysis in Nineteenth Century Philosophies of Race and Gender," in *Why Race and Gender Still Matter: An Intersectional Approach*, ed. Namita Goswami, Maeve M. O'Donovan, and Lisa Yount (Cambridge, UK: Pickering and Chatto), 2014.

17. Among many writings, see Kimberlé Crenshaw, "Mapping the Margins: Intersectionality, Identity Politics, and Violence against Women of Color," *Stanford Law Review* 43, no. 6 (1991): 1241–99, accessed April 25, 2020. doi:10.2307/1229039. For #sayhername see the African American Policy Forum, https://aapf.org/sayhername, accessed July

22, 2020. Also, Collins, *Black Feminist Thought*; Dotson, "Inheriting Patricia Hill Collins's Black Feminist Epistemology" in *Ethnic and Racial Studies* 38, no. 13 (2015): 2322–2328, 2015. Many efforts to rectify ongoing obstacles and erasures include the 2019 Black Women's Philosophers Conference in NYC held at the CUNY Graduate Center and organized by Linda Martín Alcoff and Charles W. Mills.

18. http://womenwriters.digitalscholarship.emory.edu/advocacy/content.php?level=div&id=era1_04.12&document=era1 accessed April 6, 2020.

19. A good source on Hilton is Peter P. Hinks, "To Commence a Moral World: John Telemachus Hilton, Abolitionism, and the Expansion of Black Freemasonry, 1784–1860," 40–62 in *All Men Free and Brethren: Essays on the History of African American Freemasonry*, ed Peter P. Hinks and Stephen Kantrowitz.

20. According to Horton and Horton, *Black Bostonians*, 76.4 % of the city's black population resided in Wards 2, 5, 6, and 7, about 1433 people, 4–5.

21. Grover and da Silva, *Historic Resource Study*, 69.

22. One of the best expressions of the philosophical idea of the "ideal lady." See Immanuel Kant's "Observations on the Sublime and Beautiful," and for critical analysis of this work, see Kristin Waters, "Women in Kantian Ethics," in *Modern Engendering: Critical Feminist Readings in Modern Western Philosophy*, ed. Bat-Ami Bar On (Albany, NY: SUNY Press, 1994).

23. Valerie C. Cooper, *Word, Like Fire*, 115 and Brittney Cooper, Beyond Respectability, 13. Earlier feminist formulations are found in Barbara Welter, "The Cult of True Womanhood" 1820–1860 in *Dimity Convictions: The American Woman in the Nineteenth Century* (Athens: Ohio University Press, 1976).

24. Richardson, *Stewart*, 29.

25. L. Gordon, *Africana Philosophy*, 47. The cultural relativity of color ascriptions is apparent when one considers that across cultures wedding dresses, symbols of purity, have featured many different colors, from lime-green in Korea, black in Spain, red in China, and bright colors and patterns in India and parts of Africa. See also Mary Douglas, *Purity and Danger* (1966), the white theoretical touchstone on *Purity*.

26. Brittney Cooper, *Respectability*, 13

27. Valerie Cooper, *Word, Like Fire*, 115–19.

28. A classic text, still interesting today, on the ritual performance of labor by privileged women (and others features of capitalism). See Thorstein Veblen, *The Theory of the Leisure Class*, first published in 1899.

29. Collins, *Black Feminist Thought*,178 ff.

30. For more on this topic, see Patricia Hill Collins, Brittney Cooper, Valerie C. Cooper, and Evelyn Brooks Higginbotham.

31. Mills, *Black Rights/White Wrongs: The Critique of Racial Liberalism*, (Oxford: Oxford University Press, 2017), 36; and *The Racial Contract*. Mills offers and extensive investigation of the concepts of "groups" and "individuals" in "Occupy Liberalism." Mills's thesis, congruent with the basic argument of this book attributed to Maria W. Stewart and others, is that a radical application of the principles of liberalism will lead to a more just society.

32. In addition to those authors mentioned earlier, see as an example, Anita L. Allen, "Coercing Privacy" (1999), *Faculty Scholarship at Penn Law*, 803. https://scholarship.law.upenn.edu/faculty_scholarship/803, as well as several publications by Kathryn Sophia

Belle (formerly Kathryn T. Gines), including "Black Feminist Reflections on Charles Mills's 'Intersecting Contracts,'" in *Critical Philosophy of Race, Special Issue: Charles Mills* 5, no. 1 (Spring 2017): 19–28 and "Race Women, Race Men and Early Expressions of Proto-Intersectionality, 1830s-1930s," in *Why Race and Gender Still Matter*, ed. Goswami, et. al. 15; and Falguni A. Sheth, *Toward a Political Philosophy of Race* (Albany: SUNY Press, 2009),17.

33. McLaren, *Decolonizing Feminism: Transnational Feminism and Globalization*, ed. M. McLaren (New York: Rowman & Littlefield, 2017), 2.

34. In *Feminist Politics and Human Nature* (Lanham: Rowman & Littlefield Publishers, 1983) a foundational treatise on social and political theory, Alison Jaggar argues convincingly against what she calls the abstract individualism and normative dualism (valuing the mind above the body) as the central tenets of classic liberal theory.

35. Richardson, *Stewart*, 35.

36. Collins, *Black Feminist Theory*, 49, 50, 251, 252

37. Grover and da Silva, *Historic Resource Study*, 85.

38. Horton and Horton, *Black Bostonians*, 18.

39. Ibid. 19.

40. Collins, *Black Feminist Thought*, 51.

41. David B. Landon and Teresa D. Bulger, "Constructing Community: Experiences of Identity, Economic Opportunity, and Institution Building at Boston's African Meeting House," International Journal of Historical Archeology, DOI 10.1007/s10761-012-0212-z, accessed April 6, 2020.

42. Michael Terranova was a major informant for the Grover and da Silva *Historical Resource Study*. He and Horace Seldon were instrumental in gathering information about his community many years ago and in an ongoing way. Seldon was a tireless supporter for many projects on the Black community in Beacon Hill. I was fortunate enough to meet with both, Terranova generously guiding me around the hill and pointing out sites of places that have since disappeared. Seldon's passionate opposition to racism and productive, optimistic determination to create social change through historical recognition are unparalleled. http://horaceseldon.com/.

43. See Landon and Bulger, "Constructing Community," where there is also a remarkable bibliography. Grover and da Silva note, "The African Meeting House has already been thoroughly examined in Beth Bower's excellent 1986 summary of archaeological work, which is far more than an archaeological report, and Beth Pearson's 1982 historic structure report," 67. See also "Archeology of the Meeting House: A Dig and Discovery Project in Boston, Massachusetts" sponsored by the Museum of African American History, Boston and Nantucket and the Fiske Center for Archeological Research at the University of Massachusetts, Boston, http://www.fiskecenter.umb.edu/Pdfs/AMH_Public_Booklet.pdf.

44. See George A. Levesque, *Black Boston: African American Life and Culture in Urban America, 1750–1860* (New York and London: Garland Publishing, 1994), 270. This work contains an interesting discourse about the discovery raccoons' teeth, speculating that they may have been used in ways indicative of syncretism between West African religious practices and African Baptist ones.

45. Toni Morrison, *Playing in the Dark: Whiteness and the Literary Imagination*, (Cambridge: Harvard University Press, 1992), 5.

CHAPTER THIRTEEN

1. Catharine Sedgwick, *The Life and Letters of Catharine M. Sedgwick*, by Catharine Maria Sedgwick, ed. Mary E. Dewey (New York, Harper and Brothers, 1872), 175.

2. Nathaniel Philbrick, "The True Story of the Battle of Bunker Hill," *Smithsonian Magazine*, May 2013. http://www.smithsonianmag.com/history/the-true-story-of-the-battle -of-bunker-hill-36721984/, accessed April 25, 2020.

3. Richardson, *Stewart*, 39.

4. *Wesley and Uzelac, ed., William Cooper Nell.*

5. Richardson, *Stewart*, 39.

6. http://www.aaregistry.org/historic_events/view/battle-bunker-hill-has-diverse-history.

7. Sedgwick, *Life and Letters*, 175

8. Ibid., 176.

9. Original source *Bentley's Miscellany*, vol. 34 (London, Richard Bentley, 1853), 418.

10. Frederick Douglass, *My Bondage, My Freedom*, https://docsouth.unc.edu/neh/doug lass55/douglass55.html, accessed July 23, 2020.

11. Sedgwick, 422.

12. See Christopher Cameron. *To Plead Our Own Cause: African Americans in Massachusetts and the Making of the Antislavery Movement* (Kent State University Press 2014). These cases are legally complex, but accounts such as Cameron's and others explain them carefully in detail.

13. Catharine Sedgwick, "Slavery in New England," by Miss Sedgwick, in *Bentley's Miscellany: Charles Dickens, William Harrison Ainsworth, Albert Smith*, vol. 34 (London: Richard Bentley, 1853), 421. The Elizabeth Freeman quote is taken from this essay.

14. Adrienne Rich, *On Lies, Secrets, and Silence: Selected Prose 1966–1978* (W. W. Norton Co. 1979).

15. Nell, *Patriots*, 21

16. Ibid., 23–25

17. Ibid, 21.

CHAPTER FOURTEEN

1. https://www.bartleby.com/400/poem/621.html, accessed April 8, 2020.

2. "Benjamin Banneker's . . . Almanac and Ephemeris containing the motions of the Sun and Moon, the true places and aspects of the Planets, the rising and setting of the Sun, and the rising, setting, and southing, place and age of the Moon, &c. The Lunations, Conjunctions, Eclipses, Judgment of the Weather, Festivals, and remarkable days," quoted in William Cooper Nell, *Colored Patriots*, 209–10.

3. Frederick Douglass, "What to the Slave is the Fourth of July," *The Portable Frederick Douglass*, ed John Stauffer and Henry Louis Gates, Jr. (New York: Penguin, 2016).

4. Nathaniel Paul, "African Baptists Celebrate Emancipation," in Milton C. Sernett, *African American Religious History: Documentary Witness* (Durham: Duke University Press, 1999), 187.

5. Ibid. https://www.bartleby.com/400/poem/621.html.

6. Richardson, Stewart, 40.

7. For several discussions on this and related topics, see Manisha Sinha, "To 'cast just obliquy' on Oppressors: Black Radicalism in the Age of Revolution," in *William and Mary Quarterly* 64, no. 1 (Jan. 2007); http://abolition.nypl.org/print/celebrations/, accessed April 8, 2020 and William B. Gravley "The Dialectic of Double-Consciousness in Black American Freedom Celebrations, 1808–1863." *The Journal of Negro History* 67, no. 4 (1982): 302–17. doi:10.2307/2717532. Gravely, Peter Hinks, and others have noted that there are many different dates for abolition celebrations ranging from January 1 to June 19, to July 5 and 14 to dates in September.

8. One classic compilation and analysis can be found in *American Negro Slave Revolts*, by Herbert Aptheker, first published in 1943 by Columbia University Press.

9. *Pamphlets of Protest: An Anthology of Early African American Protest Literature, 1790–1860*, ed. Richard Newman, Patrick Rael, Phillip Lapansky (New York: Routledge 2001), 47.

10. I deal extensively with the topic of hypocrisy in "Crying Out for Liberty," *Philosophia Africana* 15, no. 1 (Winter 2013): 35–60.

11. C. L. R. James published *The Black Jacobins: Toussaint L'Ouverture and the San Domingo Revolution* in 1938 and Eric Williams published *Capitalism and Slavery* in 1944.

12. Anna Julia Cooper, *Slavery and the French and Haitian Revolutionists; Attitude de la France à l'égard de l'esclavage pendant la revolution*, ed. Frances R. Keller (New York: Rowman and Littlefield, 2006).

13. For Anna Julia Cooper's most recognized work, see *A Voice From the South*, (Oxford: Oxford University Press, 1988), introduction by Mary Helen Washington. The work under consideration here is "Anna Julia Cooper's Analysis of the Haitian Revolution," Nathifa Greene, in the *CLR James Journal* 23 (Fall 2017): 1–2. Greene notes that Frances Keller translated Cooper's work as *Slavery and the French Revolutionists*" (Rowman and Littlefield, 2006), but her article relies primarily on her own translations from the French. See also Vivian May, *Anna Julia Cooper: Visionary Black Feminist* (New York: Routledge, 2007). For a book-length discussion of how disciplinary firewalls obstruct knowledge projects, see L. Gordon, *Disciplinary Decadence*.

14. Richardson, *Stewart*, 39.

15. Greene, "Anna Julia Cooper," 91, 95, 98, 96.

16. Aimé Césaire, *Discourse on Colonialism*, trans. Joan Pinkham, intro. Robin D. G. Kelley, Monthly Review Press, 1972. African Americans dominated abolitionist thought from the pre-revolutionary era, heavily influenced by actions in Haiti and throughout the Caribbean, at least until the 1830s when social and political change coupled with pressure from autonomous Black organizing helped to create white-led abolitionism. What followed was the canonically perpetrated perception that resistance to oppression was primarily a white-led enterprise. The only successful slave revolt in history is still obliterated from the general hegemonic knowledge project. Greene's reclamation of Cooper's treatise adds another piece to the puzzle of recreating a continuous narrative of historical events that respectfully embraces race and gender, both as subjects of analysis and as authors of that analysis and accords with Maria Stewart's worldview as she was writing her political essays.

17. "https://docsouth.unc.edu/church/wright/wright.html, accessed April 8, 2020.

18. Allen Chamberlain, *Beacon Hill: Its Ancient Pastures and Early Mansions* (Boston: Houghton Mifflin, 1925), 265 ff.

19. https://www.masshist.org/object-of-the-month/july-2015. See Prince Hall speech of 1897. https://www.loc.gov/resource/rbpe.0520130a/?st=text. https://www.masshist.org/object -of-the-month/july-2015 See also Sinha, *The Slave's Cause*, 133 ff.

20. Grover and da Silva, *Historic Resource Guide*, 78–79. Middleton was a community leader who was a "Horse Breaker & Coach Driver. George Middleton's success as a horse breaker and coach driver enabled him to partner with fellow entrepreneur Louis Glapion, a hairdresser, to build a house that is the oldest extant home on Beacon Hill built by African Americans. Known as Colonel Middleton, he led the Bucks of America, a black regiment that defended Boston merchants and protected local property during the American Revolution. In 1784, Middleton helped to found the African Masonic Lodge; in 1796, the African Benevolent Society; and in 1798, the African School," from *Black Entrepreneurs of the eighteenth and Nineteenth Centuries*, an interesting exhibit catalogue, https://www.maah.org/ assets/front/pdf/BlackEntrepreneursexhibitguide.pdf, accessed April 8, 2020. The parallels with today's white supremacists are evident.

21. Gravely, "The Dialectic," 306.

22. I would like to acknowledge and thank Cliff Schorer for directing me to and discussing the "Eulogy of Thomas Jefferson and John Adams by Daniel Webster, Faneuil Hall, Boston, August 2, 1826."

CHAPTER FIFTEEN

1. *Spiritual Narratives*, intro. Sue Houchins (Oxford, Oxford University Press, 1988), 23.

2. Prince, *Narrative*, 7.

3. Richardson, *Stewart*, 29; Prince, *Travels*, 10.

4. Prince, *Narrative*, 17–18.

5. *Richardson, Stewart*, 3.

6. Ibid. 3.

7. Richardson notes that at the time of their marriage James W. Stewart acknowledged "one, possible two illegitimate daughters." See appendix D.

8. Richardson, *Stewart*, "Religion," 38.

9. James W. Stewart, "shipping officer," lived at the head of Smith Court, rear of 38 South Russell Street, in 1827, according to tax records that year. Grover and de Silva, *Historic Resource Guide*, fn 66. Since James W. Stewart is recorded in the 1826 City Directory as residing at his business, the couple may have lived briefly in the rear of the building that housed his shipping office, as many of buildings on Broad Street had residential apartments.

10. See Adelaide M. Cromwell's *The Other Brahmins: Boston's Black Upper Class, 1750–1950* (Fayetteville: University of Arkansas Press, 1994). Richardson, *Stewart*, "Franklin Hall," 45.

11. Chamberlain, *Beacon Hill*, 240, 247.

12. Richardson, *Stewart*, fn. 5, 122.

13. Samuel Eliot Morison, *The Maritime History of Massachusetts, 1783–1860* (Boston: Northeastern University Press, 1979), originally published 1921, 124.

14. Richardson, *Stewart*, 4.

15. http://www.economicadventure.org/exhibits/black-entrepreneurs/brochure.pdf July 2, 2020.

16. Hinks, *Awaken*, 69.

17. David Walker, *Walker's Appeal with a Brief Sketch of his Life*, by Henry Highland Garnet, Good Press. 2019.

CHAPTER SIXTEEN

1. The phrase, "the roots of Black political thought" is already something of a misnomer, since political philosophizing emerged as soon as the first Africans were stolen and brought to the Americas. Hundreds of years of epistemic violence intentionally disrupted the conveyance of these ideas through oral traditions when the slavers mixed linguistic groups as they settled those who were kidnapped, but even these tactics failed to obliterate the traces of ancestral thought intermixed with newly generated analyses rooted in the lived experiences of newly arrived Africans and their descendants, leaving traces of African cosmologies and culture. What is missing until the second half of the eighteenth century are sufficient *written* accounts, and even these, as they emerged, are routinely overlooked or discounted as sources of thought.

2. Grover and da Silva, *Historic Research Study*, 37.

3. Italics mine. From Hinks, *Walker*, 84.

4. *Boston Directory*, 1826.

5. Thomas H. O'Connor, *The Athens of America: Boston 1825–1845* (Amherst: University of Massachusetts Press, 2006), xiii.

6. Richard Newman provides his own list of those on either side of this dispute, a list I neither endorse nor dispute, *Transformation*, 1. For a case of immediate resistance, see the example of Faneuil's ship, overtaken by its captives even before it could leave port, cited earlier. The wave metaphor as it is used to describe historical eras if often challenged and reframed, particularly with regard to feminism. Despite that, in this case the metaphor is useful, particularly for making the point about origins.

7. Sinha, *A Slave's Cause*, 1. Roughly from 1800–1820 the stabilization of institutions in Boston brought the construction of the African Meetinghouse, fostering a religious community that anchored local organizing. The Freemasons continued to meet, nurture, and cultivate their members. Visible expressions of organized resistance mounted with the work of James Forten, the Pennsylvania Abolition Society, Richard Allen, and the African Methodist Episcopal Church in Pennsylvania. The 1820s bought the Massachusetts General Colored Association, revived masonic work, and the abolitionist newspaper *Freedom's Journal*, a time period addressed in the next chapter.

8. Manisha Sinha in "To cast just obloquy," *William and Mary Quarterly*, writes, "Historians have yet to fully appreciate the alternative and radical nature of black abolitionist ideology and its origins in the revolutionary era and the early Republic. Many continue to portray black abolitionists, in Patrick Rael's words, not as "counter-hegemons" but as "co-fabricators" of northern political culture. They argue that African Americans appropriated mainstream values and ideas to construct a black protest tradition. But the terms adoption, assimilation, or appropriation hardly do justice to African Americans' intellectual and political engagement with the revolutionary tradition." Stewart, in particular, is often snubbed. For example, she is not included in the extensive collection—more than one hundred selections—in *American Antislavery Writings: Colonial Beginnings to Emancipation*, ed. James Butler, Library of America, 2012, even though her writings are more extensive and more

nuanced in their inclusion of a gender analysis than many who are included. Is this because the dates of her major works (1831–33) don't fit neatly into the standard periodization while David Walker's (1829) do? Or is it because she is a woman who also happens to include a sustained argument about gender oppression in her work?

9. See Joanna Brooks, "The Early American Public Sphere and the Emergence of a Black Print Counterpublic," *William and Mary Quarterly* 62, no. 1 (January 2005): 67–92. Among scholars who recognize the Black founders and give them their due are the contributors to the Forum, "Black Founders in the New Republic," a series of articles, including an introduction, by Roy E. Finkenbine and Richard S. Newman, *The William and Mary Quarterly*, Third Series, 64, no. 1 (January 2007): 83–94.Work reclaiming "Black Founders" continues for example, in *Black Puritan, Black Republican: The Life and Thought of Lemuel Haynes,* John Salliant (Oxford: Oxford University Press, 2003), but many other important figures have little reliable material written about them, for example, Prince Hall. And despite this promising new focus there is yet no systematic account devoted exclusively to the Black Founders in political science or philosophy, as against, according to Mary Beth Norton, the 37 new volumes between 2001 and 2011 with titles alluding to the founding fathers. (*New York Times Book Review*, May 20, 2011, "Finding More Founders.") The useful phrase "less partial and perverse" in reference to the inclusive epistemologies generated through scholarship in gender studies and ethnic studies, comes from Sandra Harding and Merrill B. Hintikka's early work in philosophy of science, *Discovering Reality: Feminist Perspectives on Epistemology, Metaphysics, Methodology, and Philosophy of Science*, Springer Netherlands, 1983.

10. Various sources assert several wives, among them Delia, and Sarah Ritchie, along with children, including Primus. Sifting out accurate information is made more difficult by the fact that several formerly enslaved men by the name of Prince Hall lived in the vicinity at the time. A comprehensive scholarly treatment of Prince Hall is sorely needed.

11. *Pamphlets of Protest*: Newman, Rael, and Lapansky. Prince Hall, "A Charge" 1797, 47.

12. Otis explicitly argues that slavery was a violation of natural law.

13. Prince Hall's manumission record is in the Boston Athenaeum. See Ezekiel Price, Notarial records, 1756–1789.

14. John Locke, *Two Treatises of Government*, ed. Peter Haslett (New York: New American Library, 1960), 446.

15. This phrase is taken from an excellent example of reclaiming Black women writers and thinkers: Teresa Zackodnik's *Press, Platform, Pulpit: Black Feminist Politics in the Era of Reform* (Knoxville: University of Tennessee, 2007).

16. Richardson, *Stewart*, 36. The term "counternarrative" is used by, among others, Manisha Sinha in "To 'Cast Just Obloquy.'"

17. Among the many works on Black nationalism a classic text is William Jeremiah Moses, *The Golden Age of Black Nationalism—1850–1925* (New York: Oxford University Press, 1978), while a more recent view can be found in Tommie Shelby's *We Who Are Dark: The Philosophical Foundations of Black Solidarity* (Cambridge, MA: Harvard University Press, 2005).

18. My extensive argument for the term Black revolutionary liberalism, along with a detailed explanation is made in "Crying Out for Liberty: Maria W. Stewart and David Walker's Black Revolutionary Liberalism" in *Philosophia Africana* 15, no. 1 (Winter 2013). An alternative designation suggested by Paget Henry is "post-colonial republicanism."

This nomenclature works well for comparative purposes in linking Black struggles in the United States to other postcolonial struggles worldwide. See *Caliban's Reason: Introducing Afro-Caribbean Philosophy*, New York: Routledge, 2000. Lucius Outlaw reminds us of the heuristic value of the idea of postcoloniality used "in order to understand the prospects for full national independence and self-determination in the areas of economic, political, social, and cultural life generally," in *On Race and Philosophy* (New York: Routledge, 1996), 33–35. Both postcolonial republicanism and Black revolutionary liberalism may be useful new introductions to the language of American political thought. In the present context there are several advantages to adopting Black revolutionary liberalism, particularly its specificity to the ideas of the time, modified and corrected.

19. Prince Hall, "A Charge, in *Pamphlets of Protest*, 47, 49.

20. Richardson, *Stewart*, 29, 38, 39.

21. For various reasons, some of the scholarship about Prince Hall and the origins of Black Freemasonry is poor and riddled with errors. For recent, excellent scholarly work, see *All Men Free and Brethren: Essays on the History of African American Freemasonry*, ed. Peter P. Hinks and Stephen Kantrowitz, foreword by Leslie A. Lewis (Ithaca: Cornell University Press), in particular the editor's introduction and "Emancipation and the Social Origins of Black Freemasonry, 1775–1800," Chernoh M. Sesay, Jr. No comparable organizations were available to women, although in this same volume, in "They are Nevertheless Our Brethren": The Order of the Eastern Star and the Battle for Women's Leadership, 1874–1926," Brittney Cooper explores the sister organizations the emerged in the later part of the nineteenth century.

22. Robert Birt, "Existence, Identity and Liberation," in L. Gordon, *Existence in Black*, 205. See also other chapters in this volume and extensive additional philosophical literature.

23. Charles W. Mills, "Occupy Liberalism! Or, Ten Reasons Why Liberalism Cannot Be Retrieved for Radicalism (And Why They're All Wrong)," *Radical Philosophy Review* 15, no. 2 (2012), 27.

24. Richardson, *Stewart*, 29.

25. Marshall, *Manhood Enslaved*.

26. Harris, "Insurrectionist Ethics,"193.

27. Cameron, *To Plead Our Own Cause*. In an important addition to the neglected study of religion and slavery in colonial America, Cameron discusses the intersection of politics, religion, and liberation movements reaching back to the Puritan legal codes in the "body of liberties," weaving in the central role of religion, particularly as interpreted by Black theorists, as it became a powerful influence intellectually, spiritually, and as a force for social change.

For those interested in the political implications of "Black hair," the "first anti-slavery tract," *The Selling of Joseph: A Memorial*, discussed by Cameron, also describes "an early formation of the ideologies of black inferiority" based on disparities "in their Conditions, Colour, and Hair." See Cameron 13–16.

28. A recent project has digitized hundreds of anti-slavery petitions: https://petitions .radcliffe.harvard.edu/massachusetts-anti-slavery-and-anti-segregation-petitions

29. http://www.historyisaweapon.com/defcon1/fourpetitionsagainstslavery.html, accessed April 9, 2020.

30. Richardson, *Stewart*, 31.

31. "Petition of a Grate Number of Blackes" to Thomas Gage (May 25, 1774). In Aptheker, ed., *A Documentary History of the Negro People in the United States*, vol. 1, pp. 8–9. From the

Massachusetts Historical Society, 5th series, vol. 3 (Boston, IB77), pp. 432ff. See also https://sourcebooks.fordham.edu/mod/1774slavesappeal.asp, accessed April 9, 2020. I have made no attempt to standardize or "correct" spellings as few standards applied at the time, and I assume that the reader is clever enough to comprehend what is written here and in similar quotations.

32. John Rawls, *A Theory of Justice* (Cambridge, Harvard University Press, 1971).

33. Carole Pateman, *The Sexual Contract* (Cambridge: Polity, 1988), 2.

34. Charles W. Mills, *The Racial* Contract (Ithaca: Cornell University Press, 199), and Pateman and Mills, *Domination and Contract* (Cambridge, Polity, 2007), 83.

35. https://royallhouse.org/belindas-petition-a-poem-by-rita-dove/.

36. See Roy E. Finkenbine, "Belinda's Petition: Reparations for Slavery in Revolutionary Massachusetts," *The William and Mary Quarterly*, Third Series 64, no. 1 (2007): 95–104, accessed April 30, 2020. www.jstor.org/stable/4491599.

37. For example, Raymond A Winbush, *Belinda's Petition: A Concise History of Reparations for the Slave Trade* (Bloomington, IN: Xlibris, 2009).

38. https://royallhouse.org/slavery/belinda-sutton-and-her-petitions/, accessed April 9, 2020.

39. Richardson, *Stewart*, 34–35.

40. https://royallhouse.org/slavery/belinda-sutton-and-her-petitions/.

41. Stewart, *Richardson*, 62.

42. Cameron, *To Plead*, 47.

43. Arlette Frund. "Phillis Wheatley, a Public Intellectual," in *Towards an Intellectual History of Black Women*, ed. Mia Bay, Farah J. Griffin, Martha S. Jones, and Barbara Savage (Chapel Hill: University of North Carolina Press, 2015), 35, 38.

44. Stefan M. Wheelock, *Barbaric Culture: Black Antislavery Writers, Religion, and the Slaveholding Atlantic* (Charlottesville: University of Virginia Press, 2016), 3.

45. Barbara Christian, "The Race for Theory," in *Cultural Critique* 6, *The Nature and Context of Minority Discourse* (Spring, 1987): 51–63. See also Toni Morrison, *Playing in the Dark*.

46. Wheelock, *Barbaric Culture*, 65.

47. Stewart, *Richardson*, 39.

48. Cameron, *To Plead*, 35.

49. https://s-usih.org/2014/06/phillis-wheatley-and-the-black-prophetic-tradition/

50. Cameron, *To Plead*, 35.

51. Tetlow, Joanne. "John Locke's Covenant Theology," *Locke Studies* 9 (2009): 167–98. https://doi.org/10.5206/ls.2009.915.

52. Richardson, *Stewart*, 39–40.

53. Moody, *Spiritual Narratives*, 53.

54. Cameron, https://s-usih.org/2014/06/phillis-wheatley-and-the-black-prophetic-tradition/

CHAPTER SEVENTEEN

1. Walker, "Speech Before the Massachusetts General Colored Association," *Freedom's Journal* (December 19, 1828).

2. James Brewer Stewart, "Modernizing "Difference": The Political Meanings of Color in Free States,1776–1840," *Journal of the Early Republic* 19, no. 4. (Winter 1999): 691–712.

3. Jacqueline Bacon, *Freedom's Journal: The First African American Newspaper* (New York: Lexington Books, 2007), 9.

4. Cooper, *Beyond Respectability*. Evelyn Brooks Higginbotham provides the first systematic treatment of the politics of respectability in *Righteous Discontent*. In recent years, movements such as Black Lives Matter and Say Her Name have explicitly rejected respectability politics as contrary to the kind of activism needed to combat the overt and deadly racism of our current culture, making for a spirited debate on the meaning and efficacy of "respectability."

5. Brewer Stewart, "Modernizing," 205.

6. Corey D. B. Walker, *A Noble Fight: African American Freemasonry and the Struggle for Democracy in America* (Urbana: University of Illinois Press, 2008).

7. Bacon, *Freedoms Journal*, 3

8. Hinks, *To Awaken*, 72.

9. Until recently, the consensus has been that the MGCA was founded in 1826. Peter Hinks suggests in his comprehensive work on David Walker and John T. Hilton that it was founded 1828.

10. *Proceedings: Agreeably to Previous Notice, a Meeting of the Colored Citizens of Boston Was Held in Southac Street Church, on Monday Evening, Dec. 17th, 1855, for the Purpose of Presenting a Memorial to Mr. William C. Nell* . . . (Boston, 1855), 20. Also found in *William Cooper Nell*, ed. by Wesley and Uzelac, 1855.

11. https://www.blackpast.org/african-american-history/1828-david-walker-necessity-general-union-among-us/, accessed April 11, 2020.

12. Bacon, *Freedom's Journal*, 84.

13. Quincy T. Mills, *Cutting along the Color Line: Black Barbers and Barber Shops in America* (Philadelphia: University of Pennsylvania Press, 2017), 43. See also Melissa Victoria Harris-Lacewell. *Barbershops, Bibles, and BET: Everyday Talk and Black Political Thought* (Princeton: Princeton University Press, 2014).

14. Bacon, *Freedom's Journal*, 2.

15. Calvin C. Herndon, *The Sexual Mountain and Black Women Writers: Adventures in Sex, Literature, and Real Life* (New York, Doubleday, 1987), 60. Moody, *Spiritual Narratives*, 27.

16. Kristie Dotson, "Inheriting," 2323–24. For an explanation of my reasons for prioritizing Black feminist analysis, see Waters, "A Journey from Willful Ignorance."

17. Mills, Quincy T. *Cutting along the Color Line*, 47.

CHAPTER EIGHTEEN

1. Richardson, *Stewart*, 30.

2. Grover and da Silva, *Historic Resource Study*, 38. I use this version rather than Hinks's because it has condensed his findings.

3. Hinks, *To Awaken*, 74.

4. The full title is *David Walker's Appeal; in Four Articles, Together with a Preamble, to the Coloured Citizens of the World, But in Particular, and Very Expressly, to Those of the United States of America.*

5. Lucius T. Outlaw, *On Race and Philosophy* (New York: Routledge, 1996), 33–34.

6. Walker, *David Walker's Appeal*, 12, 9.

7. Thomas Jefferson, *Notes on the State of Virginia*, ed. William Peden, (1781; New York, 1954), 143. His library contained works by Carl Linnaeus, Georges-Louis Leclerc, Comte de Buffon, and Johann Friedrich Blumenbach, all of whom provided various and conflicting accounts of race. Walker railed against the phrase "unfortunate difference of colour," accusing Jefferson of questioning God's choices.

8. Even earlier, René Descartes and John Locke had contributed to the idea of dividing the natural world into classes, genera, and species, and while Locke denied the existence of real essences, he nonetheless held that "*genus* and *species* are no more than abstract ideas that enable actual things to be sorted out more sensibly." Descartes's normative dualism emphasized the higher valuation of the mind or soul over the body while maintaining the connection between the physical and mental in the thinking being. These values were later mapped by others onto individuals on the basis of skin color. Montesquieu formulated an early idea of races that designated stages of historical progress, introducing connections to political liberty, economic interest, and, innovatively (albeit disastrously), the idea of climate as a determinate of race.

9. The phrase "ambidextrous philosopher," was used by Alexander Hamilton to criticize Jefferson's hypocrisy as a slave holder. See Manisha Sinha, "To 'cast just obliquy' on Oppressors: Black Radicalism in the Age of Revolution," *William and Mary Quarterly* 64 no. 1 (January 2007).

10. Hinks, *Appeal*, 19.

11. Mary Wollstonecraft, *A Vindication of the Rights of Woman* (New York, 1987), 68; John Stuart Mill, *The Subjection of Women, Essays on Equality, Law, and Education, Collected Works of John Stuart Mill*, vol. 21, ed. J. Robson (1869; Toronto, 1984), 259–348. For more on this topic, see Charles W. Mills, *The Racial Contract*.

12. Hinks, *Appeal*, 64.

13. For a wealth of essays on this topic, see ed., Darlene Clark Hine and Earnestine Jenkins, *A Question of Manhood: A Reader in U.S. Black Men's History and Masculinity*, (Bloomington: Indiana University Press, 1999).

14. See Kristin Waters, "Some Core Themes of Nineteenth Century Black Feminism," in *Black Women's Intellectual Traditions*, ed. Waters and Carol B. Conaway, and Hazel V. Carby, *Reconstructing Womanhood: The Emergence of the Afro-American Woman Novelist* (Oxford: Oxford University Press, 1987). Early discussions of gender and race are found in Angela Y. Davis, *Women, Race & Class*, and *Women, Culture, & Politics*; Patricia Hill Collins, *Black Sexual Politics: African Americans, Gender, and the New Racism* (New York: Routledge, 2004), 44. See also Jacqueline Bacon, *Freedom's Journal*.

15. Hinks, *Appeal*, 48–49. "Drain off" is Clay's term.

16. Richardson, *Stewart*, 61.

17. Hinks, *Appeal*, 53.

18. Henry Mayer, *All on Fire: William Lloyd Garrison and the Abolition of Slavery* (New York: Norton, 2008) 62.

19. Hinks, *Appeal*, Doc 4. Hinks's book provides many original documents pertaining to the dispersal of the *Appeal*.

20. Ibid. Doc 5, 96. The first phrase is from the editor, Peter Hinks. The second is from William B. Giles.

21. Doc 6, 98 The phrase "A dealer in old clothes" inspires the title of Darryl Scriven's *A Dealer of Old Clothes: Philosophical Conversations with David Walker* (Lanham, MD: Lexington Books, 2007).

22. Mayer, *All on Fire*, 83, cites the month the first edition appeared as well as the method of distribution but provides no citation. James W. Stewart, "shipping officer," lived at the head of Smith Court, rear of 38 South Russell Street, in 1827, according to tax records that year. In the introduction to Maria Stewart's first publication, *Religion and the Pure Principles of Morality, the Sure Foundation of Which We Must Build* (1831), she expressed confidence that God would protect her from her enemies, "as he did the most noble, fearless, and undaunted David Walker." See Richardson, *Stewart*, 30.

23. Hinks, *Awaken*, 79.

24. I proposed this summary of Harris's definition in a paper delivered at the 2018 Radical Philosophy Association annual meeting, "Insurrectionist Ethics and the Language of Resistance," University of Massachusetts, Lowell.

25. See Charles W. Mills, *The Racial Contract*, and *Blackness Visible: Essays on Philosophy and Race* (Ithaca: Cornell University Press, 1998); Pateman and Mills, *Contract and Domination*; Mills, "Occupy Liberalism!" *Radical Philosophy Review* 15, no. 2 (2012), part of a discussion, "Liberalism and Socialism" in the same issue.

26. Zillah Eisenstein, *The Radical Future of Liberal Feminism* (Boston: Northeastern University Press, 1993).

CHAPTER NINETEEN

1. Houchins, 24, 40.

2. The $138 bill listed among the debts accrued in the probate inventory suggests that Dr. Snow provided significant service, including medication, in trying to revive James, ultimately unsuccessfully. At $8, the assistance of Dr. Shattuck must have been relatively minor. Suffolk County Probate records for James W. Stewart, vol. 129, 1931, Massachusetts State Archives.

3. *Meditation X*, Houchins, Sue E. *Spiritual Narratives; with an Introduction. by Sue E. Houchins* (New-York: Oxford University Press, 1991), 40. Also reprinted in *Meditations X, Richardson*, 115. Stewart wrote this in reference to an experience she had as a child.

4. It is unlikely that James Stewart was interred in Granary Burying Ground or Copp's Hill due to the intense overcrowding. More likely is the "new" South End Burying Ground. For comments on the stench and more see https://www.boston.gov/sites/default/files/document-file-12–2016/hbgi_spring_2014_newsletter.pdf March 21, 2020.

5. Richardson, *Stewart*, 95.

6. Massachusetts State Archives. *A Petition for Probate and an Order of Notice*. All further relevant references in this chapter are to the probate files at the Massachusetts archives.

7. Richardson, *Stewart*, appendix D. According to Ancestry.com, there was a Fanny M. Thompson born 1805 in Plainville, Connecticut.

8. No records correspond to the information in the will read here about Laura Stuart or Phoebe Freeman.

9. See *History of Ancient Windsor*, Connecticut by Henry R. Stiles (New York: Norton, 1859) for a mention of H. Holcomb and family. Badger was notoriously litigious. In 1832 he sued Titcomb who was also mixed up in a robbery involving a turkey as payment.

10. See Richardson, *Stewart*, footnote 19, 123.

11. And yet, in the remote possibility that Maria Miller's mother was "Jared Mead's wench," Sib, she may have had three siblings as well as nieces and nephews, whom she never knew.

12. Richardson, *Stewart*, 91, "Biographical Sketch by Louis Hatton."

CHAPTER TWENTY

1. Richardson, *Stewart*, 29.

2. https://archive.org/stream/hymntunebookforuoodura/hymntunebookforuoodura _djvu.txt accessed February 7, 2021.

3. Houchins, *Spiritual Narratives*. 25–26. All references to the *Meditations* in this chapter are to Houchins.

4. Ibid, 29.

5. Ibid.

6. Ibid, xxxiii and 30. I am also put to mind here of Audre Lorde's "Uses of the Erotic as Power" in *Sister Outside*. Lorde's essay does not invoke a religious connotation, but she boldly declares that our erotic power can be used for political inspiration.

7. Valerie Cooper, *Word, Like Fire*, 30.

8. Alcoff, *Visible Identities: Race, Gender, and the Self* (Oxford: Oxford University Press, 2006), 122 ff.

9. Lewis R. Gordon, *Bad Faith and Antiblack Racism* (New York: Prometheus, 1999), 5.

10. Moody, *Spiritual Confessions*, 26.

11. George Yancy, *Black Bodies, White Gazes*, 7, 99, 166. This brings to mind many contemporary practices, for example, the subprime crisis of the 2000s in which banks lured Black borrowers into taking loans under terms that lenders knew they would be unlikely to be able to meet, only to confiscate the property and appropriate the capital invested by the borrowers.

12. Hinks, *Walker*,12

13. Cooper, *Word*, 107.

14. Yancy, *Black Bodies*, 83.

15. *Walker's Appeal with a brief sketch of his life by Henry Highland Garnet*, New York: Tobbit, 1848. https://www.gutenberg.org/files/16516/16516-h/16516-h.htm, accessed April 11, 2020.

16. Hinks, *Walker*, xliv.

17. https://biblehub.com/jeremiah/8-22.htm, accessed April 11, 2020. Emphasis mine.

18. With thanks to Valerie Cooper not only for her insightful writing about Stewart, but also for her help identifying the source of Stewart's biblical quotations.

19. Houchins, *Spiritual Narratives*, 35–36.

20. *Liberator*, https://www.accessible-archives.com/collections/the-liberator/, accessed April 11, 2020.

21. Moody, *Spiritual Narratives*, 21. In support of my contention that the introduction was written after the set of Meditations: James W. Stewart died in December 1829. In *Religion*, she identifies her conversion as experienced in 1830, the *Meditations* were written over a period of time, possibly a year, and it appears that her conversion took place around the time of her writing of Meditation III. In the Introduction she writes "it is now one year" since she was "born again," suggesting an 1831 date for the composition of the introduction.

22. Cameron, *To Plead*, 126.

23. *Liberator*, Boston, MA, Saturday, Apr. 16. 1831.

24. Aptheker, *American Negro Slave Revolts*, 295, 298, 302.

25. http://www.americanantiquarian.org/NatTurner/exhibits/show/1831reports/insurrection-of-the-slaves, accessed March 21, 2020.

26. Jacobs, *Incidents in the Life of a Slave Girl*, 58.

CHAPTER TWENTY-ONE

1. Richardson, *Stewart*, 89. Originally published as a testimonial in Stewart's 1879 *Meditations*.

2. Richardson, *Stewart* 28–29.

3. Ibid., 29.

4. David Walker, *Appeal*, ed. Hinks, 78.

5. Richardson, *Stewart*, 29.

6. Wheelock, *Barbaric Culture*, 107.

7. https://historyofphilosophy.net/walker-appeal, accessed 5 January 2020.

8. Richardson, *Stewart*, 29.

9. The phrase is from Joab, a biblical military general, "And Joab answered and said, Far be it, far be it from me, that I should swallow up or destroy," from the Book of Samuel.

10. Richardson, *Stewart*, 32.

11. See Peter P. Hinks "John Marrant and the Meaning of Early Black Freemasonry." *The William and Mary Quarterly*, Third Series, 64, no. 1 (2007): 105–16, accessed May 1, 2020. www.jstor.org/stable/4491600.

12. Jennifer Rycenga, "A Greater Awakening: Women's Intellect as a Factor in Early Abolitionist Movements, 1824–1834," *Journal of Feminist Studies in Religion* 21, no. 2 (Fall 2005): 31–59, 36.

13. Richardson, *Stewart*, 30.

14. Wheelock, *Barbaric Culture*, 101.

15. Richardson, *Stewart*, 29.

16. "David Walker and the Political Power of the *Appeal*," *Political Theory* 43, no. 2 (2015): 208–33 © 2014 SAGE Publications, Melvin L. Rogers. Note that the Constitutional covenant is a form of social contract.

17. Harris, "Insurrectionist Ethics," 192.

18. https://politicalphilosopher.net/2016/07/01/featured-philosopher-lee-a-mcbride/ See also Lee McBride, III, *Ethics and Insurrection: A Pragmatism for the Oppressed* (New York: Bloomsbury, 2021)

19. José Medina, "Pragmatism, Racial Injustice, and Epistemic Insurrection," in *Pragmatism and Justice*, ed Susan Dieleman, David Rondel, and Christopher Voparil (Oxford University Press, 2017).

20. Jacoby Adeshei Carter. "The Insurrectionist Challenge to Pragmatism and Maria W. Stewart's Feminist Insurrectionist Ethics." *Transactions of the Charles S. Peirce Society* 49, no. 1 (2013): 54. https://doi.org/10.2979/trancharpeirsoc.49.1.54. P. 54.

21. L. Gordon, *Africana Philosophy*, 93.

22. Carter, "Insurrectionist," 56. Carter points out that for Harris, and for all those exploring the connections between IE and pragmatism, *advocacy* must be motivated *by pragmatism* and *not by some other set of beliefs*, e.g., religion, etc.

23. Medina, "Pragmatism, Racial Injustice," 197–213, 203.

24. Kristin Dotson," *Transactions of the Charles Peirce Society* 49, no. 1 (Winter 2013): 74–92, 86, 81. Toni Morrison, *Beloved*, New York, Vintage, 2004. I have pointed out certain problems associated with subsuming this theory under the general rubric of "pragmatism." One consideration is that the connection is ahistoric, since Walker and Stewart were writing fifty years prior to the development of pragmatism as a theory. Further, traditional pragmatism is anything but radical. I argued these and other points at two conferences: The California Roundtable on Philosophy and Race, Loyola University, New Orleans, October 2018 and at a meeting of the Radical Philosophy Association, UMass Lowell, November 2018.

25. Medina, "Pragmatism, Racial Injustice," 208. For an analysis of "Why Sit Ye Here and Die?" see chapter ten.

26. Richardson, *Stewart*, 30–31.

27. Henderson, C. "Sympathetic Violence: Maria Stewarts Antebellum Vision of African American Resistance," MELUS: Multi-Ethnic Literature of the United States 38, no. 4 (January 2013): 52–75. https://doi.org/10.1093/melus/mlt051. 53–55.

28. Richardson, *Stewart*, 29.

29. Ibid., 40.

30. Ibid. 28, from *The Liberator*, 8 October, 1831.

CHAPTER TWENTY-TWO

1. Jacqueline Jones, *Labor of Love, Labor of Sorrow: Black Women, Work and the Family, from Slavery to the Present* (New York: Basic Books, 2010), 11.

2. Moody, 53. For the primary sources, see *Religious Experience and Journal Of Mrs. Jarena Lee: Giving an Account Of Her Call To Preach the Gospel* published in 1836 Elaw, *Memoirs Of the Life, Religious Experience, Ministerial Travels and Labours Of Mrs. Zilpha Elaw: an American Female Colour.*

3. Teresa Zackodnik provides a thorough account of Black women speaking in public in *Press, Platform, and Pulpit: Black Feminist Publics in the Era of Reform* (Knoxville: University of Tennessee Press, 2011).

4. https://www.blackpast.org/african-american-history/constitution-afric-american -female-intelligence-society-boston-1832/, accessed March 21, 2020.

5. Richardson, *Stewart*, 127, from the *Liberator*, Saturday, June 30, 1832, volume 2, issue 26, page 103, Boston, MA, United States, Library of Congress, Gale Document Number GALE|GT3005834290.

6. Anna Julia Cooper, *A Voice from the South by A Black Woman of the South*, intro. Mary Helen Washington (Oxford: Oxford University Press, 1988).

7. Anna Julia Cooper, *A Voice from the South*, originally published in 1892. New edition, intro by Mary Helen Washington (Oxford: Oxford University Press, 1988).

8. Richardson, *Stewart*, 52–54.

9. See Carol Conaway, "Mary Ann Shadd Cary: A Visionary of the Black Press," in *Black Women's Intellectual Traditions*, Waters and Conaway, 216–45.

10. *Liberator*, June 30, 1832. https://www.digitalcommonwealth.org/book_viewer/ commonwealth:8k71pk24v#1/1, accessed February 26, 2020.

11. *Liberator*, July 14, 1832.

12. Richardson, *Stewart*, 43.

13. For more on the Convention Movement see the works of Christopher Cameron, Peter P. Hinks, Manisha Sinha, and many others. The quotation is an excerpt from a lecture, "An Address on the Progress of the Abolition Cause," delivered before the African Abolition Freehold Society of Boston, and published by Garrison and Knapp.

CHAPTER TWENTY-THREE

1. Richardson, *Stewart*, 45.

2. Henry Wilson, "New England and New York City Antislavery Societies," in Henry Wilson, *History of the Rise and Fall of the Slave Power in America*, 1872, http://www.ameri canabolitionists.com/new-england-anti-slavery-society.html#Officers.

3. Ibid. Wilson lists Thomas Paul as founding member; however, Paul died in April 1831. Wilson's listing regarding Henry Grew states: "1781–1862, Boston, Massachusetts, Society of Friends, Quaker, clergyman, religious writer, reformer, abolitionist. Daughters were Mary and Susan Grew, both abolitionists. Active in abolition movements. Founding member of the New England Anti-Slavery Society, 1832. Attended the World Anti-Slavery Convention in London, England, in June 1840." This website citation is Yellin, 1994, pp. 71, 312, 333; *First Annual Report of the Board of Managers of the New England Anti-Slavery Society*, Boston, 1833, accessed March 24, 2020.ul died 13 Apr 1831 (aged 57–58). However, Cameron says he signed the Constitution—BPL 127.

4. Richardson, *Stewart*, 45.

5. Ibid., 46, 47.

6. Particular thanks go to Elena Cuffari for sharing her expertise on phenomenology and embodiment.

7. Richardson, *Stewart*, 45, 46, 48.

8. Collins, *Black Feminist Thought*, 11.

9. Houchins, *Stewart*, introduction to the *Meditations*, 24

10. Karl Marx and Frederick Engels, *The Communist Manifesto* (New York: Penguin Classics, 2002). Among earlier critics: Mary Wollstonecraft, *A Vindication of the Rights of Men* and *A Vindication of the Rights of Woman*.

CHAPTER TWENTY-FOUR

1. Advertisement in the *Liberator* reprinted in Richardson, *Stewart*, 56.

2. Richardson, *Stewart*, 64.

3. Ibid., 56. Stewart may be adopting a view of what Patrick Rael identifies as "The Fortunate Fall," a way of dealing with theodicy, of reconciling evil in the world with a good and powerful good. Rael explains this as the view that holds that while ancient Africa was "the resort of sages" and while "slavery existed as a foul blot on what was otherwise the most perfect form of government . . . possessed of free will, man might sin, but God could always bring good out of evil." God would "seek to perfect that world through the agency of his new chosen people, blacks." On this account, slavery "became the mechanism for Christianizing benighted Africa" and Black liberation, "cleansed of its national sin, the nation would finally fulfill divine vision." Patrick Rael, "Black Theodicy: African Americans and Nationalism in the Antebellum North," *The North Star: A Journal of African American Religious History* 3, no. 2 (Spring 2000): 1–24, 3.

4. Mills, *The Racial Contract*, 110.

5. Ibid., 74–75.

6. Francois Furstenberg, "Beyond Freedom and Slavery: Autonomy, Virtue, and Resistance in Early American Political Discourse," in *The Journal of American History* (Bloomington, 2003); See also James T. Kloppenberg, "The Virtues of Liberalism: Christianity, Republicanism, and Ethics in Early American Political Discourse," *The Journal of American History* (Bloomington, 1987). On this view, the predestination doctrine of some reformation theologies did not square well with Enlightenment concepts of freedom as autonomy. Initiative is not rewarded in predestination, and the idea of an American spirit of adventure for the sake of a virtuous cause required a concept consistent with individual enterprise. Kant had argued that morality was a matter literally of giving oneself the moral law through reason and free will, of "*auto-nomos.*" Furstenberg writes, "[G]rounded in property, focused on individual rights, legitimized by consent, and buttressed by contractual theory, the emergent liberal tradition assumed the existence of an autonomous human agent whose actions shape history." As a theological and moral theory in step with emergent capitalism, the identification was made of degeneracy with moral failure, prosperity with moral virtue. These combined ideologies fit well with the metanarrative of America as the prize or reward for virtuous resistance to British shackles.

7. Among the several works addressing this subject is Aptheker's classic *American Negro Slave Revolts*, the recent comprehensive work of Manisha Sinha in *A Slave's Cause*, and many in between.

8. Richardson, *Stewart*, 58.

9. Ibid., 56–57.

10. Barbara Omolade, "Faith Confronts Evil," in *Christian Faith and the Problem of Evil*, ed. Peter van Inwagen (Grand Rapids, MI: William B. Eerdmans Publishing Co., 2004), 278–79. Note the tension between scholars who identify Puritanism as a cause of slavery and those who do not. It is worth remembering that in *To Plead Our Own Cause*, Christopher Cameron argues that very early Puritan thought exemplified in the *Body of Liberties* grounds some of the early African American impulses towards equality. There is no simple story to tell here. Cameron argues regarding reformed theology that "blacks in Massachusetts initiated organized abolition in America and that their antislavery ideology had its origins in Puritan thought and the particular system of slavery that this religious ideology shaped in Massachusetts, 6–7.

11. The jeremiad is an argument form that condemns social depravity and prophesizes the end of the world. For a discussion of Stewart's use of this form, see Ebony A. Utley, "A Woman Made of Words: The Rhetorical Invention of Maria W. Stewart," in *Black Women's Intellectual Traditions*, ed. Waters and Conaway.

12. Richardson, *Stewart*, 39.

13. Hinks, *Walker's Appeal*, 26–27.

14. Richardson, *Stewart*, 59

15. Quoted in Waters, "Crying Out for Liberty," 45.

16. Ibid., 49

17. Richardson, *Stewart*, 59.

18. Ibid., 33, 60.

19. Hinks, *Walker's Appeal*, 12.

20. Richardson, *Stewart*, 62.

21. Daniel Carpenter and Colin D. Moore, "When Canvassers Became Activists: Antislavery Petitioning and the Political Mobilization of American Women," *The American Political Science Review* 108, no. 3 (2014): 479–98, accessed March 29, 2020, www.jstor .org/stable/43654388. For the access to the petitions go to: https://dataverse.harvard.edu/ dataverse/antislaverypetitionsma.

22. Richardson, *Stewart*, 33, 37, 38.

23. Ibid. 64.

CHAPTER TWENTY-FIVE

1. Ibid., 65–74.

2. Cameron, *To Plead Our Own Cause*, 126.

3. For an interesting account of Lydia Maria Child and the BFAAS, see *The Case of the Slave-Child, Med: Free Soil in Antislavery Boston*, by Karen Woods Weierman (Amherst: University of Massachusetts Press, 2019).

4. Richardson, *Stewart*, 66–67.

5. Ibid., 68. Stewart vacillates between the doctrine that salvation come through faith alone and the one that holds that grace must be combined with good works. She is a champion of good works, but in this speech asserts that it is by grace alone.

6. George Fitzhugh, "Sociology of the South," in *Defending Slavery: Proslavery Thought in the Old South*, ed. Paul Finkelman (Boston: Bedford/St. Martin's, 2003), 193. First published in 1854, these views were articulated much earlier, but flooded the presses in the 1850s.

7. Jefferson acknowledged that in ancient Rome certain slaves such as Epictetus, once freed, rose to magnificent achievement but he takes great care to explain that the accomplishments of such slaves were due to their shared race with their captors, " . . . they were often their rarest artists [and] excelled too in science . . . but they were of the race of whites. It is not their condition, then, but nature that has produced the distinction." Note that the "ancients" had no concept of whiteness.

8. Richardson, *Stewart*, 68–70.

9. Ibid., 68–69, 58.

10. Lena Ampadu, "Maria W. Stewart and the Rhetoric of Black Preaching," in Waters and Conaway, *Black Women's Intellectual Traditions*, 47. As Outlaw states, "This costly

mis-education of popular imaginations persists, as well, in historical accounts of various areas of thought (though increasingly less so in historiography related to Africa). The systematic production of ignorance and distorted, unethical "knowledge" of the peoples of Continental Africa persists in academic philosophy, especially in the training of new professionals, in the writing of canonical histories of the discipline, and in the construction of disciplinary curricula though progressive change has begun."

11. See Lucius T. Outlaw, entry on "African Philosophy," in the *Stanford Encyclopedia of Philosophy* www.plato.stanford.edu.

12. For the series on "Creolizing the Canon," edited by Jane Anna Gordon and Neil Roberts, see Rowman and Littlefield https://www.rowmaninternational.com/our-books/series/creolizing-the-canon, accessed May 1, 2020.

13. For some examples of Hall's and Allen's writings see by Richard Newman, Patrick Rael and Phillip Lapsansky eds., *Pamphlets of Protest: An Anthology of Early African-American Protest Literature, 1790–1860* (New York, 2001) and *A Documentary History of the Negro People in the United States*, ed. Herbert Aptheker (New York: Citadel Press, 1951).

14. Jacqueline Bacon, *Freedom's Journal*, 147. The historical/cultural argument for the inclusion of African Americans in civil and public life is in part an empirical one, resting on evidence much of which had been suppressed. Liberal theory relied in part on valorizing a group's historical traditions, and of course Jefferson was aware of Blumenbach's work, which could be found on his library shelves. In contrast, even with the scant material available to them, Stewart and Walker make the case for illustrious traditions of Black accomplishment as evidence of suitability for civil status.

15. Celia T. Bardwell-Jones, "Home-Making and 'World-Traveling': Decolonizing the Space-Between in Transnational Feminist Thought," in McLaren, *Decolonizing Feminism*, 158.

16. Richardson, *Stewart*, 70–72.

17. Ibid., 34.

18. The phrase, "God's trombones" comes from James Weldon Johnson's "Seven Negro Sermons in Verse. https://docsouth.unc.edu/southlit/johnson/johnson.html A contemporary musical composition was composed and performed by Chris Crenshaw who plays with Wynton Marsalis and the Jazz at Lincoln Center Orchestra https://www.jazz.org/JLCO/chris-crenshaw/.

POSTSCRIPT

1. 1835 text. quote Richardson, 48.

2. For a list of some of the other women attendees along with analysis, see Ira V. Brown, "Am I not A Woman and a Sister?" The Antislavery Convention of American Women 1837–1839," *Pennsylvania History: A Journal of Mid-Atlantic Studies* 50, no. 1 (1983): 1–19, accessed October 20, 2020. http://www.jstor.org/stable/27772873.

3. Minutes, written by Anti-Slavery Convention of American Women: 1837: New York, NY (1837); in Proceedings of the Anti-Slavery Convention of American Women, Held in the City of New-York, May 9th, 10th, 11th and 12th, 1837 (New York: William S. Dorr, 1837, originally published 1837), 1–13.

4. Richardson, *Stewart*, 93–94.

5. With thanks to Louise Knight for bringing this connection to my attention.

6. For this information, Richardson acknowledges a debt to Jean Fagan Yellin for her references to Robert J. Swan, "A Synoptic History of Black Public Schools in Brooklyn," in Charlene Claye Van Derzee, *The Black Contribution to the Development of Brooklyn* (Brooklyn: New Muse Community Museum of Brooklyn, 1977), 74. *Stewart*, xvi and preface fn. 3. At this late point in this book, it may be helpful to readers, if any, in the distant future, to note that the writing was completed during the Pandemic of 2020–21, a circumstance that made cross-verifying a few of the late references (this one in particular) difficult if not impossible as many libraries were either closed or operated on limited schedules for select patrons only.

7. Richardson, *Stewart*, "Sufferings During the War," 98.

8. Garner, "Two Texts," 156–57.

9. Richardson, *Stewart*, 96.

10. https://www.archives.gov/publications/prologue/1991/winter/war-of-1812.html.

11. Richardson, *Stewart*, 88.

12. Ibid. 85.

BIBLIOGRAPHY

Adamson, Peter, and Chike Jeffers, *History of Philosophy Without Any Gaps*, https://histo-ryofphilosophy.net/home. Accessed July 22, 2020.

Ahmed, Sara. "Declarations of Whiteness: The Non-Performativity of Anti-Racism." *Borderlands*, 3(2), 2004.

Alcoff, Linda. "A Cautionary Tale: On Limiting Epistemic Oppression." *Frontiers: A Journal of Women's Studies* 33, no. 1 (2012): 24–47.

Alcoff, Linda Martín. "Conceptualizing Epistemic Oppression." *Social Epistemology* 28, no. 2 (2014): 115–38.

Alcoff, Linda Martín. "Decolonizing Feminist Philosophy." In *Decolonizing Feminism: Transnational Feminism and Globalization*. Edited by M. McLaren, 21–36. New York: Rowman & Littlefield, 2017.

Alcoff, Linda Martín. "Epistemic Identities." *Episteme* 7, no. 2 (2010): 128–37.

Alcoff, Linda Martín. *Visible Identities: Race, Gender, and the Self*. Oxford: Oxford University Press, 2006.

Alcoff, Linda, and Elizabeth Potter, eds. *Feminist Epistemologies*. New York: Routledge, 1993.

Alford, Terry. *Prince among Slaves: The True Story of an African Prince Sold into Slavery in the American South*. Oxford: Oxford University Press, 1977.

Allen, Anita L. "Coercing Privacy" *Faculty Scholarship at Penn Law* 803.1999. Accessed May 8, 2020. https://scholarship.law.upenn.edu/faculty_scholarship/803.

Altoff, Gerard T. *Amongst My Best Men: African Americans and the War of 1812*. Introduction by Joseph P. Reidy. Put-in-Bay, Ohio: The Perry Group, 1996.

Ampadu, Lena. "Maria W. Stewart and the Rhetoric of Black Preaching: Perspectives on Womanism and Black Nationalism." In *Black Women's Intellectual Traditions Speaking Their Minds*. Edited by Kristin Waters and Carol B. Conway, 38–54. Burlington: University of Vermont, 2007.

Anzaldua, Gloria. *Borderlands / La Frontera: The New Mestiza*. San Francisco: Aunt Lute Books, 1987.

Aptheker, Herbert. *American Negro Slave Revolts*. New York: Columbia University Press, 1943.

Aptheker, Herbert. *One Continual Cry: David Walker's Appeal to the Colored Citizens of the World (1829–1830): It's Setting. Its Meaning*. New York: Humanities Press, 1965.

Aptheker, Herbert, ed. *A Documentary History of the Negro People in the United States*. Toronto: Citadel Press, 1971.

Bacon, Jacqueline. *Freedom's Journal: The First African American Newspaper*. New York: Lexington Books, 2007.

Bailey, Abigail Abbot. *Religion and Domestic Violence in Early New England: The Memoirs of Abigail Abbot Bailey*. Edited by Anne Taves. Bloomington: Indiana University Press, 1989.

Baker-Fletcher, Karen. *A Singing Something: Womanist Reflections on Anna Julia Cooper*. New York: Crossroads, 1994.

Ball, Charles. *Slavery in the United States: A Narrative of the Life and Adventures of Charles Ball, a Black Man, Who Lived Forty Years in Maryland, South Carolina and Georgia, as a Slave Under Various Masters, and was One Year in the Navy with Commodore Barney, During the Late War*. New York: John S. Taylor, 1837. Documenting the American South. University of North Carolina Chapel Hill, 1999. https://docsouth.unc.edu/neh/ball slavery/ball.html.

Bardwell-Jones, Celia T. "'Home-Making and 'World-Traveling': Decolonizing the Space-Between in Transnational Feminist Thought." In M. McLaren, *Decolonizing Feminism*, 158.

Bartlow, Dianne. "Maria W. Stewart as a Forerunner of Black Feminist Thought." In *Black Women's Intellectual Traditions Speaking Their Minds*. Edited by Kristin Waters and Carol B. Conway, 72–90. Burlington: University of Vermont, 2007.

Bay, Mia, Farah J. Griffin, Martha S. Jones, and Barbara D. Savage, eds. *Towards an Intellectual History of Black Women*. Chapel Hill: University of North Carolina Press, 2015.

Beckwith, Samuel, et al. *Centenary Memorial of the First Baptist Church Hartford, Connecticut, March 23d and 24th, 1890*. Hartford: First Baptist Church, 1890. Accessed May 8, 2020. https://play.google.com/books/reader?id=T0YBAAAAYAAJ&hl=en&pg=G BS.PA14.

Beeching, Barbara. "African Americans and Native Americans in Hartford 1636–1800: Antecedents of Hartford's Nineteenth Century Black Community." *Hartford Studies Collection: Papers by Students and Faculty* 7 (November 1993): 1–66. http://citeseerx.ist. psu.edu/viewdoc/download?doi=10.1.1.1017.3257&rep=rep1&type=pdf.

Behn, Aphra *Oroonoko: Or the Royal Slave, A True History*. London: Will Canning, 1688.

Bolster, W. Jeffrey. *Black Jacks: African American Seamen in the Age of Sail*. Cambridge: Harvard University Press, 1997.

Bower, B. A. "The African Meeting House, Boston, Massachusetts: Summary Report of Archaeological Excavations, 1975–1986." Boston: Museum of Afro American History, 1986.

Boylan, Anne M. *The Origins of Women's Activism: New York and Boston, 1797–1840*. Chapel Hill: University of North Carolina Press, 2002.

Brown, Ira V. "'Am I Not a Woman and a Sister?' The Anti-slavery Convention of American Women, 1837–1839." *Pennsylvania History: A Journal of Mid-Atlantic Studies* 50, no. 1 (1983): 1–19. Accessed October 20, 2020. http://www.jstor.org/stable/27772873.

Brown, Lois. "Out of the Mouths of Babes: The Abolitionist Campaign of Susan Paul and the Juvenile Choir of Boston." *The New England Quarterly* 75, no. 1 (March 2002): 52–79.

Busby, Margaret, ed. *Daughters of Africa*. New York: Pantheon, 1992.

Cameron, Christopher. *To Plead Our Own Cause: African Americans in Massachusetts and the Making of the Antislavery Movement*. Kent, OH: Kent State University Press, 2014.

Carby, Hazel V. *Reconstructing Womanhood: The Emergence of the Afro-American Woman Novelist*. Oxford: Oxford University Press, 1987.

Carter, Jacoby Adeshei. "The Insurrectionist Challenge to Pragmatism and Maria W. Stewart's Feminist Insurrectionist Ethics." *Transactions of the Charles S. Peirce Society* 49, no. 1 (2013): 54.

Césaire, Aimé. *Discourse on Colonialism*. Translated by Joan Pinkham. Introduction by Robin D. G. Kelley. New York: Monthly Review Press, 1972.

Chamberlain, Allen. *Beacon Hill: Its Ancient Pastures and Early Mansions*. 240–47. Boston: Houghton Mifflin, 1925.

Christian, Barbara. "The Race for Theory." *Cultural Critique* 1, no. 6 (Spring, 1987): 51–63.

Cuguano, Ottobah. *Thoughts and Sentiments on the Evil and Wicked Traffic of the Slavery and Commerce of the Human Species, Humbly Submitted to the Inhabitants of Great-Britain*. London: Ottobah Cugoano, 1787.

Cohen, Henig. "Slave Names in Colonial South Carolina." *American Speech* 27, no. 2 (May 1952): 102–7. http://www.latinamericanstudies.org/slavery/AS-1952.pdf.

Collins, Patricia Hill. *Black Feminist Thought: Knowledge, Consciousness, and the Politics of Empowerment*. Second edition. New York: Routledge, 2000.

Collins, Patricia Hill. *Black Sexual Politics: African Americans, Gender, and the New Racism*. New York: Routledge, 2004.

Combahee River Collective. *The Combahee River Collective Statement*. Boston: Combahee River Collective, 1977.

Cone, James H. *A Black Theology of Liberation*. Maryknoll, NY: Orbis Books, 2010.

Cone, James H. *The Cross and the Lynching Tree*. Maryknoll, NY: Orbis Books, 2013.

Cooper, Anna Julia. *A Voice from the South*. Introduction by Mary Helen Washington. Oxford: Oxford University Press, 1988.

Cooper, Brittney C. *Beyond Respectability: The Intellectual Thought of Race Women*. Urbana: University of Illinois Press, 2017.

Cooper, Brittney. "They Are Nevertheless Our Brethren: The Order of the Eastern Star and the Battle for Women's Leadership, 1874–1926." In *All Men Free and Brethren: Essays on the History of African American Freemasonry*. Edited by Peter P. Hinks and Stephen Kantrowitz. 114–30. Ithaca: Cornell University Press, 2013.

Cooper, Valerie C. *Word, Like Fire: Maria Stewart, the Bible, and the Rights of African Americans*. Charlottesville: University of Virginia Press, 2011.

Crenshaw, Kimberlé. "Mapping the Margins: Intersectionality, Identity Politics, and Violence against Women of Color." *Stanford Law Review* 43, no. 6 (1991): 1241–99. Accessed April 25, 2020. doi:10.2307/1229039.

Cromwell, Adelaide M. *The Other Brahmins: Boston's Black Upper Class, 1750–1950*. Fayetteville: University of Arkansas Press, 1994.

Cruson, Daniel. *The Slaves of Central Fairfield County: The Journey from Slave to Freeman in Nineteenth-Century Connecticut*. Mount Pleasant: History Press, 2007.

CT Humanities. "War of 1812." Connecticut History. Accessed February 18, 2019. https://connecticuthistory.org/topics-page/war-of-1812/.

Daly, Mary. *Gyn/Ecology, The Meta-Ethics of Radical Feminism*. Boston: Beacon Press, 1978.

Daughan, George C. *The Shining Sea: David Porter and the Epic Voyage of the U.S.S. Essex during the War of 1812*. New York: Basic Books, 2013.

Davis, Angela Y. *Blues Legacies and Black Feminism: Gertrude "Ma" Rainey, Bessie Smith, and Billie Holiday*. New York: Pantheon, 1998

Davis, Angela Y. *Women, Culture, and Politics*. New York: Vintage, 1990.

Davis, Angela Y. *Women, Race, and Class*. New York: Vintage, 1983.

Deforest, Tom. "War of 1812: Commodore David Porter and the *Essex* in the South Pacific." Historynet LLC. Accessed February 18, 2019. https://www.historynet.com/war-of-1812 -commodore-david-porter-and-the-essex-in-the-south-pacific.htm.

Delphy, Christine. *Separate and Dominate: Feminism and Racism after the War on Terror*. Translated by David Broder. New York: Verso Books, 2015.

Dillard, J. L. *Black Names*. Contributions to the Sociology of Language 13. Edited by Joshua A. Fishman. The Hague: Mouton, 1976.

Dotson, Kristie. "Inheriting Patricia Hill Collin's *Black Feminist* Epistemology." *Ethnic and Racial Studies* 38, no. 13 (2015): 2322–38.

Dotson, Kristie. "Querying Leonard Harris' Insurrectionist Standards." *Transactions of the Charles Peirce Society* 49, no. 1 (Winter 2013): 74–92.

Douglass, Frederick. *My Bondage, My Freedom*. https://docsouth.unc.edu/neh/douglass55/ douglass55.html. Accessed July 23, 2020.

Du Bois, W. E. B. *The Souls of Black Folk*. 1903. Reprint, New York: Dover Publications, 1994.

Duran, Jane. *Toward a Feminist Epistemology*. Savage, MD: Rowman & Littlefield, 1991.

Dussel, Enrique. *The Invention of the Americas: Eclipse of the Other and the Myth of Modernity*. Translated by Michael D. Barber. New York: Continuum, 1995.

Dyer, Walter. *Founding the School of Medicine of Howard University, 1868–1873*. Washington, DC: Howard University Press, 1929.

Elaw, Zilpha. *Memoirs Of the Life, Religious Experience, Ministerial Travels and Labours Of Mrs. Zilpha Elaw: an American Female Colour*. London: T. Dudley, 1846.

Egerton, Douglas R. "Forgetting Denmark Vesey: Or, Oliver Stone meets Richard Wade." *William and Mary Quarterly* 59, no. 1 (January 2002): 143–52.

Egerton, Douglas R. *He Shall Go Out Free: The Lives of Denmark Vesey*. Lanham, MD: Rowman and Littlefield, 1999.

Egerton, Douglas R., and Robert L. Paquette. *The Denmark Vesey Affair: A Documentary History*. Gainesville: University Press of Florida, 2017.

Eisenstein, Zillah. *The Radical Future of Liberal Feminism*. Boston: Northeastern University Press, 1993.

Enloe, Cynthia. *Bananas, Beaches and Bases: Making Feminist Sense of International Politics*. Berkeley: University of California Press, 2000.

Enloe, Cynthia. *Globalization and Militarism: Feminists Make the Link*. New York: Rowman and Littlefield Publishers, 2007.

Equiano, Olaudah. *The Interesting Narrative of the Life of Olaudah Equiano, or Gustavus Vassa, The African*. London: Olaudah Equiano, 1789. See second edition published in the same year via: https://play.google.com/books/reader?id=MYOo3LcFbTkC&hl=en&pg= GBS.PR1.

Ferguson, Ann. "Feminist Paradigms of Solidarity and Justice." *Philosophical Topics* 37, no. 2 (2009): 161–77.

Finkenbine, Roy E. "Belinda's Petition: Reparations for Slavery in Revolutionary Massachusetts." *The William and Mary Quarterly* 64, no. 1 (2007): 95–104. Accessed April 30, 2020. www.jstor.org/stable/4491599.

Fisher, E. T., trans. *Report of a French Protestant Refugee, in Boston, 1687*. Brooklyn: Munsell Printer, 1687. https://archive.org/details/reportoffrenchproofish/page/n5/mode/2up.

Frund, Arlette. "Phillis Wheatley, a Public Intellectual." In *Towards an Intellectual History of Black Women*. Edited by Mia Bey, Farah J. Griffin, Martha S. Jones, and Barbara Savage. Chapel Hill: University of North Carolina Press, 2015.

Furstenberg, Francois. "Beyond Freedom and Slavery: Autonomy, Virtue, and Resistance in Early American Political Discourse." *The Journal of American History* 89, no. 4 (March 2003): 1295–1330.

Gardner, Eric. "Two Texts on Children and Christian Education." *PMLA* 123, no. 1 (2008): 156.

Giddings, Paula J. *Ida: A Sword among Lions: Ida B. Wells and the Campaign against Lynching*. New York: HarperCollins, 2009.

Gines, Kathryn T. "Black Feminist Reflections on Charles Mills's 'Intersecting Contracts.'" *Critical Philosophy of Race* 5, no. 1 (Spring 2017): 19–28.

Gines, Kathryn T. "Race Women, Race Men and Early Expressions of Proto-Intersectionality, 1830s-1930s." In *Why Race and Gender Still Matter*. Edited by Namita Goswami, Maeve O'Donovan, and Lisa Yount, 13–26. London: Pickering and Chatto, 2014.

Gonzales de Allen, Gertrude. "On 'Captive' Bodies, Hidden 'Flesh' and Colonization." In *Existence in Black: An Anthology of Black Existential Philosophy*. Edited by Lewis R. Gordon, 129–36. New York: Routledge, 1997.

Gordon, Jane Anna. *Creolizing Political Theory: Reading Rousseau Through Fanon*. New York: Fordham University Press, 2014.

Gordon, Lewis R. *Bad Faith and Antiblack Racism*. New York: Prometheus, 1999.

Gordon, Lewis R. *Disciplinary Decadence: Living Thought in Trying Times*. New York: Routledge, 2007.

Gordon, Lewis R. *An Introduction to Africana Philosophy*. Cambridge: Cambridge University Press, 2008.

Gordon, Lewis R. "Shifting the Geography of Reason in an Age of Disciplinary Decadence." *Transmodernity: Journal of Peripheral Cultural Production of the Luso-Hispanic World* 1, no. 2 (2011): 96–104.

Gordon, Lewis R., ed. *Existence in Black: An Anthology of Black Existential Philosophy*. New York: Routledge, 1997.

Gordon, Jane Anna. *Creolizing Political Theory: Reading Rousseau through Fanon*. New York: Fordham University Press, 2014, 14–15.

Grant, Joanne, ed. "Preamble of the Free African Society." In *Black Protest: History, Documents, and Analyses; 1619 to the Present*. New York: Fawcett, 1986.

Gravely, William B. "The Dialectic of Double-Consciousness in Black American Freedom Celebrations, 1808–1863." *The Journal of Negro History* 67, no. 4 (1982): 302–17.

Graves, Robert, ed. *The Greek Myths*. 1955. Reprint, London: Penguin Books, 1992.

Greene, Lorenzo J. "Mutiny on the Slave Ships." *Phylon* 5, no. 1 (December 1944): 346–54.

Greene, Lorenzo J. "The New England Negro as Seen in Advertisements for Runaway Slaves." *Journal of Negro History* 29, no. 2 (April 1944): 125–46.

Greene, Nathifa. "Anna Julia Cooper's Analysis of the Haitian Revolution." *The CLR James Journal* 23, no. 1 (Fall 2017): 1–2.

Greenleaf, Jonathan. *History of the Churches of All Denominations in the City of New York from the First Settlement to the Year 1846*. New York: E. French, 1846. https://books.google.com/books?id=3DRHAAAAIAAJ&printsec=frontcover&source=gbs_ge_summary_r&cad=0#v=onepage&q&f=false.

Grosfogel, Ramón. "The Structure of Knowledge in Westernized Universities: Epistemic Racism/Sexism and the Four Genocides/Epistemicides of the Long 16th Century." *Human Architecture: Journal of the Sociology of Self-Knowledge* 11, no. 1 (2013): 73–89.

Grover, Kathryn, and Janine V. da Silva. "Historic Resource Study Boston African American National Historic Site." Boston National Historical Park Service. 2002. Accessed April 8, 2020. https://www.nps.gov/parkhistory/online_books/bost/hrs.pdf.

Harding, Sandra. *Science from Below: Feminisms, Post-colonialities, and Modernities*. Durham: Duke University Press, 2008.

Harper, Douglas. "Slavery in Connecticut." *Slavery in the North*. Accessed February 18, 2019. http://slavenorth.com/connecticut.htm.

Harris, Katherine J. "Freedom and Slavery." In *African American Connecticut Explored*. Edited by Elizabeth J. Normen, 3–12. Middletown: Wesleyan University Press, 2013.

Harris, Katherine J. "In Remembrance of Their Kings of Guinea: The Black Governors and the Negro Election, 1749–1800." In *African American Connecticut Explored*. Edited by Elizabeth J. Normen, 35–44. Middletown: Wesleyan University Press, 2013.

Harris, Leonard. "Insurrectionist Ethics: Advocacy, Moral Psychology, and Pragmatism." In *Ethical Issues for a New Millennium*. Edited by John Howie, 192–210. Carbondale: Southern Illinois University Press, 2002.

Harris, Leonard. "Walker: Naturalism and Liberation." *Transactions of the Charles S. Peirce Society* 49, no. 1 (Winter 2013): 93–111.

Harris-Lacewell, Melissa Victoria. *Barbershops, Bibles, and BET Everyday Talk and Black Political Thought*. Princeton: Princeton University Press, 2014.

Hartford Black History Project. "Emerging from the Shadows. 1775–1819: The Black Governors." Accessed February 18, 2019. http://www.hartford-hwp.com/HBHP/exhibit/03/1.html.

Heller, Agnes. "Europa, Europa." In *The European Fall: 28 Essays on the European Crisis*. Edited by Christoffer Emil Bruun, Copenhagen: Politiken, 2013.

Henderson, Christina. "Sympathetic Violence: Maria Stewart's Antebellum Vision of African American Resistance." *MELUS: Multi-Ethnic Literature of the U.S* 38, no. 4 (Winter 2013): 2–75.

Henry, Paget. *Caliban's Reason: Introducing Afro-Caribbean Philosophy*. New York: Routledge, 2000.

Herndon, Calvin C. *The Sexual Mountain and Black Women Writers: Adventures in Sex, Literature, and Real Life*. New York: Doubleday, 1987.

Herr, Ranjoo. S. "Reclaiming Third World Feminism: Or Why Transnational Feminism Needs Third World Feminism." *Meridians: Feminism, Race, Transnationalism* 12, no. 1 (2014): 1–30.

Higginbotham, Evelyn Brooks. *Righteous Discontent: The Women's Movement in the Black Baptist Church, 1880–1920*. Cambridge: Harvard University Press, 1993.

Higginson, Stephen. "A Short History of the Right to Petition Government for the Redress of Grievances." *The Yale Law Journal* 96, no. 1 (November 1986): 142–66.

Hine, Darlene Clark, and Earnestine Jenkins, eds. *A Question of Manhood: A Reader in U.S. Black Men's History and Masculinity.* Bloomington: Indiana University Press, 1999.

Hinks, Peter P., and Stephen Kantrowitz, eds. *All Men Free and Brethren: Essays on the History of African American Freemasonry.* Foreword by Leslie A. Lewis. Ithaca: Cornell University Press, 2013.

Hinks, Peter P. To *Awaken My Afflicted Brethren: David Walker and the Problem of Antebellum Slave Resistance.* University Park: Penn State University Press, 1997.

Hinks, Peter P. "John Marrant and the Meaning of Early Black Freemasonry." *The William and Mary Quarterly* 64, no. 1 (2007): 105–16. Accessed May 1, 2020. www.jstor.org/stable/4491600.

Hinks, Peter P. "To Commence a Moral World: John Telemachus Hilton, Abolitionism, and the Expansion of Black Freemasonry, 1784–1860." In *All Men Free and Brethren: Essays on the History of African American Freemasonry.* Edited by Peter P. Hinks and Stephen Kantrowitz. Foreword by Leslie A. Lewis, 40–62. Ithaca: Cornell University Press, 2013.

Hinks, Peter P. ed. *David Walker's Appeal to the Coloured Citizens of the World.* 1829. Reprint, University Park: Penn State University Press, 2000.

Holt, Thomas, Cassandra Smith-Parker, and Rosalyn Terborg-Penn. *A Special Mission: The Story of Freedman's Hospital 1862–1962.* Washington, DC: Howard University, 1975.

hooks, bell. *Feminist Theory from Margin to Center.* Boston: South End Press, 1984.

Horton, James Oliver, and Lois E. *Black Bostonians: Family Life and Community Struggle in the Antebellum North.* New York: Homes and Meier Publishers, 1979.

Houchins, Susan, Intro. *Spiritual Narratives.* Oxford, Oxford University Press. 1988.

Immerwhar, Daniel. *How to Hide an Empire: A History of the Greater United States.* New York: Vintage, 2019.

Jacobs, Donald. *Courage and Conscience: Black and White Abolitionists in Boston.* Bloomington: Indiana University Press, 1993.

Jacobs, Harriet. *Incidents in the Life of a Slave Girl.* 1861. Reprint, New York: Dover Publications, 2001.

Jaide, Don. "Oshun the African Goddess of Beauty, Love, Property, Order, and Fertility." Rasta Livewire. Last modified October 17, 2009. http://www.africaresource.com/rasta/sesostris-the-great-the-egyptian-hercules/oshun-the-african-goddess-of-beauty-love-prosperity-order-and-fertility/.

Jaggar, Alison. *Feminist Politics and Human Nature.* Lanham: Rowman & Littlefield Publishers, 1983.

Jaggar, Alison. "The Philosophical Challenges of Global Gender Justice." *Philosophical Topics* 37, no. 2 (2009): 1–15.

Jaggar, Alison. "Transnational Cycles of Gendered Vulnerability: A Prologue to a Theory of Global Gender Justice." *Philosophical Topics* 37, no. 2 (2009): 33–52.

James, C. L. R. *The Black Jacobins: Toussaint L'Ouverture and the San Domingo Revolution.* 1938. Reprint, New York: Vintage, 1989.

James, Joy. *Representations of Black Feminist Politics.* New York: St. Martin's Press, 1999.

James, Joy, and T. Denean Sharpley-Whiting. *The Black Feminist Reader.* Malden, MA: Blackwell, 2006.

Johnson, Clarence Sholé. *Cornel West and Philosophy*. New York: Routledge, 2003.

Johnson, James Weldon. "Seven Negro Sermons in Verse." https://docsouth.unc.edu/southlit/johnson/johnson.html.

Jones, Martha S. *Birthright Citizens: A History of Race and Rights in Antebellum America*. Cambridge: Cambridge University Press, 2018.

Kendi, Ibram X. *Stamped from the Beginning: The Definitive History of Racist Ideas in America*. New York: Bold Type Books, 2016.

Kerber, Linda. *No Constitutional Right to be Ladies*. New York: Hill and Wang, 1998.

Khader, Serene J. *Decolonizing Universalism: A Transnational Feminist* Ethic. Oxford: Oxford University Press, 2019.

Killens, John Oliver, ed. *The Trial Record of Denmark Vesey*. Boston: Beacon Press, 1970.

Kloppenberg, James T. "The Virtues of Liberalism: Christianity, Republicanism, and Ethics in Early American Political Discourse." *The Journal of American History* 74, no. 1 (June 1987): 9–33.

Landon David B., and Teresa D. Bulger. "Constructing Community: Experiences of Identity, Economic Opportunity, and Institution Building at Boston's African Meeting House." *International Journal of the History Archaeology* 17, no. 1 (March 2013): 119–42.

Lee, Jarena. *Religious Experience and Journal Of Mrs. Jarena Lee: Giving an Account Of Her Call To Preach the Gospel in Philadelphia*: Printed and Published for the Author, 1849.

Levesque, George A. *Black Boston: African American Life and Culture in Urban America, 1750–1860*. New York: Garland Publishing, 1994.

Lincoln, C. Eric, and Lawrence H. Mumiya. *The Black Church in the African American Experience*. Durham: Duke University Press, 1990.

Logan, Rayford W., and Michael R. Winston, eds. "'Thomas Paul, J.' Carleton Hayden." In *Dictionary of American Negro Biography*, 483. New York: W. W. Norton & Co. 1982.

Logan, Shirley Wilson. *"We Are Coming": The Persuasive Discourse of Nineteenth-Century Black Women*. Carbondale: Southern Illinois University Press. 1999.

Lorde, Audre. "The Master's Tools Will Never Dismantle the Master's House." In *Sister Outsider: Essays and Speeches*. 1984. Reprint, Berkeley: Ten Speed Press, 2007.

Lorde, Audre. "Poetry Is Not a Luxury." In *Sister Outsider: Essays and Speeches*. 1984. Reprint, Berkeley: Ten Speed Press, 2007.

Lowe, Lisa. *The Intimacies of Four Continent*. Durham: Duke University Press, 2015.

Lugones, María. "Playfulness, "World"-Travelling, and Loving Perception." *Hypatia* 2, no. 2 (1987): 3–19. doi:10.1111/j.1527-2001.1987.tb01062.x.

Maldonado-Torres, Nelson. "On the Coloniality of Being." *Cultural Studies* 21, no. 2 (April 2007): 240–70.

Mann, Regis. "Theorizing 'What Could Have Been': Black Feminism, Historical Memory, and the Politics of Reclamation." *Women's Studies* 40, no. 5 (2011): 575–99.

Marley, Bob, writer and performer. *Buffalo Soldier*. Recorded in 1978. From the album *Confrontation*, 1983.

Marshall, Kenneth E. *Manhood Enslaved: Bondmen in Eighteenth- and Early Nineteenth-Century New Jersey*. Rochester: University of Rochester Press, 2013.

Marx, Karl, and Frederick Engels. *The Communist Manifesto*. Translated by Samuel Moore. London: Penguin Books, 1967.

Massachusetts State Archives. "Suffolk County Probate Records for James W. Stewart."
Volumes 128–29, 1830–31.

May, Vivian. *Anna Julia Cooper: Visionary Black Feminist*. New York: Routledge, 2007.

Mayer, Henry. *All on Fire: William Lloyd Garrison and the Abolition of Slavery*. New York:
W. W. Norton, 2008.

McBride III, Lee. *Ethics and Insurrection: A Pragmatism for the Oppressed*, New York:
Bloomsbury, 2021.

McLaren, M. "Decolonizing Rights." In *Decolonizing Feminism: Transnational Feminism and
Globalization*. Edited by M. McLaren, 83–116. New York: Rowman & Littlefield, 2017.

McLaren, M. "Introduction: Decolonizing Feminism." In *Decolonizing Feminism:
Transnational Feminism and Globalization*. Edited by M. McLaren, 1–18. New York:
Rowman & Littlefield, 2017.

McLaren, Margaret A. *Women's Activism, Feminism, and Social Justice*. New York: Oxford
University Press, 2019.

Mead, Daniel M. *A History of the Town of Greenwich, Fairfield County, Conn., with Many
Important Statistics*. New York: Baker & Godwin, 1857.

Mead, Jeffrey B. *Chains Unbound: Slave Emancipations in the Town of Greenwich*. Baltimore:
Gateway Press, 1995.

Mead, Spencer P. *Ye Historie of Ye Town of Greenwich County of Fairfield and State of
Connecticut*. New York: Knickerbocker Press, 1911.

Medina, José. *The Epistemology of Resistance: Gender and Racial Oppression, Epistemic
Injustice, and the Social Imagination*. Oxford: Oxford University Press, 2013.

Medina, José. "Pragmatism, Racial Injustice, and Epistemic Insurrection." In *Pragmatism
and Justice*. Edited by Susan Dieleman, David Rondel, and Christopher Voparil, 197–214.
Oxford: Oxford University Press, 2017.

Melish, Joanne Pope. *Disowning Slavery Gradual Emancipation and Race in New England,
1780–1860*. Ithaca: Cornell University Press, 2016.

Menn, Stephen, and Justin E. H. Smith, *Anton Wilhelm Amo's Philosophical Dissertations on
Mind and Body*. Oxford: Oxford University Press, 2020.

Mignolo, Walter. "The Darker Side of the Renaissance: Colonization and the Discontinuity
of the Classical Tradition." *Renaissance Quarterly* 45, no. 4 (Winter 1992): 808–28. The
University of Chicago Press.

Milano, Anthony. "Republican Fatherhood: Coverture, Patriarchy, and Cultural
Constructions of Masculinity in Early National Connecticut." Master's Thesis, University
of Texas, Austin, 2014. https://search.proquest.com/openview/f42108bdf26a6b6a61f6ec51
2d309192/1?pq-origsite=gscholar&cbl=18750&diss=y.

Mills, Charles W. *Black Rights/White Wrongs*. Oxford: Oxford University Press, 2017.

Mills, Charles W. *Blackness Visible: Essays on Philosophy and Race*. Ithaca: Cornell University
Press, 1998.

Mills, Charles W. "Occupy Liberalism! Or, Ten Reasons Why Liberalism Cannot Be Retrieved
for Radicalism (And Why They're All Wrong)." *Radical Philosophy Review* 15, no. 2 (2012):
305–23.

Mills, Charles W. *The Racial Contract*. Ithaca: Cornell University Press, 1997.

Mills, Quincy T. *Cutting along the Color Line: Black Barbers and Barber Shops in America*.
Philadelphia: University of Pennsylvania Press, 2017.

Mohanty, Chandra T., *Feminism without Borders: Decolonizing Theory, Practicing Solidarity*. Durham: Duke University Press, 2003.

Monahan, Michael J. *Creolizing Hegel*. London: Rowman & Littlefield International, 2017.

Moody, Joycelyn. *Sentimental Confessions: Spiritual Narratives of Nineteenth-Century African American Women*. Athens: University of Georgia Press, 2003.

Morison, Samuel Eliot. *The Maritime History of Massachusetts, 1783–1860*. Boston: Northeastern University Press, 1979.

Morrison, Toni. *Beloved*. New York: Vintage, 2004.

Morrison, Toni. *Jazz*. London: Vintage, 2000.

Morrison, Toni. *Playing in the Dark: Whiteness and the Literary Imagination*. Cambridge: Harvard University Press, 1992.

Moses, William Jeremiah. *The Golden Age of Black Nationalism—1850–1925*. New York: Oxford University Press, 1978.

Museum of African American History. "Archeology of the Meeting House: A Dig and Discovery Project in Boston, Massachusetts." Fiske Center for Archeological Research at the University of Massachusetts: Boston. Boston and Nantucket, http://www.fiskecenter .umb.edu/Pdfs/AMH_Public_Booklet.pdf.

Museum of Connecticut History. "Connecticut's Black Governors." History and Genealogy Unit. Last modified February 2005. https://museumofcthistory.org/connecticuts-black -governors/.

Narayan, Uma. *Dislocating Cultures: Identities, Traditions, and Third World Feminism*. New York: Routledge Press, 1997.

Narayan, Uma. "'Male-Order' Brides: Immigrant Women, Domestic Violence, and Immigration Law." *Hypatia: A Journal of Feminist Philosophy* 10, no. 1 (1995): 101–19.

Nash, Gary. *Forging Freedom: The Formation of Philadelphia's Black Community, 1720–1840*. Cambridge: Harvard University Press, 1988.

National Humanities Center. *Petition of 1788 by Slaves of New Haven for the Abolition of Slavery in Connecticut*. The Making of African American Identity: Volume 1, 1500–1865. Primary Resources in U.S. History & Literature. Last modified March 2007. http://www .hartford-hwp.com/archives/45a/023.html.

National Humanities Center. "Petitions." The Making of African American Identity: Volume 1, 1500–1865. Primary Resources in U.S. History & Literature. Last modified March 2007. http://nationalhumanitiescenter.org/pds/maai/community/text4/text4read.htm.

Nell, William C. *Colored Patriots of the Revolution: With Sketches of Several Distinguished Colored Persons: to which is Added a Brief survey of the Condition and Prospects of Colored Americans*. Boston: Walcutt, 1855.

Newman, Richard S. *The Transformation of American Abolitionism: Fighting Slavery in the Early Republic*. Chapel Hill: University of North Carolina Press, 2002.

Newman, Richard S., and Roy E. Finkenbine. "Black Founders in the New Republic: Introduction." *The William and Mary Quarterly* 64, no. 1 (January 2007): 83–94.

Newman, Richard, Patrick Rael, and Phillip Lapansky, eds. *Pamphets of Protest: An Anthology of Early African American Protest Literature, 1790–1860*. New York: Routledge, 2001.

Nimako, Kwame. "Conceptual Clarity, Please! On the Uses and Abuses of the Concepts of 'Slave' and 'Trade' in the Study of the Transatlantic Slave Trade and Slavery." In *Eurocentrism, Racism, and Knowledge: Debates on History and Power in Europe and the*

Americas. Edited by Marta Araujo and Silva Rodriguez-Maeso, 178–91. London: Palgrave Macmillan, 2015.

Normen, Elizabeth, ed. *African American Connecticut Explored*. Middletown: Wesleyan University Press, 2013.

O'Connor, Thomas H. *The Athens of America: Boston 1825–1845*. Amherst: University of Massachusetts Press, 2006.

Oliver, James, and Lois E. Horton. *Black Bostonian: Family Life and Community Struggle in the Antebellum North*. New York: Holmes and Meier, 1979.

Omolade, Barbara "Faith Confronts Evil." In *Christian Faith and the Problem of Evil*. Edited by Peter van Inwagen, 278–79. Grand Rapids, MI: William B. Eerdmans Publishing Co., 2004.

Omolade, Barbara. "Hearts of Darkness." In *Words of Fire: An Anthology of African-American Feminist Thought*. Edited by Beverley Guy-Sheftall, 362–76. New York: New Press, 1995.

Ortega, Mariana. *In-Between: Latina Feminist Phenomenology, Multiplicity, and the Self*. Albany: State University of New York Press, 2016.

Outlaw, Lucius. *On Race and Philosophy*. New York: Routledge, 1996.

Parker, Edwin Pond. *History of the Second Church of Christ in Hartford*. Hartford: Belknap and Warfield, 1892. https://play.google.com/books/reader?id=BhBLoIFLN9gC&hl=en&pg=GBS.PA13.

Pateman, Carole. *The Sexual Contract*. Cambridge: Polity, 1988.

Pateman, Carole, and Charles W. Mills. *Domination and Contract*. Cambridge, Polity, 2007.

Patterson, Orlando. *Slavery and Social Death: A Comparative Study*. Cambridge: Harvard University Press, 1982.

Paul, Susan. *Memoir of James Jackson: The Attentive Obedient Scholar Who Died in Boston, October 31, 1833, Aged Six Years and Eleven Months*. Edited by Lois Brown. Cambridge: Harvard University Press, 2000.

Peterson, Carla. *Doers of the Word: African American Women Speakers and Writers in the North (1830–1880)*. New Brunswick: Rutgers University Press, 1995.

Philbrick, Nathaniel. "The True Story of the Battle of Bunker Hill." *Smithsonian Magazine*. May 2013. http://www.smithsonianmag.com/history/the-true-story-of-the-battle-of-bunker-hill-36721984/.

Pierson, William D. *Black Yankees: The Development of an Afro-American Subculture in Eighteenth-Century New England*. Amherst: University of Massachusetts Press, 1988.

Pitts, Andrea J., Mariana Ortega, and José Medina. *Theories of the Flesh: Latinx and Latin American Feminisms, Transformation, and Resistance*. Oxford: Oxford University Press, 2020.

Porter, David. *Journal of a cruise made to the Pacific Ocean, by Captain David Porter, in the United States frigate Essex, in the years 1812, 1813, and 1814: containing descriptions of the Cape de Verd island, coasts of Brazil, Patagonia, Chili, and Peru, and of the Gallapagos Islands*. Philadelphia: Bradford and Inskeep, 1815).

Porter, David Dixon. *Memoir of Commodore David Porter: Of the United States Navy*. Originally published in 1875.

Porter, David. "The Pacific Cruise 1813–1814." USS Essex Association. Accessed February 18, 2019. http://www.ussessex.org/Bravepages/frigate2.html.

Power-Greene, Ousmane K. *Against Wind and Tide the African American Struggle against the Colonization Movement*. New York: New York University Press, 2014.

Prince, Nancy. *A Black Women's Odyssey through Russia and Jamaica: A Narrative of the Life and Travels of Mrs. Nancy Prince*. Introduction by Ronald G. Walters. Princeton: Markus Weiner Publishers, 2009.

Prince, Nancy. *A Narrative of the Life and Travels of Mrs. Nancy Prince*. Boston: Nancy Prince, 1850.

Public Broadcasting Service (PBS). "Black Sailors and Soldiers in the War of 1812." *The War of 1812*. Accessed February 18, 2019. http://www.pbs.org/wned/war-of-1812/essays/black-soldier-and-sailors-war/.

Quarles, Benjamin. *Black Abolitionists*. New York: Da Capo Press, 1991.

Rael, Patrick. *Black Identity and Black Protest in the Antebellum North*. Chapel Hill: University of North Carolina Press, 2002.

Rael, Patrick. "Black Theodicy: African Americans and Nationalism in the Antebellum North." *The North Star: A Journal of African American Religious History* 3, no. 1 (Spring 2000): 1–24.

Rawls, John. *A Theory of Justice*. Cambridge, Harvard University Press, 1972.

Richardson, Marilyn, ed. *Maria W. Stewart: America's First Black Woman Political Writer*. Bloomington: Indiana University Press, 1987.

Roberts, Neil. *Freedom as Marronage*. Chicago: University of Chicago Press, 2015.

Roberts, Robert. *Roberts' Guide for Butlers and Other Household Staff*. 1827. Reprint, Bedford, MA: Applewood Books, 1993.

Robertson, David. *Denmark Vesey: The Buried Story of American's Largest Slave Rebellion and the Man Who Led It*. New York: Vintage, 1999.

Robotti, Frances Diane. *The USS Essex: And the Birth of the American Navy*. Holbrook, MA: Adams Media, 1999.

Robson, Ruthann. "Genealogy." In *Masks*. Introduction by Marge Piercy. St. Paul: Leapfrog Press, 1999.

Rogers, Melvin L. "David Walker and the Political Power of the Appeal." *Political Theory* 43, no. 2 (April 2015): 208–33.

Rycenga, Jennifer. "A Greater Awakening: Women's Intellect as a Factor in Early Abolitionist Movements, 1824–1834." *Journal of Feminist Studies in Religion* 21, no. 2 (Fall 2005): 31–59.

Said, Edward W. *Orientalism*. New York: Vintage, 1979.

Schlosser, Pauline E. *The Fair Sex: White Women and Racial Patriarchy in the Early American Republic*. New York: NYU Press, 2005.

Scott, Julius S. *The Common Wind: Afro-American Currents in the Age of the Haitian Revolution*. London: Verso, 2017.

Scriven, Darryl. *A Dealer of Old Clothes: Philosophical Conversations with David Walker*. Lanham, MD: Lexington Books, 2007.

Searle, John. *Speech Acts: An Essay in the Philosophy of Language*. Cambridge: Cambridge University Press, 1969.

Sedgwick, Catharine. *The Life and Letters of Catharine M. Sedgwick*. Edited by Mary E. Dewey. New York: Harper and Brothers, 1872. https://babel.hathitrust.org/cgi/pt?id=wu.8 9098008162&view=1up&seq=7.

Sernett, Milton C. *African American Religious History: Documentary Witness.* Durham: Duke University Press, 1999.

Sesay, Chernoh M. "Emancipation and the Social Origins of Black Freemasonry, 1775–1800." In *All Men Free and Brethren: Essays on the History of African American Freemasonry.* Edited by Peter P. Hinks and Stephen Kantrowitz. Foreword by Leslie A. Lewis, 21–39. Ithaca: Cornell University Press.

Sesay, Chernoh M. "The Revolutionary Black Roots of Slavery's Abolition in Massachusetts." *The New England Quarterly* 87, no. 1 (2014): 99–131. Accessed April 24, 2020. www.jstor .org/stable/43285055.

Shelby, Tommie. *We Who Are Dark: The Philosophical Foundations of Black Solidarity.* Cambridge: Harvard University Press, 2005.

Sheth, Falguni A. *Toward a Political Philosophy of Race.* Albany: SUNY Press, 2009.

Shorter-Bourhanou, Jameliah. "Legitimizing Blacks in Philosophy." *Journal of World Philosophies* 2, no. 2 (Winter 2017): 27–36. https://scholarworks.iu.edu/iupjournals/index .php/jwp/article/view/1258.

Simien, Evelyn. *Gender and Lynching: The Politics of Memory.* New York: Palgrave Macmillan, 2011.

Sinha, Manisha. *The Counterrevolution of Slavery: Politics and Ideology in Antebellum South Carolina* Chapel Hill: University of North Carolina Press, 2000.

Sinha, Manisha. *The Slave's Cause: A History of Abolition.* New Haven: Yale University Press, 2016.

Sinha, Manisha. "To 'cast just obloquy,' on Oppressors, Black Radicalism in the Age of Revolution." *William and Mary Quarterly* 4, no. 1 (Jan. 2007): 149–60.

Smith, E. D. *Climbing Jacob's Ladder: The Rise of Black Churches in Eastern American Cities, 1740–1877,* 1988.

Spivak. Gayatri. "Can the Subaltern Speak?," *Marxism and the Interpretation of Culture.* Edited by Cary Nelson and Lawrence Grossberg, 271–313. Urbana: University of Illinois Press, 1988.

Stallybrass, Peter, and Allon White. *The Politics and Poetics of Transgression.* Ithaca: Cornell University Press, 1986.

Stewart, James Brewer. "Modernizing "Difference": The Political Meanings of Color in Free States, 1776–1840," *Journal of the Early Republic* 19, no. 4 (Winter 1999): 691–712.

Stewart, Maria W. *An Address Delivered At The African Masonic Hall (1833).* In *Maria W. Stewart: America's First Black Political Writer.* Edited by Marilyn Richardson, 56–64. Bloomington: Indiana University Press, 1987.

Stewart, Maria W. *An Address Delivered Before The Afric-American Female Intelligence Society of America (1832).* In *Maria W. Stewart: America's First Black Political Writer.* Edited by Marilyn Richardson, 50–55. Bloomington: Indiana University Press, 1987.

Stewart, Maria W. *Cause For Encouragement (1832).* In *Maria W. Stewart: America's First Black Political Writer.* Edited by Marilyn Richardson, 43–44. Bloomington: Indiana University Press, 1987.

Stewart, Mariah W. "The First Stage of Life." In "Two Texts on Children and Christian Education." Introduction by Eric Gardner. *Modern Language Association (PMLA)* 123, no. 1 (January 2008): 162–65.

Stewart, Maria W. *Lecture Delivered At The Franklin Hall (1832)*. In *Maria W. Stewart: America's First Black Political Writer*. Edited by Marilyn Richardson, 45–49. Bloomington: Indiana University Press, 1987.

Stewart, Maria W. *Meditations*. In *Productions of Mrs. Maria W. Stewart, presented to the First African Baptist Church & Society of the City of Boston* (1835). Reprinted in *Spiritual Narratives*. The Schomburg Library of Nineteenth-Century Black Women Writers. Introduction by Susan Houchins. Oxford: Oxford University Press, 1988.

Stewart, Maria W. *Mrs. Stewart's Farewell Address to Her Friends In The City Of Boston (1833)*. In *Maria W. Stewart: America's First Black Political Writer*. Edited by Marilyn Richardson, 65–74. Bloomington: Indiana University Press, 1987.

Stewart, Mariah W. "The Proper Training of Children." In "Two Texts on Children and Christian Education." Introduction by Eric Gardner. *Modern Language Association (PMLA)* 123, no. 1 (January 2008): 159–62.

Stewart, Maria W. *Religion and the Pure Principles of Morality (1831)*. In *Maria W. Stewart: America's First Black Political Writer*. Edited by Marilyn Richardson, 28–42. Bloomington: Indiana University Press, 1987.

Strong, Nathan, Abel Flint, and Joseph Steward. *The Hartford Selection of Hymns*. Hartford: John Babcock, 1799. https://archive.org/details/hartfordselectiooostro.

Stuart, Isaac Williams. *Hartford in Olden Times: Its First Thirty Years*. Edited by W. M. B. Hartley. Hartford: F. A. Brown, 1853. https://archive.org/details/hartfordinoldentoostua/page/n9/mode/2up/search/Laugh+an'+sing+until.

Sullivan, Shannon, and Nancy Tuana, eds. *Race and Epistemologies of Ignorance*. Albany: SUNY Press, 2007.

Thornton, John. "Central African Names and African-American Naming Patterns." *William and Mary Quarterly* 50, no. 4 (October 1993): 727–42.

Trumbull, James Hammond, ed. *The Memorial History of Hartford County, Connecticut, 1633–1884*. Vol. 1. Boston: E.L. Osgood, 1886. https://babel.hathitrust.org/cgi/pt?id=ucw.ark:/13960/t1qf8tf4s&view=1up&seq=11.

University of Maryland Baltimore County. "Slave, Free Black, and White Population, 1780–1830." Center for History Education. Accessed February 18, 2019. https://userpages.umbc.edu/~bouton/History407/SlaveStats.htm.

Utley, Ebony. "A Woman Made of Words: The Rhetorical Invention of Maria W. Stewart." In *Black Women's Intellectual Traditions Speaking Their Minds*. Edited by Kristin Waters and Carol B. Conway, 55–71. Burlington: University of Vermont, 2007.

Walker, Alice. *In Search of Our Mothers' Gardens: Womanist Prose*. New York: Harcourt Brace Jovanovich, 1983.

Walker, Corey D. B. *A Noble Fight: African American Freemasonry and the Struggle for Democracy in America*. Urbana: University of Illinois Press, 2008.

Walker, David. "Speech Before the Massachusetts General Colored Association." *Freedom's Journal*, December 19, 1828.

Walker, David. *Walker's Appeal, in Four Articles; Together with a Preamble, to the Coloured Citizens of the World, but in Particular, and Very Expressly, to Those of the United States of America, Written in Boston, State of Massachusetts, September 28, 1829*. Documenting the American South. University of North Carolina Chapel Hill, 2001. http://docsouth.unc.edu/nc/walker/walker.html.

Washington Library. "Slave Religion." Center for Digital History. Accessed February 18, 2019. https://www.mountvernon.org/library/digitalhistory/digital-encyclopedia/article/slave-religion/#note3.

Waters, Kristin. "Crying Out for Liberty: Maria W. Stewart and David Walker's Black Revolutionary Liberalism." *Philosophia Africana* 15, no. 1 (Winter 2013): 35–60.

Waters, Kristin, "A Journey from Willful Ignorance to Liberal Guilt to Black Feminist Thought." *Departures in Critical Qualitative Research* 5, no. 3 (Fall 2016): 108–15.

Waters, Kristin. "Maria Stewart, David Walker and Insurrectionist Ethics." Paper presented at the Black Thought Matters Conference sponsored by the African American Intellectual History Society, Brandeis University, Waltham, MA, April 2018.

Waters, Kristin. "Past as Prologue: Intersectional Analysis from the Nineteenth Century to the Twenty-First." In *Why Race and Gender Still Matter.* Edited by Namita Goswami, Maeve O'Donovan, and Lisa Yount, 27–41. London: Pickering and Chatto, 2014.

Waters, Kristin. "Some Core Themes of Nineteenth-Century Black Feminism," In *Black Women's Intellectual Traditions Speaking Their Minds.* Edited by Kristin Waters and Carol B. Conway. Burlington: University of Vermont, 2007.

Waters, Kristin. "Women in Kantian Ethics." In *Modern Engendering: Critical Feminist Readings in Modern Western Philosophy.* Edited by Bat-Ami Bar On, 117–26. Albany: SUNY Press, 1994.

Waters, Kristin, ed. *Women and Men Political Theorists: Enlightened Conversations.* Malden, MA: Blackwell Publishers, 2000.

Waters, Kristin, and Carol B. Conaway, eds. *Black Women's Intellectual Traditions Speaking Their Minds.* Edited by Kristin Waters and Carol B. Conway. Burlington: University of Vermont, 2007.

Weierman, Karen Woods. *The Case of the Slave-Child, Med: Free Soil in Antislavery Boston,* University of Massachusetts Press, 2019.

Wells-Barnett, Ida B. *The Red Record.* New York: New York Age Print, 1895. https://www.gutenberg.org/files/14977/14977-h/14977-h.htm.

Wells-Barnett, Ida B. *Southern Horrors: Lynch Law in All Its Phases.* New York: New York Age Print, 1892. https://www.gutenberg.org/files/14975/14975-h/14975-h.htm.

Welter, Barbara. "The Cult of True Womanhood, 1820–1860." In *Dimity Convictions: The American Woman in the Nineteenth Century.* Athens: Ohio University Press, 1977.

Wesley, Dorothy Porter, and Constance Porter Uzelac, eds. *William Cooper Nell, Nineteenth-century African American Abolitionist, Historian, Integrationist: Selected Writings from 1832–1874.* Baltimore: Black Classic Press, 2002.

Wheatley, Phillis. *Poems on Various Subjects, Religious and Moral.* Denver: W. H. Lawrence, 1887. https://www.google.com/books/edition/Poems_on_Various_Subjects_Religious_and/KLFBAAAAYAAJ?hl=en&gbpv=1&printsec=frontcover.

Wheelock, Stefan M. *Barbaric Culture: Black Antislavery Writers, Religion, and the Slave-holding Atlantic,* Charlottesville: University of Virginia Press, 2016.

Whitehill, Walter Muir. *Boston: A Topographical History.* Cambridge: Harvard University Press, 1959.

Willard, Asaph. *Plan of the city of Hartford: from a survey made in 1824.* Hartford: Surveyed and published by D. St. John and N. Goodwin, 1824. Map. Library of

Congress. Digital Collections: Maps. https://www.loc.gov/resource/g3784h.ct003489/
?r=-0.8,0.352,2.601,1.428,0.

Williams, Eric. *Capitalism and Slavery*, Chapel Hill: University of North Carolina Press, 1944.

Williams, Patricia J. *The Alchemy of Race and Rights: Diary of a Law Professor*. Cambridge:
Harvard University Press, 1991.

Wilson, Henry. "New England and New York City Antislavery Societies." In Henry Wilson,
History of the Rise and Fall of the Slave Power in America, 1872. http://www.american
abolitionists.com/new-england-anti-slavery-society.html#Officers.

Wollstonecraft, Mary. *A Vindication of the Rights of Men, In A Letter To The Right
Honourable Edmund Burke; Occasioned By His Reflections On The Revolution In France*.
London: Joseph Johnson, 1790. https://www.google.com/books/edition/A_Vindication_
of_the_Rights_of_Men/p9bAAAAQAAJ?hl=en&sa=X&ved=2ahUKEwicxsqtncrpAhW
VJ8oKHSfaD6gQiqUDMAB6BAgAEAI.

Wollstonecraft, Mary. *A Vindication of the Rights of Woman: With Strictures on Political and
Moral Subjects*. London: Joseph Johnson, 1792.

Yancy, George. *Black Bodies, White Gazes*. Lanham: Rowman & Littlefield, 2017.

Yancy, George. *Look, a White!: Philosophical Essays on Whiteness*. Philadelphia: Temple
University Press, 2012.

Yee, Shirley J. *Black Women Abolitionists: A Study in Activism 1828–1860*. Knoxville:
University of Tennessee Press, 1992.

Yellin, Jean Fagan, and John C. Van Horne, eds. *The Abolitionist Sisterhood: Women's Political
Culture in Antebellum America*. Ithaca: Cornell University Press, 1994.

Young, Iris M. *Responsibility for Justice*. Oxford: Oxford University Press, 2011.

Zackodnik, Teresa. *Press, Platform, Pulpit: Black Feminist Politics in the Era of Reform*.
Knoxville: University of Tennessee, 2007.

INDEX

abolition: Black abolitionists, 66, 100–101, 131, 139, 148, 161, 207, 240, 260n5, 282n8; first wave of, 8, 12, 158–59, 173–75; Maria W. Stewart and, 7–8, 168, 220, 228, 238, 246; and masonic movement, 164–65, 177–78. *See also* abolitionist newspapers; antislavery movement; antislavery societies

abolitionist newspapers, 7, 178–79; *Freedom's Journal*, 109, 165, 177–79, 181–82, 243, 270n24, 282n7; the *Liberator*, 3, 7, 50, 206–7, 223, 234, 270n24

Adams, John, 7, 148, 151, 159

Adamson, Peter, 111, 213, 250

"Address Delivered at the African Masonic Hall, An" (Maria W. Stewart), 233–34

advocacy, 9, 50, 191

Africa, 27–32, 50, 77–78, 242–43, 258n4, 295n10; colonization to, 176, 188, 243; cosmologies, 33, 36, 171, 282n1; North, 5, 30, 74–75, 77, 132; traditions in US, 56–58, 60–61, 125, 215; West, 27, 29, 55, 110, 170, 268n24

Afric-American Female Intelligence Society, 114, 221, 223, 227, 234

African Americans: Afric', 10, 108, 161, 171, 211, 220; Freemasons, 120–21, 160–62, 164, 174, 176–78, 183–85, 282n7; Intellectual History Society (AAIHS), 251, 260n5. *See also* African Baptist Church; African Meeting House; African Methodist Episcopal (AME) church; African religious societies; Black activism; Black communities

African Baptist Church, vii, 100, 110, 155–56, 173–74, 201, 256n9

African Day, 7, 142, 145–46, 148, 154, 163, 176

African Masonic Halls, 156, 158, 162, 174, 184, 234, 281n20

African Meeting House, 13, 120, 126–27, 255n1; Maria Stewart at, 103, 116–17, 155–56; speeches at, 222, 241, 246. *See also* African Baptist Church; churches

African Methodist Episcopal (AME) church, 35, 88, 91–92, 225, 247, 264n6, 282n7; Richard Allen and, 87–88, 91, 100, 225

African religious societies, 22, 102, 116, 243

"African Rights and Liberty" (Maria W. Stewart), 27, 165, 233–39, 257n20

agency: Black, 56–59, 62, 159, 178, 208; of enslaved people, 25–26, 28

Alcoff, Linda Martín, 30, 180, 203

Algeria, 75, 77, 269n8

Allen, Richard: and Free African Society, 87–88, 93–94; influence of, 98, 100, 120, 159, 235, 243, 259n5

American Colonization Society (ACS), 81, 189, 206–7, 228, 237, 243

American Revolution: African American soldiers in, 6, 21, 54–56, 65, 81, 120, 131–32, 138, 219, 268n6; Black resistance amidst, 158–63, 166, 172, 174, 177, 214–15, 229; Black veterans of, 21, 111, 137, 139; Boston in, 105–6, 130–31, 133; Peter Salem in, 130–31, 137; Prince Hall and, 130, 137, 143

ancestors, ix, 23, 32, 91, 130, 153

anti-Black racism, 11, 49, 78, 92, 174, 217

ABOUT THE AUTHOR

Kristin Waters is author of many journal articles and book chapters, editor of *Women and Men Political Theorists: Enlightened Conversations*, and coeditor with Carol B. Conaway of *Black Women's Intellectual Traditions: Speaking Their Minds*. She is professor of philosophy, emerita at Worcester State University and resident scholar at the Women's Studies Research Center, Brandeis University.

CPSIA information can be obtained
at www.ICGtesting.com
Printed in the USA
JSHW020824210622
27293JS00002B/79